STUDIES IN THE TRANSMISSION OF TEXTS & IDEAS

1

EDITOR IN CHIEF

Gerd VAN RIEL

EDITORIAL BOARD

Anthony DUPONT
Michèle GOYENS
Marleen REYNDERS

SUBMISSIONS
SHOULD BE SENT TO

Marleen REYNDERS
marleen.reynders@kuleuven.be

Cover illustration:
Bible of Anjou, Maurits Sabbebibliotheek,
KU Leuven (Belgium), fol. 309r.
© KU Leuven, Maurits Sabbebibliotheek, photo by Bruno Vandermeulen

D/2014/0095/142

ISBN 978-2-503-55268-2

Printed on acid-free paper

Analysis of Ancient and Medieval Texts and Manuscripts: Digital Approaches

Edited by
Tara ANDREWS and Caroline MACÉ

BREPOLS

TABLE OF CONTENTS

9

TARA ANDREWS – CAROLINE MACÉ

INTRODUCTION

Within the field of digital textual studies there is a stereotype, unjust but tenacious, that for all the work of image scanning, transcription, and creation of ever larger online archives of text, there is little that can be done with them that is novel – that, for all the digitization work of the past few decades, the result has been little more than the ability to make better concordances. How (if at all), ask the skeptics, has the digital turn truly changed the nature of our research, particularly in the field of medieval scholarship where our collections are almost never large enough to justify the term 'big data'? In short, when the transcription is made and the edition published online, to what research use can our texts be put?

This collection of articles aims to give an up-to-date overview of the use of computer-assisted methods in several fields of scholarship dealing with ancient and medieval texts and manuscripts (from codicology and palaeography to textual criticism and literary or historical studies), across the boundaries of language and period. In moving away from theoretical debates about what the field of 'digital humanities' is or should be, we hoped to get a clearer picture of what textual scholars can achieve when they use computers for their research needs and purposes, and what their expectations may be in terms of the technology and developments in computational methodology.

The overview we are offering here is far from complete – that would be impossible, and it was not our goal – but in many respects we find it very stimulating. All kind of new avenues of

10.1484/M.LECTIO-EB.5.102562

research are emerging, thanks to the creativity of scholars and to their interest in what digital means can offer. The research landscape that we are depicting here would have been unthinkable even 10 years ago, and it is still a dynamic landscape whose transformations are difficult to predict. It is only possible to draw some general trends from the very diverse contributions to this volume, all of which testify to the dynamism of textual scholarship.

A first trend we can discern is the implementation of methods of analysis taken from other fields of science (chemistry, physics, biology), in order for example to study the physical characteristics of manuscripts (Rabin) or to identify relationships between manuscripts that contain versions of the same text. Experiments in the field of stemmatology are the subject of several papers within this volume (Heikkilä, Roelli, Camps and Cafiero, Cantera), and each of these articles offers a quite different approach. This shows that, far from being an old-fashioned and moribund philological activity, this sub-field of textual scholarship is flourishing in the digital environment.

Statistical methods of various sorts have been applied to textual scholarship for a long time; this is by no means a new phenomenon. Even so, we see an ever-increasing sophistication of the use of statistics, not only to formulate questions that have easy mathematical answers, but more and more to address questions that have always been of interest to textual scholars but often considered impossible to answer. Several articles in this volume illustrate many ways in which statistics can fruitfully be used to interrogate textual data, from paleography and epigraphy (Castro, Hoenen, Luján and Orduña) to authorship attribution (Van Dalen-Oskam, Stella), robustly linked data and intertextuality (Andrist, Spinazzè, Rubenson, Tupman and Jordanous), and historical research (Romanov). It has become very clear that, in several fields of textual scholarship as well, we need even larger corpora of data than exist as present and appropriate tools with which to explore them. This may be the key to how we can revive and surpass the scholarship of the nineteenth century. In many ways, twentieth-century scholarship has been dominated by theory, rightly casting into doubt many of the (false) certainties built by nineteenth-century positivism. Yet today we see that very few of those theories have survived the last millennium, whereas we may be in a position now to revise and renew our visions of the past thanks to a new way of looking at data.

At the heart of science perhaps lies a constant effort to free ourselves as much as possible from all kinds of fascinations, not only ideological illusions but also from a specific and peculiar fascination with the object under study or with the tools used in its study. In that respect we can offer here a quite mature picture of science in our field. The time when scholars were doing statistical analysis of their texts for the sake of statistics may be considered definitely over. For the same reason this volume showcases comparatively fewer tools, which quickly become outdated, than other comparable collections of papers. Our authors focus rather on practices and methodologies – the sort of analysis that can be done once the tools and data are in place.

One of the new ways of looking at data is enhanced by the possibility of linking it. This is an intellectual activity that has always been key to scholarship: making meaningful links between isolated facts, isolated texts, isolated languages. In the past those links existed in scholars' minds, to be expressed in carefully-formulated arguments within the pages of academic journals. The direct connection and presentation of linked data, and the scholastic openness and accessibility it implies, is one of the most interesting novelties in the world of digital scholarship.

Finally, another tendency is clear: through digital forms of publication we are moving away from traditional forms of dissemination of our research through print-based media, wherein academic publishers are the gatekeepers. But here we need to be careful: although some have argued convincingly for the shortcomings of the current system of research publication, it is too easy to discount the fact that academic publishers fulfill several functions for which we have not yet found a workable or convincing replacement. First and most directly, publishers handle the layout, typography, and physical dissemination of works of scholarship; at present the digital alternative usually requires the scholar to become expert at (or hire experts for) the design, implementation, and maintenance of the necessary infrastructure. Second is the sociological distinction between what is of an adequate academic or scholarly standard and what is not. This is a debate in its own right – there are as many ways to argue that the categories are unjustified as there are rationales for their maintenance – but the arguments for and against an office of 'gatekeeper of academic quality' must be heard in their own right, independent of the question of new technological forms of publication. These are the two points that are the most crucial to understanding how we can make a successful shift from traditional modes of academic publication to freely-accessible resources on the web, and what role academic publishers will play in that shift.

We are very much aware that our book does not cover all possible aspects of digital textual scholarship. We hope nevertheless that this overview of some of the research projects that currently exist and are still evolving may stimulate further developments and encourage junior (and not so junior) researchers to carry on, and to add new results and new questions to those which have been presented here.

ACKNOWLEDGEMENTS

The articles contained in the present book were presented during a workshop organized on April 2-3, 2012 in Leuven and Brussels. This workshop was financially supported by the *Tree of Texts* project, a CREA ('creative research') project (3H100334), funded by the KU Leuven from 1/10/2010 to 30/9/2012), by the COST Action *Interedition* ‹http://www.interedition.eu›, by the ESF Research Networking Programme COMSt (Comparative Oriental Manuscript Studies), by the Flemish Royal Academy of Belgium (KVAB - contactforum) and by the Faculty of Arts of the KU Leuven.

In addition to the funding bodies, we would also like to thank the members of our scientific committee, who actively participated in the process of selection of the proposals and in the evaluation of the papers: Aurélien Berra (Université Paris-Ouest), Thomas Crombez (Universiteit Antwerpen), Juan Garcès (Göttingen Centre for Digital Humanities), Tuomas Heikkilä (University of Helsinki), Torsten Schaßan (Herzog August Bibliothek Wolfenbüttel), Frederik Truyen (KU Leuven), Dirk Van Hulle (Universiteit Antwerpen). We are also grateful to Brian Garcia (KU Leuven), who assisted us with the copy-editing of the proceedings, and Thomas Leibundgut (Universität Bern), who assisted with the preparation of the final volume.

STEMMATOLOGY

TUOMAS HEIKKILÄ

THE POSSIBILITIES AND CHALLENGES OF COMPUTER-ASSISTED STEMMATOLOGY. THE EXAMPLE OF *VITA ET MIRACULA S. SYMEONIS TREVERENSIS**

In search of the original text

The basic principles of textual criticism – or stemmatology – have been understood and applied for centuries: The roots of today's thoroughly computerized discipline can be traced back to the Middle Ages. For medieval writers copying the texts by hand, the complicated copying chains of important literary works, and the scribes' unavoidable mistakes and *lapsus pennae* were self-evident and normal phenomena. It was just as easy to understand the logic of tracing the copying chain of the manuscripts backwards, from a copy to its exemplar again and again until one arrives at the original version of the text. Even though the principle was known, and Medieval and Renaissance scholars, like Erasmus of Rotterdam (1466-1536) or Julius Caesar Scaliger (1484-1560), tried to compare the different versions of the same text with each other in order to find its original contents, applying the principle turned out to be exceedingly difficult, and in the case of a more complex textual tradition practically impossible.

The nineteenth century saw the birth of a number of new scholarly disciplines, and methods of textual criticism were developed much further, hand in hand with the methodological work

* I am deeply indebted to Dr Teemu Roos (University of Helsinki) for his insightful comments and for running the Symeon data on different computer-assisted methods. I would also like to thank Yuan Zou, MA, (University of Helsinki) for her many computer runs with Semstem and RHM, and Dr Philipp Roelli (Universität Zürich) for the R&B results.

10.1484/M.LECTIO-EB.5.102563

done in the fields of history and philology. Many of the improvements were carried out by Karl Lachmann (1793-1851), and, some generations later, by Paul Maas (1880-1963), who shaped a method based on a selection of *errores significativi* or *Leitfehler*, i.e. significant errors of the copyists or the important variants between the versions. In their quest to find the original version of a text Lachmann, Maas and their followers aimed at eliminating unnecessary textual witnesses from the stemmata, and thus narrowed down number of the text versions under scrutiny.[1] They focused solely on the finding of the original version of the text. The Lachmannian-Maasian method really struck a chord, and they have been eagerly followed by philologists in different fields for generations. However, the shortcomings of the method have been just as evident as its advantages, and traditional textual criticism has been faced with fierce criticism. To sum up, the most important points of the critics have been the tendency of the method to provide only bifurcating stemmata, the subjective nature of choosing the *errores significativi* and emendating the text, as well as the inability to deal with the numerous cases of contamination – a scribe would use several exemplars when writing his/her copy. These points have been considered to be significant weaknesses of the method.[2]

The past decades have witnessed a new and innovative use of computers in the field of study of the texts. Especially after Peter Robinson's and Robert O'Hara's pathbreaking *Textual Criticism Challenge* on the Old Norse *Svipdagsmàl* textual tradition in 1991,[3] both the use of computers and an emphasis on multidisciplinarity have been part of the toolkit of a textual critic or a stemmatologist. The basic principles of finding textual relations based on similarities and differences of the versions are still the same as in the Lachmannian-Maasian method, but in many respects the new computer-aided approach has directed the discipline back to its roots. It is no longer necessary for a scholar to choose (more or less subjectively) a selection of variants or read-

---

[1] On the principles of the Lachmannian-Maasian methods, see Lachmann 1842, prologue; Maas 1957; Kristeller 1981; Delz 1997, p. 51-73.
[2] See, e.g., Quentin 1926; Bédier 1928, p. 161-196, 321-356; Donaldson 1970, p. 107.
[3] Robinson & O'Hara 1992.

ings considered important, and to eliminate a set of manuscripts or textual versions from his or her material, for computers allow us to scrutinize the whole textual tradition. At the same time, the scope of the discipline has widened. Whereas, e.g., Lachmann and Maas were first and foremost interested in finding the archetype, the quasi-mythical original, authentic and immaculate version of a text, their modern successors are at least equally interested in revealing the whole copying tradition of the same text.

Previous trends of computer-aided stemmatology

Much has happened in the field of stemmatology during the past two decades. There is a multitude of computer-aided methods in use, and scholars are reporting encouraging results. Since the processes of textual variation resemble those of biological evolution, many methods of computerized phylogenetics used previously within the field of evolutionary biology have been borrowed.[4] This approach has proven to be successful,[5] and the best methods include distance-matrix-based methods (e.g. neigbour-joining), parsimony methods, and model-based methods, like maximum likelihood and Bayesian inference.[6] Most of the relevant phylogenetic methods are available in the PAUP, PHYLIP and SplitsTree packages in their different versions.[7]

There are several scholarly projects developing and applying different methods to textual traditions, and the last five years have seen the first stemmatological algorithms specially developed for building trees on textual data, namely the RHM, Semstem, and Roelli-Bachmann method (henceforth: R&B). RHM uses an algorithm for stemmatic analysis based on a minimum-information criterion and stochastic tree optimization.[8] Unlike most earlier methods, RHM does not require significant preprocessing of the data other than the almost inevitable collation and regularization

---

[4] For general overviews, see, e.g. Cavalli-Sforza & Edwards 1967; Felsenstein 1982; Semple & Steel 2003.

[5] Robinson & O'Hara 1992; Spencer et al. 2004; Roos & Heikkilä 2009.

[6] See, e.g., Saitou & Nei 1987; Yang & Rannala 1997; Ronquist & Huelsenbeck 2003.

[7] Swofford 2003; ‹http://www.splitstree.org›; Huson & Bryant 2006; ‹http://evolution.genetics.washington.edu/phylip.html›; Felsenstein 2004.

[8] Roos et al. 2006; Roos & Heikkilä 2009, p. 432-433.

needed for every method, but instead operates directly on aligned text files, thus being more user-friendly. Semstem, based on a structural expectation-maximization (structural EM) algorithm, in turn, is the first computer-aided method able to estimate general latent tree structures.[9] This is a major improvement and an important step towards a more realistic way of shaping stemmata which depict textual traditions, since the earlier methods are usually restricted to bifurcating trees where all the extant texts are placed in the leaf nodes. One further method well worth taking into account is R&B, since it has returned impressive results on real-life data sets.[10]

In spite of the occasional criticism towards the approach that it is too unrealistic, the artificial textual traditions created by simulating a copying process are very important in developing computer-assisted methods, since they allow a study of the advantages and challenges of a given method *in vitro*, and make it possible to compare the results of different approaches. Still, in order to provide us with a reasonable comparison to real-life textual traditions, the artificial data sets have to be as realistic as possible: Should one want to simulate, e.g., a typical Medieval textual tradition, the artificial set of data has to include a multitude of different versions, omissions and additions within the text, a high number of missing witnesses, multifurcation, missing internal nodes and so on.

One should bear in mind that just as the success of classical textual criticism is dependent on the skills and experience of the scholar, the performance of computer-assisted methods relies to a great degree on various aspects, e.g. the normalization of the readings of textual witnesses, or the correct alignment of the text. This makes it challenging to compare the results of several scholars with each other, be they based on classical or computer-aided approaches. Comparing the results acquired traditionally with pen and paper and those of computers is a slightly provocative aspect when developing new methods, and many scholars have been reluctant to do such a 'man vs. machine' comparison. On the other hand, the lack of comparison implies the difficulties of

[9] Roos & Zou 2011.
[10] Roelli & Bachmann 2010. See also Philipp Roelli's contribution in this volume.

the classical textual criticism to cope with such vast and complex textual traditions that computerized methods normally deal with. We know that the classical approach may give excellent results, especially when applied to fairly small traditions, but these results may vary significantly.[11]

The performance of different computer-aided methods has been tested and compared on several occasions.[12] The overall conclusion is mixed, as the performance of a given method varies depending on the data set and the way, or ways, in which performance is measured. In general, the previous comparisons indicate that three methods outperform others when it comes to the correctness of the stemmata of artificial data sets, constant good results, and the capacity to deal with complex textual traditions: Semstem, RHM, and PAUP with the parsimony criterion. It should be mentioned, however, that whereas the success in finding the correct stemma is the most important feature of a method, there are other aspects to be taken into consideration, especially usability, the amount of data the method requires and the required degree of preprocessing the data. It is worth mentioning that R&B has not been included in previous comparisons of different methods, and we thus lack knowledge of its performance on artificial data sets.

Vita et miracula s. Symeonis Treverensis

Artificial data sets are being used and new computer-assisted methods of stemmatology are being developed in order to solve real-life scholarly challenges. In this article, a high Medieval hagiographical text, *Vita et miracula s. Symeonis Treverensis*, has been chosen as an example. This serves a twofold purpose: on one hand, it elucidates the possibilities of the stemmatological approach, and, on the other, it gives important insights into the text on Symeon for a critical edition the present author is currently preparing. On the grounds of previous comparisons of different methods, the emphasis of this article is on Semstem, RHM, R&B, PAUP

---

[11] See, e.g., the different results of two traditional approaches on the same material: Baret et al. 2006; cf. Roos & Heikkilä 2009, p. 422.

[12] Baret et al. 2006; Roos & Heikkilä 2009; Roos & Zou 2011.

(parsimony criterion, MP, and neighbor-joining, NJ), and NeighborNet, based on which a stemma of the text will be shaped.

The *Vita et miracula s. Symeonis Treverensis* (BHL 7963-7964) is a lengthy eleventh-century hagiographic text of the life and miracles of St Symeon, who died in the German town of Trier in 1035. The life of Symeon of Trier is well documented in a *vita* written by his close friend, Abbot Eberwinus.[13] According to his hagiography, Symeon was born in Sicily; his family was Christian in spite of Syracuse being under Muslim rule since 878. The future saint's father was Greek, and Symeon was taken to a school in Constantinople as a seven-year-old boy. Having seen the Western pilgrims pass Constantinople on their way to the Holy Land, Symeon became interested in visiting the holiest places of pilgrimage in the East. Later on, he spent a lengthy period of time in the Holy Land, found a Christian calling, and was gradually drawn more and more into the religious life. During the following years, he acted as a pilgrims' guide, served a hermit on the banks of the Jordan, joined the monastery of St Mary in Bethlehem, was consecrated a deacon, moved to the monastery of St Catherine on Mount Sinai, and lived as a hermit on the shores of the Red Sea and on Mt Sinai.[14]

In the early 1020s, Symeon was commissioned to travel from Mt Sinai to Rouen, to collect a charitable donation promised to the monastery by Richard II, the Duke of Normandy. Symeon's voyage turned out to be full of adventures: he was attacked by pirates on the River Nile, and, later on in Belgrade, apprehended on suspicion of being a Byzantine spy. Soon released, Symeon finally arrived to Rouen – only to discover that the local duke had died and his descendants wanted to know nothing about a gift to the monastery of St Catherine. Disheartened, Symeon retired to the town of Trier, where he decided to return to the hermitical way of life and lived for his remaining years as a recluse in the Porta nigra, the Roman town gate of the city.[15]

According to his *vita,* Symeon lived in Trier for seven years, during which time he accomplished numerous miracles and

---

[13] *Vita et miracula s. Symeonis,* p. 86-92.

[14] *Vita et miracula s. Symeonis,* p. 89C-90D.

[15] *Vita et miracula s. Symeonis,* p. 91A-92C.

gained a saintly reputation among the local clergy. When he died in 1035, the local archbishop wanted to have him canonized and ordered a hagiographic life and a miracle collection to be written. The first version of the *vita* and a small *miracula* were ready just a couple of months after the death of the saint, and they were subsequently sent to Rome for the canonization of Symeon. The pope was impressed, and Symeon became the second saint in history to receive papal canonization. Porta nigra, where the saint had lived and was buried, was turned into a church, and the local clergy began to propagate the cult of St Symeon.[16]

Concerning the texts on Symeon, the canonization and the first steps of the cult of the saint were the beginning of a new phase. More and more miracles were added to the original *miracula* over the next half century, and, consequently, the *Vita et miracula s. Symeonis* is a very complex text. In fact, we can identify no less than five different layers of writing – i.e. five different subsequent writers – in the *miracula*.[17]

The *Vita et miracula s. Symeonis* found vast dissemination during the Middle Ages. There are nearly sixty Medieval manuscripts still preserved, most of which date from the eleventh and twelfth centuries.[18] This is an astonishingly high number, taking into consideration the fact that Symeon remained a relatively unknown saint whose cult did not achieve great popularity outside Trier. When comparing the dissemination of Symeon manuscripts to that of, e.g., his relics, references to him in ecclesiastical calendars and the evidence on his liturgy, it soon becomes clear that Symeon's cult and his *vita* and *miracula* were not disseminated together. The texts were naturally needed for the proper veneration of St Symeon, but their diffusion clearly exceeded the needs of his modest cult. Whereas the cult of Symeon seems to have been restricted mainly to the neighbouring areas of Trier, the texts on him found readers throughout Western Christendom, from Rome to Utrecht and from the shores of the English Channel to eastern Austria.[19]

[16] Heikkilä 2002, p. 132-146.
[17] Heikkilä 2010.
[18] For the shelf marks and descriptions, see Heikkilä 2002, p. 148-168. For the sigla corresponding to the manuscripts, see the list in the end of the article.
[19] Heikkilä 2002, p. 197-261.

Consequently, the *Vita et miracula s. Symeonis* seems to have had other values to readers and listeners in addition to the normal theological and instructive values of a hagiographical text. The texts described the exotic East, the Holy Land and Biblical places that were very much in people's minds during the eleventh and early twelfth centuries when the texts found their widest dissemination, and it was just the exotic contents of the *vita* and *miracula* that made them interesting to the general public. Consequently, the study of the texts may provide us with interesting insights not only into the fields of religious and cult history, but also into textual history and literary taste. In studying these questions, stemmatology may well prove invaluable.

Interpreting a stemma

For the sake of simplification, and in order to gain a clearer picture of the possibilities of computer-aided stemmatology on St Symeon material, the tradition of text versions contained in nearly 60 medieval manuscripts has been narrowed down to 28 versions, representing presumably the oldest and most interesting layer of the material. As another restriction, this experiment uses just the first 10 chapters of the text (out of a total of 43);[20] the material covers about 20-22% of the maximum length of the text and less than half of the textual witnesses. The length of the single transcriptions varies from 1200 to 1600 words, of which about 230 are parsimony-informative, i.e. their variants contribute to the shaping of a stemma. This selection is large enough to obtain justified results. In retrospect, it would have been reasonable to include a *passus* here and there throughout the whole text to be able to identify exemplar shifts, for instance, but as this article uses the material produced during the ongoing editing of the text, and only the beginning of the text has hitherto been collated, such an approach was not applied.

---

[20] The chapters are numbered according to the seventeenth-century Bollandist edition (*Vita et miracula s. Symeonis*) of the text; the medieval manuscripts do not have any chapter numbers. Some of the text versions contain a prologue by Eberwinus. As the Roelli-Bachmann (R&B) method is uneasy with large *lacunae*, the prologue was omitted from the stemmatological analysis when using the method in question.

Obviously, as this is a real-life data set and the textual tradition has never been scrutinized by stemmatological means, we
lack the 'right answer' how the correct stemma of the Symeon
text should look. However, known textual witnesses have been
roughly clustered (mainly) according to the length of the text
in previous scholarship, and tentative sub-branches of a stemma
within the clusters have been proposed.[21] This provides us with
at least some background to evaluate the results of different approaches of computer-aided methods.

Six different computer-assisted methods were used to gain
further knowledge of the textual tradition of *Vita et miracula s.
Symeonis:* RHM, Semstem, R&B, PAUP (maximum parsimony
(MP) and neighbor-joining (NJ), and NeighborNet (NNet)).
Some exactly identical groups or pairs of text versions were
found by all the used methods, and some were suggested by several but not all computer-assisted methods:

- PAIRS:
  - M – Pa (all)
  - Eb – Max (all)
  - Au – Om (all)
  - Ep – T (RHM, R&B, MP, NJ, NNet)
  - C – F (RHM, R&B, MP, NJ)
  - Ei – R (RHM, R&B, MP)
  - E – Mc (RHM, Semstem, R&B)
  - E – O (R&B, NJ, NNet)
  - A – BB (RHM, R&B)
  - P – X (RHM, Semstem)

- GROUPS:
  - Ei – R – Z (RHM, R&B, MP)
  - E – Mc – O (RHM, Semstem, R&B, NJ, NNet)

- BRANCHES:
  - M – Pa & Eb – Max & Ech & V (all)
  - Ep – T & E – Mc & O (all)
  - A – BB & Au – Om & C – F & N (RHM, R&B, partly
    NJ, NNet).

---

[21] Heikkilä 2002, p. 195.

The results of the different methods applied to the St Symeon material vary somewhat. The trees provided by RHM and R&B are very similar, whereas the others show greater differences between them. As the methods are based on different approaches and use different algorithms, it is the similar findings shared by all the methods that attract one's attention most. The pairs and branches of text versions found by every method are obviously the easiest parts of the tree to identify with certainty; this is ascertained both by the study of the texts using traditional textual criticism and by bootstrapping the RHM results.

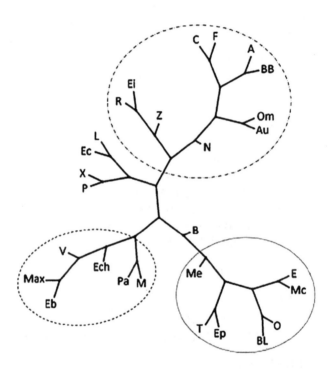

FIGURE 1: The stemma proposed by RHM.

In addition to the identical parts of the textual tradition, all the methods are able to identify three large groups that are very similar from one result to the other. Figures 1-6 show the groups and their members. A look at the contents of the text versions and

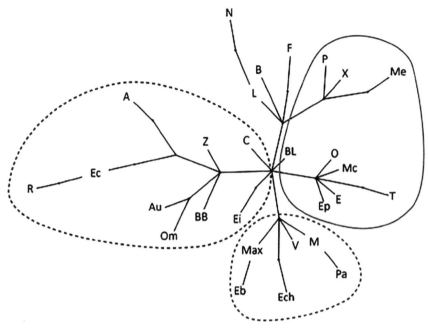

FIGURE 2: The stemma proposed by Semstem.
One of equally probable stemmata is chosen.

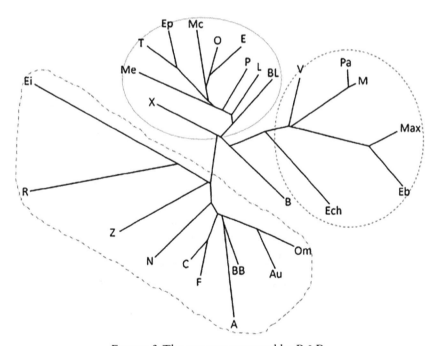

FIGURE 3: The stemma proposed by R&B.

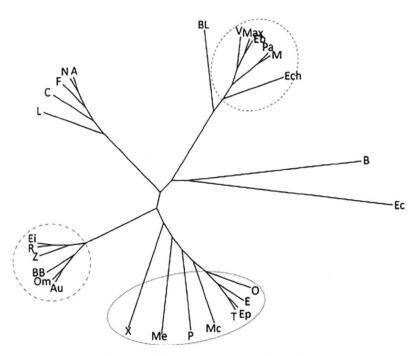

FIGURE 4: The stemma proposed by MP.

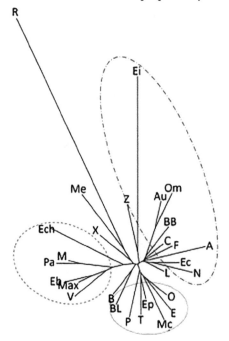

FIGURE 5: The stemma proposed by NJ.

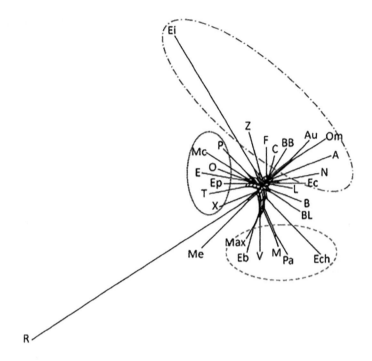

FIGURE 6: The stemma proposed by NeighborNet.

the manuscripts in which they are contained reveals a substantial threefold correlation between the members of each group: the length of the text, the date of the manuscript, and the provenance of the manuscript.[22]

With just one exception, the texts of the first group all end after c. 33 (hence the group is dubbed '33'); the majority of the second group ends after c. 34 (group '34'); and the third group contains mixed material (therefore henceforth 'mixed'). The finding is significant from the viewpoint of the study of the textual tradition, and the strong correlation of the findings gives credence to the hypotheses of the computer-assisted methods since the text material used in the experiment only contained cc. 1-10

---

[22] Self-evidently, the age of a manuscript does not necessarily tell us about the antiquity of the text version it contains or vice versa. Still, manuscript studies provide us with a great deal of information which contextualizes the text and its copying and such approaches are thus a powerful tool in studying a textual tradition.

31

of the *Vita et miracula,* and the methods had no way of 'knowing' at which point each version would end.

Group 33	RHM	Semstem	R&B	MP	NJ	Ends after c.	Century of ms.
	BL	BL	BL		BL	33	XII
	E	E	E	E	E	33	XI
	Ep	Ep	Ep	Ep	Ep	43	XI ex. / XII in.
			L			33	XI ex. / XII in.
	Mc	Mc	Mc	Mc	Mc	33	XI
	Me	Me	Me	Me		33	XV in.
	O	O	O	O	O	33	1062-66
		P	P	P	P	33	XI
	T	T	T	T	T	33	XI
		X	X	X		33	XIII ex./ XIV in.

Group 34	RHM	Semstem	R&B	MP	NJ	Ends after c.	Century of ms.
	A	A	A		A	27	XI ex. / XII in.
	Au	Au	Au	Au	Au	34	XIII
	BB	BB	BB	BB	BB	34	XI /2
	C	C	C		C	34	XI ex. / XII in.
		Ec			Ec	8	1051-81
	Ei	Ei	Ei	Ei	Ei	34	XII
	F		F		F	22	XI ex. / XII in.
	N		N		N	26	XII in.
	Om	Om	Om	Om	Om	34	XII
	R	R	R	R		11	XVII ex. / XVIII in.
	Z	Z	Z	Z	Z	34	1120-25

Group Mixed	RHM	Semstem	R&B	MP	NJ	Ends after c.	Century of ms.
	Eb	Eb	Eb	Eb	Eb	35	XV
	Ech	Ech	Ech	Ech	Ech	43	XII
	M	M	M	M	M	43	XIII in.
	Max	Max	Max	Max	Max	35	Post 1235
	Pa	Pa	Pa	Pa	Pa	33/34	XV ex. / XVI in.
	V	V	V	V	V	34	XV

FIGURE 7: Groups of text versions identified by computer-assisted methods.

The study of the extant manuscripts, i.e. the carriers of the textual witnesses, corroborates the hypothesis of the three major groups further (for detailed dating of the manuscripts, see fig. 7). The manuscripts of group 33 contain practically all of the oldest manuscripts, whereas a typical representative of group 34 is some generations younger. The manuscripts of the mixed group, in turn, represent the most recent layer of all the manuscripts. This is something one would expect based on previous scholarship on the different redactions of *Vita et miracula*.[23] Despite some occasional younger copies of the text blurring the big picture, the tendency is very clear: the manuscripts of the earliest redactions are older than those of the later ones.

The provenances of the manuscripts reveal yet another interesting pattern (see fig. 8). The carriers of the text versions of group 33 are to be found within the borders of the German part of the Holy Roman Empire, mainly concentrating east of Trier. The manuscripts of group 34, in turn, were written within a much broader geographic area, stretching from the shores of the English Channel to the Alps and beyond, whereas the provenances of the mixed group concentrate in the vicinity of Trier. These results which provide a geographical dimension to the stemmatological study are of utmost interest for anyone studying the dissemination of the *Vita et miracula*, the spreading of the cult of St Symeon, and the cultural contacts involved.

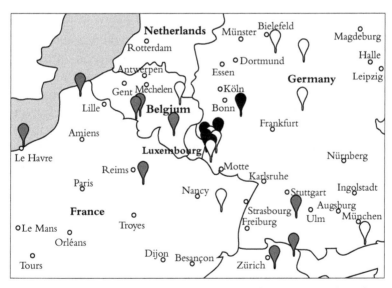

FIGURE 8: The provenances of manuscripts. White corresponds with group 33, gray with group 34 and black with the mixed group.

[23] See Heikkilä 2010.

Interestingly, the results achieved by using several computer-assisted methods correspond rather well with the preliminary rough grouping of the text versions by previous scholarship based on classical textual criticism.[24] On one hand, many parts of the sub-stemmata proposed earlier are found by the computerized methods, and many of the findings of RHM, Semstem, R&B, MP and NJ related to groups 33 and 34 were suggested by the classical method, as well. There are differences, too, and especially the mixed group remains a mystery to be solved by future studies: is it a real sub-branch of the stemma or just a false result created by the algorithms that do not comprehend the contents of the text? Was it a result of multiple contamination, or do some of the versions represent a text abridged from a longer version?

Finding the archetype, the 'original' version of the text, is the crucial question of the classical approach of textual criticism. The common challenge with the computer-assisted methods is, however, that they leave the tree describing the relationships between the textual witnesses unrooted, i.e. they do not take a stand on the direction of the copying relations and, thus, on the location of the archetype within the tree. Nevertheless, the direction of an edge between two nodes or leaves of a tree is in most cases relatively easy to deduce on the grounds of the variants; some changes within the text are likely to have happened in one direction and not the other. In other words, the classical approach of textual criticism is needed to refine the results of the computer-assisted methods. In our Symeon example, the original archetype is doubtless found within group 33. In this case, however, the question of the archetype is multifaceted, since the different redactions of the text suggest a series of authoritative, slightly differing versions that were copied over and over again.

Main challenges of computer-assisted methods

After our example, let us now turn back to more general observations on the possibilities and challenges of computer-assisted stemmatology. In spite of the developing work on computer-assisted stemmatological methods, they are still in their infancy

---

[24] Heikkilä 2002, p. 195.

and are far from being perfect tools for a textual scholar. The main challenges can be roughly categorized under five points:[25]

1. The methods presently used result in an unrooted tree, i.e. the scholar still has to find the root, or archetype, or 'original' version of the text manually, using traditional methods. This is, however, not an insuperable difficulty, since in most cases the contents of the text as well as the palaeography and codicology of the textual witnesses provide the scholar with a multitude of hints that point him or her in the right direction. A far bigger challenge is the fact that the results of a stemma of any real-life Medieval textual tradition are always too simplistic in comparison to the truth, whatever method we choose to use, be it computer-assisted or not. It is obvious that the Medieval manuscript traditions of a popular text like the *Vita et miracula s. Symeonis* were much more complex than the extant copies seem to represent. In other words, our trees representing the textual tradition are missing a plethora of both outer leaves and inner nodes.

2. Despite numerous efforts, the present methods have difficulties in dealing with contamination, i.e. cases in which a version of a text was copied from two or more model exemplars. It should be mentioned, however, that network methods like NeighborNet provide a scholar with insights into contamination as well (see fig. 6). Still, the inability of most methods to identify contamination is a problem, since it is considered to have occurred relatively frequently in textual traditions copied by hand.[26] It is possible that the Symeon tradition presented above has contaminated witnesses, but none of our methods is able to detect such cases. Of the manuscripts of our material, two (T and V) are put together from parts that originated from different *codices*,[27] which inevitably indicates an exemplar shift within the text, although it does not occur within

---

[25] See Howe et al. 2012, p. 51-67.
[26] This is the prevailing assumption of manuscript and textual scholars. However, it might be useful to ponder more precisely how e.g. a medieval copyist would have worked in practice when copying the same text from several exemplars.
[27] Einsiedeln, Stiftsbibliothek, MS 323 (1065), p. 83-105; Trier, Stadtbibliothek, MS 1353 / 132 8°, fol. 27r-36v; Heikkilä 2002, p. 163.

our material (the first 10 chapters of the text) of this experiment in either of the cases. This form of contamination can be found and tackled rather well by computerized methods,[28] but the thorough study of manuscripts has not lost its paramount significance. In other words, multidisciplinarity is called for.

3. Most methods, be they phylogenetic or based on other principles, tend to produce only bifurcating trees, whereas it is obvious that most textual traditions are and were much more complex; the text of an exemplar could be copied a myriad number of times. Hence, none of the results of RHM, R&B, MP and NJ are totally accurate but rather give a general idea of the relationships between the text versions. Some of the most recently developed methods, especially Semstem, look very promising and seem to tackle the challenge and be able to shape multifurcating trees, but a thorough assessment of the trustworthiness of their results requires further work.

4. As a part of their heritage from the phylogenetic methods of evolutionary biology, computer-assisted methods produce trees in which the extant text versions are located in the leaf (outer) nodes and none are to be found in the internal nodes. In real-life copying traditions, however, it is not true that none of the extant manuscripts or text versions are ancestors of some other still-existing manuscripts or texts. Semstem is, to my knowledge, the first computer-aided method to handle the challenge.[29] In the Symeon material, Semstem suggests four places in which there are text versions of existing manuscripts as internal nodes of the tree. One of them, the relationship between versions *Max* and *Eb* (see fig. 2) is probably correct and can be verified by means of classical textual criticism, whereas the others remain more questionable.

5. Albeit the best computer-aided methods perform very well on the artificial textual data-sets and the stemmata they provide are up to 75-85% correct on the simple artificial traditions,[30] it

---

[28] See, e.g., Windram et al. 2005, p. 189-204.

[29] More work is being done on this aspect of stemmatology: see, e.g., the method proposed by J.-B. Camps and F. Cafiero in this volume.

[30] On the measuring of the performances of different methods by average sign distance, see Roos & Heikkilä 2009, p. 421-422.

is hard to estimate the reliability of the results on real-life textual traditions.[31] Many methods are not consistently good on all the data, most performing well on small data sets but struggling on more complicated ones.[32] It remains clear that most of the real copying patterns are and were much more complex than even the biggest artificial sets of data, and, consequently, the results are bound to be less convincing. Furthermore, the results of the computer-assisted methods are much affected by the number of missing nodes and the number of *lacunae* within the text[33] – and it is evident that in the typical tradition of a Medieval text like *Vita et miracula s. Symeonis* we only have few exemplars of the multitude of versions and copies that were once available.

Conclusion

The applying of several computer-assisted methods on a set of nearly 30 Medieval text versions of *Vita et miracula s. Symeonis Treverensis* resulted in identifying three groups of manuscripts. The groups probably represent three branches of the stemma depicting the textual tradition of the *vita* and *miracula* and the geographical dissemination of the work. The result suggests that the work was disseminated in three waves: 1) a text version ending after c. 33 was copied especially east of Trier in the eleventh century; 2) a text version ending after c. 34 was popular west and south of Trier somewhat later; and 3) a mixed group of text versions was copied in the vicinity of Trier during the last centuries of the Middle Ages.

It is evident that the new methods of computer-assisted stemmatology are very useful in shaping the stemmata of textual traditions. One important caveat is, however, that the algorithms and computer programs designed and used to facilitate the work

---

[31] It should be mentioned, however, that bootstrapping can be used to evaluate the trustworthiness of individual branches of bifurcating stemmata; the higher the bootstrap value, the more probable the existence of the hypothetical branch in the real stemma.

[32] In a recent comparison, RHM was found to be consistently good, whereas the performance of most of the phylogenetic methods seemed to vary more significantly; see Roos & Heikkilä 2009.

[33] See esp. Roos & Zou 2011, p. 6-7.

of a textual scholar only do what they are told to do. There are few scholars who genuinely command the methods, sources, and aims of several disciplines. Hence, one of the challenges of multidisciplinary scholarship uniting the efforts of a more traditional textual scholar with those of a, say, computer scientist, is the need for transparency: the mutual understanding of the aims, prerequisites and materials of the disciplines involved.

In many cases, transparency is a synonym for the easy usability of a method. Both RHM and Semstem allow a scholar to easily acquaint him- or herself with the text of the hypothetical internal nodes necessary for the existence of the proposed tree. This is an invaluable tool to prove the hypotheses of the algorithms: if the proposed text of the internal node makes contental and grammatical sense, the solution is possible and the hypothesis provided by the algorithm is well worth taking into closer consideration. R&B has a similar feature, as it provides the scholar with a list of possible *errores significativi;* modifying the list and weighing certain variants allows him or her to interact with the computer-assisted tree building. Should one be preparing a critical edition of a text, this is an important feature, as it helps to quickly distinguish the important variants within the text from the insignificant ones. Still, any choice of variants adds to the danger of subjectivity, and a scholar has to be very careful when choosing the variants.

From a textual scholar's point of view, it is precisely the interoperability between the computational methods and the traditional ones concentrating on the textual contents that is of paramount significance within computer-assisted stemmatology. As our Symeon example shows, the computer-assisted methods of today do not give a shortcut to the real, correct stemma of a textual tradition, but rather show aspects, individual text versions, and branches of the tree that are of special interest or require more attention. Furthermore, they emphasize the understanding of the textual contents and are, thus, another powerful and important tool a textual scholar should add to his or her toolkit.[34]

Despite the promising results of our experiment on *Vita et miracula s. Symeonis,* one should not be overly confident – at least not yet. In their present state, the computer-assisted methods are

---

[34] See Howe et al. 2012 with similar results.

already an invaluable aid for a textual scholar, since they result in interesting, formally justified hypotheses, but they do not give exhaustive answers on the textual tradition and its development. The results of the classical approach, in turn, are often very good on a small textual tradition but struggle with larger ones and require vast amounts of textual data to be excluded – by means of *recensio*, isolating the witnesses that are probably closest to the archetype – in order to achieve reliable results.

As the computer-assisted and classical approaches use the same material and fundamentally the same principles, it would be foolish not to use both in studying the development history of a text and its tradition. It is crucial not to rely blindly on the results provided by a computer-assisted method and to verify the results of every single node of a stemma with the text, but it is equally useful to take advantage of the computational power of the new approaches. The strength of computer-assisted methods is and remains their capability to deal objectively with very large sets of data in a short space of time.

Sigla of the Manuscripts

A   Bruxelles, Bibliothèque Royale, MS II. 1050, fol. 64r-75r.

Au   Bruxelles, Bibliothèque Royale, MS II. 1146, pag. 89-102.

B   Bruxelles, Bibliothèque Royale, MS 207-208, fol. 259r-262r.

BB   Bern, Burgerbibliothek, MS 24, fol. 238r-242v.

BL   London, British Library, MS Add. 18359, fol. 105r-116r.

C   Châlons-en-Champagne, Bibliothèque municipale, MS 56, fol. 64r-77r.

E   Trier, Stadtbibliothek, Codex 118/106, fol. 296v-309v.

Eb   Trier, Stadtbibliothek, Codex 1167/469, fol. 171r-181r.

Ec   Luxembourg, Bibliothèque nationale, MS 264, fol. 380vb-381rb.

Ech   Paris, Bibliothèque nationale de France, MS lat. 9740, fol. 172v-180v, 182r-195r.

Ei   Einsiedeln, Stiftsbibliothek, MS 247 (379), pag. 430-456.

Ep   Epinal, Bibliothèque municipale, Codex 147 (olim 67), fol. 95v-104v.

F   Paris, Bibliothèque nationale de France, MS lat. 2628, fol. 144v-152r.

L   Bruxelles, Bibliothèque Royale, MS 9290, fol. 118r-122r.

M   Trier, Stadtbibliothek, Codex 1384/54 8°, fol. 2r-13r.

Max   Trier, Stadtbibliothek, Codex 1151/454, Band II., fol. 140v-145r.

Mc   München, Bayerische Staatsbibliothek, Clm 18625, fol. 18v-28r.

Me   Trier, Stadtbibliothek, Codex 2002/92, fol. 191r-199r.

N   Namur, Musée des arts anciens, MS 12, fol. 217v-221v.

O   London, British Library, MS Add. 22793, fol. 31v-42r.

Om   Bruxelles, Bibliothèque Royale, MS II. 932, fol. 113ra-118rb.

P   Città del Vaticano, Biblioteca Apostolica Vaticana, Cod. Reg. lat. 481, 95a-103v.

Pa   Paris, Bibliothèque nationale de France, MS lat. 10875, fol. 103r-113v.

R   Roma, Biblioteca Vallicelliana, Codex P. 196, fol. 114v-119v.

T   Einsiedeln, Stiftsbibliothek, MS 323 (1065), pag. 83-105.

V   Trier, Stadtbibliothek, Codex 1353/132, fol. 27r-36v.

X   Bruxelles, Bibliothèque des Bollandistes, MS 209, fol. 9v-16v.

Z   Stuttgart, Württembergische Landesbibliothek, Cod. bibl. 2° 57, fol. 247r-252v.

Bibliography

Ph. V. Baret, C. Macé & P. Robinson (2006), 'Testing Methods on an Artificially Created Textual Tradition', in C. Macé, et al. (eds.), *The Evolution of Texts. Confronting Stemmatological and Genetical Methods*, Pisa & Roma: Istituti editoriali e poligrafici internazionali (Linguistica computazionale, XXIV-XXV), p. 255-281.

J. Bédier (1928), 'La Tradition Manuscrite du *Lai de L'Ombre*. Réflexions sur l'Art d'Éditer les Anciens Textes', in *Romania*, 54, p. 161-196, 321-356.

L. L. Cavalli-Sforza & A. W. F. Edwards (1967), 'Phylogenetic analysis – Models and estimation procedures', in *American Journal of Human Genetics*, 19, p. 233-257.

J. Delz (1997), 'Textkritik und Editionstechnik', in F. Graf (ed.), *Einleitung in die lateinische Philologie*, Stuttgart & Leipzig: Teubner, p. 51-73.

E. T. Donaldson (1970), *Speaking of Chaucer*, London: Athlone.

J. Felsenstein (1982), 'Numerical methods for inferring evolutionary trees', in *Quarterly Review of Biology*, 57, p. 379-404.

J. Felsenstein (2004), *Inferring Phylogenies*, Sunderland (MA): Sinauer Associates.

T. Heikkilä (2002), *Vita et miracula s. Symeonis Treverensis. Ein hochmit-telalterlicher Heiligentext im Kontext*, Helsinki: Academia Scientia-rum Fennica (Annales Academiae Scientiarum Fennicae, 326).

T. Heikkilä (2010), 'Hagiographers' Workshop. The Writing of a Me-dieval Miracle Collection Reconstructed', in *Mediävistik*, 22.

C. J. Howe, R. Connolly & H. Windram (2012), 'Responding to Crit-icisms of Phylogenetic Methods in Stemmatology', in *SEL. Studies in English Literature 1500-1900*, p. 51-67.

D. H. Huson & D. Bryant (2006), 'Application of phylogenetic net-works in evolutionary studies', in *Molecular Biology and Evolution*, 23(2), p. 254-267.

P. O. Kristeller (1981), 'The Lachmann Method: Merits and Limita-tions', in *TEXT*, 1, p. 11-20.

K. Lachmann (1842), *Testamentum Novum Græce et Latine. Carolus Lachmannus recensuit. Philippus Butmannus, Ph. F. Græcæ Lectionis Auctoritatis, apposuit I*, Berlin: G. Reimer.

H. Quentin (1926), *Essais de Critique Textuelle*, Paris: August Picard.

P. Robinson & R. J. O'Hara (1992), 'Report on the Textual Criticism Challenge 1991', in *Bryn Mawr Classical Review*, 03.03.29, p. 331-337.

P. Roelli & D. Bachmann (2010), 'Towards generating a stemma of complicated manuscript traditions: Petrus Alfonsi's *Dialogus*', in *Re-vue d'histoire des textes*, p. 307-331.

F. Ronquist & J. P. Huelsenbeck (2003), 'MRBAYES 3: Bayesian phy-logenetic inference under mixed models', in *Bioinformatics*, 19, p. 1572-1574.

T. Roos, T. Heikkilä & Petri Myllymäki (2006), 'A Compression-Based Method for Stemmatic Analysis', in *Proceedings of the 2006 conference on ECAI 2006: 17th European Conference on Artificial Intelligence*, Amsterdam: IOS Press, p. 805-806.

T. Roos & T. Heikkilä (2009), 'Evaluating methods for computer-assisted stemmatology using artificial benchmark data sets', in *Liter-ary and Linguistic Computing*, 24, p. 417-433.

T. Roos & Y. Zou (2011), 'Analysis of Textual Variation by Latent Tree Structures', in *Proceedings of IEEE 11th International Conference on Data Mining*, Vancouver: IEEE, p. 567-576.

N. Saitou & M. Nei (1987), 'The neighbor-joining method: A new method for reconstructing phylogenetic trees', in *Molecular Biology and Evolution*, 4, p. 406-425.

C. Semple & M. A. Steel (2003), *Phylogenetics*, Oxford: Oxford Univer-sity Press.

M. Spencer, E. A. Davidson, A. C. Barbrook & C. J. Howe (2004), 'Phylogenetics of artificial manuscripts', in *Journal of Theoretical Biology*, 227, p. 503-511.

D. L. Swofford (2003), *PAUP**: *Phylogenetic Analysis using Parsimony (*and other methods)*, Version 4, Sunderland (MA): Sinauer Associates.

'Vita et miracula s. Symeonis Treverensis' (1867), in *Acta Sanctorum Junii I*. Parisiis et Romae: Palme, p. 86-92.

H. F. Windram, C. J. Howe & M. Spencer (2005), 'The Identification of Exemplar Change in the Wife of Bath's Prologue Using the Maximum Chi-Squared Method', in *Literary and Linguistic Computing*, 20(2), p. 189-204.

Z. Yang & B. Rannala (1997), 'Bayesian phylogenetic inference using DNA sequences: A Markov chain Monte Carlo method', in *Molecular Biology and Evolution*, 14, p. 717-724.

PHILIPP ROELLI

PETRUS ALFONSI, OR: ON THE MUTUAL BENEFIT OF TRADITIONAL AND COMPUTERISED STEMMATOLOGY

Introduction

In a previous publication[1] I studied the manuscript tradition of Petrus Alfonsi's *Dialogus* with the goal to be able to group its witnesses into an approximate *stemma codicum* and to give recommendations to the editors for a significantly reduced set of manuscripts from which to edit the text.[2] A very fast method consisting of both traditional and newly developed computerised methods was used to achieve this goal. After resuming the project and previous research, the present article intends to undertake an assessment of the validity of those results and will propose some improvements in the algorithm used. This is now facilitated by more reliable data based on much longer text samples transcribed by the editors and a traditionally elaborated stemma of theirs. The conclusion will summarise the benefits of this method for the edition of texts transmitted by many witnesses in general.

[1] See Philipp Roelli & Dieter Bachmann 2010. A similar, experimental automated procedure is now proposed by J.-B. Camps and F. Cafiero in this volume (p. 69 ff.); I would, however, approach their way of automatically finding the root with caution. They also offer some historical background about the stemmatic method.

[2] The editors are Carmen Cardelle de Hartmann, Darko Senekovic and Thomas Ziegler who started their work in 2010. Their edition is now well advanced and is likely to see the light in the year 2015. For the very generous access to all their data and the fruitful collaboration I thank them heartily.

10.1484/M.LECTIO-EB.5.102564

Background

Petrus Alfonsi was a Jewish convert from Spain who chose to be baptised in Huesca in the year 1106, changing his name from Moses to that of the saint of the day of his conversion (June 29, the apostle St Peter) and taking the second part of his name from his godfather Alfonso I of Aragón. He became an early propagator of Arabic lore and science for Latin Western Europe.[3] One of his two major works is the so-called *Dialogus*,[4] in which he justifies his conversion in a dialogue between himself before ('Moses') and after ('Petrus'). In the course of the argument a wide range of topics from Arabic learning, familiar to Alfonsi but not to his readers, comes under scrutiny. Besides these, there are also many references to contemporary Judaism completely unknown to his Latin readers. Interestingly, although Moses is compelled to repeatedly admit that Petrus's arguments are superior, the dialogue does not end in his conversion.

Alfonsi's familiarity with Arabic and Jewish lore may be the main cause for the work's subsequent huge popularity: in total we know of nearly 100 extant witnesses, more than seventy of which contain the more or less complete and non-redacted text. Fifteen of them still belong to the twelfth century,[5] after which the interest in the text does not wane until the sixteenth century. In contrast to many other anti-Jewish polemical writings, this one seemed to contain something timeless. The oldest manuscripts stem from Northern France and England where Alfonsi taught after his conversion. Paradoxically, the text's popularity made modern scholarship shirk from the laborious task of establishing a critical edition of the text. Besides the reprint of its *editio princeps* (gy)[6] from 1536 in Migne's *Patrologia latina* there has hitherto only been one attempt to produce a better text, made in a very ambitious PhD

---

[3] For the actual state of research cf. C. Cardelle de Hartmann 2011.

[4] The work does not seem to have had a title in the archetype, in the prologue it is simply referred to as *Opus sequens*. For background on this work compare the forthcoming volume by Cardelle de Hartmann and Roelli 2014.

[5] One of them from Chartres (Bibliothèque de la Cathédrale 127 [130]) is no longer extant: it fell pray to World War II.

[6] For the manuscript sigla see the list below (p. 48-52). The editors will publish a full and more detailed list of all manuscripts (including traces of lost ones) in their edition.

project by Klaus-Dieter Mieth, based for practical reasons on the manuscripts in Berlin and Paris.[7] The dissertation was never published on the book market and is therefore quite rare. Our research on the manuscript tradition suggests that his key manuscript (B1) belongs to a subsequently revised branch of the tradition.

Previous Research

In order to arrive at a preliminary result I transcribed a short set of text samples[8] from all witnesses and used software tools that Dieter Bachmann and I developed for that occasion. After the time-consuming process of getting hold of reproductions of all known witnesses, I was able to complete the transcription of those samples in less than a month's work. In order to plot a tree (an unrooted stemma) we used a combination of the common 'diff' algorithm (tuned for our circumstances) with a novel approach that tries to weight more significant variants (such approaching *Leitfehler*-status) more heavily. In this new experimental procedure the algorithm checks for any pair of potentially significant variants whether all four combinations of either's presence and absence occur among the witnesses. If only three of these four combinations occur, we took this to indicate that the changes from presence to absence (or *vice versa*) in both these loci of the examined pair happened exactly once each in the tradition (for an example, cf. table 1). Those variants that happened only once in a given tradition, and that are not easily revertible by thinking scribes or by coincidence, are the significant ones.[9] The next step counts the number of cases with only three combinations for a given candidate with all others. The higher that number, the more significant the variant.[10] As our text sample was rather short we could hardly

---

[7] K.-D. Mieth 1982.

[8] Mieth 1, 10-29; Mieth 3, 14-39; Mieth 143, 15-23 in total comprising 521 ± 10 words or 2943 ± 52 characters. The entire text contains some 370,000 characters.

[9] Note that the empty field in this procedure does not indicate which two variants are the original ones.

[10] For more details and an example of this procedure we refer to our previous publication (cf. p. 318). J.-B. Camps and F. Cafiori in this volume (p. 54) use a similar method, they speak of 'closed configurations' and 'conflicting variant locations' when all four combinations are found.

expect to find variants that would really deserve the term *Leitfehler* in a strictly Lachmannian sense. But we take this notion to be a quantitative one: a variant can be more or less useable as a *Leitfehler*, and should therefore be more or less weighted by our algorithm. For clarity we will refer to these algorithmic *Leitfehler* in quotes. Our procedure in further detail, *n* being the number of witnesses:

- Generate a list of words occurring between 2 and (n-2) times in the sample ('candidate' variants);

- Find the good and bad combinations for each candidate, those with only three or all four combinations of presence and absence occurring.

Our previous way of calculating a score for each 'Leitfehler' was:

- Penalise variants occurring in few witnesses by dividing by $\sqrt{k}$.[11]

- Divide this number by the total number of relevant cases of difference: $k*(n-k)$, where k is the number of occurrences or cases of absence, whichever happens to be smaller;

- Use the best, that is lowest/highest[12] scoring, among these variants with a higher weight in the diff-based algorithm.

The following steps are new improvements:

- We assign the 'Leitfehler' with the best score a maximum value (e.g. 10), and the others values between 1 and that maximum value (linearly according to their score). This removes the cut-off chosen *ad hoc* before.[13]

- In the meantime I found a much simpler and faster calculation formula yielding similar (even slightly better) results: for any good combination square the lowest among the three non-

---

[11] Without this step variants that occur in only two or three witnesses get a large advantage. Imagine a case with +A in 2 manuscripts, -A in all others, then the probability that these two manuscripts have both either +B or -B by coincidence is already 50%. The square root was chosen heuristically.

[12] Depending on whether the bad or good cases are used.

[13] Thus words with scores higher than 1 will be used with higher weight in the diff-based algorithm. The maximum number used is specified for the trees below.

zero values and add it to both candidates' scores. Compare numbers for both methods in the appendix, there referred to as old and new score.

	+ *intueor*	- *intueor*
+ *plebeiorum*	A2, A3, Ca, Fi, J1, Ld, P1, P3, P4, P5, V4 (11)	A1, An, Ar, Au, B2, Be1, Be2, Br, CC, Cp, Do, Go, gy, Ha, Hb, He, J2, Kn1, Kn2, L2, L3, Li, Mu, Ob, Ol, Or, P2, P6, Pr1, Sa, Sd, T2, Ut, V2, V3, V5, V6, V7, Wi, W2, Zu (41)
- *plebeiorum*	(none)	B1, Bo, Cr, D1, D2, In, Kr, L4, Ls, Me, Mi, P7, Pm, Po, Pr3, T1, Ta, To, V1 (19)

TABLE 1: An example for our method comparing presence and absence of potential *Leitfehler*. Two good ones are shown having one combination represented in no manuscript.

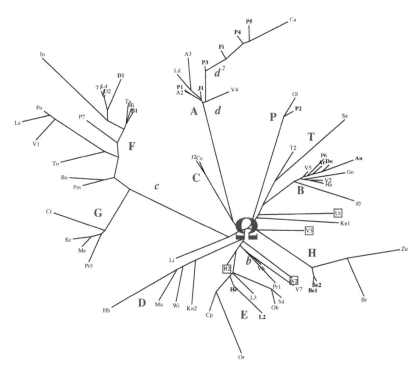

FIGURE 1: A tree generated with our best settings (using hand-picked *Leitfehler*) from our previous publication but now including nine newly discovered manuscripts. The archetype (Ω) had to be positioned manually. The heavily altered texts of A1 and Au were not plotted. Solitary manuscripts are boxed.

In order enable the reader to compare our result from 2010 to the stemma, the old algorithm (without the additional steps in the above list) was used to plot fig. 1 (cf. note 16 below), but in the appendix a completely automatically generated tree plotted with the new algorithm using all steps from the above list for the same text sample is included (fig. 5). The two new steps improve our result considerably. Compare the rather unconvincing fully automated plot (fig. 3 in our previous publication, printed here as fig. 6) to the current one (fig. 5 below). Now only few details are worse than in fig. 1 which additionally used handpicked *Leitfehler* and some others are indeed better.[14]

The following manuscripts of the *Dialogus* were used in Roelli & Bachmann 2010. The group names from the present publication are included. They differ from the ones I used then as for practical reasons the groups were renamed by the editors.

Manuscript	Sig.	Group	Ff.	Age[15]
Paris, Bibliothèque de l'Arsenal 769	A1	a^1?	158r–179r	XIII 1/4
Paris, Bibliothèque de l'Arsenal 941	A2	d^1	53r–98v	XII/XIII
Paris, Bibliothèque de l'Arsenal 553	A3	d^1	20r–98v	1451
Antwerp, Museum Plantin Moretus lat. 2/M 15.3	An	a^{2a-1}	77v–124v	XII 3/3
Arras, Bibliothèque municipale 1016 (ex 432)	Ar	a^{2a-1}	1r–41r	XII 2/3 or 2/4
Augsburg, Universitätsbibliothek Cod. II. 1 fol. 41	Au	-	157r–214v	XV
Berlin, Staatsbibliothek zu Berlin – Preußischer Kulturbesitz, Phillips 1721	B1	c^1	1r–132v	XII 3/5 or 4/5

---

[14] Some minor groups like d^2 or the position of the solitary Ut are better depicted in the manual plot; e.g. the position of gy or B2 in the automated plot.

[15] In order to save space the dating system gives the possible interval by a 'fraction' number for those witnesses dated newly for our previous publication. 1/2, e.g., means first half of the century given by the Roman number. Century dates in Arabic numbers are taken from the extant manuscript catalogues. Precise numbers are given for dated mss.

Berlin, Staatsbibliothek zu Berlin - Preußischer Kulturbesitz, Hamilton 21	B2	- 1r-42v	14th
Bern, Burgerbibliothek cod. 188	Be1	a^{2b}	35r-89r	XII 3/3
Bern, Burgerbibliothek cod. 111	Be2	a^{2b}	169r-217v	XII 4/4
Burgo de Osma, Biblioteca Capitular 35 (28)	Bo	c^1	7r-139r	1380
Brugge, Bibliotheek van het Grootseminarie MS 26/91	Br	a^{2b}	1-104v	XIII 2/2
Cambrai, Bibliothèque municipale 166 (161)	Ca	d^2	154r-197r	late 14th
Cambridge, Corpus Christi College 309	Cc	a^{2a}	37r-78v	XIII 1/3
Cambridge, Pembroke College 244	Cp	a^{1a}	49v-91v	14th
Cracow, Biblioteka Jagiellońska 1197	Cr	c^2	23r-118v	15th
Dijon, Bibliothèque municipale 228 (ex 190)	D1	c^1	2r-92r	XII 4/4
Dijon, Bibliothèque municipale 230 (ex 192)	D2	c^1	2r-101v	XIII 1/2
Douai, Bibliothèque municipale 199	Do	a^{2a-1}	95r-158v	XII 3/4
Cambridge, Fitzwilliam Museum, McClean Collection 120	Fi	d^2	1r-129v	XII 3/3
Göttingen, Niedersächsische Staats- und Universitäts-bibliothek, Luneb. 12	Go	a^{2a-1}	1-66v	15th
Cambridge Mass., Harvard College Library, MS Judaica 16	Ha	a^{2a1}	1r-182r	XV 2/4
Hereford, Cathedral Library P. 2 IV	He	a^{1a}	1r-108v	XII 3/3
Cambridge, St. John's College, E. 4 (James 107)	J1	d^1	117r-180v	XII 3/3
Cambridge, St. John's College, D. 11 (James 18)	J2	a^{2a}	1r-64v	XII/XIII
Klosterneuburg, Stiftsbibliothek 352	Kn1	a^1	101r-146v	14th
Klosterneuburg, Stiftsbibliothek 826	Kn2	a^{1a-1}	87r-207r	1391

49

Kremsmünster, Stiftsbibliothek 82	Kr	c^2	1r–68v	15th
London, British Library, Harley 3861	L2	a^{1a}	1ra–93vb	XII 3/3
London, British Library, Royal 15 C II	L3	a^{1a}	116ra–177rb	early 13th
London, British Library, Additional Ms 15404	L4	c^1	31r–144r	XIII 2/2
Leiden, Bibliotheek der Rijksuniversiteit, Scaliger 42	Ld	d^1	1r–104v	XIII
Liège, Bibliothèque Générale de l'Université 360 (cat. 351)	Li	a^{2a}	139r–198v	15th
Lisbon, Biblioteca Nacional, Alcobaça 148 (CCXLI)	Ls	d^1	1r–123r	XIII 1/4
Melk, Stiftsbibliothek 1059	Me	c^2	p. 25–160	1414
Munich, Bayerische Staatsbibliothek, Clm 28225	Mu	a^{1a-1}	81r–168r	XIII 1/2
Oxford, Bodleian Library, Bodley 801	Ob	a^{1a}	206r–268v	15th
Oxford, Bodleian Library, Laud. Misc. 356	Ol	a^{1a-1}	1r–120r	15th
Oxford, Bodleian Library, Rawlinson C. 322	Or	a^{1a}	1r–60v	14th
Paris, Bibliothèque nationale de France, lat. 10624	P1	d^1	63v–171r	XII 3/3
Paris, Bibliothèque nationale de France, lat. 10722	P2	a^{1a-1}	3r–76v	XII 3/5
Paris, Bibliothèque nationale de France, lat. 5080	P3	d^2	145r–205r	XII 1/4
Paris, Bibliothèque nationale de France, lat. 14069	P4	d^2	49r–113v	XII 2/3
Paris, Bibliothèque nationale de France, lat. 15009	P5	d^2	205r–255r	XII 3/3
Paris, Bibliothèque nationale de France, lat. 3359a	P6	a^{2a-1}	2r–61v	XIII/XIV
Paris, Bibliothèque nationale de France, lat. 16523	P7	c^1	2r–61r	14th
Paris, Bibliothèque Mazarine 980	Pm	c^1	93r–129v	XIV 1/2
Porto, Biblioteca Pública Municipal do Porto 34 (43)	Po	c^{1a-1a}	1r–73r	XIII 1/4

Prague, Archiv Pražského hradu C.XCV	Pr1	b	14r–37v	14th
Prague, Archiv Pražského hradu N.XLI	Pr3	c^2	56r–110v	early 15th
Salamanca, Biblioteca Universitaria 2579	Sa	a^{2b}	4r–130v	16th
Santo Domingo de la Calzada, Biblioteca Capitular 2	Sd	a^{1a}	96r–141r	XIII 1/2
Troyes, Bibliothèque municipale 509	T1	c^1	1r–57v	XIII 1/2
Troyes, Bibliothèque municipale 1720	T2	a^{2b}	1r–68v	XIII 1/2
Tarragona, Biblioteca provincial, Códice Misceláneo 55 (olim 126)	Ta	c^{1a}	109r–215v	XIII
Tortosa, Biblioteca de la Catedral 15	To	c^{1a-1}	1r–115r	XIII 2/2
Utrecht, Bibliotheek der Rijksuniversiteit 257 (eccl. 195)	Ut	-	156r–205v	1466
Vatican, Biblioteca Apostolica Vaticana, Vat. lat. 988	V1	c^{1a-1a}	80r–155v	1455
Vatican, Biblioteca Apostolica Vaticana, Pal. lat. 425	V2	a^{2a-1}	1r–72v	1392
Vienna, Österreichische Nationalbibliothek 1623	Wi	a^{1a-1}	1r–83r	early XIV
Zurich, Zentralbibliothek MS C 125	Zu	a^{2b}	1r–88r	XIII 1/2

EDITIO PRINCEPS (BASED ON A LOST MANUSCRIPT):

Coloniae apud Ioannem Gymnicum: *Petri Alphunsi ex Iudaeo Christiani Dialogi* (ed. prin.)	gy	a^{2a-1}	-	1536

New insight

Since our last publication, owing mostly to Darko Senekovic's heuristic skills, nine more manuscripts containing the complete text were newly discovered. Although none of them is very old, it seems that some of them will prove to be important for the *constitutio textus*. Moreover, thanks to these discoveries a new group

51

(below called **b**) emerges together with the previously isolated manuscript Pr1. What follows is a list of their provenance, sigla to be used, age and group they will be assigned to:

MANUSCRIPT	SIG.	GROUP	FF.	AGE[15]
Heidelberg, Universitäts-bibliothek, Cod. Sal. VII 102	Hb	a^{1a-1}	1r-79r	mid 13th
Innsbruck, Universitäts- und Landesbibliothek Tirol, 560	In	c^{1a-1}	25ra-93v	13/14th
Milano, Biblioteca Ambrosiana, Q. 29 sup.	Mi	c^1	1r-127	14/15th
Vaticano, Biblioteca Apostolica, Vat. Lat. 1294	V3	-	37v-246v	1370
Vaticano, Biblioteca Apostolica, Vat. Lat. 5379	V4	d^2	1r-41v	13th
Vaticano, Biblioteca Apostolica, Pal. Lat. 399	V5	a^{2a-1}	PDF p. 18-139	14th
Vaticano, Biblioteca Apostolica, Ottob. Lat. 254	V6	b	48r-209v	1461
Vaticano, Biblioteca Apostolica, Arch. Cap. S. Pietro G 30	V7	b	1r-46v	15th
Wien, Österreichische Nationalbibliothek, Ser. n. 12841	W2	-	PDF p. 1-94	15th

Now we have a total of 71 manuscripts to take into account, among which eleven are incomplete. Manuscripts still from the twelfth century are printed in bold face in the figures to give the reader some timescale. Senekovic and I transcribed the previously used text portions from the new manuscripts (cf. table 2, nos. 1-3). Fig. 1 was generated with the same settings as in the previous publication's best plot.[16] The new plot resembles the best older plot very closely (except for the additional manuscripts, of

---

[16] For practical reasons the list of hand-picked *Leitfehler*-candidates that were used, was slightly changed to: *accurrit, adheserat, aduersionis, citra-ad, compositor, cotidie, delegeris, dominus, elatorem, expositor, intueor, iudeorum, parebit, pecora, peperit, plebeiorum, plebis, propter, quantum, rectam, segregabuntur, similiter, supradicta, uie, uiri*. They were again weighted 30 times more than other variants. This choice im-

course). The new super-group names (lower-case letters) the editors now believe to be accurate, and the group names from our previous publication are added to the plot. The newly discovered super-group *a* (not marked in the plot in fig. 1) is spread through different parts of the plot, comprising all the upper-case groups in the plot not assigned to any lower case group.

	INCIPIT	MIETH PAGE	TITULUS	NO. OF CHARS.	NO. OF MS.	REMARKS
1	*dixit sequentis operis*	1,10-1,29	prol.	1 285	all	1-3 for previous article
2	*a tenera igitur pueritie*	3,14-3,39	1	722	all	
3	*multum certe sue tibi*	143,15-143,23	12	626	all	
4	*dixerunt ut ipsemet nosti*	29,16-32,33	1	8 670	24	
5	*quod ad presentem pertinuit*	46,12-58,4	3	30 274	22	entire *titulus*

TABLE 2: Existing transcriptions of portions of our text. For transcriptions 4-5 the editors chose heads of groups and manuscripts that were difficult to group. B2 was chosen at random as reference to indicate the amount of text in characters.

The editors have transcribed more text from the manuscripts that looked most profitable for the *constitutio textus* in our previous stemma. Table 2 summarises the transcriptions now at our disposal. The first three short samples were used in the previous publication. The samples to be used in the remainder of the present contribution were largely transcribed by the editors while elaborating their stemma and preparing their critical text; especially important is sample 5, using the text of one entire book (called in this work *titulus*) which makes up about one tenth of the full text amount. We plotted trees with the new data from samples 4 and 5. Again, we prepared the transcribed data by standardising the

proved our result very slightly, as can be seen by comparing fig. 6 in our previous publication to our fig. 1 here.

variable parts of mediaeval orthography.[17] With these transcriptions and some probing in other *tituli*, the editors have worked out a stemma by traditional means, mostly based on *lacunae* (and sometimes additions) as shared errors (*Bindefehler*) between the groups. Their current best result is shown in a simplified way in fig. 2. Bold lines indicate few differences, dotted lines many differences between items. Thus, e.g. L2, though apparently far removed from the origin (being mostly separated from it by bold lines) is in fact much closer to it than (e.g.) A1 or Kn1. The entire stemma may still be subject to minor changes before the text's final publication, but it is mostly the positions that are marked by dotted boxes where significant uncertainty remains. The gray divisions and manuscripts in fig. 2 indicate parts of the stemma our algorithm did not detect satisfactorily (in fig. 1); the hatched ones will become detectable by the aid of the larger text samples – these are discussed below.

The editors differentiate now four major groups:

1. *a* the biggest group splits into a^1 (our old groups E, P, D, and manuscript Kn1: in total 14 items), and a^2 (our old groups B, C, T, H: 18 items) – in total, close to half of the tradition. Up until now only two common eye-skips as shared errors in the entire *titulus* 11 were found to link the two subgroups, and one may thus wonder whether they could not have happened by coincidence independently in both groups. Thus, within all our text samples a^1 and a^2 appear as two separate groups: a^1's text is very close to that of the archetype; a^{2b} and our old group C, on the other hand, changed the text significantly.

2. *b* this new group consists of the previously solitary manuscript Pr1 and the newly discovered V6 and V7 (3 items). All its manuscripts are recent, but must needs go back to a good, early copy.

---

[17] There are many numerals in sample 4, so besides the usual suspects (y, h, nasals before consonants that may appear as m or n) I standardised those to normal Roman numbers (from varieties like *ducentos* vs. *cc* vs. *cc^os* vs. *ii centos* ... → *cc*). This approach proved to be good as indeed there were some real differences between some of the numerals that separate the tradition well.

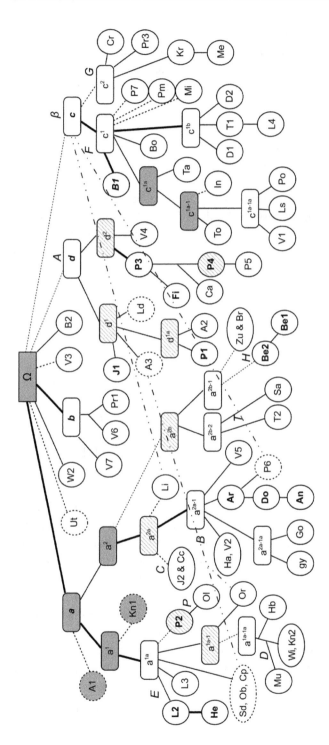

Figure 2: The editors' current *stemma codicum* based mostly on *titulus* 3. Bold lines show few alterations, dotted ones many; dotted witnesses' positions remain uncertain. Dots and dashes indicate likely cases of contamination.

3. *c* our previous 'hyparchetype β' consisting of groups F and G (19 items), now called c^1 and c^2. This group's text was slightly redacted at an early stage; it circulated mostly among Cistercian abbeys. Mieth's edition is based mostly on one of its manuscripts (B1).

4. *d* our old group A which can now clearly be split into two subgroups d^1 and d^2 (11 items). This text also represents an early redaction mostly of improvements in the Latin language.

Besides these four groups, six solitary manuscripts remain, three of which exhibit a strongly altered text, Ut and even more so Au and A1 (the latter possibly belonging to *a*),[18] plus B2, V3 and the newly discovered W2. More and more definite results about the manuscript tradition will be published by the editors in the introduction to their edition.

Problems and mistakes in our tree

One glance at fig. 1 and 2 suffices to see that the main problem with the previously suggested tree lies in the 'upper branches', i.e. those bifurcations close to the archetype. The editors discovered many of these divisions by the help of rare *Leitfehler* that were not present in our very restricted text sample. In this case the necessary information was simply not present and the algorithm had no chance to arrive at the correct dependencies. More interesting, from the point of view of improving the algorithm, are the rare cases of 'leaves' on a wrong 'branch'. These will be studied below. Caution concerning the branch lengths is in order: although our algorithm in principle produces branches proportional to the actual differences between witnesses, our (be it automatic or hand-picked) choice of Leitfehler disturbs this. Imagine a single medium strongly divergent manuscript (from the centre of the plot). It will have a relatively short branch. But if we add a close relative to the sample, our algorithm should find shared errors between these two and remove them further from the centre. A good example for this is Pr1 now joined to V6 in fig. 3 – there

---

[18] This manuscript lacks *titulus* 11, so the presence of the two cases of eye-skip cannot be checked.

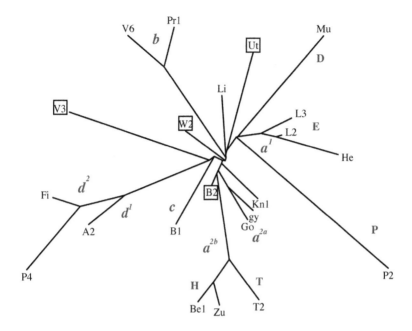

FIGURE 3: Plot for sample 4 (cf. table 2) for selected manuscripts making use of the best automatically found 'Leitfehler', maximally weighted 20 times more than other variants.

this new group is further from the centre than B1 whose text is in fact much more divergent.

For the new samples 4 and 5 I generated trees shown in fig. 3 and 4, the former with our old procedure, the latter fully automatically. Fig. 3 now resolves H and T as one well-defined group, moves P and D close to E, and He looks very much like a direct descendent of L2 (which is very probable). Manuscripts T2, Zu, Be1 were not plotted in fig. 4 as they omit more than half the text in this *titulus*. So while they clearly form a group, their inclusion would distort the rest of the plot. Other dependencies could here be detected: P1 and A2 against J1, and all of them against d^2; Li moves now close to a^2. The editors have already reconstructed a tentative archetypal text for *titulus* 3. To see how it behaves in our algorithm, we included this new 'witness' (called OM): it figures indeed close to the point where the major groups intersect, though with a slight preference for V7 and thus group *b*, which seems to have an especially good text.

Details

Let us now quickly sift through the major groups in order to locate the main problems. Among the four major groups, two (*c* and *d*) have such a strongly diverging text that it might tempt one to speak of redactions. These marked divisions were detected clearly by our algorithm and our small data sample. The structure within these two groups (excepting some sub-structures) seems to be quite accurate in our generated plot with the conspicuous exception of P4.[19] The smallest of the major groups *b* was detected, although it ends up close to our former group E as both are conservative compared to the rest. The remaining group *a* proved to be the most difficult to detect. Real *Leitfehler* between Ω and *a*, and similarly between *a* and its subgroup a^1, were not present in our small sample, so the group structure could not be detected; nevertheless the two major subgroups E and B were correctly separated but their fellows D & P and C, T & H, respectively, were not detected as belonging together. These five groups all altered their text quite significantly, so our algorithm placed them all over the tree. Previously, our hand-probing led us to believe that groups H and P represent a hyparchetype we called α. This could not be confirmed. In fact the assumption rested on a very small empirical basis: P was based on an eye-skip it had in common with *c*, but which apparently happened twice independently; for H it depended on the missing two words *uel superare*, which seemed to tie the group to *c*, but this apparently also happened twice independently. So the conclusion reached by philological means was clearly unwarranted: in fact, the algorithm's result (though also imprecise) was here better than my own. Within a^{1a-1} group P (in our plots represented by P2) often changes or even omits words. Compared to its particular errors, its number of shared errors with D (Mu) is very small which made its placing difficult. The manuscripts of group D were subjected to a redaction of its language, often consisting merely of alterations in the word order.[20] Among a^{1a} D and P are by far the most divergent parts, so the algorithm failed to arrange these groups correctly.

---

[19] As shown in our previous publication. For P4 compare its discussion below.
[20] For example in our small text sample: *dispositione et uoluntate* becomes *uoluntate et dispositione*, or *uiuos iudicare et mortuos* becomes *uiuos et mortuos iudicare*.

The only shared error for these groups in our samples 1-3 is *accurrit* against *peruenit*.[21] Even in the larger text sample 4 there are very few shared errors.[22] Nevertheless, fig. 3 shows a closer (albeit uncertain) relation between P2, Mu and E. This is a group that could hardly be detected with that small an amount of text; even with more text it remains difficult for the above reasons: a human expert seems necessary in such cases. H and T are easier to detect: they form a new definitive group with the new data plotted in fig. 3. B2 tends to be slightly misplaced as being closer to group E than it really is. This happened because B2 and E are both very conservative and thus share many old variants that were not well enough separated from true *Leitfehler* by our algorithm. Let us now have a quick look at the three manuscripts that deviated most in our plots:

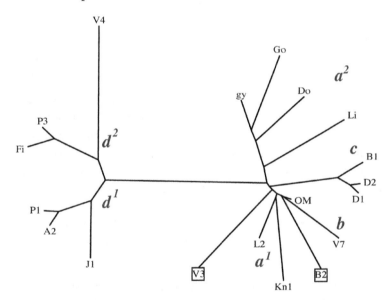

FIGURE 4: Plot of sample 5 with the best automatically identified variants, weighted maximally 20x more according to their score. OM is the editors' critical text. This sample is very robust: the result for 2x to 100x more weight is nearly identical.

This latter change happened at least three times independently in our tradition, posing serious problems to any algorithm.

[21] Which is even absent in Wi and Kn2 (within D).

[22] The shared errors between P2 and Mu: they lack *pariter* in *te mecum pariter salutiferis,* and have *dicitur* instead of *legitur* (this one together with their kin L2 and He).

Li   This manuscript tended to fluctuate in all our plots (compare fig. 3 and 4, the latter closer to what we believe to be true). There are readings that clearly go with c (*propter quid* in our first sample), but no strong shared variants in our text with a^2, though quite a few minor ones agreeing with it. In the more extended data set (no. 5) Li has the very strong variant *resurgent* against *reliqua* together with c but for most variants groups with a^2. So it seems to be contaminated by c though belonging in the main to a^2. A much more sophisticated algorithm would be needed to detect contamination.

Ut   Ut often goes its own ways, although in several *loci* it appeared to be related to T2 (and thus T); in our sample 4 *resolui* (against *reuolui*) and *risisse* (against *ridisse*), on the other hand, it can definitely not be part of that group as it does not share most of its many changes, like the large lacuna in *titulus* 3. What makes things worse is its lack of the two cases of eye-skip that 'define' group a. Its idiosyncratic text might go back to the archetype independently, but this needs to be studied further by traditional means.

P4   Previously, this manuscript looked contaminated as it fluctuated between our groups A (now d) and P. Fortunately for our algorithm – but to our embarrassment – the cause of this fluctuation lay in the fact that the transcription of our sample contained many mistakes, so many indeed, that it seems that something went wrong in the process of formatting the text. Once all the mistakes were corrected, the manuscript showed its true nature very clearly: it belongs to group A between P3 and P5.[23] This event reminds us how crucial clean input data is for any attempt to reconstruct a stemma!

One may wonder about the many branches on the stemma apparently tracing back directly to the archetype. This does not seem to be an artifact or mistake in our procedure. Fortunately, we know quite a lot about the publication of books in Alfonsi's time from his more famous contemporary Anselm of Canterbury.[24] Drafts were written on wax tablets that were then copied to parchment, be it by the author himself or by scribes. As Alfonsi

---

[23] The subsequent numbering is purely coincidental.
[24] Cf. R. Sharpe 2009.

seems to have been a sought after master and his text suited the Latin audiences' interest in Arabic lore, his wax tablets may well have been copied several times, possibly even in a corrected form by some scribes who took into account that Alfonsi probably learnt his Latin late in life.[25]

Conclusions

We have seen that the main problem in our previous publication was the small sample size. This, however, was intentional since the transcription from a large number of witnesses is the bottle neck with regard to labour, and a compromise between sample size and labour expense must be sought. Another issue is the accuracy of input data: correct transcriptions and a consistent policy of standardisation. Apart from these obvious factors that deteriorated our results, we have met others that could give us clues as to how to improve our software: in the very long sample 5, several excellent *Leitfehler* were not detected because their words occurred several times in the sample.[26] An easy remedy we are about to implement is to run the diff algorithm on the sample before choosing the *Leitfehler* candidates; in this way we will remove (for this step) all words with no variation which will reduce the problem significantly. A related matter concerns very long *lacunae* like those in a^{2b} in sample 5. As more than half of the text was missing there, our algorithm could not deal with the situation well. The pragmatic solution here was to use no witnesses with very long *lacunae* and to place them manually. Short *lacunae* on the other hand were well detected as shared errors as long as at least one of their words was not present in the sample elsewhere.

Let us note in passing that an editorial approach that takes into account only old manuscripts would in our case have completely overlooked group *b* (with its especially good text) together with the solitary manuscripts B2, V3, W2 and Ut as they are all late: *recentiores non deteriores*! Despite the fact that it is often hard to tell whether a variant may pass as a true *Leitfehler* (we have met

---

[25] This is Carmen Cardelle de Hartmann's hypothesis about the work's early circulation.

[26] E.g. the eye-skip *uos de sepulchris uestris populus meus et inducam* occurring exclusively in a^2. All its words occurred also somewhere else in this long sample.

several that seemed likely – such as the aforementioned cases of eye-skip – but finally turned out to have occurred independently more than once in the tradition), an approach which accords variants more weight proportionally to their stemmatic significance seems to improve purely statistical approaches considerably. This said, it is nonetheless clear that our approach is still in an experimental phase and will need to be studied in more depth. In our concrete case our procedure will make it possible to edit a text with more than 70 witnesses and of a total length of some 370,000 characters, or 140 Migne pages critically by a team of three part-time editors in less than three years. These figures might entice other editors to embark on similar projects for previously neglected popular mediaeval texts. Let us finish by recapitulating this procedure in the hope of inspiring similar projects.

Our method

Although the scenario of programming an algorithm that would produce the correct *stemma codicum*, upon input of all completely transcribed witnesses, is an interesting theoretical problem – whether possible or not seems hard to determine at present – such an algorithm would hardly be of much use for editors in most cases, as the limiting factor in the production of a critical edition is nearly always the time and effort involved in the very transcription of witnesses (leaving aside the problem of gaining access to them). On the other hand an algorithm such as ours, able to achieve a decent result with a very small text sample, may be very useful and time saving. Its result enables the editors to form a picture of the entire tradition with only slight inaccuracies, given only seconds of calculating power. Let us summarise here algorithmically how we propose to edit such texts. The procedure was successful for our text and may be so for others as well. Only the first steps rely on computerised methods; their aim is to reduce the amount of witnesses in order to allow the editor to proceed traditionally.

1. Transcribe a small sample from all witnesses[27] in standardised orthography;

2. Generate a list of *Leitfehler*-candidates and plot tentative trees with our software (which we will happily share);

3. Check whether the 'Leitfehler' make sense, and (if necessary) improve the list manually and so improve the manuscript groupings;

4. Choose a subsample of witnesses containing the most promising ones in each group as well as the solitary and unclear ones;[28]

5. Transcribe more text from these, plot more trees, and also (if necessary) align the transcriptions, trying to find solid *Leitfehler* and creating a stemma of the subsample;

6. Use the solid *Leitfehler* that were identified to confirm the other witnesses' grouping (if impossible, go back to step 5 and transcribe the additional text for the problematic witness[es] as well);

7. Choose the subset of witnesses to be used in the critical edition;

8. Edit the text critically from them.

Bibliography

C. Cardelle de Hartmann (2011), 'Pedro Alfonso y su Dialogus: estado de la cuestión', in J. Martínez Gázquez et al. (eds.), *Actas del V Congreso Internacional de Latín Medieval Hispánico (Barcelona, 7-8 de septiembre, 2009)*, Florence: Sismel.

C. Cardelle de Hartmann & P. Roelli (2014), 'Petrus Alfonsi and his Dialogus. Background, context, reception', Acts from the congress in Zurich, September 3-4, Micrologus Library, Florence: Sismel.

K.-D. Mieth, 'Der Dialog des Petrus Alfonsi. Seine Überlieferung im Druck und in den Handschriften. Textedition' (unpublished doctoral thesis, Freie Universität Berlin, 1982).

---

[27] Preferably from more than one *locus* in the text, as the exemplar may have been shifted in some witnesses. Less than some 500 words each does not seem advisable.

[28] In our case a reduction from 71 to about a dozen witnesses was possible.

P. Roelli & D. Bachmann (2010), 'Towards Generating a Stemma of Complicated Manuscript Traditions: Petrus Alfonsi's Dialogus', in *Revue d'histoire des textes*, 5, p. 307-321.

R. Sharpe (2009), 'Anselm as Author, Publishing in the Late Eleventh Century', in *Journal of Medieval Latin*, 19, p. 1-87.

SOME NUMERIC DATA
FROM OUR LEITFEHLER-CALCULATION

This section evaluates the automatically found 'Leitfehler' in the already previously used short samples (1-3 in table 2), and shows the completely automated tree mentioned above (page 50). Table 3 shows the best scoring variants for samples 1-3; the first number is the number of manuscripts that either do or do not have the variant, whichever of the two is fewer. The last two numerical columns show the variants' relative scores according to my previous and my current calculation (mentioned above p. 48f). The numbers were standardised to a maximum of 10 arbitrary units, the larger the better, with the intention of giving the best ones a weight of ten times that of an insignificant variant. The right part of the table studies the variants' value as *Leitfehler*. When several variants had the same scores (and thus were present in the same manuscripts), they were printed in the column to the right to save space. (+) and (-) indicate whether the variant's presence or absence is shown in the next column.

For valid *Leitfehler* we would expect to find in the column to the right only one group each, but group separation still works reasonably well in case of two or even three major groups sharing the variant by coincidence. Solitary manuscripts that should belong to a known group, on the other hand, are a bad sign for a candidate. None among the best scoring 25 variants are completely useless stemmatologically; those printed in bold face were used in the hand-pick for fig. 1 above. Nonetheless further studies with larger text samples seem necessary to evaluate our new calculation method better.[29]

---

[29] Note that all but one (*peperit*) of the variants I used for the handpicked plots appear in the first 100 of more than 300 candidates. Most of the others in the top 50 or so could be added to the hand-pick without detriment to the result. We chose to include mainly variants that separate major groups, not only two or three manuscripts from the rest, as these groups were easily detected anyway.

variant	no.	old score	new score	pres./ abs.	groups	other variants with the same occurrences and numbers
intueor	11	8.02	**10.00**	(+)	*d*	*climatis, delegeram*
expositor	9	4.82	8.39	(+)	c^{lb}, B1, Mi, Ta, To	
elatorem	7	6.73	8.34	(+)	ca. half c^l: B1, D1, D2, Mi, L4, Ta, P7	
accurrit	11	5.18	8.20	(+)	a^{la} (not Kn2, Wi)	
apparebit	16	6.56	7.94	(+)	$a^{2\text{-}al}$, **T**, **D**, Ut	
pecora	11	4.76	7.40	(+)	$a^{2\text{-}al}$ (not An), **T**, Ut	
poteris	11	3.47	7.19	(+)	*d* (not A3), Sa	
citra	21	6.87	7.05	(–)	a^2, *b*	
parebit	18	4.92	7.00	(–)	$a^{2\text{-}al}$, **T**, **D**, Ut	
		4 more				
plebeiorum	19	7.31	6.32	(–)	*c*	*plebis, cotidie, rectam, iudeorum*
		2 more				
peruenit	19	6.95	6.29	(–)	a^{la}, C, A3, J1, Ld; W2	
supradicta	14	6.88	6.29	(+)	$a^{2\text{-}al}$, **P**, Zu, Kn1	
dominus	5	5.32	6.07	(+)	d^2 (not V4)	*pueritie*
		2 more				
assidue	21	7.21	5.34	(–)	*c* , Kn1	
uiri	16	6.07	5.31	(+)	*d*, c^{lb}, In	
		6 more				
aduersionis	4	3.87	4.62	(+)	**H**	
similiter	21	6.93	4.58	(–)	*c*, **P**	
		2 more				
segregabuntur	4	3.05	4.48	(+)	**D**	
adheserat	4	5.32	3.69	(–)	**H**	
			10 more, after *superare* only selected words are shown			
superare	24	7.81	3.25	(–)	*c*, Br, Zu	
quantum	34	**10.00**	3.06	(–)	*d*, a^2, Kn1, V3	
compositor	17	5.46	2.71	(–)	*c*, Sa	
propter	21	7.04	2.70	(+)	*c*, Kn2, Li	
recte	22	7.22	2.56	(–)	*c*, Sa, P6	
mortuusque	3	6.71	2.56	(–)	$c^{la\text{-}la}$	
credere	2	6.63	1.05	(–)	Sd, Ob	*nomine*
peperit	2	6.03	0.98	(–)	**P**	*ipsum, fecerit, atque*

TABLE 3: The best automatically detected 'Leitfehler' and their properties (for samples 1-3). Variants in bold print were included in our handpick for fig. 1.

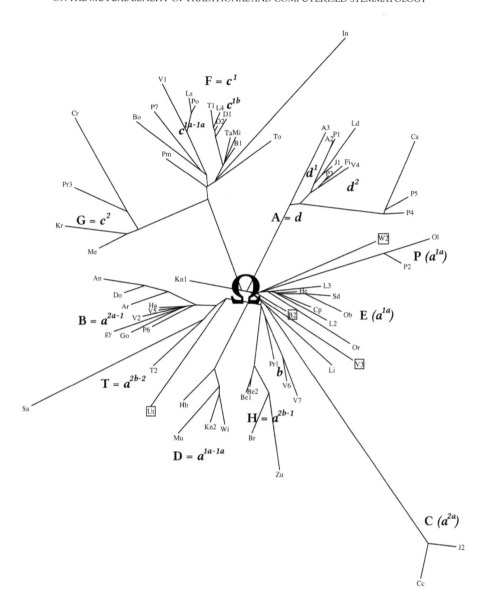

FIGURE 5: Fully automated plot of samples 1–3, using a weight of 20 times for the best 'Leitfehler' and proportionally less for the others, according to their scores. Cf. p. 48 above.

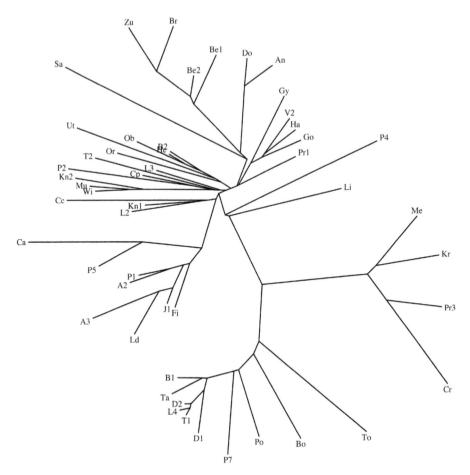

FIGURE 6: Fully automated plot published as fig. 3 in previous publication. Comparing it to figure 5 shows the latter's improvement.

JEAN-BAPTISTE CAMPS – FLORIAN CAFIERO

GENEALOGICAL VARIANT LOCATIONS AND SIMPLIFIED STEMMA: A TEST CASE*

Introduction

The method to be presented here relies upon text-genealogical principles inspired by the Lachmannian or neo-Lachmannian tradition,[1] and attempts to computerise them, following and ex-

---

* Sources used for this article are available at http://graal.hypotheses. org/625. Readers are welcome to contact the authors at jbcamps@hotmail.com or florian.cafiero@polytechnique.edu.

[1] The hesitation in terminology here deserves some explanation. Parts of what is traditionally considered the 'Lachmannian method' do not stem from Karl Lachmann, but from other philologists and scholars. Stemmata themselves did not appear in Lachmann's work; the idea of elaborating a genealogy of manuscripts based on their common readings (though not yet common errors) goes back to the eighteenth century and scholars such as Bengel (see particularly in Bengel 1763, p. 20-21, where he states that the entire tradition of the New Testament could be summarised in a *tabula genealogica*, a statement presented along with the concept of elimination of singular readings inside each family), and the first actual stemmata appeared almost concurrently in Schlyter and Collins 1827, Zumpt 1831, I, p. xxxviii, and Ritschl 1832, p. xxx. Even after stemmata became common, Lachmann never took the time to draw any in his editions, perhaps considering them an unnecessary simplification, in contrast to some of his followers such as Karl Nipperdey. The confusion between the work of Lachmann and the method of the 'common errors', often erroneously attributed to him, seems to go as far back as the 1860s and contributions by Goebel in 1860 and by Boeckh in 1877 (see Fiesoli 2000, part. p. 261 and 370). However, the idea that only the 'common errors' (and not 'common readings') have a genealogical value is to be attributed to Gaston Paris in 1872, although not clearly stated and theorised until Paul Lejay, first in a review of a work by Sabbadini in 1888 ('dans sa liste de variantes, il [M. Sabbadini] introduit de bonnes leçons de *B H b* qui ne prouvent rien. Si, en effet, *B H b* ont une bonne leçon contre une faute ou plutôt une innovation de *M*, cela ne peut prouver seulement que le copiste de *M*,

10.1484/M.LECTIO-EB.5.102565

tending the procedure first proposed by E. Poole in the 70s (Poole 1974, 1979). More than the application of computerised methods to philology, this method seeks to extend philology through the aid of the computer.[2] It favours interaction between philologist and computer, and requires the former's critical judgement at some points.[3]

After a careful selection of variant locations,[4] needed to eliminate contamination and polygenesis (the two major factors that could impede the elaboration of a stemma), we will then proceed to produce a stemma that is, at least at first, a simplification. It is of course to be noted that a stemma is by its very nature a simplification. In particular, Weitzman 1985, p. 82 notes that:

> The stemmatic method involves the following assumptions: (i) the author nowhere left variant readings; (ii) every manuscript (except the original) was copied from a single source; (iii) no two copyists originated the same error independently;

comme tout autre, a ses fautes personnelles,' p. 282); and then more clearly even in an other review from 1903 ('Une famille de manuscrits est constituée par leurs fautes communes, ou, si l'on préfère ce terme plus exact, par leurs innovations communes. Ainsi, l'existence d'une série de leçons correctes et authentiques dans plusieurs manuscrits ne peut prouver que ces manuscrits dérivent d'une source commune. Les fautes seules sont probantes,' p. 171). In a strict sense, Lachmann's originality resides more in his intent to reconstruct the text of the archetype mechanically, without having to appeal to critical *judicium*. Nonetheless, the term of 'Lachmannian' is broadly used to qualify a philologic current of thought whose foundations go back earlier than our German scholar, and that was further developed and enriched after him by famous philologists such as G. Paris, p. Collomp, G. Pasquali or p. Maas, to name but a few. See the enlightening works on the genesis of this method by Timpanaro 2003, and Fiesoli 2000. For the history of the elaboration of the principle of 'common errors', see Reeve 1998 or the shorter and less precise summary by Froger 1968, p. 41-42.

[2] As such, it seeks to take into account the question of Duval (2011) on computerised stemmatological methods: 'Quel éditeur pourra juger du degré de confiance à placer dans des algorithmes complexes, dont il ne maîtrise pas les soubassements?'.

[3] It is in that regard similar in perspective to the contribution in this volume by P. Roelli, 'Petrus Alfonsi or On the mutual benefit of traditional and computerised stemmatology'.

[4] A variant location (*lieu variant*), sometimes called a 'place of variation' is to be understood as a 'part of a text in which the extant text versions show one or more different ('competing') variants' (Salemans 1996), or more precisely in our case, as the largest textual unit showing stable common variation among witnesses and opposing at least one witness to the others, be it at the word- or syntagm-level; it is to be noted that it corresponds to the way variants are commonly displayed in the critical *apparatus* of an edition (i.e. attached to a common *lemma*).

(iv) errors were not removed by conjecture; (v) every relevant manuscript (i.e. a manuscript that survives or leaves extant progeny) except the original introduced at least one new error, at a point where no relevant manuscript had yet erred; (vi) of the errors introduced by a given relevant manuscript, at least one can be identified by critics as an error.

It is obvious that, in most text traditions, this will never be strictly the case. This is why we will, in the first instance, focus all our efforts on the removal of all variant location that do not fit these principles (i-iv) – and it is in that sense that the stemma produced will have to be considered a simplification. Moreover, we choose not to postulate any supposedly lost manuscript that is not strictly necessary to represent the genealogy of the extant ones. We will, on the other hand, have to assume that rule (v) – the introduction of at least one new error by each of the 'relevant manuscripts', an error that should be at this point found only in this manuscript[5] – always applies. Fortunately, as we shall see, our method is not bound by rule (vi) as it is based only on disagreements.

The Method: Selecting readings – Preliminaries

To establish our first selection of variant location and readings, a few things need to be said about the nature of the texts with which we intend to work. As medieval vernacular works, they are usually characterized by what has been called a '*tradizione attiva*' (Varvaro 1970, p. 87) – that is, a tradition in which scribes feel at liberty to introduce modifications to the text in order to 'improve' it according to their own perception or tastes. In many cases they are even expected to do so, for instance, to adapt the text to the uses or tastes of their region, time, or a particular audience. The most obvious examples of such modifications are

---

[5] Contrarily to Weitzman, we think that the error in itself should be unique to this manuscript at this point, not that the existence of an error should be unique; this new error could coexist with other different errors found elsewhere in the tradition at the same variant location, and still play the role Weitzman attributes to it. On the other hand, there is a need to add another principle, that could be formulated as: 'every relevant manuscript has kept intact at least one of the errors belonging to its source' – a principle slightly different from (iv) as it excludes any modification to the error, not just its being removed by conjecture.

diachronic or diatopic variations, such as graphical change induced to give a word a more modern or locally appealing aspect. At this level, this kind of transformation may even not necessarily be conscious. Of course, they can also happen on a larger scale and be the outcome of a fully conscious intention to transform, interpolate, or rewrite parts of the source[6]

This phenomenon – be it called '*mouvance*' (Zumthor 1972) or, perhaps more properly considering the written more than oral nature of this transformation, '*variance*' (Cerquiglini 1983) – results in each medieval copy being what Cesare Segre calls a 'diasystem', that is, a compromise between two or more systems: the system of the original and that of the scribes. Those two systems interact with each other and result in a compromise inherent to each medieval copy, a new system including its own form of variation (Segre 1976, 1979).

Moreover, the texts are heavily transformed by the process of text copying itself. A good understanding of this process, which is in itself interesting, also enables us to gain a better understanding of text variation, and, eventually, of text genealogy. In that case, books like Louis Havet's *Manuel de critique verbale* (Havet 1911) are highly valuable: his catalogue of errors can also be read as a fundamental study on what text copying in the Middle Ages was, and we strongly believe that any stemmatological method must be grounded in sound knowledge of the mechanisms of text copying, especially in what concerns the genesis of variations and errors.

In this regard, we can only sympathize with Marichal's regret (1979, p. 287) that there is no equivalent to Havet's book for vernacular languages, apart from several attempts, of limited broadness, such as the one found in Robert Marichal's editions of Marguerite de Navarre's texts:[7]

> Les latinistes ont le *Manuel de critique verbale* de Havet [...].
> Pour la langue vulgaire, nous n'avons rien. [...] C'est un travail
> long et fastidieux, démoralisant parce qu'il est très complexe;
> il requerrait d'ailleurs la collaboration d'un psychologue.

---

[6] See the summary of these questions, done from the point of view of scribal behaviour in Camps 2012.

[7] See the 'Catalogue des fautes' in Marichal 1956 and in Marichal 1971.

Mais il ne paraît pas douteux qu'un gros catalogue, bien fait, fondé sur de nombreux textes variés, nous donnerait une compréhension beaucoup plus profonde de la psychologie d'un copiste et permettrait d'aboutir à une pondération statistique des variantes.

It would indeed certainly be a very fruitful project to build a database of errors that could be used to identify the mechanisms inherent to text variation – the environmental, psychological, and textual factors inseparable from text copying – and its impact would certainly be broader than stemmatology. Beyond the weighting of readings hinted at by Marichal, such a catalogue would be very helpful (including what was mentioned above) to help in the elaboration of sets of text-genealogical rules, such as the inspiring one from Salemans 1996.

The Method: Selecting readings – Encoding and selection of variant locations

The first step is of course to create a database and select the readings. According to the aforementioned principles, and to eliminate the most likely cases of *polygenesis* – what Havet (1911, § 1614) calls '*rencontres*', and Salemans (1996) or Schmid (2004) 'parallelisms'[8] – we differentiate between:

1. *indicative readings* (useful for dating, localisation or work on the scribe's system), such as simple graphical changes, synonymisms, diachronic or diatopic variations, flexional changes in tense or case, simple inversions, which are excluded from the database;

2. *potentially genealogical readings* characterised by:

   a) being not easily reproducible independently;
   b) being not easily corrigible through conjecture;

---

[8] Contrarily to what Salemans 1996, p. 8, n. 5 affirms Havet does not uses the term of '*parallélisme*' with the same meaning as he does. For Havet 1911 § 543, a '*parallélisme*' is a scribal error ('*confusion de passage*') due to analogies in two close parts of a text: 'Lorsque deux portions de texte voisines ont des analogies, les auteurs s'efforcent d'y varier l'expression; les copistes, au contraire, tendent à l'uniformiser [...]'.

c) producing a semantic alteration;
d) being somehow meaningful by themselves (a reading 'must fit inconspicuously in context' [Salemans 1996], a rule also referred to as elimination of 'nonsense readings' [Colwell 1969; Duplacy 1979; Epp 1967], or, to quote Maas [1957, p. 32]: 'Besonders sicher kenntlich als Trennfehler sind solche Fehler [...], die in ihrer Umgebung gar nicht als Fehler erkannt werden, also keinen Anreiz zu konjekturaler Beseitigung geben konnten'); it results, for instance, in the exclusion of nonexistent words.

Amongst potentially genealogical readings, a distinction must be made between: (i) readings that are potentially genealogical *only in certain configurations, i.e.* singular readings (SR) or omissions; (ii) readings shared by at least two manuscripts, or common readings (CR).

When, for a given potentially genealogical variant location, we have at least two different potentially genealogical readings, each of which is shared by at least two manuscripts (*i.e.,* two different CR), we can assume the presence of at least one genealogically usable significative error or *Leitfehler* (Maas 1937).[9] Since we do not want to have to judge *ex ante* which (if any) reading is original and which is innovated or erroneous, we will work only on textual disagreements (and not on agreements), in which case – assuming no *varianti di autore* (Pasquali 1934, p. 396 ff.) – we assume that at least one of those readings is not original and that we are thus left with one usable separative error – *errores separativi* or *Trennfehler* (Maas 1937)[10] – of course, with three different CR, we can assume two usable separative errors.

[9] This can be compared, in some regards, to Salemans 1996, p. 19, fourth genealogical rule and his notion of 'type-2 variation' ('Only if all text versions show at a place of variation exactly two genealogically significant variants, and if each variant does occur in at least two text versions, can these variants be directly used for the determination of the structure of the stemma [...]. This fundamental variation is called a 'type-2' variation'), with the important difference that we see a limitation to binary variant locations as dangerous, and that our method allows to take into account variant locations containing more than two CR, and, to some extent, also to take singular readings into account.
[10] Since we will not group manuscripts if they share one CR, but instead, will separate them if they are opposed on two different CR, we are freed from the traditional Lachmannian necessity to differentiate between an original reading,

Or to say it more formally, let R_a be the set of manuscripts containing the same Reading a, let L be a variant Location such as $L=\{R_a,...,R_i\}$, and S the number of Separative errors:

$$\forall L, \exists (R_a, R_b), (Card(R_a)>1) \wedge (Card(R_b)>1) \Rightarrow 1 \leq S \leq 2 \qquad (1)$$

We will see later how the disagreements can be used to build the stemma. For now, nonetheless, as Schmid 2004 tries to demonstrate, a set of text-genealogical rules for the selection of variant readings does not suffice to rid oneself completely from accidental common variations (polygenesis, also called *rencontres* or 'parallelisms'). Moreover, we are still left to face the most terrifying foe of every text-genealogist, i.e., *contamination*, against which, to use the very famous quotation of Maas 1937, p. 294, '*ist noch kein Kraut gewachsen*' (or in an even less optimistic way: '*ist kein Kraut gewachsen*', Maas 1957, p. 31). To that end, we will make use, at first, of a quite archaic medical principle to be able to produce a (simplified) stemma: *amputate that what you cannot treat*.

The application of our method must be strict, making it necessary for all non-genealogical or contaminated readings to be properly filtered out using our aforementioned principles; after this first selection *by individual examination*, we then proceed to a second algorithmic selection.

The Method: Selecting readings -
Detecting genealogically unusable variant locations

The principle

Once we have selected potentially genealogical variant location, we need to assess which ones truly are, and which ones result from either left out cases of polygenesis or contamination. To this end we shall make use of an algorithmic selection of variant location based on an inspiring article from Poole (1979). Its principle is both easy to understand and very powerful. Variant locations are systematically compared two by two. For the sake of the demonstration, we can picture this as a table, figuring the dif-

the sharing of which has no genealogical weight, and a 'common error', implying parentage.

ferent readings of the first variant location (where in this example three variant readings are found, labelled 1-1 to 1-3), and those of the second variant location (four variant readings, labelled 2-1 to 2-4). Each combination, extant in at least one manuscript, of a reading from the first variant location with a reading from the second variant location is marked in the table (fig. 1 and 2).[11] As long as there is no 'closed configuration', no problem arises, and the two variant location may both correspond to a possible genealogy (1). On the other hand, as soon as there is a closed configuration, there is a problem (either polygenesis or contamination), because this configuration cannot correspond to a normal genealogical tradition (2).[12]

FIGURE 1: Crossing the readings of two potentially genealogical variant locations: table (left) and an example of a possible genealogy it could correspond to (right).

FIGURE 2: Conflicting variant locations: table (left) and absence of a possible normal genealogy (right).

---

[11] To take a virtual example for clarity's sake, for the first table, we could have a first variant location: cuer *AB* iex *DE* chief *C*, and a second: esragement *AD* forment *C* estraingement *B* per engien *E*. For the second, we could have a first variant location: cuer *AB* iex *DE* chief *C*, and a second: esragement *AD* forment *C* estraingement *BE*.

[12] Our approach can be compared to the procedure proposed by Roelli in his contribution in this volume (see the 'Previous Research' section); they actually seem more or less equivalent, with a slight difference in the treatment of *lacunae*, when there are exactly two different readings for each of the considered variant location, but tend to differ in other cases.

This 'closed configuration' can also be formalised as: let x, y be readings of the first variant Location L and x', y' readings of the second variant Location L', such as: $L = \{x, y, ...\}$, $L' = \{x', y', ...\}$, let $M = \{m_1, ..., m_k, ..., m_n\}$ be the set of all manuscripts, and G the group of genealogical variant locations:

$$\begin{cases} \{x, x'\} \in m_k \\ \{x, y'\} \in m_{k'} \\ \{x', y'\} \in m_{k''} \\ \{y, y'\} \in m_{k'''} \\ (k, k', k'', k''') \in [1;n]^4 \end{cases}$$

$$\Rightarrow (L \not\subseteq G) \vee (L' \not\subseteq G) \tag{2}$$

In that case, the two variant locations are considered to be 'conflicting' with each other, and at least one of them is genealogically unusable at that point.

This is, we think, a typical example of how traditional stemmatic methods can be extended by the use of the computer: it allows one to perform a number of comparisons that would not be possible manually, while still following the same principles.

We then implement a method allowing us to determine, as often as possible, which of these conflicting variant locations are genealogical and which are not.

Representing conflicts

To represent the conflicts between variant locations, we create a graph $G=(V,E)$, where $V(G)$ is the set of all the conflicting variant locations, and $E(G)$ the set of all links between these variant locations. A link $\{u, v\}$ is drawn between two variant locations u and v if and only if u and v are in conflict with each other. The network is obviously not oriented. We choose not to add any weights in this network, thus assuming that all the conflicts between variant locations are of the same significance. We then implement an algorithm to deduce from this graph G appropriate variant locations to build our stemma.

STEP 1: *isolate the most conflicting variant locations.* Variant locations which are most in conflict with other variant locations can be of two types: some may actually participate in the normal genealogy – the numerous variant locations in conflict with them being non-genealogical. However, most of them should be non-genealogical themselves, containing random parallelisms or contaminated readings, thus hardly of any use to build our stemma. Poole (1979) described this situation with this metaphor: Picture a room full of people, some of them drunk, some of them sober. The drunken one can crash into everybody, while the sober ones will not initiate a crash by themselves; thus, two sober persons will never crash into each other. To define which are the most conflicting variant locations (the probable 'drunken' ones), different approaches might be adopted. A simple method would be to define a threshold above which the number of links pointing towards a variant location is such that the variant location is considered 'over-conflicting'. It is, however, hard to think that there actually exists an absolute number of conflicts that should be considered abnormal. A simple and classic solution would be to set a threshold, not on the degree of a node, but on its degree centrality[13] C_i, defined as:

$$C_i = \frac{deg(u)}{n\text{-}1}$$

where n denotes the number of nodes in the graph G. Yet, taking into account the number of nodes might not be the best way, as what interests us is not only the number of variant locations, but also how many conflicts there are between them. This is why we chose to set a threshold on another index, computed as follows:

$$C_i = \frac{deg(u)}{e\text{-}deg(u)}$$

where e denotes the total number of conflicts. The threshold, based on the second index, has been chosen here on a heuristic basis.

STEP 2: *isolating variant locations in conflict with the over-conflicting variant locations.* In the second step of our algorithm, we make the obvious assumption that a variant location that is in conflict with the 'over-conflicting variant locations' as defined above has

---

[13] In Graph theory, the degree of a node is the number of links (here representing conflicts) drawn between this node and other nodes of the graph.

reasonable chances to be reliable. This is why we call these variant locations 'potentially reliable'.

STEP 3. *Determining reliable variant locations.*

3.a. Conflicts between 'potentially reliable variant locations'. Since it is impossible to determine if variant locations that are 'potentially reliable' but are in conflict with each other are really reliable or not, if two potentially reliable variant locations are in conflict, they are both deleted (fig. 3 left); another possibility is of course to resort to the critical judgement of the philologist and examine these cases individually, if feasible.

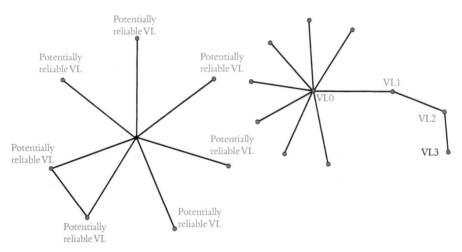

FIGURE 3: Non-assessable variant locations.

3.b. *Path superior or equal to 3.* The nature of a variant location whose minimal path to an over-conflicting variant location is superior or equal to 3 is not assessable (fig. 3 right): a variant location connected to a 'potentially reliable' variant location is not reliable. These variant locations have a distance 2 to an over-conflicting variant location; and variant location connected to them may be either reliable or not (being in conflict with a weakly rejected variant location does not help to decide whether a variant location is reliable or not). Again, these variables shall be either eliminated by the algorithm, or examined individually by the expert.

Algorithmic Aggregation method:
Benign and severe disagreements

The aggregation method is based not on agreements, but on disagreements, with an important difference to be made between *benign* and *severe* disagreement between two manuscripts:

1. A benign disagreement is a disagreement between two manuscripts, on two readings of which at least one is a singular reading or a omission. This kind of disagreement involving a singular reading does not necessarily signify that one manuscript could not have shared the same model as the other, or that one could not have been copied from the other;

2. A severe disagreement is a disagreement between two manuscripts, on two readings both shared with at least one other manuscript. Since we consider only disagreements, the concurrence of two different readings means that at least one of them is erroneous or innovated and thus constitutes a *Trennfehler* (see above, section 1.1.2, p. 8).

Algorithmic Aggregation method: Grouping manuscripts

To build the stemma, the algorithm goes through the following steps:

1. Manuscripts that have no severe disagreement between each other form a group.

2. For each group a virtual model of it is constituted. For each variant location:

   a) if all manuscripts agree on one reading, this reading is assigned to the virtual model.

   b) if not:

      i. if all, except one, are singular readings or omissions (or *lacunae*), the non-singular reading is assigned;

      ii. if all are singular readings or omissions (or *lacunae*): the reading of the model is not assessable.[14]

---

[14] We recommend that these cases, very rare in our experience, be system-

3. All manuscripts of the group are then compared to this virtual model:

   a) if a manuscript of the group has no benign disagreement with the model, it is the model of the group;

   b) if several manuscripts can correspond to the model, there is not enough data to decide;

   c) if none can be the model, then the model is outside the group, and the virtual model will be compared in the same fashion to all extant and virtual manuscripts outside the group;

   d) if again none can be the model, then it is assumed that the model is a lost manuscript.

4. Once all groups are formed, child manuscripts (*codices descripti*) are removed, and the algorithm goes back to step one, until the top of the stemma is reached.

Let a and b be two different manuscripts, L a variant location, and R readings:

$$(\exists L=\{\{R_a,R_i,...\}\{R_b,R_j\}\})\Rightarrow\{a,b\}\in G \tag{3}$$

G being a group of manuscripts. For this group, to reconstruct the model m:

$$G=\{a,b,...,i\},j\notin G$$
$$\forall L,R_a=R_b=R_i\Rightarrow R_m=R_a \tag{4}$$
$$\forall L,R_a\neq R_b=R_i\Rightarrow R_m=R_b \tag{5}$$
$$\forall L,R_a\neq R_b\neq R_i,R_a=R_j\Rightarrow R_m=R_a \tag{6}$$

For manuscript a and model m

$$(\exists R_a\neq R_m)\Rightarrow a=m \tag{7}$$

atically examined individually, because they can contain interesting information about the state of the tradition at this level. In some cases, this impossibility of assessing the reading of the model is solved at aggregation step 3(a), if a manuscript of the group is identified with the reconstructed model.

Algorithmic Aggregation method: Orientation

The stemma's orientation is obtained through the progressive resolution of severe disagreements and their transformation into benign disagreements, through the *eliminatio codicum descriptorum* to which we proceed at each step as well as the ensuing transformation of some of the common readings into singular readings.

To summarise, two things are necessary to have an orientation, a bottom and a top. The bottom – meaning here the absence of extant descent – is provided by the singular readings: following our definition of benign disagreements, manuscripts with the most singular readings inside each family are likely to be grouped first, and thus provide us with the bottom. This is legitimate since we expect manuscripts to transmit to their descendants at least one of their errors or innovations.

For a manuscript that would directly descend from the original or archetype while still having an important number of singular readings and no extant descent, we can reasonably assume – an assumption equally necessary to traditional stemmatological methods – that it would also have kept some of the original readings, sharing at least one of them with at least one other family while at least one other family does not, the direct result of which would be a severe disagreement that would only be resolved when all the other families have been reduced to their archetype, so that our manuscript would still be grouped in time and at its rightful place.

The top is obtained by the reconstruction of the model of each group and its comparison to the extant manuscripts: a manuscript completely corresponding to the virtual reconstructed model has good chances to *be* that model – it could also of course be an almost exact copy of it, but in that case the editorial difference would be almost negligible.

As we climb up the branches of the stemma, the amount of data (i.e. the number of disagreements between manuscripts and therefore the number of presumed errors) consequently decreases, and so does the certainty of the orientation and of the links between manuscripts. This becomes most appreciable at the very top of the stemma, where the number of disagreements (both severe and benign) can be extremely low (hence the necessity to use as much data as possible). Moreover, at the last step, the method will encounter a difficulty if there are three or fewer manuscripts left: with fewer than four manuscripts, it will no longer be possible to use severe disagreements as a way to determine the potential existence of two groups without resorting to a critical judgement on the quality of the readings. It will be the same if the tradition is bipartite – this is of course not particular to our method and is a, perhaps *the*, fundamental stumbling block of the Lachmannian method itself and has been abundantly noted as such, most famously by Bédier 1928 who saw in it sufficient reason to reject the method *en bloc*. As the two manuscripts will have at this stage only singular readings, the parentage of one over the other will be impossible to assess for the algorithm. It is then recommended that, in this case, the decision over the parentage of one over the other, or their sharing a common lost model, be made by the expert, who should probably also consider the possibility of two different redactions of his work by the author.

Testing the Method on a fictional modern corpus

The first tests of the method were done on a database provided by Matthew Spencer and Heather F. Windram (Spencer et al. 2004) for the Computer-Assisted Stemmatology Challenge held in 2009 in Helsinki (Roos and Heikkilä 2009). It consists of 21 copies by volunteer scribes of 'the first eight paragraphs (834 words, 49 sentences)' (Spencer et al. 2004, p. 504) of the Middle High German poem *Parzival* by Wolfram von Eschenbach, translated to English by A. T. Hatto (Eschenbach 1980), of which 5 copies were removed. We were thus able to test our method and to compare it to the actual tradition. The network of conflicts between variant locations is represented on fig. 4 (for the sake of evaluation by the reader, nodes figuring non-genealogical variant locations are printed in red, nodes figuring genealogical ones in green).

83

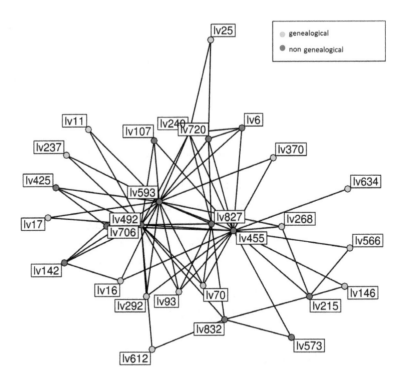

FIGURE 4: Network of conflicts for the *Parzival* test sample.[15]

Our principles led us to keep the truly genealogical variant locations 11, 16, 17, 25, 70, 93, 146, 237, 268, 292, 370, 566, 612, 634 but also the actually non-genealogical 6, 107, 425, 573; and to suppress the truly non-genealogical 142, 215, 240, 455, 492, 593, 706, 720, 827, 832 while suppressing none actually genealogical (24 successes and 4 errors; error rate, 14.29%).

Then, the stemma was constructed and compared to the true stemma (fig. 5, where the original is the central node adjacent to *p9*). The differences concerns manuscripts 2 and 8, and the model of {1,4}

---

[15] In this figure, as well as in fig. 7, the variant locations are named with an arbitrary alphanumeric identifier (the letters 'lv' followed by the order number of the variant location in the database).

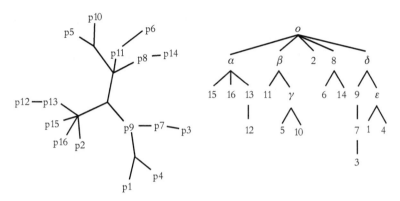

FIGURE 5: True stemma of the corpus (left) and our stemma (right).

Testing this Method on a medieval corpus

Though testing our method on a fictional modern corpus yielded interesting results on its accuracy, and since our method rests
heavily on the concept of variation linked to the modalities of
production and copy of medieval (vernacular) texts, it was necessary to give it a test in 'real combat conditions'. Facing the
inability to find a medieval tradition of a vernacular romance
text whose original or archetype would be known to us – a
fact which would have enabled us to judge our accuracy by the
editorial results of our stemma – we consequently decided to
test it against a quite undisputed stemma produced by a major
philologist and chose the edition by Segre (1957) of the *Bestiaires
d'Amors* by Richart de Fournival, a thirteenth century (*c.* 1250)
Picard prose text, of roughly 1,000 lines. Its manuscripts are divided into two groups (according to Segre): manuscripts *IDKO-
BEAHCJ* deriving from archetype *y* in a mostly uncontaminated
tradition for which C. Segre drew the stemma on fig. 6; and a
group of contaminated manuscripts *FGVMQP* deriving from a
second archetype (*x*).

We chose to work on the mostly uncontaminated tradition
(manuscripts deriving from *y*), first on a sample from the beginning up to p. 9 of the edition (which makes up 120 potentially
genealogical variant locations and roughly 7% of the text) – a
sample that proved sufficient to display the more general groupings of the manuscripts but lacked precision inside the α family),

85

resulting in $\{\{I,D,K,\{O,B\}\},\{C,\{A,H\}\}\}$ – before being led to increase the size of our sample, to be able to include manuscripts E and K (that have long *lacunae* in the beginning of the text), by adding p. 18-30 of the edition (in total up to 20% of the text and almost 300 variant locations).

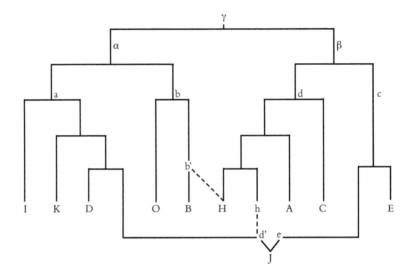

FIGURE 6: Segre's stemma for the *Bestiaires*.[16]

The network of conflicts between variant locations (fig. 7) shows here a much more complex situation: along with the opposition – usual in uncontaminated closed traditions – between, as over-conflicting central nodes, clearly non-genealogical variant locations and, as peripheral nodes in conflict with them, probably genealogical variant locations,[17] we also find secondary and more

---

[16] Richart de Fournival (1957), p. 104.

[17] Our index led us to label as over-conflicting nine variant locations (13, 88, 100, 101, 143, 166, 206, 247, 267), some of them already considered by us to be doubtful and presenting a risk of polygenesis, among which some were bordering with synonymisms, such as variant locations 88 (7,9,5 in Segre's edition: hommes *IKBAC* chevaliers *DO* amis et de ses milleurs hommes *H*) or 166 (19,9,1: repondre *OC* esconser *others*), while others concerned small variations on frequent words, such as 101 (8,5,3: vous *IO* vous ja *DKBAC* vous point *H*), or the addition of a formula often repeated in this work, for 267 (28,2,7: ki est de tel nature ke *E* qui de tel nature est ke *H* ke *others*) and in one instance provided an interesting case of polygenesis, perhaps including both a dialectal variation and

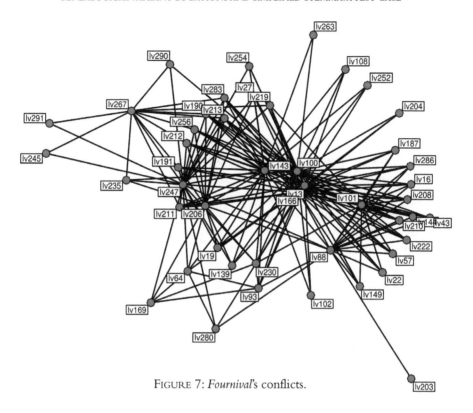

FIGURE 7: *Fournival*'s conflicts.

peripheral nodes, that, while themselves in conflict with the central nodes (a fact that tends to indicate their genealogical status),
also are conflicting with each other. This concerns, by order of
centrality, variant locations 64, 93, 169 and 230 (3 conflicts each
with non central variant locations), and 280 (2 conflicts), and this
situation, that the algorithm cannot resolve, is worthy of a closer
philological examination. If we exclude from the start variant location 93,[18] the conflicts revolve around *D*, and an opposition between a configuration *DB(O)* vs. others (variant locations 64 and
230) or *DK* vs. others (variant locations 169 and 280). A group-

---

a palaeographic error, for 247 (26,6,1: parties (partie *D* perties *C*) *DEC* perchies
(perchie *IJK*) *others*).

    [18] Already labelled by us as 'doubtful' in the database, this variant location
seems to offer a good case of possible polygenesis (7,11,5 in Segre's edition: il
amaine *IK* il an meine *OB* il a (en a *A*) amene (menes *A* amenes avoec soi *H*)
DAHC) and showing a grouping (*DAHC*) in contradiction with the place given
elsewhere to *D*.

ing *DBO*, proposed by Holmberg with precautions,[19] has since been refuted by Vitte (1929) in favour of two distinct groups *BO* and *IDK*, and by Segre (1957) in favour of a grouping *I KD OB* (more precisely $\{\{I,\{K,D\}\},\{O,B\}\}$), before being put forward again by Speroni (1980).[20]

According to which variant location we choose to eliminate, we will find ourselves either with a stemma following the Holmberg-Speroni solution (fig. 8 left)[21] or the Vitte-Segre (fig. 8 right). This choice cannot be made by the algorithm, nor by quantitative criteria, since there is in our sample a strict equivalence of the number of cases. The only option is to submit it to a critical evaluation, and it seems, as it did to Speroni, that the variant location backing *DB(O)* vs. others[22] show less risk of polygenesis than the one backing *DK* vs. others.[23]

The placement of *J* together with *E* is consistent with Segre's assessment (1957, p. XCVI) that 'sino a p. 51 *J* s'accorda constantemente con β, mentre da p. 51 in avanti l'accordo è, se non fedelissimo, abbanstaza costante, con α', and that *J* descends for its first part from a parent of *E*, and for the second from a parent of *D* contaminated by a parent of *H*.[24]

---

[19] He states that 'B und O gehören ihrerseits trotz mancher verschiedenheit nahe zusammen [...] Der letzgenannten gruppe am nächsten steht vielleicht D' (Holmberg 1925, p. 147-148).

[20] Speroni (1980, p. 349-352) proposes indeed a return to Holmberg's hypothesis of a *DBO* group, and backs this hypothesis by a cross examination of the readings uniting *DBO* and those uniting *IDK* or *DK*, that he judges more likely to be casual or to go back to α, and by the study of the newly found MS *W*, which is according to him to be integrated in a *DWOB* group.

[21] In our stemmata the dotted lines represent the stage of the aggregation method where a manual intervention was necessary.

[22] Variant locations 64 (6,1,6: enmpire *DB* ampite *O* ne peire *AHCIK missing by material loss EJ*) and 230 (25,4: es (as *O* en *B*) iex *DOB* maint (et maint *J*) en (el *AH*) cuer *others*).

[23] Variant locations 169 (20,2,3: puist redescaucier *DK* ait deschaussiet *O* puist descauchier *others*) and 280 (29,2,2: regarder *I* regarder mon malade (malage *D*) *DK* regarder moi malade *BAH* moi regarder *C* moi regarder malade *OEJ* – which, if we do not take inversions into account, opposes *DK* to others, with a lacuna in *I*, and, for the second part in *C*). Both of these two variant locations barely fit into our selection principles and seem to offer stronger possibilities of polygenesis.

[24] Despite the erroneous statement (inversion) by Bianciotto 2009, p. 103, that 'La copie *J* a la particularité d'avoir emprunté à deux modèles, d'abord à α pour un peu moins de la moitié du texte, puis à β dans la suite'.

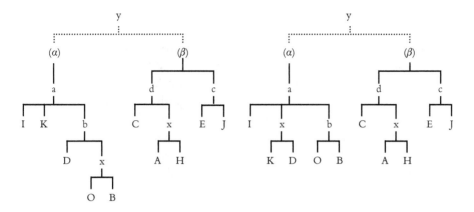

FIGURE 8: Our two stemmata for the *Bestiaires* based on an extended sample.

A more important difference between our stemmata and Segre's concerns the exact relation between *b* and *a* (a relationship that has not yet, to our knowledge, been questioned since[25]). In both instances our sample did not contain any disagreement *a* vs. *bβ* that would have led our algorithm to distinguish *a* and *b* as descendants from the same lost model (Segre's *α*). On the contrary, in both cases, we only had disagreements *b* vs. *aβ*, that did not preclude *a* from being the model for *b*.

It is obvious that, due to the limited size of our sample, our stemmata cannot really be perceived as disagreeing with Segre's. Since we only took into account a 20% sample (as opposed to Segre, who accounted for the full text), we would, in any case, need to extend our database, and to take into account the five manuscripts discovered since 1957[26] before being able to formulate – or not – another hypothesis.

---

[25] Even the quite controversial contribution by Ham 1959 – mostly disproved by Segre 1961 – did not alter it, despite its apparent lack of taste for so-called 'needless complications'.

[26] Among these, *W* seems to be close to *D* in a *WDOB* group and *Y* to *H* in the *d* group, Speroni 1980, while *S* and *T* would both belong to the contaminated manuscripts descending from the second archetype *x*, Vitale-Brovarone 1980. A fifth manuscript, called 'T' by Roy 2006 and *R* by Bianciotto 2009, is probably a close parent of *C*, be it either its direct ascendant (for Roy) or not (for Bianciotti).

Further work

The next step in improving our method is to find a way to take contamination into account. An obvious way to do this might be to return to the non genealogical variant locations, once the stemma is drawn, and there try to distinguish polygenesis from genuine contamination. This could perhaps be achieved through statistical evaluation: for example, consistent agreements between a manuscript and a family outside its own, verified against a random distribution through various statistical tests. Another improvement, suggested by Poole (1979), could be to reincorporate formerly conflicting variant locations when they cease to be, due to the progressive *eliminatio codicum descriptorum*. Nonetheless, such a procedure, valid in cases of contamination, could prove dangerous in cases of polygenesis – it also falls within the scope of the philological debate about whether a variant location that is obviously in its whole non-genealogical when the totality of the tradition is considered can be attributed meaning in establishing the relationships at another level (inside a single family or at a certain level of the stemma).[27]

Apart from the assessment of contamination, the most important source of improvement to this method would surely be its testing against all sorts of *corpora*, both fictional and medieval, and its systematic comparison to either known true stemma or to the stemma achieved through traditional means.

Bibliography

D'A. S. Avalle (1958), Review of Segre (1957), in *Cultura Neolatina*, 18, p. 77-88.

J. Bédier (1928), 'La tradition manuscrite du *Lai de l'ombre*: réflexions sur l'art d'éditer les anciens textes', in *Romania*, 54, p. 161-196 and 321-356.

J. A. Bengel (1763), *Apparatus criticus ad Novum Testamentum*, Tubingae.

J.-B. Camps (2012), 'Le Scribe face au texte: Regards sur quelques cas

---

[27] For some elements on this debate, here surrounding the precise case of the *Bestiaire d'Amours*, see the aforementioned contributions by Ham (1959), Segre (1961), and the point of view of Avalle (1958).

de doute et sur des formes de pensée philologique au Moyen Âge', in *Questes*, 23, p. 65-84.

B. Cerquiglini (1983), 'Éloge de la variante', in *Langages*, p. 17-69, in part. 25-35.

Cicero (1831), *Ciceronis Verrinarum libri VII*, ed. C. T. Zumpt, Berlin.

E. C. Colwell (1969), 'Method in Classifying and Evaluating Variant Readings', in *Studies in Methodology in Textual Criticism of the New Testament*, Leiden: Brill (New Testament Tools and Studies, 9), p. 96-105.

J. Duplacy (1979), 'Préalables philologiques à la classification automatique des états d'un texte', in J. Glenisson et al. (eds.), *La pratique des ordinateurs dans la critique des textes*, Paris: CNRS Éditions, p. 23-33.

F. Duval (2011), 'Conflit d'interprétations: typologie des facteurs de choix éditoriaux', in *Les enjeux intellectuels des pratiques d'édition (Paris les 4, 5 et 6 mai 2011)*, Paris.

E. J. Epp (1967), 'The Claremont Profile Method for Grouping New Testament Minuscule Manuscripts', in B. L. Daniels & M. J. Suggs (eds.), *Studies in the History and Text of the New Testament in Honor of K. W. Clark*, Salt Lake City: Univ. of Utah Press, p. 27-38.

W. von Eschenbach (1980), *Parzival*, trans. A. T. Hatto, New York: Penguin Books.

G. Fiesoli (2000), *La genesi del lachmannismo*, Firenze: Sismel.

R. de Fournival (1957), *Li bestiaires d'amours di maistre Richart de Fornival e li response du bestiaire*, ed. C. Segre, Napoli: R. Ricciardi.

R. de Fournival (2009), *Le Bestiaire d'amour et la Response du Bestiaire*, ed. G. Bianciotto, Paris: H. Champion (Champion classiques).

Dom J. Froger (1968), *La critique des textes et son automatisation*, Paris: Dunod (Initiation aux nouveautés de la science).

E. B. Ham (1959), Review of Segre (1957), in *Romance Philology*, 13, p. 461-466.

L. Havet (1911), *Manuel de critique verbale appliquée aux textes latins*, Paris.

J. Holmberg (1925), *Eine mittelniederfränkische Übertragung des Bestiaire d'Amour: Sprachlich untersucht und mit altfranzösischem Paralleltext*, Uppsala: Almqvist & Wiksell (Uppsala universitets årsskrift, 2).

P. Lejay (1888), Review of 'R. Sabbadini, *La critica del testo del De officiis di Cicerone e delle poesie pseudo-virgiliane secondo due nuove codici*', in *Revue critique d'histoire et de littérature*, 26, p. 281-283.

P. Lejay (1903), Review of 'Aeli Donati quod fertur Commentum Terenti... Recensuit Paulus Wessner', in *Revue critique d'histoire et de littérature*, 56, p. 168-172.

G. Lozinski (1925), 'Un fragment du *Bestiaire d'Amour* de Richard de Fournival', in *Romania*, 51, p. 561-568.

C. Lucken (2010), 'Les manuscrits du *Bestiaire d'Amours* de Richard de Fournival', in O. Collet & Y. Foehr-Janssens (eds.), *Le recueil au Moyen Âge. Le Moyen Âge central*, Turnhout: Brepols, p. 113-138.

P. Maas (1937), 'Leitfehler und stemmatische Typen', in *Byzantinische Zeitschrift*, 37, p. 289-294.

P. Maas (1957), *Textkritik 3., verbesserte und vermehrte Auflage*, Leipzig: Teubner.

Marguerite d'Angoulême, *La Navire, ou Consolation du roi François Ier à sa sœur Marguerite*, ed. R. Marichal, Paris: Champion, 1956 (Bibliothèque de l'École des Hautes études. Sciences historiques et philologiques, 306).

Marguerite d'Angoulême, *La coche*, ed. R. Marichal, Genève & Paris: Droz & Minard, 1971 (Textes littéraires français, 173).

R. Marichal (1979), 'Conclusion', in J. Glenisson et al. (eds.), *La Pratique des ordinateurs dans la critique des textes*, Paris: CNRS Éditions, p. 285-288.

La vie de saint Alexis: poème du XIe siècle et renouvellements des XIIe, XIIIe, et XIVe siècles publ. avec préfaces, variantes, notes et glossaires, ed. G. Paris & L. Pannier, Paris: A. Franck, 1872 (Bibliothèque de l'École des hautes études, 7).

G. Pasquali (1934), *Storia della tradizione e critica del testo*, Florence: Le Monnier.

E. Poole (1974), 'The Computer in Determining Stemmatic Relationships', in *Computers and the Humanities*, 8, p. 207-216.

E. Poole (1979), 'L'analyse stemmatique des textes documentaires', in J. Glenisson et al. (eds.), *La Pratique des ordinateurs dans la critique des textes*, Paris: CNRS Éditions, p. 151-161.

M. D. Reeve (1998), 'Shared innovations, dichotomies, and evolution', in A. Ferrari (ed.), *Filologia classica e filologia romanza: esperienze ecdotiche a confronto*, Spoleto, p. 445-505.

Thomae Magistri sive Theoduli Monachi Ecloga vocum Atticarum, ed. F. Ritschl, Halle, 1832.

T. Roos & T. Heikkilä (2009), 'Evaluating methods for computer-assisted stemmatology using artificial benchmark data sets', in *Literary and Linguistic Computing*, 24, p. 417-433.

B. Roy (2006), 'Un nouveau manuscrit du Bestiaire d'Amours', in C. Galderisi & J. Maurice (eds.), *'Qui tant savoit d'engin et d'art': mélanges de philologie médiévale offerts à Gabriel Bianciotto*, Poitiers: Université de Poitiers, Centre d'études supérieures de civilisation médiévale, p. 205-213.

B. J. P. Salemans (1996), 'Cladistics or the Resurrection of the Method of Lachmann. On Building the Stemma of Yvain', in P. van Reenen & M. J. P. van Mulken (eds.), *Studies in Stemmatology*, Amsterdam: Benjamins, p. 3-70.

D. C. J. Schlyter & D. H. S. Collins (1827), *Corpus iuris Sueo-Gothorum antiqui...*, Stockholm.

U. Schmid (2004), 'Genealogy by chance! On the significance of accidental variation (parallelisms)', in P. van Reenen et al. (eds.), *Studies in stemmatology II*, Amsterdam: Benjamins, p. 127-143.

C. Segre (1961), 'Questions de méthode: à propos du Bestiaire d'amours', in *Romance Philology*, 15, p. 124-129.

C. Segre (1976), 'Critique textuelle, théorie des ensembles et diasystème', in *Bulletin de la classe des lettres et des sciences morales et politiques de l'Académie royale de Belgique*, 62, p. 279-292.

C. Segre (1979), 'Les transcriptions en tant que diasystèmes', in J. Glenisson et al. (eds.), *La Pratique des ordinateurs dans la critique des textes*, Paris, p. 45-49.

M. Spencer et al. (2004), 'Phylogenetics of artificial manuscripts', in *Journal of theoretical biology*, 227, p. 503-511.

G. B. Speroni (1980), 'Due nuovi testimoni del *Bestiaires d'Amours* di Richard de Fournival', in *Medioevo Romanzo*, 7, p. 342-369.

S. Timpanaro (2003), *La genesi del metodo del Lachmann*, 4th ed., Torino: Utet.

A. Varvaro (1970), 'Critica dei testi classica e romanza, problemi comuni ed esperienze diverse', in *Rendiconti della Accademia di Archeologia Lettere e Belle Arti*, 45, p. 73-117.

A. Vitale-Brovarone (1980), 'Un testimone sconosciuto ed uno recuperato del Bestiaire d'Amours', in *Medioevo Romanzo*, 7, p. 370-401.

S. Vitte (1929), 'Richard de Fournival. Étude sur sa vie et ses œuvres suivie de l'édition du bestiaire d'amour, de la Réponse de la Dame et des Chansons' (thèse pour le dipl. d'arch. paléogr., non publiée, Paris: École nationale des chartes).

M. Weitzman (1985), 'The Analysis of Open Traditions', in *Studies in Bibliography*, 38, p. 82-120.

P. Zumthor (1972), *Essai de poétique médiévale*, Paris: Éditions du Seuil (Poétique, 4).

APPENDIX

THE MANUSCRIPTS OF RICHART
DE FOURNIVAL, *LI BESTIAIRES D'AMOURS*[28]

A Paris, BnF, fr. 25566 (*olim* 72; La Vallière 81; Debure 2736; anc. petit fonds 2736)

B Paris, BnF, fr. 412 (*olim* Lancelot 9; Lancelot 125; Regius 7019[3])

C Paris, BnF, fr. 12786 (*olim* suppl. fr. 319)

D Paris, BnF, fr. 12469 (*olim* suppl. fr. 540,1)

E Paris, BnF, fr. 1444 (*olim* B 23; ancien fonds 7534)

F Paris, BnF, fr. 24406 (*olim* La Vallière 59; ancien petit fonds 2719)

G Paris, BnF, fr. 15213 (*olim* 3579; suppl. fr. 766)

H Dijon, Bibl. Municipale, MS 526 (*olim* Collège des Godran, 299)

I Paris, Bibl. Sainte-Geneviève, MS 2200 (*olim* N. 7; B. b. 2; 41; R. l. in-4°. 17)

J Arras, Bibl. Municipale, MS 139(657) (*olim* Bibliothecæ monasterii Sancti Vedasti Atrebatensis, 1628. K. 2.)

K Bruxelles, KBR, 10394-414

L London, BL, Harley MS 273

M New York, Pierpont Morgan Library, MS M.459

O Oxford, Bodleian Library, MS Douce 308

P Firenze, Biblioteca Mediceo-Laurenziana, Plut. LXXVI, 79

Q Firenze, Biblioteca Mediceo-Laurenziana, Ashb. 123 (*olim* Libri 50)

R Switzerland, private collection (manuscript *T* for Roy 2006)

S Genève, Bibl. publique et universitaire, *Comites latentes* 179

T Torino, Biblioteca Nazionale, L.III.22

V Wien, ÖNB, cod. 2609

W Milano, Biblioteca Ambrosiana, cod. I. 78 sup.

Y Milano, Biblioteca Braidense AC.X. 10

p Saint-Petersbourg, private coll. Likhatchev as of 1925 (one leaf fragment of 46 lines found in a binding, transcribed in Lozinski 1925)

[28] For a description of these manuscripts, see Richart de Fournival (1957), particularly 'I manoscritti', p. XXXIII-LXV, to be updated concerning *RSTWY* by Speroni (1980), Vitale-Brovarone (1980), Roy (2006), Richart de Fournival (2009) and Lucken (2010); for the *p* fragment, see Lozinski (1925).

ALBERTO CANTERA

THE PROBLEMS
OF THE TRANSMISSION
OF THE AVESTAN TEXTS
AND THE TOOLS FOR AVESTAN
TEXT CRITICISM (TATEC)*

Introduction

The Avestan manuscripts contain the recitatives of several Zoroastrian liturgies that are today still celebrated. These liturgies took
shape around the sixth century BC, long before they were written
down for the first time. In the process of their creation texts of
different dates and serving different functions were amalgamated;
place and date of the different texts included in these rituals are
not known. From the dialectological point of view, the languages
in which they are composed can be classified among the Eastern
Iranian languages. The oldest parts of these liturgies are composed in a language that is as archaic as the Vedic language of the
Rg-Veda, or even older.

The Avestan texts were composed orally and transmitted
mainly in that way until the invention of the Avestan script. This
script is a modification of the Pahlavi script – in which the Middle Persian Zoroastrian texts are written – with some letters tak-
en from the alphabet of Christian Middle Persian and even from
the Greek alphabet. With these materials a very precise phonetic
script was created for accurately transcribing the recitatives of
the Zoroastrian liturgies. The date for the creation of the Avestan script is controversial, but the span can be limited between

---

* For a more detailed philological argumentation of the issues discussed
in this paper, cf. Cantera 2012a. For a general description of the Avestan manuscripts, their history and typology, cf. Geldner 1886 and Cantera 2011 with
further bibliography. For a relatively recent description of the transmission, cf.
Kellens 1998.

10.1484/M.LECTIO-EB.5.102566

the sixth century and the first moments after the Islamization of Iran. Oral transmission, however, still played a very important role even after the invention of the Avestan script.

The manuscripts

Today we know of more than 300 manuscripts, including Avestan texts, but the true number is probably much higher since the tradition of producing manuscripts has continued until recently and the production of copies of parts of Avestan manuscripts is part of the instruction of Zoroastrian priests. The oldest manuscript is perhaps MS 2000 (K7),[1] which according to the date of the colophon was written in the second half of the thirteenth century. Other colophons, however, mention copies going back to the tenth century. In fact, most of the extant manuscripts were copied in the seventeenth century and above all in the eighteenth century, even though there are a few manuscripts that were copied in the fourteenth and sixteenth centuries.

The extant manuscripts in Avestan language contain, with few exceptions, the transcription of the recitatives of several Zoroastrian rituals. There is a great typological variety of manuscripts depending on their contents, function, and place of publication. According to the kind of rituals they include, the Avestan manuscripts can be divided in two different types:

1. Manuscripts of the long liturgy, somewhat comparable to the Christian missals. They mainly include the complete recitative of one of the different variants of the long liturgy we know (Yasna, Wīsperad and intercalation ceremonies);

2. Lectionaries or manuscripts including collections of ceremonies that could be held outside the Fire temple and by private citizens or priests of a lower rank.

According to their function, the manuscripts can be classified as:

1. Liturgical manuscripts, including not only the Avestan recitative of the long liturgy but also directions for the ritual which

[1] For the sigla of the mansucripts s. ⟨http://ada.usal.es/img/pdf/Numbers.pdf⟩

are in different languages depending on the time and place of the copy;

2. Exegetical manuscripts, in which the Avestan recitative of the liturgy is translated into Pahlavi or Sanskrit;

3. Combined manuscripts, which include directions for the ritual as well as the Pahlavi translation

The relationship between these three types of manuscripts is controversial. Traditionally, it has been thought that the liturgical manuscripts were dependent on the exegetical manuscripts with Pahlavi translation (Westergaard 1852: 23; Geldner 1886: 1.xix). Today some researchers (including myself), inspired by Kellens 1998, believe that the situation is different. The descriptions of rituals we find in the manuscripts, including ritual directions and Avestan recitatives, go back at least to Sasanian times (224-651 CE) and originally were transmitted orally. The exegetical manuscripts derive (with the exception perhaps of the exegetical manuscripts of the Wīdēwdād) from the liturgical ones. For the Yasna – or, the standard ceremony of the long liturgy – a combined manuscript was created around the tenth century in which the Pahlavi translation, copied from a different manuscript, was added to the Avestan recitative and the ritual directions. It seems likely that all the Pahlavi manuscripts of the Yasna derive from this combined copy, although this is not certain with regard to the manuscripts of the family of Mihrābān's Pahlavi Yasna (copied in India in the fourteenth century). Only the exegetical manuscripts of Yasna include the complete ceremony. The rest include only the sections of the respective liturgies that do not appear in the Yasna liturgies, and therefore need to be translated. In the case of the intercalation ceremonies, only the intercalated texts appear in the exegetical manuscripts.

After the Islamization of Iran, an important part of the Zoroastrian community migrated to Gujarat and was established there. Although the contact between both communities of Zoroastrians have always been frequent, we can speak of two separate communities with independent transmissions. For the earlier centuries, we have reports of Indian priests going to Iran seeking manuscripts as well as Iranian priests travelling to Gujarat to copy some of the oldest manuscripts, which are still available today. An autochthonous Indian tradition arose quite soon as well. Around the twelfth century, Nēryōsang composed a partial translation of the Yasna into Sanskrit and we have ritual Indian manuscripts from the middle of the sixteenth century, earlier than in Iran (besides K7 that is 300 years older).

The history of the Avestan written transmission

The last analysis of the Avestan transmission based on the autopsy of manuscripts was done 125 years ago by the German scholar K. F. Geldner, who is responsible for the last nearly complete edition of the Avesta (Geldner 1886), for which he used around 135 manuscripts. Every analysis of the Avestan transmission performed subsequently is based on the data provided by Geldner and the autopsy of a very limited number of Avestan manuscripts available in facsimiles. Some 15 years ago, when working on the edition of an Avestan text, I decided to try to locate and see for myself the extant Avestan manuscripts. I soon realized the importance of such an enterprise and postponed the edition I had started. Since then I have worked primarily on searching for, digitizing, and analyzing the Avestan manuscripts. I started with a project centred on the manuscripts of the Avestan text I was editing – the Wīdēwdād. An outcome of this project was the creation of the webpage Videvdad.com (‹http://www.videvdad.com›). Five years ago I decided to expand the project to all Avestan texts. Thus I started the Avestan Digital Archive (‹http://www.avesta-archive.com›), with the aim of digitizing, indexing, and publishing all available manuscripts of the Avesta in the Avestan Digital Archive. Since then we have located more than 300 manuscripts, digitized approximately 120, indexed and published about 60 online.

This direct work with the manuscripts has shown that many established ideas about the transmission of the Avesta, repeated again and again after Geldner's Prolegomena to his edition, have proved to be false and that today a new edition of the Avesta is needed. In fact, we have reasons to repeat the work done by Geldner in almost every step of the editorial process.[2] In this short paper, I will describe the problems posed by Geldner's *stem-*

[2] These weak points of Geldner's edition are reviewed in three different pa-

mata and introduce the tools I have developed for trying another approach to this problem. Nevertheless, a quick view of Geldner's conception of the nature of the Avestan texts and their transmission is necessary in order to understand the problems concerning the analysis of the Avestan manuscripts.

Geldner's view of the transmission follows that of his predecessor, Westergaard (1852: 22s.). The Avesta was compiled in Sasanian times, but our manuscripts do not go directly back to this Sasanian archetype, but rather through (in the words of Westergaard) 'the Yazd-original, no doubt an exact image of the Sasanian', from which all the extant manuscripts derive. This view in three steps was at the basis of the most intensive work on the Avestan transmission carried out in the second half of the twelfth century at the Institute for Indo-European Linguistics at the University of Erlangen, represented especially by K. Hoffmann and J. Narten,[3] and by H. Humbach. Hoffmann carried out a deep analysis of the Avestan alphabet and discovered many original features of the Avestan script at the time of its invention which were already confused in the oldest manuscripts. Hence he drew the conclusion that these were the features of the Sasanian archetype, the first written copy of the Avesta with the actual Avesta script. Since then, the intensive editorial work done in the last few years has consisted mostly in restoring the Sasanian aspect to the text transmitted in the manuscripts in a more modern shape.[4] Furthermore, Hoffmann and Humbach have found several mistakes of the written transmission common to all the manuscripts of the different text types, such that they posited the existence of one hyparchetype of the long liturgy and one of the short liturgies.

The dependence of our manuscripts on the Sasanian archetype was rightly questioned by Kellens (1998). According to him, our manuscripts do not derive from the supposed Sasanian archetype or Great Avesta, but from a collection of rituals, the ritual Avesta. In contrast, the existence of the hyparchetypes was not

pers in the volume *The transmission of the Avesta*: Hintze 2012, Andrés-Toledo 2012, and Cantera 2012b.

[3] Cf. especially Hoffmann 1969, 1971, 1989; and Humbach 1973.

[4] A list of the new 'editions' produced on the basis of Geldner's edition with occasional use of some manuscripts in the last 40 years can be consulted in Hintze 2012.

put into question until my presentation at a conference held in Salamanca, in September 2009 (Cantera 2012a). The methodology leading to the hyparchetypes is exactly the same as that used by Geldner for his analysis of the relationship between the single manuscripts – that is, the Lachmannian principle that agreement in error supposes a genetic relationship between the witnesses attesting this error. Geldner bases his analysis of the relationship of the manuscripts on lists of common variants shared by two or more manuscripts. In addition to the general criticism against this methodology formulated during the twentieth century, there is a special feature of the Avestan transmission that makes Lachmannian principles especially inappropriate for the analysis of the relationship between the Avestan manuscripts. Thus, the following criticism of this methodology applied to the Avesta will show the inadequacy of the method used by Geldner for the analysis of the relations between manuscripts, and by Hoffmann and Humbach for determining the existence of hyparchetypes.

Interferences between the oral-ritual and the written transmission

The Avestan manuscripts essentially contain the recitatives of a series of liturgies that have been performed at least from Sasanian times on, and that are partly performed still today. The liturgical manuscripts were used mainly in the priestly schools for teaching the correct performance of the ceremonies and their recitatives.[5] Their use in the proper ceremonies was not allowed with the exception of the Wīdēwdād ceremony, the longest one, and even then only for the proper Wīdēwdād text that is intercalated in the standard liturgy. The recitative of the rituals was known by heart and manuscripts were used mainly as a tool for the instruction of priests.

This fact has conditioned enormously the way the manuscripts were produced. Geldner admitted a very limited influence of the ritual:

> The copyists knew the majority of their text by heart. The oral text, however, had become more corrupted than the

---

[5] The colophons mention four different uses of these manuscripts: to be read; to be taught in the priestly schools; to be recited in the ceremonies; and finally to be copied.

written text and keeps constantly crossing the latter. Scribes who read and copied word for word from the text before them, ran less danger than those scribes who grasped the entire sentence and wrote it off before looking at the copy before them (Geldner 1886).

In fact the influence of the ritual is far stronger. Ritual practice and copying of manuscripts are linked processes and influence each other reciprocally; in the production of the manuscripts both the process of copying from a written source and the ritual practice are involved. Each manuscript moves between these two poles. Some manuscripts show, indeed, a clear influence of the oral-ritual text. In fact, some of them even seem to be copied not from a written source, but from an oral dictation or as a transcription of the ritual practice. A clear example is the oldest known Yasna Sāde,[6] MS 100 (B3), copied in the second half of the sixteenth century. Let us compare, for instance, Y1.3 in three different liturgical manuscripts:

B3 (230)

niuuaēδaiēme. asnīaēibiiō. ašahe. ratubiiō. ḫāuuanēašaoni. ašahe. raθβe.niuuaēδaiēme. . šauuaŋhēe. vīšiiāeca. ašaoni. ašahe. raθβe. niuuaēδaiēme. miθrahe. vōuru.gaoiiaoi̯tōiš. hazaŋhra.gaošahe. baēuuarǝcasmanō. aōxtō.nām[anō. y]azatahe. rāmanō. xᵛāštr[ahe.]

I announce ⟨and include in the litany⟩ (the sacrifice for Ahura Mazdā) for the daily articulations of Order; for the morning articulation of the Order that supports Order. I announce ⟨and include in the litany⟩ (the sacrifice for Ahura Mazdā) for the (articulation) that grants success and is clanic. I announce ⟨and include in the litany⟩ (the sacrifice) for the god Miθra of broad pastures, thousand ears and ten thousand eyes with mention of his name and the sacrifice) for Rāman who bestows grazing.

110 (K11)

niuuaeiδaiieimi. hǝnkāraiiemi. asniiaeibiiō. ašahe. ratubiiō. hā uuanēe. ašaoni. ašahe. raθβe. niuuae. sāuuaŋhēe. vīsiiāica. ašaone. ašahe. raθβe. niuuae. miθrahe. vouru.gaōiiaōi̯tōiš. hazaŋhara.gaōšahe. baeuuarǝ.cašmanō. aoxtō.nāmanō. yazatahe. rāmanō. x̌āstrahe.

---

[6] MS 100 (B3) has no date since the final pages containing the colophon are missing, but it is the indirect ancestor of MS 230 (L17) (see below). MS 230 (L17) bears the date 1556, but its colophon is likely the copy of the lost colophon of MS 100 (B3). The manuscript is published in the Avestan Digital Archive.

4010[7]

ńiuuaēδaiiemi. hanākāraiiemi. asniiaēibiiō. aṣ̌ahe. ratubiiō. [...]
hāuuanə̄e. aṣ̌aōne. aṣ̌ahe. raθβe. ńiuuaēδaiiemi. hanākāraiiemi. sā
uuaŋhə̄e. vīsiiāica. aṣ̌aōne. aṣ̌ahe. raθβe. ńiuuaēδaiiemi. hanākā
raiiemi. miθrahe. vouru.gaōiiaōịtōiš. hazaŋhrō.gaōš̌ahe. baēuuarə.
caš̌manō. aōxtō.nāmanō. yazatahe. rāmanō. xᵛāstrahe.

I have marked in bold and underlined the writings that reflect the
way in which this text was recited at the time when these manuscripts were copied, and that differ from the way in which they
appear in other manuscripts with a greater dependence from the
written transmission. The most correct variants are offered clearly
by MS 4010, the second oldest Iranian liturgical manuscript of
Wīdēwdād. Among the Indian Sādes the variants of MS 110 (K11)
(written 1647) are less influenced by the oral-ritual transmission
than those of MS 100 (B3), although MS 100 (B3) is probably
older. Many features of MS 100 (B3) reveal, indeed, a clear influence of the recitation, such as the systematic use of *ī* for *ii*; -*āeca* for
-*āica* in *vīsiiāica*; the total confusion between *s*, *š̌* and *ṣ̌* (*š̌āuuaŋhə̄e* for
sāuuaŋhə̄e, *vīṣ̌iiāeca* for *vīsiiāica*, °*casmanō* for °*caš̌manō*, etc.), whereas
MS 110 (K11) limits the confusion to the usual Indian writing
aṣ̌ahe for *aṣ̌ahe*; or the form *hāuuanēaš̌aoni* for *hāuuanə̄e. aṣ̌aoni*. This
manuscript could be a trustworthy record of the recitation of the
Yasna ceremony in the sixteenth century in Gujarat, written down
under the influence of the exegetical manuscripts of Mihrābān,
but adapting them to the ritual practice and the actual recitation.
In opposition to the theory of Sasanian archetype and of the hyparchetypes, it is more likely that ceremonies were written down
at different times and in different places, and that all our copies of
different ceremonies do not go back to *one* single copy.

Furthermore, the influence of ritual practice is not limited to
phonetic deviations from the old copies. Liturgical manuscripts
do not pretend to be accurate copies of old originals, but authoritative guides for the correct performance of the ritual. Accordingly, conscious changes introduced in a priestly school are
reproduced as a matter of fact in the manuscripts copied under
the influence of this school, disregarding the text found in the

---

[7] In the VS manuscripts this passage does not appear as such, but I have taken
the first sentence from VS1.2 and the second from VS1.3.

original written source of the copyist. The greater or lesser generalization of these new readings depends on the influence of the priestly school over other schools and priestly families. Thus, in Y 30.1 the change of *mazdāθā* (*'you consider'*) into *mazdā. θβā* (*'and you Mazdā'*) in all IndVS but MS 4200 (B2) is obviously the result of an analysis of the transmitted form as *mazdā* and the personal pronoun *θβā*, and not a simple transmission error: it represents a conscious decision. This new reading nevertheless became almost universal in India. It appears in all the liturgical manuscripts and even in some of the late exegetical manuscripts like MS 415 and MS 420 and in the Sanskrit manuscript MS 680. In MS 530 (M1) the copyist first wrote the variant he knew from the ritual, *mazdā.θβā*, and then corrected it himself with the form that appeared in his original, *mazdāθā*. Among the Sades only MS 4210 (B2), the oldest Videvdad Sade (1626), retained the original *mazdāθā*. This does not mean, however, that all manuscripts but B2 are genealogically related – this variant simply became trendy after 1626, the date of MS 4210 (B2).

The intricate relationship between written copies and ritual practice, between unconscious mistakes in the written transmission and conscious corrections, can be seen in an example that I have given elsewhere (Cantera 2010). In V3.41 the liturgical manuscripts appear divided into three groups and none of them corresponds with the text of the exegetical manuscripts:

ORIGINAL TEXT	EXEGETICAL MANUSCRIPTS	LITURGICAL MANUSCRIPTS		
		A (4200, 4210, 4240, 4260)	B (4250, 4370, 4400)	C (4320, 4360, 4410, 4420, 4510, 4515[8])
spaiietidraošəm	*spaiieti draošəm*	*spaiieti draošəm*	*spaiieti draošəm auuaynīm*	*spaiieti draošəm*
spaiieti				*spaiieti*
yātuynīm	*spaiieti*	*spaiieti*	*spaiieti*	*auuanīm*
spaiieti	*ašauuanīm*	*yātuynīm*	*yātuynīm*	*spaiieti*
ašauuanīm		*spaiieti*	*spaiieti*	*yātuynīm*
		ašauuanīm	*ašauuanīm*	*spaiieti*
				ašauuanīm

TABLE 1

8 Formerly known as G42; cf. Cantera 2010.

The origin of these variants is clear. In an unknown liturgical manuscript with the division of lines as shown here, one line was skipped:

> *daēna. māzdaiiasniš. narš. āstauua*
> *nahe. baṇdəm. spaiieite. draošəm.*
> **spaiieite. yātuynīm. spaiieiti. aš**
> *auuaynīm. spaiieite. nasuspaēm.*

(The Vision obtained in the sacrifice to Mazdā forgives to the man who has praised it the bonds; she forgives the brand marking; she forgives the killing through (black) magic; she forgives the killing of a supporter of Order; she forgives the throwing of a corpse).

The copyist wrote the beginning of the new line (*auuaynīm*), then noticed his error, marked *auuaynīm* with deletion dots and then continued writing the correct text:

> *daēna. māzdaiiasniš. narš. āstauua*
> *nahe. baṇdəm. spaiieite. draošəm.*
> *a̤ṳ̤ṳ̤a̤y̤n̤ī̤m̤. spaiieite. yātuynīm. spaiieiti.*
> *aša̤ṳ̤ṳ̤a̤y̤n̤ī̤m̤. spaiieite. nasuspaēm.*

Later copyists did not notice the presence of the deletion dots and thus the text B arose that appears in MS 4370 (L5) and MS 4400. Then the pseudo-philological reflection of a school introduced *spaiieiti* before *auuaynīm* in order to make this incorrect text 'understandable'. This occurred in the seventeenth or eighteenth century, and from then on this variant became almost universal. In the reformist school of Nawsari this variant spread even into the exegetical manuscripts of the family of MS 4600 (L4) and a new Pahlavi translation was even created for this invented text. In this fortunate case, the textual evidence allows us to distinguish between the variant of the 'written' transmission that spreads into other manuscripts only by way of copying, and the variant created consciously within a school that contributed to its generalization through manuscripts and through priestly teaching and reciting. It shows also that a reading originated through a transmission error could enter the ritual practice.

The newly created variants (or at least some of them) were integrated into all the manuscripts created in this school and, of course, into its ritual praxis. And if this school was authoritative enough, they spread to other schools. Hence, the manuscripts sharing this reading do not necessarily have any genetic relationship: they share what is just a more or less trendy variant within the Zoroastrian ritual community. In this context the textual homogeneity of the Avestan manuscripts can be, in fact, the reflection of a ritual homogeneity within the Zoroastrian community. Travelling priests and the transportation of manuscripts may have been responsible for such uniformity.

This has important consequences for our view of the Avestan transmission. Regarding the prehistory of the written transmission, it is possible that the common readings that are adduced as proofs of the different archetypes (only one in the case of the long liturgy, for example) may, in fact, be variants that entered the ritual practice and spread over wide areas through the influence of certain priestly schools. Hence, we would lack evidence for postulating unlikely hyparchetypes for manuscripts of very different text types.

Thus the very specific problems of the Avestan manuscripts can be summarized as follows:

1. Common readings do not necessarily point to a direct genealogical relationship, but can also be the result of membership in a ritual community. Some common readings spread, indeed, over very wide areas. Manuscripts are often copied from other manuscripts, but adapted to the way in which the ritual was celebrated in the place and time where the new manuscript was produced. There is a very close interaction between written copies and actual ritual practice.

2. Manuscripts of a text type (a liturgical manuscript of a concrete ceremony) can serve as a basis for the production of a manuscript of a different text type (a different ceremony sharing with the first important sections of the Avestan recitative). The different parts were supplied by the ritual knowledge of the priests producing the new manuscript.

The Tools for Avestan Text Criticism (TATEC)

Under these circumstances, I have tried to find a method that can provide a better solution to the problems posed by the Avestan transmission beyond Geldner's approach. Significant common errors cannot be the only basis for the analysis, since they may reflect not only a genetic relationship, but also a position in the same sphere of influence of ritual practice. Thus, one-to-one relations are not adequate for the representation of the complex process of copying the Avestan manuscripts. Ritual practice often conditions the shape of a manuscript as well as its written source. A manuscript can be copied in Nawsari, India, under the sphere of influence of a specific priestly school from an Iranian original sent there a century before. The resulting manuscript would share features with the Iranian manuscripts of the same text type, but also with other manuscripts copied in the same priestly school of the same or different text type.

When examining the variety of new methodologies approaching the problems of genealogical relations between manuscripts in an extremely contaminated transmission, I gave special consideration to two significant factors:

1. the ability to represent multivectorial relations, that is, the ability to represent the different sources involved in the creation of a manuscript (the likely written source and the ritual sphere[s] of influence);

2. the integration of tested traditional philological tools for the evaluation of single readings in the methodology.

The philological method allows us in some privileged cases to know with a high degree of certainty the original reading in a passage and the history of at least some of the subsequent readings. Frequently, computer-assisted stemmatology neglects the positive information that traditional philological tools can provide. Traditional methods allow not only recognition of significant common errors,[9] but also identification of the *original* reading presupposed

---

[9] This can be done as well through some algorithms (cf. Roelli in this volume).

by the rest of readings – and in some fortunate cases we can even reconstruct the relative chronology of the different readings. This is obvious in the two instances mentioned above. In Y30.1 the original reading is without any doubt *mazdaθā* whereas *mazda. θβā* and *mazdaδāta* are independent new readings. In the case of V3.41 the philological tools allow us to discover the exact relative chronology of the different variants. By failing to integrate this information in the building of the stemmata, this very important chronological data is wilfully neglected in favour of a completely automatic process; this is, in my view, a serious limitation of many automated or semi-automated genealogical or stemmatological methods.[10]

A noteworthy exception is the Coherence-Based Genealogical Method (CBGM) developed at the Institut für Neutestamentliche Textforschung. There is an abundant bibliography on this method (Mink 2000; Mink 2003; Mink 2004; Wachtel 2008), therefore it is not necessary to present it here.[11] I will limit myself to a brief introduction of the main features of the Tools for Avestan Text Criticism (TATEC) that I am developing under the inspiration of the CBGM, with the assistance of the software developers Flagsolutions (Salamanca, Spain). The TATEC is available for everyone at ⟨http://ada.usal.es/analizador⟩.

The basis for comparison is at the moment Excel datasheets with aligned transcriptions of the different manuscripts[12] like the following (cf. fig. 1, p. 110).

The Tools present the researcher with the different readings of each place of variation; the researcher is able to evaluate the relevance of each reading and, if possible, the dependence of each reading in order to build 'local stemmata' or 'sub-stemmata' which are the basis of the genealogical comparison in the Coher-

---

[10] Roelli (in this volume) presents a very interesting method that combines the benefits of traditional and computerised stemmatology. Nevertheless, in his approach the philological capacities for determining (at least sometimes) the relative chronology of the different readings are not taken sufficiently into account.

[11] Extensive online information is to be found at the page of the Institut für Neutestamentliche Textforschung of Westfälische Wilhelms-Universität Münster (⟨http://egora.uni-muenster.de/intf/projekte/gsm_en.shtml⟩).

[12] In the context of the Avestan Digital Archive, we have transliterated 8 complete manuscripts of the same text type (Pahlavi-Widewdad). At the present, we are transliterating selected parts of around 130 manuscripts..

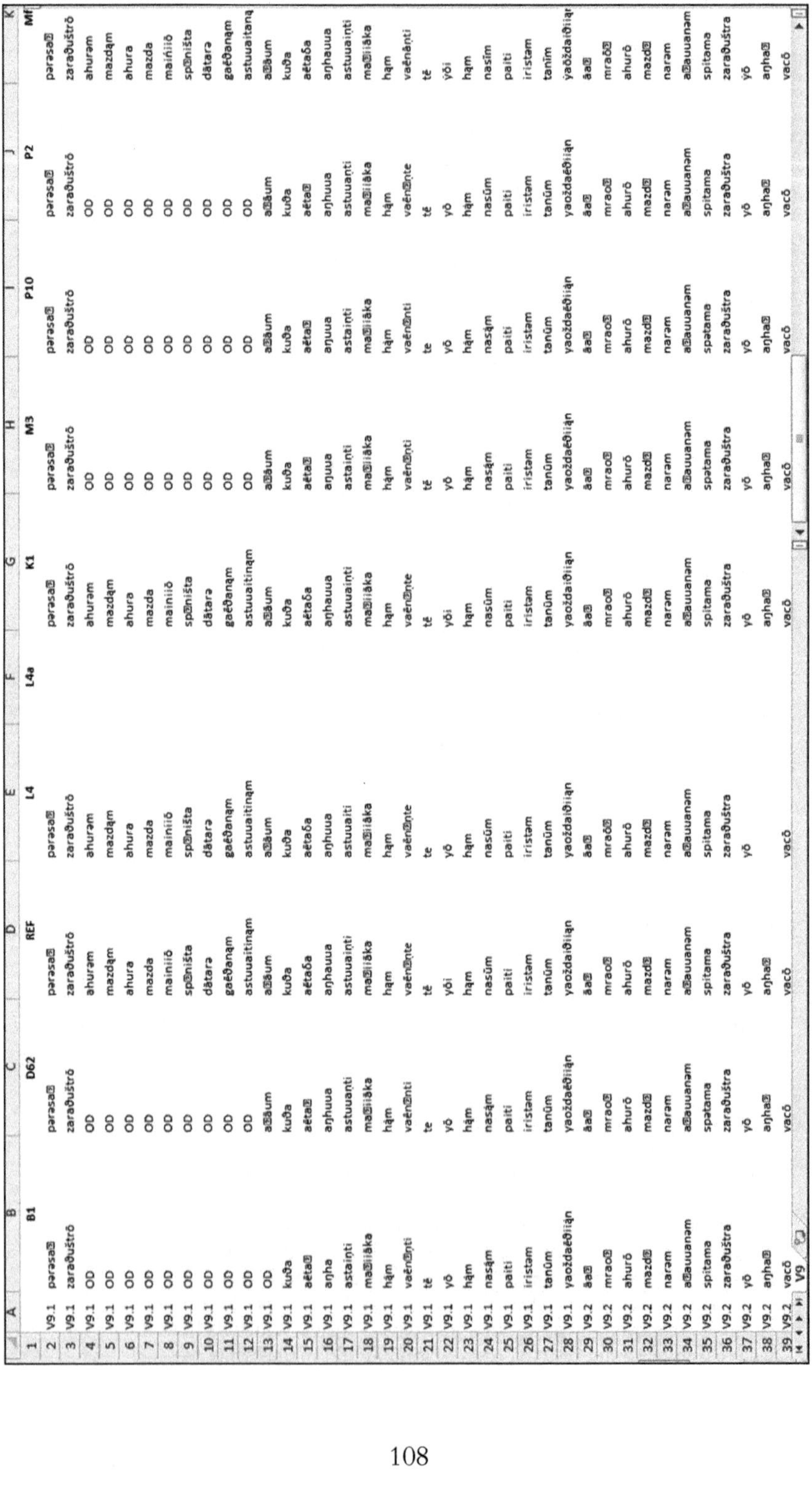

	A	B	C	D	E	F	G	H	I	J	K
1		B1	D62	REF	L4	L4a	K1	M3	P10	P2	Mf
2	V9.1	parəsa□	parəsa□	parəsa□	parəsa□		parəsa□	parəsa□	parəsa□	parəsa□	parəsa□
3	V9.1	zaraθuštrō	zaraθuštrō	zaraθuštrō	zaraθuštrō		zaraθuštrō	zaraθuštrō	zaraθuštrō	zaraθuštrō	zaraθuštrō
4	V9.1	OD	OD	ahurəm	ahurəm		ahurəm	OD	OD	OD	ahurəm
5	V9.1	OD	OD	mazdąm	mazdąm		mazdąm	OD	OD	OD	mazdąm
6	V9.1	OD	OD	ahura	ahura		ahura	OD	OD	OD	ahura
7	V9.1	OD	OD	mazda	mazda		mazda	OD	OD	OD	mazda
8	V9.1	OD	OD	mainiiō	mainiiō		mainiiō	OD	OD	OD	maińiiō
9	V9.1	OD	OD	sp□ništa	sp□ništa		sp□ništa	OD	OD	OD	sp□ništa
10	V9.1	OD	OD	dātarə	dātarə		dātarə	OD	OD	OD	dātarə
11	V9.1	OD	OD	gaēθanąm	gaēθanąm		gaēθanąm	OD	OD	OD	gaēθanąm
12	V9.1	OD	OD	astuuaitinąm	astuuaitinąm		astuuaitinąm	OD	OD	OD	astuuaitaną
13	V9.1	OD	a□āum	a□āum	a□āum		a□āum	a□āum	a□āum	a□āum	a□āum
14	V9.1	kuθa	kuθa	kuθa	kuθa		kuθa	kuθa	kuθa	kuθa	kuθa
15	V9.1	aēta□	aēta□	aētaδa	aētaδa		aētaδa	aēta□	aēta□	aēta□	aētaδa
16	V9.1	aŋha	aŋhuua	aŋhauua	aŋhuua		aŋhauua	aŋuua	aŋuua	aŋhuua	aŋhauua
17	V9.1	astaiṇti	astuuaṇti	astuuaiṇti	astuuaiti		astuuaiṇti	astaiṇti	astaiṇti	astuuaṇti	astuuaiṇti
18	V9.1	ma□iiāka	ma□iiāka	ma□iiāka	ma□iiāka		ma□iiāka	ma□iiāka	ma□iiāka	ma□iiāka	ma□iiāka
19	V9.1	hąm	hąm	hąm	hąm		hąm	hąm	hąm	hąm	hąm
20	V9.1	vaēn□ṇti	vaēn□nti	vaēn□ṇte	vaēn□ṇte		vaēn□ṇte	vaēn□nti	vaēn□nti	vaēn□ṇte	vaēnāṇti
21	V9.1	tē	te	tē	te		tē	tē	te	tē	tē
22	V9.1	yō	yō	yōi	yō		yōi	yō	yō	yō	ẏōi
23	V9.1	hąm	hąm	hąm	hąm		hąm	hąm	hąm	hąm	hąm
24	V9.1	nasąm	nasąm	nasūm	nasūm		nasūm	nasąm	nasąm	nasūm	nasīm
25	V9.1	paiti	paiti	paiti	paiti		paiti	paiti	paiti	paiti	paiti
26	V9.1	iristəm	iristəm	iristəm	iristəm		iristəm	iristəm	iristəm	iristəm	iristəm
27	V9.1	tanūm	tanūm	tanūm	tanūm		tanūm	tanūm	tanūm	tanūm	tanīm
28	V9.1	yaoždaēθiiąn	yaoždaēθiiąn	yaoždaiθiiąn	yaoždaiθiiąn		yaoždaiθiiąn	yaoždaēθiiąn	yaoždaēθiiąn	yaoždaēθiiąn	ẏaoždaiθiiąr
29	V9.2	āa□	āa□	āa□	āa□		āa□	āa□	āa□	āa□	āa□
30	V9.2	mrao□	mrao□	mrao□	mraō□		mrao□	mrao□	mrao□	mrao□	mraō□
31	V9.2	ahurō	ahurō	ahurō	ahurō		ahurō	ahurō	ahurō	ahurō	ahurō
32	V9.2	mazd□	mazd□	mazd□	mazd□		mazd□	mazd□	mazd□	mazd□	mazd□
33	V9.2	narəm	narəm	narəm	narəm		narəm	narəm	narəm	narəm	narəm
34	V9.2	a□auuanəm	a□auuanəm	a□auuanəm	a□auuanəm		a□auuanəm	a□auuanəm	a□auuanəm	a□auuanəm	a□auuanəm
35	V9.2	spitama	spətama	spitama	spitama		spitama	spətama	spətama	spitama	spitama
36	V9.2	zaraθuštra	zaraθuštra	zaraθuštra	zaraθuštra		zaraθuštra	zaraθuštra	zaraθuštra	zaraθuštra	zaraθuštra
37	V9.2	yō	yō	yō	yō		yō	yō	yō	yō	ẏō
38	V9.2	aŋha□	aŋha□	aŋha□			aŋha□	aŋha□	aŋha□	aŋha□	aŋha□
39	V9.2	vacō	vacō	vacō	vacō		vacō	vacō	vacō	vacō	vacō

FIGURE 1.

ence-Based Genealogical Method. When possible, the relevance of the different readings is evaluated. We distinguish four different degrees of relevance:

- r = reading is just an orthographic variation of another attested reading. Thus *aetaδa* is just a reading of *aētaδa* and is encoded accordingly as r-b, which means that *aetaδa* is just a reading of (b) *aētaδa*.

- 1 are banal variants of single letters, such as the usual variation between *ī* and *ii* or the confusion between *ar*, *ər*, *r*, etc.

- 2 are haplologies, dittographies, metatheses, accumulations of changes of level 1, etc.

- 3 is reserved for aberrant variants that are quite unlikely to arise independently.

The information of the dependency is encoded as well and stored in a database. Here you see the encoding of a very simple example in which there are only three readings attested and there is a clear lineal dependence:

(a) varədaϑəmca: B1,D62,REF,K1,M3,P10,P2	a
(b) varədasəmca: L4,T44,E10,G25	2-a
(d) EMPTY: L4a	
(c) varədsīmca: G34	1-b

FIGURE 2.

The information encoded can be read as a 'local stemma' in which *varədaθəmca* is the original reading:

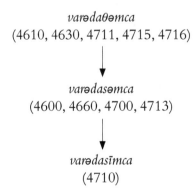

varədaθəmca
(4610, 4630, 4711, 4715, 4716)

↓

varədasəmca
(4600, 4660, 4700, 4713)

↓

varədasīmca
(4710)

109

	A	B	C	D	E	F	G	H	I	J
1					Agreements V					
2	K1	Total of words	Total agreements	Percentage	Agreements 1	Percentage	Agreements 2	Percentage	Agreements 3	Percentage
3	B1	15194	13359	87.92%	219	1.44%	45	0.3%	12	0.08%
4	P10	15299	13079	85.49%	184	1.2%	48	0.31%	12	0.08%
5	M3	15316	13085	85.43%	206	1.34%	49	0.32%	13	0.08%
6	L4	9692	7861	81.11%	87	0.9%	30	0.31%	4	0.04%
7	D62	15384	12137	78.89%	150	0.98%	42	0.27%	9	0.06%
8	D62REP	278	210	75.54%	17	6.12%	0	0%	1	0.36%
9	L4a	5562	4077	73.3%	6	0.11%	0	0%	0	0%
10	P2	15179	10918	71.93%	103	0.68%	25	0.16%	9	0.06%
11	G34	13673	8575	62.71%	62	0.45%	13	0.1%	3	0.02%
12	Bh11	5447	3397	62.36%	3	0.06%	1	0.02%	1	0.02%
13	ML630	923	571	61.86%	0	0%	1	0.11%	0	0%
14	R354	923	571	61.86%	0	0%	1	0.11%	0	0%
15	B4	923	570	61.76%	0	0%	1	0.11%	0	0%
16	Bh4	923	570	61.76%	0	0%	1	0.11%	0	0%
17	R263	923	570	61.76%	0	0%	1	0.11%	0	0%
18	K10	923	570	61.76%	0	0%	1	0.11%	0	0%
19	P1251	923	570	61.76%	0	0%	1	0.11%	0	0%
20	Pr1	923	570	61.76%	0	0%	1	0.11%	0	0%
21	Bh1	923	570	61.76%	0	0%	1	0.11%	0	0%
22	G11	923	570	61.76%	0	0%	1	0.11%	0	0%
23	F11	923	570	61.76%	0	0%	1	0.11%	0	0%
24	G103	923	570	61.76%	0	0%	1	0.11%	0	0%
25	Bh2	923	570	61.76%	0	0%	1	0.11%	0	0%
26	Bh3	923	570	61.76%	0	0%	1	0.11%	0	0%
27	D68	923	570	61.76%	0	0%	1	0.11%	0	0%
28	G102	923	570	61.76%	0	0%	1	0.11%	0	0%
29	G125	923	570	61.76%	0	0%	1	0.11%	0	0%
30	L3	923	570	61.76%	0	0%	1	0.11%	0	0%
31	R368	923	570	61.76%	0	0%	1	0.11%	0	0%
32	R361	923	568	61.54%	0	0%	1	0.11%	0	0%
33	P1079	914	562	61.49%	0	0%	1	0.11%	0	0%
34	Z.Or.1434	914	562	61.49%	0	0%	1	0.11%	0	0%
35	P1976	914	557	60.94%	0	0%	1	0.11%	0	0%
36	T44	15247	9233	60.56%	56	0.37%	11	0.07%	4	0.03%
37	Mf2	2858	1728	60.46%	12	0.42%	1	0.03%	0	0%
38	AQ	2844	1710	60.13%	28	0.98%	1	0.04%	0	0%
39	G25	6833	4058	59.39%	24	0.35%	6	0.09%	1	0.01%

FIGURE 3.

The information stored in the databases allows us, in the first instance, to make queries about the index of agreement of the different manuscripts. They show a purely quantitative index of agreement between the different manuscripts, but also the number of agreements in readings that have been already evaluated according to their relevance (cf. fig. 3).

The manuscripts of lines 3 to 12 + line 36 belong to the same text type as K1, the manuscript that serves as basis for the comparison. The oldest manuscripts of this text type are two copies (mss. 4600 [L4] and 4610 [K1]) by the same copyist, Mihrabān Kayxōsrō that according to their colophons go back to the same source. There is a clear group of manuscripts that have a higher

110

index of agreement with K1 than with MS 4600 (L4). There are likely to be copies from K1: MS 4711 (MS 4711 (B1)), MS 4715 (M3) and MS 4716 (P10). The rest are probably copies from MS 4600 (L4). This is confirmed by the index of agreement of MS 4600 (L4):

The index of agreement of ms 4600 (L4) with the manuscripts copied from MS 4610 (K1) is higher than with its own copies. However, the agreements of level 3 help us to identify some copies of MS 4600 (L4). All the numbers of agreement are active links that show the agreements shared by the compared manuscripts. Thus we can see that whereas all the agreements of level 3 of MS 4711 (B1) with MS 4600 (L4) are in common with MS 4600 (K1, fig. 5),

	A	B	C	D	E	F	G	H	I	J
1					Agreements V					
2	L4	Total of words	Total agreements	Percentage	Agreements 1	Percentage	Agreements 2	Percentage	Agreements 3	Percentage
3	K1	9946	8063	81.07%	87	0.87%	30	0.3%	4	0.04%
4	B1	10613	7909	74.52%	88	0.83%	26	0.24%	3	0.03%
5	M3	9713	7210	74.23%	90	0.93%	26	0.27%	4	0.04%
6	P10	9728	7213	74.15%	86	0.88%	28	0.29%	3	0.03%
7	G34	10650	7680	72.11%	147	1.38%	43	0.4%	6	0.06%
8	D62	9703	6897	71.08%	81	0.83%	23	0.24%	3	0.03%
9	Bh11	4961	3333	67.18%	14	0.28%	1	0.02%	1	0.02%
10	P2	9517	6330	66.51%	67	0.7%	13	0.14%	4	0.04%
11	T44	11005	7131	64.8%	112	1.02%	29	0.26%	5	0.05%

FIGURE 4.

Pre-genealogical coherence

Go to index Exportar

Párrafo	Palabra (L4 - B1)	Coherencia	Otros
19.1-40	duždå	3	duždå: D62,REF,K1,M3,P10,P2,L1,P1,L5,FK1,T44,E10,G34,O2,M2,Bh11 :L4a dauuažå: Mf2 dužå: B2,T46 daožå: L2 daojå: E4 duždå: G25 duuažå: AQ
13.1-20	hazaṇrayna	3	hazaṇhuδarayna: D62 hazaṇrayna: REF,K1,M3,P2,T44,E10 :L4a hazaṇhrayyna: P10 hazaṇharayna: G34 hazaṇraja: G25

FIGURE 5.

Data | Passage | Pregenealogical coherence | Genealogical coherence | Quality

Pre-genealogical coherence

Go to index Exportar

Párrafo	Palabra (L4 - G34)	Coherencia	Otros
19.1-40	duždå	3	**duždå:** B1,D62,REF,K1,M3,P10,P2,L1,P1,L5,FK1,T44,E10,O2,M2,Bh11 : L4a **dauuažå:** Mf2 **dužå:** B2,T46 **daožå:** L2 **daojå:** E4 **dužðå:** G25 **duuažå:** AQ
9.21-37	pasca	3	**paitiša:** B1,Mf2,L1,P1,L2,AQ **pasca:** D62,REF,K1,M3,P10,P2,L5,FK1,T44,D62REP : L4a **paitiš:** B2,T46,E4,E10,O2,M2
9.39-18	pasca	3	**pasauuō:** B1,M3,Mf2,L1,P1,B2,T46,O2,AQ **pasuuō:** D62,REF,K1,P10,P2,L2,E4,L5,FK1,T44,E10,M2 : L4a,D62REP
13.36-3	asmanō	3	**ipimnō:** B1,D62,M3 **isəmnō:** REF,K1 : L4a **ipiminō:** P10 **βimanō:** P2 **asmanō:** T44,E10,G25
13.43-14	tarasca	3	**jatarasca:** B1,D62,REF,K1,M3,P10,E10,G25 : L4a,P2 **tarasca:** T44

FIGURE 6.

The situation is different in the case of the manuscript 4710 (G34), a copy of 4600 (L4):

Here appears the reading *asmanō* that characterizes all the copies of MS 4600 (L4) and furthermore *tarasca* for *jatarasca* that is shared exclusively by both. Besides, the highest index of agreement of MS 4710 is with MS 4600 (L4), so that MS 4710 is very likely a copy of MS 4600 (L4) (72.08%).

However, this method for grouping manuscripts does not allow us to know the relative chronology of the witnesses, except in the fortunate case that external data can indicate which the original source is. To be able to introduce the chronological factor, we use queries about the amount of prior and posterior variants of a manuscript in comparison with the others. The numbers of prior and posterior variants are calculated on the basis of the 'local-stemmata' stored in the database. Thus if we compare the number of prior variants of K1 with the other exegetical manuscripts of the Wīdēwdād and especially with the manuscripts of this group closer to it according to the pre-genealogical index of agreement (MS 4711 (B1), MS 4715 (M3) and MS 4716 (P10)), we obtain the following results:

- Prior variants of K1:

K1	Total	Total <y <<O	%Total <y <<O	Total <y <<No	%Total <y <<No	<	%<	<1	<2	<3
B1	1687	57	3.38%	8	0.47%	61	3.62%	5	3	0
L4	1627	67	4.12%	2	0.12%	68	4.18%	2	0	0
M3	1686	71	4.21%	7	0.42%	74	4.39%	3	1	1
P10	1691	87	5.14%	10	0.59%	85	5.03%	5	3	0
L1	1645	110	6.69%	2	0.12%	100	6.08%	1	0	0
D62	1675	116	6.93%	15	0.9%	118	7.04%	9	3	1
T44	1691	149	8.81%	9	0.53%	130	7.69%	3	3	0
E10	1675	165	9.85%	10	0.6%	149	8.9%	8	0	0
G34	1592	173	10.87%	5	0.31%	151	9.48%	2	1	0

(Chronology 1: V — sheet: archivo)

FIGURE 7.

- posterior variants of K1:

K1	Total	Total >y >>O	%Total >y >>O	Total >y >>No	%Total >y >>No	>	%>	>1	>2	>3
B1	1687	12	0.71%	1	0.06%	13	0.77%	1	0	0
M3	1686	9	0.53%	0	0%	9	0.53%	0	0	0
P10	1691	31	1.83%	0	0%	31	1.83%	0	0	0
D62	1675	39	2.33%	0	0%	39	2.33%	0	0	0
L4	1627	52	3.2%	2	0.12%	54	3.32%	2	0	0
P2	1684	42	2.49%	0	0%	42	2.49%	0	0	0
T44	1691	48	2.84%	0	0%	48	2.84%	0	0	0
E10	1675	59	3.52%	0	0%	58	3.46%	0	0	0
G34	1592	50	3.14%	1	0.06%	51	3.2%	1	0	0

(sheet: archivo (1))

FIGURE 8.

The percentages of prior variants of K1 in comparison with MS 4711 (B1), MS 4715 (M3) and MS 4716 (P10) are higher by far than the percentages of the posterior variants, so that we might

113

conclude that K1 is the oldest witness in this group. If we make the same query about MS 4715 (M3), the results are less clear, but informative enough:

- Prior variants of MS 4711 (B1)

	A	B	C	D	E	F	G	H	I	J	K	
1					Chronology 1: V							
2	B1	Total	Total < y << O	% Total < y << O	Total < y << No	% Total < y << No	<	% <	< 1	< 2	< 3	
3	K1	1687	12	0.71%	1	0.06%	13	0.77%	1	0	0	
4	M3	1714	25	1.46%	5	0.29%	30	1.75%	3	1	1	
5	P10	1719	36	2.09%	9	0.52%	41	2.39%	6	2	0	

archivo (3)

FIGURE 9.

- subsequent variants of MS 4711 (B1)

	A	B	C	D	E	F	G	H	I	J	K	
1												Chronolc
2	B1	Total	Total > y >> O	% Total > y >> O	Total > y >> No	% Total > y >> No	>	% >	> 1	> 2	> 3	
3	K1	1687	55	3.26%	9	0.53%	60	3.56%	6	3	0	
4	M3	1714	7	0.41%	5	0.29%	12	0.7%	3	2	0	
5	P10	1719	25	1.45%	2	0.12%	27	1.57%	2	0	0	

archivo (2)

FIGURE 10.

MS 4711 (B1) seems to be younger than MS 4610 (K1), but older than MS 4715 (M3) and MS 4716 (P10). The data are apparently less clear in the case of MS 4716 (P10), but if we make a query about which are the prior variants of MS 4716 (P10), we will discover that the picture is disturbed by the decision of the evaluator that almost all prior variants of MS 4716 (P10) are the enclitic pronoun *hē* that appears in MS 4716 (P10) as *hē*, but in MS 4715 (M3) as *he* (with short *e*). This information can help the evaluator of the data for changing his former evaluation of these readings. Therefore, I consider it very important that the numbers are hyperlinks that point to the data behind the numbers, so that the researcher may discover and correct potential anomalies.

These data allow us to know the textual flow, that is, the relative chronological position of each witness among all the witnesses analyzed. The combination of these dates with the indices of agreement is the basis for the selection of the potential ancestors of each manuscript and for establishing dependence hypothesis for all the witnesses. The dependences are not one-to-one.

A manuscript can be related to different manuscripts in different ways (simple process of copy, belonging to the same priestly school, contamination, etc.) and a global stemma must represent the most important relations of each manuscript as well as the intensity of the relation. An algorithm remains to be developed for the establishment of a global stemma on the basis of the index of agreement and of the different local stemmata obtained through the traditional linguistic and philological tools. Nevertheless the available tools are already useful for the analysis of the relationship of single manuscripts and are of great help for the editorial work.

The TATEC offers further possibilities, such as a search for omissions and additions, or a tool for advanced collation, but I hope to have shown its most essential features. It is a set of tools that combines the evaluation of each variant by the specialist with quantitative analysis and assists in the analysis of the relative chronology of each witness on the basis of the local stemmata built by the specialist. The next step will be the production of an algorithm that allows the different relations of dependency between the manuscripts to be determined, combining the data of the quantitative analysis and of the local stemmata obtained through the traditional philological tools.

The result will offer a more realistic picture of the complex processes of the Avesta transmission, over and above the simplistic stemmata produced by Geldner solely on the basis of the agreement in error, since errors spread in the Avestan transmission not only through the process of copying from written sources, but also through the influence of ritual practices.

Bibliography

M. A. Andrés-Toledo (2012), 'A critical revision of Geldner's critical edition', in A. Cantera (ed.), *The transmission of the Avesta*, Wiesbaden: Harrassowitz, p. 433-438.

A. Cantera (2010), 'Lost in transmission: The case of the Pahlavi-Vīdēvdād manuscripts', *Bulletin of the School of Oriental and African Studies*, 73, p. 179-205.

A. Cantera (2011), 'Breve tipología e historia de los manuscritos avésticos de la liturgia larga', *Aula Orientalis*, 29, p. 199-243.

A. Cantera (2012a), 'Building trees: genealogical relations between the manuscripts of Videvdad', in A. Cantera (ed.), *The transmission of the Avesta*, Wiesbaden: Harrassowitz, p. 207-276.

A. Cantera (2012b), 'Why do we really need a new edition of the Avesta', in A. Cantera (ed.), *The transmission of the Avesta*, Wiesbaden: Harrassowitz, p. 439-477.

K. F. Geldner (1886), *Avesta. The sacred books of the Parsis*, Stuttgart: Kohlhammer.

A. Hintze (2012), 'On editing the Avesta', in A. Cantera (ed.), *The transmission of the Avesta*, Wiesbaden: Harrassowitz, p. 419-432.

K. Hoffmann & J. Narten (1989), *Der Sasanidische Archetypus. Untersuchungen zu Schreibung und Lautgestalt des Avestischen*, Wiesbaden: L. Reichert.

K. Hoffmann (1969), 'Zur Yasna-Überlieferung', *MSS*, 26, p. 35-38.

K. Hoffmann (1971), 'Zum Zeicheninventar der Avesta-Schrift', *Festgabe Deutscher Iranisten zur 2500 Jahrfeier Irans*, Stuttgart: Hochwacht Druck, p. 64-73.

H. Humbach (1973), 'Beobachtungen zur Überlieferungsgeschichte des Awesta', *Münchener Studien zur Sprachwissenschaft*, 31, p. 109-122.

J. Kellens (1998), 'Considérations sur l'histoire de l'Avesta', *Journal Asiatique*, 286, p. 451-519.

G. Mink (2000). 'Editing and Genealogical Studies: the New Testament'. *Literary and Linguistic Computing*, 15, p. 51-56.

G. Mink (2003), 'Was verändert sich in der Textkritik durch die Beachtung genealogischer Kohärenz?', in W. Weren & A. D. Koch (eds.), *Recent Developments in Textual Criticism. New Testament, other Early Christian and Jewish Literature*, p. 39-68.

G. Mink (2004), 'Problems of a Highly Contaminated Tradition: the New Testament. Stemmata of variants as a source of a genealogy for witnesses', in P. van Reenen, A. den Hollander & M. van Mulken (eds.), *Studies in Stemmatology II*, p. 13-85.

Ph. Roelli (2014), 'Petrus Alfonsi or On the mutual benefit of traditional and computerised stemmatology', in T. L. Andrews & C. Macé (eds.), *Analysis of Ancient and Medieval Texts and Manuscripts: Digital Approaches*, Turnhout: Brepols, p. 32-32.

Wachtel, K. (2008), 'Towards a Redefinition of External Criteria: The Role of Coherence in Assessing the Origin of Variants', in H. A. G. Houghton & D. C. Parker (eds.), *Textual Variation: Theological and Social Tendencies?*, Piscataway: Gorgias Press, p. 109-127.

N. L. Westergaard (1852), *Zendavesta, or The religious books of the Zoroastrians*. Copenhagen: Berling brothers.

STATISTICS AND STYLISTICS

ARMIN HOENEN

SIMULATION OF SCRIBAL LETTER SUBSTITUTION*

Introduction

While a wide array of different algorithms have already been developed in phylogeny and by Robinson and O'Hara, were first applied to the field of stemmatics, other algorithms like the Coherence Based Genealogical Method (Wachtel 2011), mentioned in the previous article written by A. Cantera still remain to be explored computationally.[1] Since 1992, a lot of research has been conducted, today there are specialised methods of stemmatology such as RHM. Utilising RHM T. Roos et al. consider not only word pairs when comparing manuscripts but with them their corresponding contexts.[2] Roelli et al. successfully incorporate the significance of a line skip into stemmatological algorithms.[3] Still, computerised stemmatology faces some problems and criticism, largely reflected by Christopher J. Howe et al.[4]

One of the problems of traditional and computerised stemmatology is the verification of results. Once a computer or a human being has figured out a stemma, how can this result be verified, when the true historical stemma is unknown? In order to cope with this problem, scholars have tried to use artificial traditions. An artificial tradition is one, in which the stemmatic

---

[1] Robinson & O'Hara 1992; for the Coherence Based Genealogical Method cf. Wachtel 2011.

[2] Roos et al. 2006.

[3] Roelli et al. 2010.

[4] Howe et al. 2012.

10.1484/M.LECTIO-EB.5.102567

relationships between the texts are exactly known, because the texts have been artificially – mostly by volunteers – generated whilst recording their true relationships. With such an artificial tradition at hand, a stemma-generating algorithm can be evaluated. To date three artificial traditions are most famous (all three referred to in Ph. V. Baret et al.).[5] All of these were produced by hand, that is by human volunteers, who copied the texts. The papers give reasons for producing an artificial tradition by hand, while it is not explicitly stated why the computer generation of such a tradition is not pursued. The present paper aims to take the first step in producing such a computer generated artificial tradition by constructing and testing a baseline approach, an endeavour which, to the best knowledge of the author has not been undertaken so far.

Automatic Tradition Generator (ATG)

Producing artificial traditions by hand is very labor intensive and consequently such corpora to date do not exceed a certain size. Additionally, they could be biased by the difference in setting and orthographic education of modern scribes and medieval ones. T. Roos et al. detected differences in the performance of RHM on artificial traditions and real historic examples largely due to contamination.[6]

On the other hand producing a realistic artificial tradition by means of an algorithm is a very difficult task. Firstly, when copying automatically similar changes must be introduced to the manuscripts as have been introduced in former times by humans, such that a typology of these changes and their prototypical distributions could be useful. Such a typology however could differ considerably with the tradition.[7]

Thereby, an ATG must generate a realistic distribution of all types of deviations within a corpus. Effects such as the accumulation of errors in a copy's copy must be reproduced. In other

---

[5] Baret et al. 2004.
[6] Roos et al. 2006.
[7] If it were universal, a machine learning approach could be thinkable, where an algorithm is trained on the distributions of typed variants in one corpus and used on any other.

120

words, the algorithm first takes an input manuscript, proceeds ideally from the beginning to the end and in the manner of a human copyist introduces certain changes to the copy it produces, according to predetermined parameters. By applying this process a number of times, discarding some of the material produced in order to produce a simulation of historical loss, ATG should arrive at an output corpus, that features characteristics similar to those found in real historical corpora. Among one another, will a body of historical corpora display similarities in any non-trivial characteristic? From where do we pull the ideal characteristics that we want reproduced, needed to calibrate our model? Advisably not from the same tradition we want to later evaluate although methods such as bootstrapping may have beneficial effects. Unfortunately, looking into biology, we do not find exactly the same problem, as there the restricted input alphabet of four letters encoding the four nucleic acids is not object to a comparable variety of different substitution processes as is written text in an alphabet that contains 26 letters. Additionally, the number of linguistic levels such as letter, morpheme, word, clause, sentence and their interrelationships are highly complex and as a whole lack suitable known counterparts in DNA.

One potential solution is to take multiple traditions and explore similarities in the distributions of changes and variants, abstracting to universal properties. The ultimate abstraction of universal properties would be closely correlated to a cognitive model of the copy process of which an outline is provided in Appendix A. In the next section, we try to construct a first ATG based on the aforementioned assumptions.

Simulations

In this section, we begin simulating a copy process, changing our paradigm iteratively. We then compare our results to an actual data corpus. Our first working unit will be the letter, as we start from the smallest units copied in a copy process.[8]

---

[8] Probably the word is a more realistic unit for observations. However, not only does single-letter copying occur in one letter words as well as, probably when a scribe is not able to read the language, but also the distribution of letters could carry the same characteristics as the distribution of words, simply repre-

We start from a maximally naive simulation. As an input text we take the *Human Rights Bill*, an error or mutation rate of 1 in 50 was chosen (the choice of which is arbitrary). The first hypothesis for the automatic scribe is that each letter, when a copy error occurs, is replaced by any one other letter of the given alphabet implying equiprobability of letter exchanges.

After one copy
no one shall be hzld in slavery or serqitude; slavery and the slave trcde shall be prohibited in all their forms.

After five copies
no oze sqall be held in seavery or servitwde; blavery and the slave crade shahl be prohibited gn hll their forms.

After fifty copies
gh oce sfdlo we kebt zs sttdzry oj gjrvibudbf skyvwrq anm tye sbakz teazx jzwkl ka pfbhjffteq in acu uvpid oorys.

Figure 1: Naive scribe simulation. All letters are exchanged with all other letters, error rate of 1 in 50. Human Rights Bill, English, lowercase, article 4.

The output of the simulation (fig. 1) is no longer legible after a few copies. Hence, we reject this hypothesis and in the second step assume that only those letters which are visually similar are being exchanged. The replacements are thus limited to sets of visually similar letters, judged automatically for their similarity according to values from a letter discriminability matrix, which describes the visual discriminability of any letter pair in the given alphabet.

Mueller and Weidemann compare 55 papers from 1886 until today describing 74 experiments with the majority using psycholinguistic approaches (*c.* 82%) to establish a letter discriminability matrix for the Latin alphabet.[9] Jacobs et al. present a discriminability matrix based on saccade latency times for lowercase letters, which we used here.[10] We only allowed replacements with the

senting another level of observation and is in this sense worthy to be investigated, since then any further investigation would be rendered close to obsolete.
[9] Mueller & Weidemann 2011.
[10] Jacobs et al. 1989, p. 100.

2-3 most similar letters (for example ⟨i⟩ and ⟨l⟩).[11] For historical corpora however, it must be noted, that since there are no speakers to obtain such a matrix from experimentally, other means of establishing them would have to be explored should the method be successfully applicable.[12][13]

After one copy
no one shall be subjected to torture or to cruel, inhuman or degrading treatment or punishment.

After five copies
na one shall be sudjoctep to torture ot to cruel, inhuman or degtading treatment or pwnishment.

After fifty copies
wq que ehail pc subieered tq icrrupg ot ta etucl, juhhnan ot degrebtwg treajwghr or dwntshmani.

FIGURE 2: Less naive scribe simulation? The letters are being exchanged with the most probable substitutes according to an observed letter discriminability matrix by Jacobs et al. (1989). Human Rights Bill, English, lowercase, article 5.

At this point the simulation does not improve significantly, which calls in question a purely letter-similarity-driven alternation in copy process chains. Units greater than letters should thus be investigated in subsequent research. This does not come as a surprise since for instance phenomena such as grammatical reanalyses, language change and modernisation have no direct connection with letters or letter similarity. The next simulation alters letters only according to a fixed set of possible substitutes which are phonologically similar. The sets were composed by the author and always included the voiced and unvoiced variant of a

---

[11] Arguably, the matrix is unrealistic for historical data in that it is based on lower case computer font letters, but since the text used features the same letter shapes, the simulation is consistent.

[12] The predominant non-psycholinguistic approach is examining the visual appearances of letters by defining graphical recognition units like "belly + bar" ('b','p'), "ascenders" ('d') and so forth, see Jacobs 1989.

[13] As an alternative, we chose expert's intuition and compared the distributions of differences which turned out to be similar to those found in the mentioned experiments with native speakers.

phoneme or *feature combination* and in some instances additionally included direct *featural neighbours* of place or manner of articulation (examples encompassing 'd' and 't' or 'm' and 'b').

After one copy
everyone has the right to a standard of living adequate for the health
and well-being of himself and of his bamily

After five copies
everyome haj thi right lo a standard ob living adequate for the health
and well-being of himsjlb and of his family

After fifty copies
ivelyomi has tei right ta a jramlarl of livime adekvadi mar the hjalth
amr vell-mijng ob eimjelb amd am his bamily

FIGURE 3: The letters are being exchanged with letters usually representing similar phonemes. Human Rights Bill, English, lowercase, article 25(1) excerpt.

Our model does not have any correction function included prohibiting for instance geminates at the beginning of words. Yet the outcome after 50 copies is probably a little more readable than in the previous simulations.[14]

The next simulation targeted orthography. Orthographically similar units were substituted instead of letters. We adopted the model of *basic* and *contextual* spellings for English which is described in greater detail in Van Berkel and allowed exchanges of one, two or three letter units only with such units, that could represent the same phoneme in the English orthography (for instance exchanging ‹ay› and ‹eigh›).[15] Each such orthographic unit had the probability based but not entirely similar to the classification in Van Berkel.[16] In our model all basic spellings amounted to 50%, all contextual spellings amounted to 30% and all word specific spellings amounted to 20%. As an example, if a word was chosen to be altered by the Math.random function in the Java programming language, a unit present in the word such as ‹a›, is

---

[14] Being accustomed to strong accents, someone might be able to deduct the word "forms" from "falmj", certainly not from "kakmc".
[15] Van Berkel 2006.
[16] Van Berkel 2006.

exchanged by another unit that could equally represent the phoneme usually represented by ‹a›, such as ‹ai›. For instance, ‹lady›
would have been changed to ‹laidy›. Then a basic correction
ensured that a word did not start with a geminate and would not
contain too many geminates. The model overgenerated geminates through successive substitutions.

After one copy
no one may be compelled to belong to an association.

After five copies
no one may be compelled to belong to ang association.

After fifty copies
no oune mai be scompelled tough beloange too aing assoseiation.

FIGURE 4: Orthographic units are being exchanged with other such units
which can represent the same phoneme. Human Rights Bill, English, lowercase, article 20(2) excerpt.

There are many things that can be elaborated in this model such
as a strict chunking into orthographic units before application
of the substitution process. Nevertheless, even after 50 copies for
the first time, the output is close to readable. The scribes could
thus even in unstandardised orthographic environments keep the
information transmission intact by a constant orthographic rule
system. In unstandardised writing, this implies that certain spelling alternatives could have been permissible in any or most contexts and would not necessarily have been perceived as erroneous. English, being a deep orthography,[17] might not be the most
prototypical example, since the number of acceptable alternative
spellings could exceed that of other orthographies by far trigger-
ing particular compensatory strategies. The phonological simula-

---

[17] The concept of orthographic depth refers, for instance, to the degree to
which a writing system uses grapheme-to-phoneme or phoneme-to-grapheme
conversion rules that are not based on a one to one representation. Additionally
consistency of representation is a factor for orthographic depth. For instance, the
representation of /ʃ/ by ‹sh› employs two letters for one phoneme. This representation is not absolutely consistent, since different orthographic units, such as ‹ch›
as in ‹chef› can also represent the same phoneme. In this sense, English is a rather
deep orthography (see for instance Katz & Frost 1992).

tion was already nearly legible and at this point the distributions of corresponding substitutions of real historical and artificial traditions shall be consulted.

Letter-based Investigation of Corpora and Final Simulation

Our first corpus is the Yasna ceremony of the Avesta, which was also the subject of the previous article by Alberto Cantera. The actual corpus we are looking at is a collation of 7 manuscripts of the Yasna ceremony (Pt4, Mf4, Br2, K5, J2, K7, P1, K4) from the Avesta as stored in the TITUS website).[18] Each of the manuscripts is compared to one another, in order for every possible pair of words at each position to be evaluated although they do not necessarily represent items that stand in any stemmatic relationship. The reason for choosing all word pairs is the fact that a genuine stemmatic relationship is unknown. This makes the results harder to interpret. Any word pair was compared with Meyer's Diff algorithm as implemented in the java-diff-utils[19] library.[20] The algorithm produces a letter based alignment of the two words. We obtain a table with distributions of letter divergences for each letter pair.[21] The correspondence patterns obtained in this way for the Avestan matrix showed two tendencies:

a. vowels were deviating at a higher rate
b. vowels were exchanged by vowels, consonants by consonants.

The question is whether this pattern was due to the Avestan phonology and/or writing system or if this was a more general observation. Consequently, we computed the same distribution tables for the datasets available alongside the publication of Roos

---

[18] Gippert 2002.

[19] ⟨http://code.google.com/p/java-diff-utils/⟩

[20] The algorithm aligns for instance the word pair 'since' and 'sense' in a way that one difference i:e and one difference c:s is counted.

[21] A second visual letter similarity matrix was build through the intuition of an expert, which carried similar characteristics. Note, that at this point, we do not focus on phonological, phonetical, motoric or graphemic units' similarities, but solely on the contribution of visual grapheme similarity. The importance of the other factors is not meant to be neglected with this narrow focus.

et al.[22] In all of these traditions, the probability that two vowels at aligned places in any manuscript pair disagree is higher than that of consonantal disagreement. The reasons might be manifold. At this point, this is of no concern to a successful simulation of an artificial corpus nor without further elaboration a generalisable statement. In consequence, we try to reproduce a similar pattern in our final simulation. This time keeping the letter (and not graphemic unit) based simulation, the phonological one and limiting the transitions by reproducing the distribution of two times more vowel : vowel than consonant : consonant shifts. Vowel to consonant transitions were not permitted, simulating a more sophisticated correction function.

After one copy
everyone has the right freely wo participate in the cultural life af the community, to enjoy the arts and to share on scientific advancement and its benefits.

After five copies
everyone has thi right fraely to larticipite in the uultural life ef xhe cummunity, to anjoy the arts end to shore in sciebtific advincement aed its benefots.

After fifty copies
ivaraenu uis taj reaei freqln ko qartexieate sa gha cegtocal eafe ie the mimkwniah, zu aduup tiu urtm inu tu shora en xcuoceafor oavin-cumadt abi its banewaiz.

FIGURE 4: Graphemes typically representing vowels are replaced slightly more often and by graphemes typically representing phonologically similar vowels, same for consonants. Human Rights Bill, English, lowercase, article 27(1).

The last simulation did not improve the performance and the simulation based on orthographic units remains the most convincing one. There, the basic unit was graphemic and not restricted to one letter. At this point the letter should be abandoned as basic unit in order to progress along the scale of linguistic units.

---

[22] Roos et al. 2006.

127

Discussion and Conclusion

In order to create artificial corpora automatically, a simulation of a copyist has been attempted. The starting point was the basic hypothesis, that a simulation reproducing distributions on the most basic unit, the letter is sufficient. The outputs produced relating to different substitution hypotheses suggest that phonological and orthographic phenomena play a role in preserving the message of a text throughout its copy history, since these simulations were the most compelling ones. A look into five corpora, three artificial and two historical ones made it plausible that vowels are less stable than consonants. The hypothesis that for Avestan the pattern was only due to a high similarity of the vowels in the writing system can be doubted as the same patterns also occur in the Latin alphabet, where a letter discrimination matrix presented by Jacobs showed no similar visual similarity patterning.[23] From the simulation based on the same visual letter similarity matrix it could also be shown, that visual similarity patterns are not the only source of scribal errors.

Adjusting simulations by looking at distributional data from historical and artificial corpora and abstracting principles showed to have merit for copyist simulation. Nevertheless, all simulations lacked a clear readability after 50 copies, a possible hint towards the importance of higher levels of distributory analyses, such as the graphemic unit, the morpheme or the word. With a number of fifty, the copy chain of the simulation might have been too long. It remains to be judged by paleographical and philological expertise which of the variants simulated are similar to real world examples.

Whether from the distributional data of the corpuses, a hypothesis such as "scribes are more likely to correct errors which concern vowel to consonant changes, since those are more likely to produce nonwords" is too far-fetched equally remains to be verified. In this the study is to be viewed as clearly preliminary. The study does not imply that for stemmatological purposes it is necessary to discard or keep certain errors. With regard to this question, the only conclusion that can be drawn is: since qualita-

[23] Jacobs 1989.

tively different deviations seem to exist, a weighting could make sense.[24] Furthermore could an *error distribution analysis* per manuscript lead to a *copy circumstance model*, that is a model where from the distribution of error types (such as vowel to vowel, vowel to consonant, gemination etc.), factors such as "proficiency of the scribe", "mother tongue of the scribe" or "concentration of the scribe" could be deducted (possibly aided by information of the collophones[25] and other sources[26]) and then used in some way for stemma construction. The aim of the study was a first step in producing artificial traditions with known stemmata in great numbers in order to provide test cases for the development of a potent stemmatology.[27] Although this goal is yet to be reached and could not be completed by examining the letter level, the study could show that investigating and reproducing seemingly universal characteristics of distributions can have a positive effect on a copyist simulation. The next step and at the same time perhaps the biggest shortcoming of this study would presumably be the word level and variant level investigation of distributions.

Bibliography

C. Bartholomae (1895-1901), 'II. Awestasprache und Altpersisch', in W. Geiger & E. Kuhn (eds.), *Grundriss der iranischen Philologie*, Strassburg: Trübner, p. 152-248.

Ph. V. Baret, C. Macé, P. Robinson (2004), 'Testing Methods on an Artificially Created Textual Tradition', in *Linguistica Computazionale*, 24-25, p. 255-281.

A. van Berkel (2005), 'The Role of the Phonological Strategy in Learning to Spell in English as a Second Language', in V. J. Cook & B. Bassetti (eds.), *Second Language Writing Systems*, Clevedon: Multilingual Matters, p. 97-121.

---

[24] A local stemma of variants as proposed by the CBGM method can be understood as a kind of weighting.

[25] For instance, a copy made for a king could be produced more carefully than one for the local theatre. Coleman 2005 discusses the illustrations of *Cité de Dieu* and their relation to the recipient of the copy.

[26] L. Canfora 2002 mentions for instance that library exemplars differ from private ones.

[27] At present many comparative studies use the same artificial datasets all based on the Latin alphabet.

L. Canfora (2002), *Il copista come autore*, Palermo: Sellerio.

A. Cantera (2012), 'Building Trees: Genealogical Relations Between the Manuscripts of Wīdēwdād', in A. Cantera (ed.), *The Transmission of the Avesta*, Wiesbaden: Harrassowitz, p. 279-346.

J. Coleman (2005), 'Aural Illumination: Books and Aurality in the Frontispieces to Bishop Chevrot's *Cité de Dieu*', in M. Chinca & C. Young (eds.), *Orality and Literacy in the Middle Ages*, Turnhout, Belgium: Brepols (Utrecht Studies in Medieval Literacy, 12), p. 223-252.

S. Costard (2011), *Störungen der Schriftsprache*, Stuttgart: Thieme.

J. I. Glass et al. (2006), 'Essential Genes of a Minimal Bacterium,' in *PNAS*, 103, p. 425-430.

J. Gippert (2002), 'The avestan language and its problems', in *Proceedings of the British Academy*, 116, p. 165-187.

J. Gippert (2012), 'The Encoding of Avestan - Problems and Solutions', in *Journal for Language Technology and Computational Linguistics*, 27(2), p. 1-24.

Z. Han, Y. Zhang, H. Shu, Y. Bi (2007), 'The Orthographic Buffer in Writing Chinese Characters: Evidence from a Dysgraphic Patient', in *Cognitive Neuropsychology*, 24, p. 431-450.

K. Hoffmann (1986), 'Avestisch ṣ̌', in R. Schmitt & P. O. Skjærvø (eds.), *Studia grammatica iranica – Festschrift für Helmut Humbach*, München: Kitzinger, p. 163-183.

K. Hoffmann & J. Narten (1989), *Der Sasanidische Archetypus – Untersuchungen zu Schreibung und Lautgestalt des Avestischen*, Wiesbaden: Reichert.

C. J. Howe, R. Connolly, and H. F. Windram (2012), 'Responding to Criticism of Phylogenetic Methods in Stemmatology', in *SEL Studies in English Literature*, 52, p. 51-67.

D. Hudson & D. Bryant (2006), 'Application of Phylogenetic Networks in Evolutionary Studies,' in *Mol. Biol. Evol.*, 23, p. 254-267.

A. M. Jacobs (1989), 'Perception of Lowercase Letters in Peripheral Vision: A Discrimination Matrix Based on Saccade Latencies', in *Perception & Psychophysics*, 46, p. 95-102.

T. Jügel (2012), 'Peculiarities of Avestan Manuscripts for Computational Linguistics', in *Journal for Language Technology and Computational Linguistics*, 27(2), p. 25-38.

L. Katz & R. Frost (1992), 'Reading in different orthographies: The orthographic depth hypothesis', in R. Frost & L. Katz (eds.), *Orthography, phonology, morphology, and meaning*, Amsterdam: New Holland, p. 67-84.

S. T. Mueller & C. Weidemann (2011), 'Alphabetic Letter Identification: Effects of Perceivability, Similarity, and Bias', in *Acta Psychologica*, 139, p. 19-37.

P. Robinson & R. O'Hara (1992), 'Report on the Textual Criticism Challenge 1991', in *Bryn Mawr Classical Review*, 3, p. 331-337.

P. Roelli & D. Bachmann (2010), 'Towards generating a stemma of complicated manuscript traditions: Petrus Alfonsi's Dialogus', in *Revue d'histoire des textes*, 5, p. 307-321.

T. Roos, T. Heikkilä, and P. Myllymäki (2006), 'Compression-Based Method for Stemmatic Analysis', in *Proceedings of the 17th European Conference on Artificial Intelligence*, Amsterdam: IOS Press, p. 805-806.

T. Shallice (1988), *From neuropsychology to Mental Structure*, Cambridge: Cambridge Univ. Press.

M. de Vaan (2003), *The Avestan Vowels*, Amsterdam & New York: Rodopi.

K. Wachtel (2006), 'Reconstructing the Initial Text of the *Editio Critica Maior* of the New Testament Using the Coherence-Based Genealogical Method', in *Journal for the Study of the New Testament*, 29, p. 229-235.

APPENDIX A

A COGNITIVE MODEL
FOR A BETTER STEMMATOLOGY

In order to understand copying prior to producing simulations, it is beneficial to investigate the copy process from a cognitive perspective. For the reader familiar with cognitive models, the appendix outlines characteristics of such a model for the copying process. Copying involves reading and writing in a concatenative chain. First the scribe reads a unit (word, portion of a sentence, letter etc.), then he/she writes it down. Therefore, a model for copying must start with a model for reading or in dictation copies or copies from text learned by heart from auditory input.

The model will be based on the most widespread contemporary model of reading, the *dual route model*, according to which there are two routes of reading a written word. Costard (2011) adopted the model in fig. 1 from Shallice (1988). One route is *lexical*, that is, the recognition of the word triggers the direct retrieval in the mental lexicon, where the general meanings of words are stored. This route is assumed for familiar words. It means that the word shape has been encountered and connected to the same meaning so often, that another encounter of the same word shape makes this very meaning accessible to the reader almost instantaneously.

The *segmental route* on the other hand is based on letters or graphemic units. In the segmental route, a reader fails to find the word in the mental lexicon or is so unfamiliar with the word, that the retrieval is unsuccessful, and the letters are converted into the proper sounds one by one according to grapheme phoneme conversion rules. In the beginning of learning to read, the student only has the segmental route at his/her disposal.

A writer essentially needs to put into letters the words he hears in his mental (or in case of a dictation in the real) ear.[28] For copying, we assume the same two major routes of processing, lexical and segmental. We present some possible pathways within this model, that could connect reading and writing, details given in the respective captions.

---

[28] For some time, the receptors themselves store the imprint of a sensual activation.

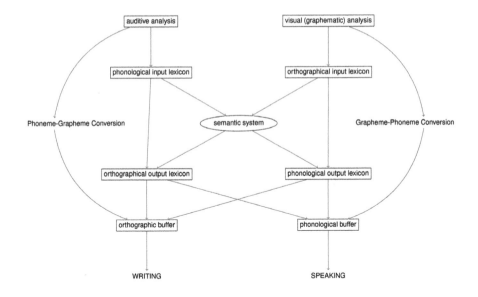

FIGURE 1: The dual route model of reading and writing.

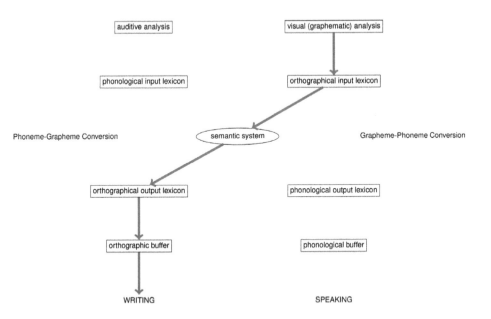

FIGURE 2: The lexical route that applies in copying. A visual input is retrieved in the lexicon and the writing of this same entry is triggered.

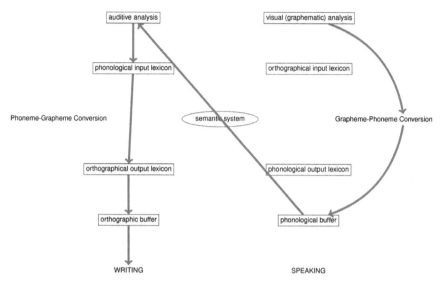

FIGURE 3: A segmental route. Here the word is not immediately recognized, typically for words with a low natural frequency of occurrence. The word is read from the letters/graphemic units one by one (segmental route) e.g. into the working memory. From the visual shape it was not retrieved in the lexicon, but now the read out version is and is written down accordingly.

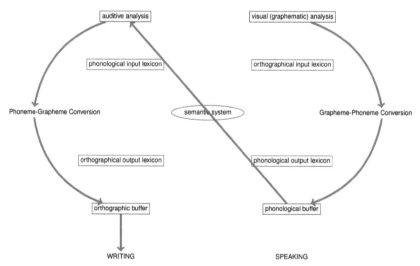

FIGURE 4: Another segmental route. Here the retrieval upon reading failed, the letters are converted into phonemes and appended to one single auditive shape which is again not found in the lexicon and is hence reconverted one by one into letters upon writing.

134

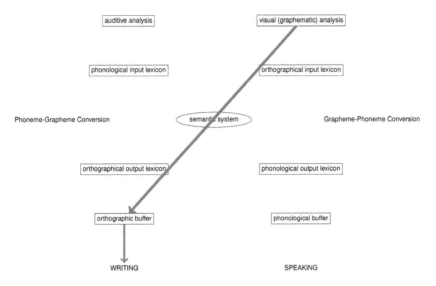

FIGURE 5: Yet another segmental route. Instead of converting anything phonologically at all, the visual shape is directly taken as input for the orthographic output buffer, hence a lexical retrieval is not even attempted. This route portrays a rather automatic and thoughtless copying similar to repainting.

We tried to choose the most plausible routes for a copying process on the basis of the dual route model since there is virtually no literature available on the cognitive modeling of the copy process. This preliminary construction of possible pathways in copying starting in an adjacent field[29] serves an illustrative purpose. It is possible and maybe even probable that copying itself proceeds along different pathways depending on factors such as word frequency, position, length and proficiency of the scribe. If so, and the figures gave evidence that different pathways exist, the errors made – both in quality and quantity – could be understood in a better way, such that a model of the circumstances surrounding the copy could be constructed from the observed types of error. If such a model were possible phenomena such as one scribe copying the same manuscript twice in two subsequent

[29] There are many more possible pathways and new feedback loops like an online comparison to the visual or auditory imprint left in the receptors for correction of the written letters.

years, once making many mistakes and arriving at a low similarity with the ancestor and once making few mistakes and arriving at a higher similarity could be understood and even modeled for the purpose of creating a more precise stemmatology.

To elaborate on this, if certain errors are such, that they occur predominantly then, when a certain cognitive pathway is chosen and this pathway is connected with low attention or non comprehensive reading (such as our pathway in fig. 5, where visual discriminability could be much more important than otherwise), then the number of such errors/deviations, could allow us to compute a coefficient of "copyist concentration" on the particular copy. Furthermore, determining the level of concentration applied in making a copy would enable us to identify those edges in a stemma, which generated bigger differences. Additionally, such information could be valuable for the set-up of local word stemmata since the significance of such a variant and the number of independent occurrences could be interrelated.

Apart from that, cognitive science, therapy of aphasia, writing acquisition and many other adjacent fields could profit from a cognitive model of the copy process.[30]

Last but not least, the automatic creation of an artificial tradition is a task, that could be performed with much more ease alongside such a model.

---

[30] Nevertheless, the peculiarities of a shift of primary orality through literacy with large oral residues and the steady decline of these, or the transition from orality to handwriting and on to print are domain specific factors for stemmatological research as is the standardisation process of orthography and it's influence on stemmata, these processes need to be addressed and combined with cognitive factors as well as other stemmatologically relevant information elsewhere. In this sense, stemmatology is at the very beginning of development.

APPENDIX B

BACKGROUND INFORMATION
ON THE AVESTAN ALPHABET

The Avestan alphabet is one of the few alphabets in the world which did not gradually develop but which was purposely invented, certainly in the Sasanian era (i.e., AD 224-651). Following from an analysis of the composition of the Avestan alphabet, which will be discussed in what follows, it is quite possible to narrow the timeframe to the fourth century AD.[31]

The purpose of inventing the Avestan script was to gain an adequate tool for preserving the original sound of the holy texts of the Zoroastrian religion, the text corpus of which is called 'the Avesta'. Before, the Avesta was transmitted orally, and the non-native speakers felt the need of writing it down in a most detailed way. In fact, the Avestan script is very close to a phonetic transcription, i.e., it was not phonemes which were written down but phones. This explains the high amount of characters, viz. 51, seven of which have orthographic variants.[32] Starting from Proto-Iranian, we expect six vowels (/ă, ĭ, ŭ/, i.e., long and short /a/ etc.), as Old Persian has it, but in Avestan we find 15: ‹ă, ĭ, ŭ, ĕ, ŏ, å, ā̊, ą, ə̃›.[33] The phonematic status of all of them is not entirely clear, i.e., whether the sound change is due to a sound law or to the pronunciation of reciters.[34] The 21 expected consonants (/b, p, f, g, k, x, d, t, θ, m, n, r, w, y, č, ǰ, s, z, š, ž, h/) are enhanced to 36 in Avestan: ‹b, β, p, f, g, ġ, γ, k, x, x́, xᵛ, d, δ, t, θ, ṭ, m, m̨, n, ņ, ń, ŋ, ń̃, ŋᵛ, r, v, y, č, ǰ, s, z, š, ž, ś, ṣ̌, h›. We are quite certain that several characters only represented allophones of one another, e.g., ‹ṇ› only appears in front of consonants, ‹ń› in palatal context, and ‹n› is the neutral representation of /n/. While the three characters of /š/ are mostly used randomly in the manuscripts: ‹ś› is the palatal variant of ‹š›, and the character ‹ṣ̌› probably represented originally a different phoneme, because it is

---

[31] Hoffmann & Narten 1989, p. 34.

[32] The variants ‹y› and ‹ẏ› later became a feature for telling Iranian from Indian manuscripts apart. Originally, ‹ẏ› may have represented /y/, and ‹y› represented /ž́/ (i.e., palatal /ž/), cf. Bartholomae 1895-1901, p. 153 § 267/1 and p. 162 § 271/I.

[33] Parantheses contain the phonological representation of characters, angle brackets the graphological one. For a survey on encoding Avestan characters see Gippert 2012.

[34] Cf. de Vaan 2003.

the result of a sound change of /rt/ after accentuated syllables via a devoiced /ṛ/ to /š/.[35]

The inventor(s) of the Avestan script used Middle Persian scripts as *vorlage* for the Avestan alphabet.[36] 12 characters and two ligatures[37] were directly taken from the Pahlavi cursive, and three characters come from the alphabet of the psalter. Further 14 characters are derived by means of diacritics or by little alternations from the characters which served as *vorlage*. The remaining characters were invented or derivated from existing characters in an unclear way.[38]

When it comes to stipulate the probability of characters being confused, one has to bear in mind that confusion may not only take place due to visual but to phonological similarities as well. There are differing orthographic conventions, e.g., writing ‹uu› or ‹β› for the bilabial glide /w/. If the use of the one or the other representation of the sound is consistent, such a difference is helpful to postulate different habbits of writing, which may be a hint for the existence of different writing schools. However, this grouping of manuscripts does not exclude direct relations of manuscripts of different writing schools because a scribe could have simply transferred the orthographic conventions of the one manuscript into his own he was using for the copy.

Phonological differences may be the result of assimilation processes. For example, in palatal context /a/ may alternate with /e/ (e.g., *-iiami* vs. *-iiemi*), although the shapes of these letters differ completely. Such cases could reveal a relationship of manuscripts, however, it is also possible that a scribe having the sound of recitation in mind deliberately or unconsciously changed the *vorlage*.[39] Some characters are derivations of others, e.g., ‹h› consists of ‹a› plus a bow. Thus, they are partly uniform, still, they differ significantly because ‹h› is much broader and longer than ‹a›. Other characters are indeed easily confused in the manuscripts, such as ‹xᵛ›, which equals jointly written

[35] Hoffmann 1986.

[36] Middle Persian was mainly written in a derivation of the Aramaic script, which is represented in several different stages: especially by the inscriptions, the psalter, and the so-called Pahlavi script of Zoroastrian texts.

[37] The ligature being the *vorlage* of /ā/ is particularly interesting, because it is one of the few cases where we can date sound changes despite the historical orthography of Middle Persian. ‹ᵓg› /āg/ and ‹ᵓy› /āy/ (both written the same) developed to /ā/, so their ligatures could be taken to represent /ā/ by the inventor(s) of the Avestan script. If the Avestan script was invented in the fourth century AD, this sound change must have had already proceeded.

[38] For a detailed survey on the Avestan script, its invention, and the phonological value of characters see Hoffmann & Narten 1989.

[39] For examples see Cantera 2012, p. 300 ff.

‹an›; ‹ū› and ‹ī›, which differ only in the angle of their bows; ‹γ› and ‹δ›, which differ only at the top, which is a loop to the left for ‹γ› and a loop to the right or a hook for ‹δ›. For the latter the probability of confusion of characters is very high, for the first it is possible though less likely. Variations which may be due to phonological similarities have to be examined individually. In order to enable users to rate the exchangeability of characters, a letter discrimination matrix was set up, including values for visual similarity and phonological permutability.[40]

---

[40] See Jügel 2012, p. 29 ff. for a more detailed representation of the letter discrimination matrix of Avestan.

KARINA VAN DALEN-OSKAM

AUTHORS, SCRIBES, AND SCHOLARS. DETECTING SCRIBAL VARIATION AND EDITORIAL INTERVENTION VIA AUTHORSHIP ATTRIBUTION METHODS

Introduction

One of the most intriguing subdisciplines of Digital Humanities is non-traditional authorship attribution. This branch focuses on applying computational methods to digitized texts in order to find out who is the most probable author of a text with contested or unknown authorship. It is the approach of digitized texts with computer software that makes this subdiscipline 'non-tradition-al'; for hundreds of years scholars have tried to solve authorship problems in a 'traditional' way, reading the texts closely and look-ing for text-internal as well as text-external clues that could lead to the most probable author. Text-internal clues might include the use of certain words or phrases that are felt to be unique for a certain author. Text external pointers could be private corre-spondence or diaries containing explicit or circumstantial evi-dence about the authorship.[1]

Most non-traditional approaches to authorship attribution deal with comparing the vocabulary and the word frequen-cies of the texts under investigation. This is the case for a well-known and successful procedure such as Burrows's Delta, but also the most common multivariate approaches, cluster analysis, and principal components analysis.[2] These methods – which will

---

[1] For a good overview of traditional methods see Love 2002. For an overview of non-traditional approaches from a mostly technical perspective see Holmes 1994 and Stamatatos 2009.

[2] For Burrows' Delta see Burrows 2002, 2003, and Hoover 2004a, 2004b.

10.1484/M.LECTIO-EB.5.102568

be described in more detail below – need not be used for authorship attribution only. In my article, *The Secret Life of Scribes*
(Van Dalen-Oskam 2012), I applied cluster analysis and principal
components analysis to a corpus of samples from different copies
of the same Middle Dutch text to compare those copies to each
other. Burrows' Delta, furthermore, was found to be a probable
help in zooming in on the exact differences that were reflected
in the statistical results. My aim in that research was to gain more
insight into the work of scribes – some of the questions which
arose included: How much do copies of the same text differ from
each other? Can we find any trends in, for instance, copies from
different time periods or from different geographical regions? In
which parts of the vocabulary are most differences to be found?
The application of non-traditional authorship attribution methods did indeed help to visualize the main similarities and differences. The methods rendered significantly more information
than a traditional approach such as close reading, and as such
opened up new perspectives for further research.[3]

The exploration of copies of the same text showed that they
all measurably differed from each other. It also became clear that
there are different ways in which the copies differ, which may be
attributed to such things as language idiosyncrasies of the scribes,
the state of their exemplar, the wishes of the patron, or the expectations of the intended audience. There is another factor, however, whose influence can be measured in a comparable way: the
scholar in his or her role as editor. The application of non-traditional methods of authorship attribution to distinguish scribes
from a scholarly editor is the topic of the current contribution.
I will apply cluster analysis and principal components analysis on
one of the samples analyzed in *The Secret Life of Scribes* combined
with the critical edition of one of the copies, in order to visualize
the differences of this edited version. I will then explore whether
the use of the intermediate results of a Delta analysis may help to
pinpoint those words where the diplomatic transcription and the
edited text differ from each other to achieve further insight into
the changes made by the editor.

---

[3] See Kestemont 2011 for a state of the art in non-traditonal Middle Dutch
authorship attribution.

A synchronous approach

The research reported on in 'The secret life of scribes' was done on a corpus of five text episodes from the Middle Dutch *Rijm-bijbel* (i.e. *Rhyming Bible*), also known as *Scolastica*, written by the Flemish author Jacob van Maerlant, who finished his text in 1271.[4] The 35,000 pairwise rhyming verse text is an adaptation/translation of Peter Comestor's *Historia Scholastica*, presenting a selection of the material from the Old Testament, followed by the gospel harmony from Comestor's work. Van Maerlant did not continue with the Acts of the Apostles, but added a much shortened version of Flavius Josephus's *De bello judaico* (i.e. *The Jewish War*). This makes of his *Scolastica* a work explicitly revolving around the life and death of Jesus Christ, with the Old Testament functioning as prefiguration of Jesus, and *The Jewish War* as the revenge taken on the Jews for their murder of Jesus.

We do not have the autograph, but have only copies (or copies of copies, etc.) from a later date. The oldest manuscript, dated around 1285 and probably written in or near Bruges, was manufactured still during van Maerlant's lifetime, but there are no indications whatsoever that he had a hand in it. Fourteen other manuscripts have survived, of which two only contain the Old Testament part (I and O) and one only has the Old and New Testament part, leaving out *The Jewish War* (H). The youngest of the manuscripts dates from the last quarter of the fifteenth century (more details can be found in Table 1). Apart from these manuscripts, many fragments have come down to us, but these have not been included in the research reported here.

The five selected samples from the text deal with different female protagonists and are distributed throughout the whole text: an episode about Eve at the beginning of *Scolastica*'s Old Testament part, the story of Deborah from later in the Old Testament, Judith's murder of Holofernes from the Old Testament Apocrypha, a passage dealing with Mary, Martha, and with Mary Magdalene from the New Testament, and finally from the last section (*The Jewish War*) the episode of Transjordanian Mary. In this con-

---

[4] Some of the details mentioned in this section are also described in Van Dalen-Oskam 2012. More can be found in my dissertation (in Dutch), which dealt with this text, Van Dalen-Oskam 1997.

tribution I will use this last episode in order to illustrate the measurements that were done, and add an extra version to the analysis:
the edited text of the sample from one of the manuscripts.

Only two of the manuscripts are available in a (relatively)
modern edition. The oldest manuscript, C, was edited by Maurits
Gysseling and published in 1983. Gysseling presented a strictly
diplomatic edition, which in Dutch terminology means that the
text from the manuscript is presented as far as possible in modern characters, keeping to the spelling in the manuscript, not
changing interpunction or capitalization, and italicizing solved
abbreviations. Emendations based on common sense or on other
manuscript readings are rare and are kept to the footnotes, leaving the 'wrong' readings in the main text (unfortunately, Gysseling himself sometimes diverged from this rule). These editorial choices made Gysseling's edition a prime source for the new
Dictionary of Early Middle Dutch, which describes the vocabulary
of Middle Dutch as it occurs in (nearly) all surviving documents
written in the thirteenth century.[5] The other manuscript that has
been edited – and which is the particular focus of this paper – is
manuscript A. It was edited by the Flemish priest J. David, who
published his four-volume edition in 1858-1861. In his introduction, David lists the six manuscripts that he had access to. None
of these, he states, have a perfect text, so that he had to compare
the available manuscripts to find the correct readings. For his
edition, he chose A as the basis. He was under the impression
that A was the oldest of the six; he misjudged the age of C, one
of the other manuscripts he used. Furthermore, he found it the
most complete, and in general the least corrupted manuscript. In
his edition, he followed A from start to finish, listing, as he states,
important variants in footnotes, or, 'in places where this seemed
imperative, replacing a word with a word from one of the other
readings'.[6] He added chapter titles alternately from two other
manuscripts, occasionally adding a word; this was done for the
reader's convenience only, since David clearly admits that these
chapter headings are not original – that is, they were added later

---

[5] See Van Dalen-Oskam & Depuydt 1997 on the key importance of diplomatic transcriptions as the basis for lexicographical work.
[6] *Rymbybel*, ed. David, Vol. 3, p. XXXIII.

and not by van Maerlant himself.[7] Although David does not explicitly mention this, he also adapted spelling, interpunction and capitalization (not quite consistently, however). David does not explicitly state that he strives to reconstruct Maerlant's original text. His edition is, one could say, a slightly touched up version

JACOB VAN MAERLANT'S *SCOLASTICA*

Ms	KEPT IN	DATE	GEOGRAPHICAL INFORMATION
A	Berlin (PrKult. Germ. Fol. 662)	Dated 1331	Flanders
Ad	Edition by J. David	Published in 1858-1861	Not applicable
B	Brussels (KB, 19545)	Around 1300	Flanders
C	Brussels (KB, 15001)	Around 1285	Flanders
D	The Hague (KB, 76 E 16)	Mid 14th century	Flanders
E	The Hague (KB, 129 A 11)	Around 1400	Flanders
F	The Hague (KB, KNAW XVIII)	Around 1400	Utrecht
G	Groningen (UB, 405)	Around 1339	Brabant
H	Leiden (UB, BPL 14c); OT+NT	Around 1465	Guelders
I	Brussels (KB, 720-722); OT	Around 1450	Southern Low Countries
J	Leiden (UB, Ltk 168)	Around 1451	Low Countries
K	London (BL, Add. 10.044)	1370-1385	Low Countries
L	London (BL, Add. 10.045)	Dated 1393	Low Countries
M	The Hague (MM, 10 B 21)	Around 1330	Utrecht
N	The Hague (MM, 10 C 19)	Dated 1453	Southern Low Countries
O	The Hague (KB, 75 E 20); OT	Around 1475	Low Countires

TABLE 1: The fifteen manuscripts of *Scolastica* used in the analysis. OT: Old Testament, NT: New Testament. More information about the names, dates and geographical location of the manuscript can be found in Van Dalen-Oskam 2012, Section 3. See the Appendix to this chapter for more information.

[7] *Rymbybel*, ed. David, Vol. 3, p. xxxv.

of the text in A and certainly not a critical edition in the sense of
the term in Anglo-Saxon textual scholarship. In Dutch medievalist scholarship, however, the term 'critical edition' is specifically
used for editions such as David made of A.

For my analysis I had to transcribe the chosen samples from
the thirteen other manuscripts and collate and correct those
made by Gysseling and by David.[8] My transcription followed the
rules set by Gysseling. Abbreviations were solved according to full
forms, when available, or when not available to the most common form in Middle Dutch dialects. I included the edition by
David of manuscript A in my corpus of copies to be compared
and addressed this version as Ad. From David's text I removed
the modern interpunction, such as the quotation marks used for
dialogue. Additionally, I lemmatized all samples with Modern
Dutch headwords. Spelling differences can be used to distinguish
between the different scribes, as is shown by Kestemont and Van
Dalen-Oskam (2009). Scribal differention in spelling, however, is
not my purpose in the research presented here, which has a more
literary and stylistic aim. In doing the measurements on the lemmas, I expected the measurement results would show only those
differences that had a relatively high probability of being related
to less superficial differences between the copies. From this point
of view, spelling differences tend to be noise, distracting from the
most interesting, possibly content-related, differences.

My aim was to deal with all the different copies on the level of
the episode – comparing all Eve samples to each other, and all Judith samples to each other, etc. My assumption was that when all
70 samples were taken together, the evaluation of measurement
results would always lead to the question of whether or not the
differences in topic of the different episodes would skew the results. I estimated that it would be better to proceed immediately
to take a look on the episode level. Furthermore, I wanted to
approach the different copies from a pseudo-synchronic perspective. I wanted to compare their vocabulary and word frequencies without yet taking into account any possible dependencies
between manuscripts, starting out from a purely descriptive perspective and postponing any kind of interpretation in that direc-

---

[8] For this work I received help from my colleague Willem Kuiper.

tion as long as possible so as not to influence the measurements results in any way. It may be useful at some point to draw up a stemma for these manuscripts, but for the moment the research into the variation is still in too early a stage. In one of the next phases of research, however, a stemmatological approach may be appropriate.

Results

Twelve of the fifteen manuscripts contain the last chosen sample about Transjordanian Mary. The thirteenth sample is David's edition of manuscript A, named Ad here. The thirteen samples were submitted to cluster analysis and principal components analysis twice, once on the texts in their original spelling and once on the lemmas. An application of Burrows' Delta Procedure was used to have a first look at the most significant differences between A and Ad.

Cluster analysis is useful for exploration of the data because the objects are grouped in a tree-like visualization according to their level of similarity, in this case based on the vocabulary (words and frequencies) of the texts. The higher the similarity between two manuscripts, the lower they will be connected in the graph – the vertical axis in the graph normally shows the similarity percentage. I made use of The Intelligent Archive and Excel to prepare the data, and Minitab 16 for the multivariate analysis and the graphs; the software ignored the (very scarce) interpunction in the transcribed texts.[9] In the cluster analysis, the selected linkage method was Ward, and the distance measure Squared Euclidian, showing 2 clusters.

Principal components analysis groups objects according to different (unknown) components which are mathematically calculated. The first component reflects the characteristic in which the objects differ most from each other. I selected the correlation analysis and calculated the first two components.

[9] For The Intelligent Archive, see ⟨http://www.newcastle.edu.au/school/hss/ research/groups/cllc/intelligent-archive.html⟩ (accessed 18 May 2012). See for a description of the steps in the use of Excel and Minitab David L. Hoover's homepage, at ⟨https://files.nyu.edu/dh3/public/ClusterAnalysis-PCA-T-testing InMinitab.html⟩ (accessed 18 May 2012).

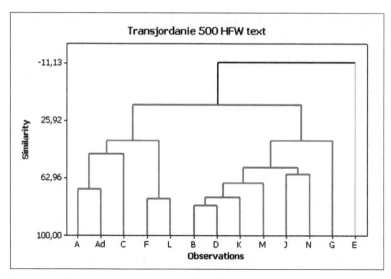

FIGURE 1: Cluster observations based on the 500 highest frequency words (original spelling).

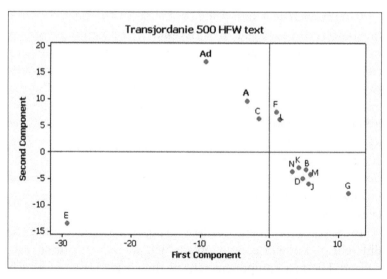

FIGURE 2: Principal components analysis based on the 500 highest frequency words (original spelling).

The Transjordania sample in the twelve medieval manuscripts together had about 15,000 word occurrences (tokens), distributed over 1624 different word forms (types). When lemmatized, 578

148

different lemmas were counted. The cluster analysis and principal components analysis were all done on the 500 highest-frequency words; for the measurements on the original texts this meant that two-thirds of the types (those that had the lowest frequencies, usually only one) are not taken into account, and for the measurements on the lemmas fewer than one-sixth were left out.

Fig. 1 shows the cluster observations on the original spelling of the thirteen samples. It shows two branches, one with twelve of the samples and one with only manuscript E. Manuscript A and its edited version Ad show up as most similar to each other (and not each to other manuscripts) in the big cluster. It is significant, however, that two other couples are more similar to each other than A and Ad – namely F and L, and B and D.

Fig. 2 plots the scores of the principal component analysis. This shows more about the nature of the differences: manuscript E shows up as differing widely on the first component, which means that most of the variation between the samples occurs in relation to E as opposed to the rest of the group. Manuscript A is on the fringes of the other medieval samples, and its edited version Ad could even be described as an outlier on the second component. This implies that the second most important variation is most apparent in the placement of Ad in relation to the other manuscripts except E. Since here the spellings of the samples are measured, Ad's position may be the result of the normalizations in spelling its editor David made. Since, as I already stated, I am not interested in a further analysis of the spelling, I will refrain here from an in-depth analysis of the exact differences.

The measurements on the lemma version of the text, in which word forms of the original text are each represented with their dictionary entry, show a slightly different picture. In fig. 3, the cluster observations only shows manuscript L changing to another branch of the big cluster, breaking the close bond between F and L that we found in fig. 1. Again, A and Ad are closely linked, and again two other sets show to have a higher similarity to each other than A and Ad, namely K and N, and again B and D. Since B and D are so close together in both graphs, this could be an indication to check whether B (dated around 1300) might be the exemplar of D (dated about half a century later). The levels of similarity in all cases are clearly higher than in the graph based on the original spellings in fig. 1, which suggests that simple spelling variation has indeed been taken out of the calculation, thus showing a clearer view on the content of the samples.

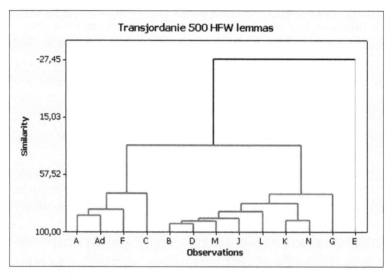

FIGURE 3: Cluster observations based on the 500 highest frequency lemmas.

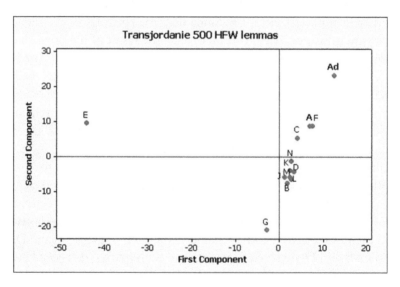

FIGURE 4: Principal components analysis based on the 500 highest frequency lemmas.

Fig. 4 shows the scores of the principal components analysis done on the lemmas. The overall picture is the same as in fig. 2, but unlike in the cluster observation in fig. 3, the differences between the manuscripts seem larger than in the analysis on the original texts. Manuscript E differs even more from the rest of the group on the first component, which could imply that E may partly differ from the rest on the content level. This would be very interesting to investigate further. The other manuscripts range along differences on the second component, in which Manuscript Ad is on one of the fringes. Manuscript A now is much closer to manuscript F than in fig. 2. This suggests that the work of the editor, David, may have influenced Ad also on a content level.

For each of the samples, Burrows' Delta was also calculated based on those lemmas which belong to the 150 highest-frequency lemmas in all of the *Scolastica* samples.[10] The frequency of each of these lemmas in each of the samples was compared to the mean frequency of the same lemma in all of the Transjordania samples and expressed in a z-score for each lemma. The sum of the absolute differences in z-scores for all lemmas was the basis for one overall Delta score for each of the samples. In Table 2 the Delta scores for the Transjordania sample in all of the manuscripts including Ad (fourth column from the left) are sorted from lowest to highest. As in the multivariate analyses above, manuscript E differs most from the Transjordania mean, showing up at the bottom of the list. Manuscript C is equally distant from the others as in the cluster observations and the principal components analysis. The other manuscripts show up in a different order than we would have expected from the earlier results. Repetition of the Delta measuments using all lemmas may show a different result, but we will not check at this point for reasons that will shortly become clear.

The calculation sheets used to apply Delta may be of help in finding those high frequency lemmas in which a sample shows the most significant distance from the Transjordania samples as a whole; to explore the differences between two different samples I will use a more straightforward method which I will go into

---

[10] Thanks are due to my colleague Meindert Kroese for his help in the Delta calculations.

151

Manuscript	Count	Sum	Mean(= Delta)	Stdev
D	124	13,18916	0,106364	0,121879
M	123	18,79219	0,152782	0,217608
G	123	18,84784	0,153234	0,183041
N	124	19,09586	0,153999	0,205476
A	125	19,87923	0,159034	0,220671
J	122	20,23095	0,165827	0,226914
B	123	20,44522	0,166221	0,255509
K	126	23,12421	0,183526	0,239512
Ad	125	23,06153	0,184492	0,272803
F	123	23,90563	0,194355	0,276584
L	121	24,40428	0,201688	0,237924
C	124	34,86691	0,281185	0,34115
E	122	76,22532	0,624798	0,712894

TABLE 2: Delta (column 4) from lowest to highest for each Transjordania episode compared to all Transjordania episodes together, including the edited version Ad of manuscript A. The second column has the amount of lemmas the sample contains from the 150 lemmas with the highest frequency in all of the *Scolastica* samples.

shortly. Looking at the lemma Delta scores for the outlier manuscript E, we find almost 80 lemmas in which E has a significantly higher or lower absolute difference from the mean compared to the rest of the Transjordania samples. Several nouns and verbs are in this list, which I will not go into here. I do want to turn attention to A and Ad, which both have just eighteen lemmas with a comparably high absolute difference from the mean score. When we then compare the lemma list scoring the highest differences for both A and Ad, we mostly find the same lemmas differing a great deal from the mean of all Transjordania episodes together, such as DEZE ('this'), OOK ('also'), ZULLEN ('shall'), TE ('to'), NU ('now'), and KIND ('child'). A and Ad only differ more widely from each other in a few lemmas. A shows a rather lower absolute difference for HOREN ('to hear') and a higher one for OF ('or'), ALS ('if'), and EEN ('a'). Ad has a higher absolute difference compared to the mean for UIT ('out'), DOEN ('to do'), JERUZALEM ('Jerusalem'), and HETEN ('to order'), and a higher absolute difference for AAN ('at'). Some are due to use in the added chapter headings in Ad (such as an extra occurrence of JERUZALEM). Others reflect added words in an emendation (such as A: Noit man dies ghenoot › Ad: Noit man *horde* dies ghenoot, 'One never [heard] of something comparable'). In small samples, such as the ones we had to use for this research, even one or two extra occurrences of a lemma influences the general perspective – which is exactly what we want when studying *copies of the same text.*

A Delta analysis taking all lemmas into account would surely have yielded differences in lower frequency lemmas as well. But there is a more straightforward way to visualize the exact differences between A and Ad. An automatic comparison of all lines of the two samples only showing the lemmas in A and in Ad does the trick. We then find many more changes involving lemmas which fell below the threshold of 150 highest frequency lemmas in the complete corpus.

The examples in Table 3 clearly show that, true to the nineteenth-century editorial norms with which he was familiar, J. David emended the text by replacing or adding words (or lemmas), just as he stated. His emendations are not always necessary from a purely linguistic point of view, although they are for the

Manuscript A	Critical edition Ad	Translation
.vij. daghe	.vj. daghe	'seven days' › 'six days'
Die noort poorte onder gheuen si some	Die noortpoorte onder groeven si some	'Some of them under??? the North gate' › 'Some of them undermined the North gate'
Die ioeden ne constent niet ghewreken	Die Joeden ne constent niet ghemeken	'The Jews could not avenge that' › 'The Jews could not ?make that'
Ter poorten die stont open	Ter oost poorten die stont open	'To the gate which was open' › 'To the eastern gate which was open'
Jn dnrerste poorte	Jn dinderste temple	'To the inner gate' › 'To the inner temple'

TABLE 3: Some of the changes made by J. David in his critical edition based on manuscript A.

most part quite understandable given knowledge of the textual context. In some cases, he seems to have worsened the reading rather than improving it.

Evaluation

The aim of this contribution was to find out whether the edited text as produced by a modern (in this case: nineteenth-century) editor can be distinguished from the text in its medieval appearances, using non-traditional authorship attribution methods. The results, described in section 3, show that this can indeed be done. In the graphs resulting from several multivariate methods applied to word and lemma frequencies, the work of the nineteenth-century editor clearly differs from the medieval versions of the same text. The edited text is most similar to its medieval original text, as the cluster analysis showed. However, some of the other medieval manuscripts are more similar to each other than A and Ad. The principal components graphs show the edited text Ad on the fringes of the main group of manuscripts, but still clearly belonging to this group rather than taking its own, lonely place somewhere else, as does the visibly idiosyncratic manuscript E. What should we conclude from this?

From a methodological point of view I am convinced that when we want to analyze medieval text versions, we need to use the texts in their original form, transcribed diplomatically from the original manuscripts or printed texts. In the *Scolastica* test case it would seem that the edited text, Ad, has been proven to be a hybrid text by its distance from its original, A, in the graphs – or, perhaps better stated, by the fact that it does not have the closest relationship to its original. Sceptics may object that the use of the multivariate approaches is not very convincing when we can also compare A and Ad automatically and thus find the possibly content-related differences very easily (i.e., when we have lemmatized them). My reply would be that although this can be done very easily, only the graphs I have presented place the results in the much needed context of the relative distances between all of the surviving versions of the same sample. The graphs based on cluster analysis and principal component analysis show calculated, weighted, distances between the different copies. The main result for the edited version Ad is that the distance between A and Ad is larger than the distance between some of the other manuscripts. A bottom-up approach that begins with only the comparison of A to Ad and then adds the other versions does not seem easy to implement.

A philological approach to the test case suggests that the editor was just another scribe. This, however, may not be a very useful conclusion. Turning this around may be more rewarding. In her article *The Scribe as Editor*, Elspeth Kennedy reported on her analysis of scribal variation in manuscripts of the Prose Lancelot. While preparing an edition of the first part of this work, she observed 'that the scribe did not necessarily regard himself as a purely passive copyist whose only concern was to reproduce faithfully the text before him, only deviating from it through involuntary error.' The methods Kennedy used can be called traditional, but her ultimate aim was the same as my own: 'to analyse the types of alteration made, to see whether there is any kind of recognizable pattern in motives and methods and to try to determine what kind of attitudes towards the text are revealed.[11] A close look at her material showed that scribes freely made corrections to the text. Kennedy then wondered: 'In order to do this did scribes rely purely on native wit and memory of other romances or parts of the cycle, or on marginal corrections by readers, or did they actually compare texts as would a modern editor?'[12] She continues: 'While not true redactors, for they have not fundamentally remodelled the text, the scribes were often 'editors' in the sense that they seem to have aimed at producing a text which would be agreeable to their readers. [...] By the 15th century we even have scribes from time to time comparing two or more versions, trying to reconcile different readings and picking a sentence now from one MS, now from another, on a small scale it is true, but rather in the manner of some nineteenth-century 'critical' editions.'[13]

The *Scolastica* measurements, presented above, in a way confirm Kennedy's findings. It may therefore be useful to rethink the

[11] Kennedy 1970, p. 523.
[12] Kennedy 1970, p. 529.
[13] Kennedy 1970, p. 531.

value and aims of modern text editions, as well as to take medieval scribes more seriously as editors who made equally carefully-considered choices in the mediation of the text they were copying for a specific audience, just as our nineteenth-century editor did. The graphs presented here can point the way to those manuscripts that need to be examined first to get a better view on what our medieval colleagues found important in their jobs.

Bibliography

J. Burrows (2002), 'Delta: a Measure of Stylistic Difference and a Guide to Likely Authorship', in Literary and Linguistic Computing, 17, p. 267-287.

J. Burrows (2003), 'Questions of Authorship: Attribution and Beyond', in Computers and the Humanities, 37, p. 5-32.

J. David (ed., 1858-1861), Rymbybel van Jacob van Maerlant: Met voorrede, varianten van hss., aenteekeningen en glossarium, 3 vols, Brussels: M. Hayez, Drukker der Koninlyke Akademie.

D. I. Holmes (1994), 'Authorship Attribution', in Computers and the Humanities, 28, p. 87-106.

D. L. Hoover (2004a), 'Testing Burrows's Delta', in Literary and Linguistic Computing, p. 19 and 452-475.

D. L. Hoover (2004b), 'Delta Prime?', in Literary and Linguistic Computing, 19, p. 477-495.

E. Kennedy (1970), 'The scribe as editor', in Mélanges de langue et de littérature du Moyen Age et de la Renaissance offerts à Jean Frappier, Professeur à la Sorbonne, par ses collègues, ses élèves et ses amis, Genève: Librairie Droz, p. 523-531

M. Kestemont (2011), 'What Can Stylometry Learn From Its Application to Middle Dutch Literature?', in Journal of Dutch Literature, 2, p. 46-65.

M. Kestemont & K. Van Dalen-Oskam (2009), 'Predicting the past: memory based copyist and author discrimination in medieval epics', in T. Calders, K. Tuyls, M. Pechenizkiy (eds.), BNAIC 2009. Benelux Conference on Artificial Intelligence. Proceedings of the twenty-first Benelux conference on artifical intelligence, Eindhoven, October 29-30, 2009, Eindhoven, p. 121-128.

H. Love (2002), Attributing Authorship: An Introduction, Cambridge: Cambridge Univ. Press.

M. Gysseling (ed., 1983), Corpus van Middelnederlandse teksten (tot en met het jaar 1300) uitgegeven met medewerking van en van woordindices voorzien door W. Pijnenburg. Reeks II, *Literaire handschiften*, Vol. 3 *Rijmbijbel/tekst*, Leiden: Martinus Nijhoff; Vol. 4 *Rijmbijbel/indices*, Leiden: Martinus Nijhoff (Bouwstoffen voor een woordarchief van de Nederlandse taal).

E. Stamatatos (2009), 'A Survey of Modern Authorship Attribution Methods', in *Journal of the American Society for Information Science and Technology*, 60, p. 538-56.

K. Van Dalen-Oskam (1997), *Studies over Jacob van Maerlants Rijmbijbel*, Hilversum: Verloren (Middeleeuwse Studies en Bronnen, 57).

K. Van Dalen-Oskam (2012), 'The secret life of scribes. Exploring fifteen manuscripts of Jacob van Maerlant's *Scolastica* (1271)', in *Literary and Linguistic Computing*, 27(4), p. 355-372.

K. Van Dalen-Oskam & K. Depuydt (2007), 'Lexicography and Philology', in K. Van Dalen-Oskam et al. (eds.), *Dictionaries of Medieval Germanic Languages. A Survey of Current Lexicographical Projects (Selected Proceedings of the International Medieval Congress, University of Leeds, 4-7 July 1994)*, Turnhout: Brepols, p. 189-197.

APPENDIX

THE MANUSCRIPTS IN MORE DETAIL

A   Berlin, Staatsbibliothek der Stiftung Preussischer Kulturbesitz, Germ. fol. 662

B   Brussels, Koninklijke Bibliotheek Albert I, 19545

C   Brussels, Koninklijke Bibliotheek Albert I, 15001

D   The Hague, Koninklijke Bibliotheek, 76 E 16

E   The Hague, Koninklijke Bibliotheek, 129 A 11

F   The Hague, Koninklijke Bibliotheek, KNAW XVIII

G   Groningen, Universiteitsbibliotheek, 405

H   Leiden, Universiteitsbibliotheek, BPL 14c

I   Brussels, Koninklijke Bibliotheek Albert I, 720-722

J   Leiden, Universiteitsbibliotheek, Ltk 168

K   London, British Library, Add. 10.044

L   London, British Library, Add. 10.045

M   The Hague, Museum Meermanno, 10 B 21

N   The Hague, Museum Meermanno, 10 C 19

O   The Hague, Koninklijke Bibliotheek, 75 E 20

FRANCESCO STELLA
in collaboration with
LUCA VERTICCHIO *and* STEFANIA PENNASILICO

GENERIC CONSTANTS AND CHRONOLOGICAL VARIATIONS IN STATISTICAL LINGUISTICS ON LATIN EPISTOLOGRAPHY*

Introduction

The application of computational linguistics to research on liter-ary language and style has seen a rapid development in recent years, giving rise to topical university courses and specialized journals such as the International Journal of Corpus Linguis-tics, ICAME-*Journal*,[1] *Literary and Linguistic Computing, Natural Language Engineering, Computer and the Humanities, La Revue in-formatique, Statistique dans les sciences humaines, Digital Humanities Quarterly* and others, in addition to online discussion forums like *Humanist*.This scholarship has determined statistical methods that are relatively stable for modern languages. But still far more rare and sporadic – aside from isolated studies or experiments being carried out in laboratories like the *LASLA* in Liège – have been applications of computer analysis to ancient languages, proba-bly on account of the level of technical knowledge required for such research,[2] or else due to the influence of a pseudo-humanist

---

* An Italian version of this paper, with some modifications, has been pub-lished in Biville, Lhommé & Vallat 2012, p. 491-506.

[1] International Computer Archive of Modern and Medieval English (Ber-gen).

[2] In Italy, notable work in this field includes some recent research of Maurizio Lana and Guido Milanese and the projects of Marco Passarotti and Andrea Bozzi at the CNR in Pisa in the 1980s. In recent years other invaluable work – that taken up by the Perseus Project of Tufts University – has been developed con-cerning syntactic analysis by the Centro Interdisciplinare di Ricerche per la Computerizzazione dei Segni dell'Espressione (CIRCSE) at Università Cat-tolica (‹http://centridiricerca.unicatt.it/circse_index.html›); see Passarotti 2011.

10.1484/M.LECTIO-EB.5.102569

prejudice against quantitative stylistics. Only in the last few years have these methodologies really begun to take off, as has been demonstrated by the reports of Dominique Longrée and Celine Poudat, Bela Adamik and Caroline Philippart.[3]

In a prior study (Stella 2008a) I applied stylometric procedures to Latin texts in an attempt to credit certain authors with works of uncertain authorship, such as the *Epistolae duorum amantium*, a collection of anonymous love letters from the twelfth century. Now I would like instead to propose an experimental analysis of *generic language* – understood as literary genre on a group of Latin texts that do not constitute a unified *corpus* but are definable as a sequence of *corpora*, because each was produced by a single author in a single style, and all of them belong to what literary historians usually call the epistolary genre, the outlines of which Cugusi has well analyzed.[4] This proposal is based on the conviction that this collection of data can make a valuable contribution to our understanding of the historical development of Latin – one not provided by other kinds of linguistic study – and that only today's technology puts us in a position to carry out relatively sophisti-cated surveys on extended bodies of texts instead of small sam-ples, as has been done in the past. The primordial condition of these techniques in Latin studies makes it nevertheless necessary to identify a proper methodology which, while measuring up to the complexity of Latin linguistics scholarship, does not mire the research in exclusively mathematical analyses.

The Data

The study I will present involves the computational analysis of the lexicon of epistolary corpora in Latin dating to the ancient republican period, the imperial age, late antiquity, the high and late medieval periods, and the humanistic period. Naturally the aim is to survey possible constants of genre in comparison with

---

For a technical overview, without applications to concrete authors or texts, see Bamman & Crane 2009, and Denooz & Rosmorduc 2009.

[3] Biville, Lhommé & Vallat 2012.

[4] Cugusi 1983. Even for a genre so rigorously defined, ancient rhetoricians identify between 21 (Demetrius) and 41 (Libanius) *typoi* that represent genuine subgenres.

possible constants of author or epoch. The texts included in the enquiry were the letters of Cicero, Pliny the Younger, Augustine, Alcuin of York († 804), Abelard († 1142), and Petrarch († 1374).

The Program

The program we used is *Analisi lessicale*, a simple but relatively powerful tool developed by Carlo Poli and Giorgio Carboni in 1998 based on MS Access to study Italian grammar and still available online.[5] The same kind of research can be reproduced and extended with the much more up-to-date tools available on the Canadian site *TAPoR* (Text Analysis Portal for Research) alongside many other tools, such as the many free software programs available for making concordances. A common characteristic of computational humanistic research is indeed the extreme fragmentation of methods, owing to the fact that once a humanist goes to the trouble to learn how to use one program, he does not want to lose any time using other ones and will continue to prefer the first one encountered. The core task of all these programs, obviously, is the indexing of the words in a text, understood as linguistic strings separated by a space, as well as the ordering of results in alphabetical lists, by frequency, concordance, collocation, and phrase strings of two or more terms. *Analisi lessicale* has the advantage that it provides simple methods for comparing texts side by side or in larger groupings, and thus is well-suited both for analyses for attribution purposes and for analyzing corpora.

Previous Studies

Studies on linguistic aspects of the concept of literary genre have begun circulating in recent years, starting with Swales 1990. In 1999, Maria Wolters and Mathias Kirsten published an ex-

---

[5] ‹http://web.tiscalinet.it/divulgator/analsilessicale.html›. Similar, more sophisticated software like *Hyperbase* or *TAPoR* or *Stylometry with R* or *Juxta*, even in their latest versions, are not able to do operations like extracting the words shared or not shared by two or more authors in the same simple way as this tool does. A new program provisionaly called *Lexicon* has been developed in 2014 from *Analisi Lessicale*, now on trial at the address ‹www.himeros.it›.

periment that categorized genre on the basis of the presence of specific parts of speech,[6] applied to the LIMUS corpus of 500 contemporary German texts of around 2000 words each, based on very wide genre classes, such as political texts, juridical texts, economic texts, narrative texts, and so on, which we would define more as thematic classes than literary genres. Their results are presented in a series of algorithms difficult for non-experts in statistics to comprehend but vague enough to declare bankrupt any analysis based on linguistic categories that are too generic – while also confirming that the choice of sample affects the results, and the function words, the finite verb forms, just as with nouns, are less frequent in certain textual categories like academic texts. In the ACM SIGIR 2007 Workshop[7] in Amsterdam on *Plagiarism Analysis, Authorship Identification and Near-Duplicate Detection*, Jussi Karlgren and Gunnar Eriksson presented a paper (*Authors, Genre, and Linguistic Convention*) that started from the same problem we faced in researching the authors of the *Epistolae duorum amantium*: how to distinguish the linguistic characteristics of an author from those of a genre, in order to determine, for instance, whether the language, or at least the lexicon, of one author varies from one genre to another more or less than one finds between one author and another. In other words, does the language of Cicero as orator differ from that in his letters to a greater or lesser extent than the average language of Cicero differs from that of Livy or Virgil? What has more linguistic implications – the genre, the author, or the period? Karlgren and Eriksson undertook a measurement of adverbs and clause types in various genres of newspaper articles in a year of the *Glasgow Herald*, concluding that adverbs are found in each subgenre but their collocation or placement is subject to individual choice, and adding to these stimulating results their own problematization of the concept of genre.

The firmest methodological basis therefore, besides the seminal works of John Sinclair,[8] remains to be found in the explora-

---

[6] Wolter & Kirsten 1999; the criteria used were TTR, Sentence Length (Words per Sentence), Word Length (characters per word) and POS frequency.

[7] *Association for Computing Machinery's Special Interest Group on Information Retrieval*. After this paper was delivered and edited (2011), other conferences on this topic have been held, whose proceedings we could not take into consideration.

[8] Especially Sinclair 1991, 2003, 2004.

tions carried out by Douglas Biber[9] in *Variation across Speech and Writing*, where the author lists the frequencies of dozens of variables, from ratio type/tokens (i.e., the relations between forms and occurrences) to the presence of certain verb tenses, or conjunctions, or clauses, all divided by several specifically recognizable genres: among these, one table is dedicated to 'personal letters'. Among the most recent studies, the anthology edited by Tony McEnery and Richard Xiao-Yukio, *Corpus-Based Language Studies* (2006), proposes an extremely detailed grid of statistical operations on texts collected in *corpora*; but even in this anthology the method adopted for diachronic and comparative analysis is always based on Biber 1991 and Bybee & Hopper 2001.

None of these studies examines corpora of ancient texts, and among the few previous studies in the field that we can cite is the work of Xuan Luon and Sylvie Mellet (2003) on the corpus of Latin historians,[10] which demonstrates how the use of specific syntactic features is distributed in the *corpus Caesarianum* and in other Latin historiography: verbal tenses and moods, parts of speech, and use of cases clearly separate Caesar and his epigone from Sallust, Tacitus, and Curtius Rufus, while displaying subdistinctions as well, such as those between the *Bellum Hispanicum* and the other works in the Caesarian corpus.

Our enquiry further widens the chronological span considered in comparison with the model of Luon and Mellet, posing also the question of possible generic continuity from classical Latin through imperial, medieval, and humanistic periods, and delving more specifically into individual characteristics such as lexical choice; in this way we also broach the question of relations of stylistic or lexical dependence among authors, or of greater lexical proximity among a humanist author and a medieval or classical one.

---

[9] Biber 1991, p. 246 ff.

[10] The English abstract reads (Luon & Mellet 2003): 'The calculation of intertextual distance is generally performed by studying lexical parameters. We will in the first place examine whether it is possible or not to apply one of the available methods to grammatical parameters, then we explain our own method, based on an ordinal classification table rather than a multiple contingency table. To present this methodology, we use Latin texts extracted from a lemmatized and tagged corpus. The different results will be compared and evaluated.'

This experiment is part of the DIGIMED project,[11] which focuses on digital philology of medieval texts and of computational analysis of texts in general; my work on applying computational analysis to attributions for the *Epistolae duorum amantium* provided further confirmation of the fact that any piece of data only becomes significant if and when it is comparable. In the case of the 'two lovers' the comparison was between these anonymous epistles and data from possible authors. However, in order to evaluate whether the data resulting from comparison are significant, one needs to have a reference value: for instance, to measure how far an author deviates from the mean for his period or the genre he is working in, one needs to know the mean for a period or genre, the standard value of the frequency for a term in a certain context. It is exactly these baselines that are lacking for Latin literature, and in coming years we would like to contribute to establishing them. Breaking ground in this area has thus been one of the aims with our experiment on representative samples of Latin epistolary literature, with classical alongside medieval and humanist Latin. Our epistolography data was collected by Luca Verticchio and Stefania Pennasilico, whom I gratefully acknowledge as coauthors on this paper.

Procedural Protocol

1. Our texts were identified and downloaded from digital libraries of reliable quality, while acknowledging the many limitations in philological rigor of collections like the *Patrologia Latina*, to which nevertheless in many cases no alternatives exist.

2. We selected samples of roughly the same length and provisionally saved them as Word files. The length was around 57,000 words per sample, a size large enough for evaluation purposes and to yield sufficiently reliable results, considering that the samples used by Wolters and Kirsten (1999) were around 2,000 words and ended up being of limited effectiveness in demonstrating their argument. The samples are normalized by eliminating editorial notes, special signs and characters and, in our case, restor-

---

[11] ‹http://www.tdtc.unisi.it/digimed/›.

ing the diphthongs in medieval and humanist texts that lacked them, replacing *y* or *j* with *i*, and so on. The edited files are then converted into .txt format. At this point they are ready for lexical analysis. Different from the method used by other researchers, the procedure does not involve that most unpleasant phase in any statistical operation on language, that is, the mark-up or tagging, but instead works directly with texts in the form that some computing specialists call a 'blind reading' of the text and which Sinclair continues to recommend for directly operating on raw data.[12] This limits the range of possible operations while leaving open many other potential avenues, but it also simplifies and significantly speeds up the process and shifts more responsibility onto interpretation of the data.

3. The program carries out its Normalization with a specific command, and generates a new file that reports the number of words in a single sample. This new file is then subjected to a frequency calculation with another dedicated command: one thus obtains a list of forms in order of frequency, direct or reverse, absolute or relative. From this it is possible to extract the empty terms or 'function words', such as prepositions or conjunctions, which are considered crucial for identifying the unconscious traits of an author's style or diction that escape authorial control and are habitually independent from genre. In our case, S. Verticchio and L. Pennasilico chose *adhuc, amplius, autem, enim, itaque, maxime*, and *quidem*, since these words came into the discussion concerning possible authors of the *Epistolae duorum amantium*, but obviously other words could have been chosen. The tables (fig. 1) show that even the ten most common terms in each author, which should be the same for all because they represent links of a system – i.e., a characteristic of *langue* and not *parole*[13] – have slightly different frequencies and positions in each author, and it might prove interesting to see whether and how the ranked positions of single terms differ.

---

[12] Sinclair 2004, p. 192: 'In corpus-driven linguistics you do not use pretagged text, but you process the raw text directly and then the patterns of this uncontaminated text are able to be observed.'
[13] In connection with this, an objective basis for comparison exists in the form of the Latin frequency database, which calculates frequencies for the 1,000 most frequent Latin words; it can found on the website maintained by Claude Pavur at Saint Louis University.

CICERONE			PLINIO			AGOSTINO			ALCUINO		
Termini	Ricorrenze	Frequenze	Termini	Ricorrenze	Frequenze	Termini	Ricorrenze	Frequenze	Termini	Ricorrenze	Frequenze
et	1486	2,57E-02	et	1521	2,64E-02	et	1986	3,44E-02	et	2455	4,29E
in	1110	1,92E-02	in	990	1,72E-02	in	1535	2,66E-02	in	1950	3,41E
non	893	1,54E-02	ut	816	1,42E-02	non	1354	2,35E-02	est	666	1,16E
ut	850	1,47E-02	non	804	1,40E-02	est	922	1,60E-02	ut	641	1,12E
te	794	1,37E-02	est	636	1,10E-02	ut	707	1,23E-02	non	612	1,07E
me	703	1,21E-02	quod	631	1,10E-02	quod	639	1,11E-02	qui	466	8,15E
ad	680	1,17E-02	cum	452	7,85E-03	sed	578	1,00E-02	ad	416	7,28E
est	661	1,14E-02	quam	422	7,33E-03	qui	499	8,66E-03	de	380	6,65E
quod	659	1,14E-02	sed	377	6,54E-03	si	496	8,60E-03	sed	362	6,33E
cum	612	1,06E-02	me	376	6,53E-03	ad	458	7,94E-03	te	296	5,18E
sed	579	9,99E-03	enim	372	6,46E-03	de	406	7,04E-03	si	293	5,12E
de	516	8,91E-03	si	356	6,18E-03	cum	404	7,01E-03	quod	291	5,09E
esse	473	8,17E-03	etiam	356	6,18E-03	que	390	6,76E-03	dei	285	4,99E
quam	468	8,08E-03	que	316	5,49E-03	enim	351	6,09E-03	deo	261	4,57E
si	460	7,94E-03	qui	302	5,24E-03	autem	338	5,86E-03	per	257	4,50E
			mihi	302	5,24E-03						

FIGURE 1.

4. One can also calculate the ratio of type/tokens, i.e. forms/ occurrences,[14] which is usually a valuable index for assessing the richness of an author's vocabulary. The most effective statistic on the semantic level for this purpose would be a comparison of words rather than forms, but this would involve lemmatizing the indexed data, which requires an extra stage of labor that is rather long and complex, since, as is well known, automatic lemmatizers for Latin are limited to just a small portion of the classical lexicon and would be extremely hazardous with the great number of rare words and ambiguous forms. The results therefore remain relatively crude on the semantic level, but the uniformity of procedure and the large sample size nonetheless assure us of the usefulness of the comparison even though it is limited to forms.

5. A further analysis examined the presence of Locutions, i.e. collocations – or better, the particular kind of collocation called a 'cluster'[15] – of consecutive terms, a valuable tool whether to probe an author's phraseology or to test continuity or revival from one author to another, or again to evaluate the unconscious association of favorite terms by any one author. These tables, which the program calls Locutions [*locuzioni*], can process sequences of 2, 3, 4, or any number of words, due to the expedient of programming the computer to link individual words with underscores. The Locutions table can then be submitted to calculate frequencies, which gives an ordered list by frequency, on which the linguist can then exercise critical reflection.

6. Finally the characteristic operation of this program is carried out, which is the analysis of the overlap or exclusion of shared forms or locutions for each author, compared with one other author or with groups of other authors. The contrary operation is also tested: that is, the identification of terms belonging to a single author and not present in others, which establishes a kind of index of individual leftovers. In the simple terminology of the program these operations are defined as AxB and A-B: e.g., 'Alcuin x Augustine' marks terms the two authors share, while 'Alcuin-

---

[14] Note that the meaning of 'type' and 'token' varies across semiotic, philosophical, and linguistic discourses. We refer here to what Sinclair calls 'word-forms'.

[15] On TAPoR they are called 'fixed phrases.'

Augustine' collects the terms in Alcuin that are NOT found in Augustine.

The program and the possibilities of stylometry allow for many other operations as well, but these seem sufficient to obtain the first elements for evaluation.

Results

The results are contained in about 100 *Access tables*, around 220 MB in size, which present the outcomes of the described operations for each pair of authors and for each couple of pairs and so on for the whole series. The data one can obtain are infinite. Let us extract just a few.

1. (fig. 1) In all the authors the 5 MOST FREQUENT TERMS, even if in different order, are: *et, in, non, est, ut*, with the exception of Cicero and Abelard. In Cicero, in place of *est*, the third most frequent term, we find *te*, a sign of a strongly relational character of his letters and their nature as authentic rather than fictional or reworked epistles. This example shows us *e contrario* how not even the presence of the second-person singular pronoun is able to act as a stable marker of a genre that on the level of communicative status is characterized primarily by the presence of an addressee. The lower frequency of *te* in the statistics for Pliny instead corresponds to how his epistles tend more toward a collection of reflections than a dialogue with an interlocutor. In Abelard *ad* appears fifth instead of *ut*, which we could interpret as a sign of the decline of clauses governed by *ut* (in favor of *quia* and *quoniam*, for instance), and of influence by the increase in functions of *a* in vulgar French, which might have had a feedback effect on *ad*. But naturally other explanations are also possible.

2. (fig. 2) Among the EMPTY TERMS we considered, the one most used by all authors is *enim*, with the exception of Abelard who most often uses *autem*; the highest frequency of *enim* is observed in the three most ancient authors. *Autem* occurs in Augustine just less than *enim*, while it is little used by Pliny and Alcuin. The least frequent term in nearly all the authors is *amplius*, and only Abelard makes regular use of it. In general, in Alcuin all the terms are quite infrequent, and this may be one trace that helps to de-

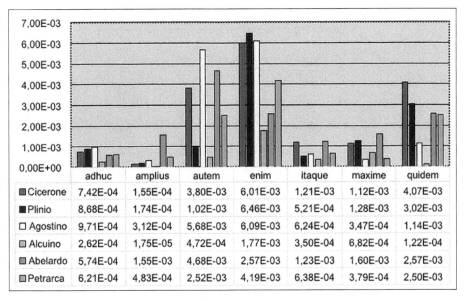

	adhuc	amplius	autem	enim	itaque	maxime	quidem
▣ Cicerone	7,42E-04	1,55E-04	3,80E-03	6,01E-03	1,21E-03	1,12E-03	4,07E-03
▪ Plinio	8,68E-04	1,74E-04	1,02E-03	6,46E-03	5,21E-04	1,28E-03	3,02E-03
☐ Agostino	9,71E-04	3,12E-04	5,68E-03	6,09E-03	6,24E-04	3,47E-04	1,14E-03
▨ Alcuino	2,62E-04	1,75E-05	4,72E-04	1,77E-03	3,50E-04	6,82E-04	1,22E-04
▨ Abelardo	5,74E-04	1,55E-03	4,68E-03	2,57E-03	1,23E-03	1,60E-03	2,57E-03
☐ Petrarca	6,21E-04	4,83E-04	2,52E-03	4,19E-03	6,38E-04	3,79E-04	2,50E-03

FIGURE 2.

fine a more nominal style, where forms of conjunction and adverbial forms are proportionally low, creating a kind of communication where the traces of an individualized language are less easily identifiable. One also gets a curious sort of ideal contrast between a classical and humanistic Latin characterized by enim and an Augustinian and Abelardian Latin rich in *autem* and, taken together, an initial indication that Petrarch's lexicon is closer to classical Latin than to Augustine's – though so loved by him – and to medieval Latin.

3. (fig. 3) The authors who show the most variation in forms (i.e., the type/token relation, how many forms divided by how many occurrences) are Petrarch (27.44%) and Pliny (26.54%); low variety is found instead in Cicero (20.58%) and Alcuin (20.83%). The statistical data for Petrarch are thus closer to those of the postclassical, rather than classical and medieval, writers. Cicero and Alcuin tend to use few forms more often – i.e., they privilege a more limited vocabulary.

4. (fig. 4) With regard to shared lexicon and continuity of genre: from the percentage based on the total number of terms in the more recent author, one notes that in general each author shows

169

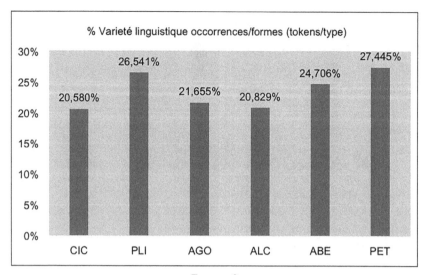

FIGURE 3.

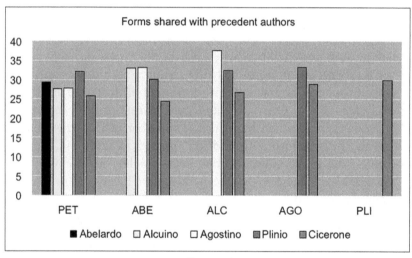

FIGURE 4.

more terms in common with his immediate predecessor, with the exception of Petrarch who has the most terms in common with Pliny. This fact may indicate two things: first, that the force of a relation of imitation is stronger than the force of a generic standard, admitting that – as the studies of Cugusi show[16] – an

[16] Cugusi 1989, p. 391-392 and 1983, p. 90-91 talks about 'consciousness of genre'.

entity of this sort can be defined. From this perspective it is no surprise that the value of shared terms is high (37.55%) between Alcuin, who did not know Cicero's letters, and Augustine, who along with Jerome was the openly avowed model for the Carolingian abbot, while the lowest value is between Abelard and Cicero (24.42%). The second explanation may be that time is the predominant factor, except in the case of an author like Petrarch, who aims precisely to rupture chronological contiguity and wants to recuperate the style of a different period. The percentage of common terms calculated based on the total terms of the more ancient author ranges from 25.28%, the terms Pliny has in common with Alcuin, which marks the greatest distance, to 39.43% for Alcuin with Abelard, the greatest proximity. Notable here are the similar values for all the authors in relation with Petrarch (32.82-36.88%). This consistency is found also in locutions.

What reflections can we glean from this? In our view this point tends to confirm the specificity of Petrarchan language[17] in relation both to classical and medieval diction, while the high degree of sharing with Alcuin and Abelard can be explained by the Augustinian basis common to both. In addition there is certainly a common basis between the two authors independent of Augustine, which – barring imitative relationships between them – seems to point to a certain consistency in the specifically medieval lexicon.

On the statistical level, however, it should be noted, again, that these kinds of data only become meaningful when compared with a median value; but to know the average values of common forms in Latin texts would require a frequency index for all the authors. For now, this big corpus of data is found only on the horizon of hopes, and so for the moment we are restricted to comparisons between certain authors or groups of authors.

5. Linguistic data, however, do not always obediently fall into line with historical-cultural schemes that we try to impose on them. In the statistics for Abelard, for example, we have one broadly predicted result – viz., an indication of the most shared terms

---

[17] It is also possible that the data are partially altered by the presence of metrical epistles in the samples, which employ a markedly more literary vocabulary.

with Augustine, who is an undisputed model for the French philosopher; another result that was predictable, viz., a very high rate
of shared terms with Alcuin, almost equal to that with Augustine,
and here we might ask whether this fact derives from the Augustinian lexicon of Alcuin himself or from the medieval language of
Abelard; and finally, an unexpected result: a very high percentage
shared with Petrarch (32.82%), nearly as high as for the first two.
One would naturally wish to analyze this Petrarchan lexicon that
coincides with Abelard but does not derive from Augustine. How
do we explore it? We generate a table AbexPet-Ago – i.e., we ask
the program to tell us how many of the 4,655 forms shared by
Petrarch and Abelard are not found already in Augustine: there are
1,865 forms, an impressive proportion. What sort of language is
it? One might hypothesize that here Petrarch shares with Abelard
the intellectual language of twelfth-century theology, which does
not overlap with Augustine's lexicon. In reality, we find much
more and much less than this: among the terms common to Abelard and Petrarch but absent in the sample of Augustine's letters
we find, in order of frequency (fig. 5), *fortuna, scribens, meminit,
urbe, sequi, amicorum, prouidere, demum, commemorat, uirginum, ex-
tremum, inuidia, professionis, siquidem, iuvenis, ceterum, senectus, arte,
solitudine, alto, cibis, mulieris, Seneca,* and *Augustini.*

Each one of these words opens onto a cultural world and leads
to reflections no doubt provisional and calling for further study
but nevertheless strongly provocative. For example, the theme of
writing and art *(scribens, arte)* comes to light, uniting Abelard and
Petrarch in what can be described as the stylistic self-conscious-
ness of medieval epistolary culture, so far removed from the Late
Antique epistolography and so focused on the content of the
opinions and information being exchanged. We rediscover the
obsession with memory – an Augustinian theme in his treatises
but little present in his epistolary exchanges – which is a powerful force in cultural formation for Abelard and Petrarch. Again:
urbe takes us back to the urban tumult of the twelfth-fourteenth
centuries familiar to wandering intellectuals like Abelard and Petrarch; and *amicorum* and *invidia*, which shed light on academic
debates and the social dynamics of that intellectual climate, just
as in *professionis* one glimpses the flowering of liberal professions

Termini	Ricorrenze	Frequenze
fortuna	37	4,51E·04
scribens	31	3,78E·04
meminit	28	3,42E·04
sepius	26	3,17E·04
urbe	25	3,05E·04
i	24	2,93E·04
sequi	24	2,93E·04
amicorum	23	2,81E·04
nunquid	22	2,68E·04
providere	21	2,56E·04
demum	20	2,44E·04
commemorat	20	2,44E·04
virginum	20	2,44E·04
extremum	19	2,32E·04
exitum	19	2,32E·04
primis	19	2,32E·04
quin	19	2,32E·04
invidia	18	2,20E·04
professionis	18	2,20E·04
siquidem	18	2,20E·04
quecunque	18	2,20E·04
iuvenis	17	2,07E·04
septem	17	2,07E·04
summam	17	2,07E·04

FIGURE 5.

in the university age to which Petrarch is both heir and adversary. On an entirely different level, the presence of *siquidem* identifies a conjunctive particle typical of medieval philosophical language and even more of Petrarch, but rare in classical and late antiquity; and so on. Statistical linguistics affords us a glimpse so penetrating as well as so powerful in plumbing the depths of the expressive tools of a writer, a thinker, and a human being.

Also deserving explanation is the fact that the highest proportion of sharing is found between Alcuin and Abelard. Considering the strong thematic differences between the two letter-writers, this result can be interpreted as evidence of a relative homogeneity of medieval Latin with patristic Latin.

173

6. (fig. 6) Let us see now whether the data on collocations of locutions confirms the tendencies identified for single terms. In
general, word clusters reveal a greater commonality between Augustine and the later authors, pinpointing, in other words, the
moment when a phraseology coalesced into a fairly stable form.

PLI	56306	X ALC	81	0,144
ALC	55001	X PLI	81	0,147
CIC	56369	X ALC	114	0,202
ALC	55001	X CIC	114	0,207
PLI	56306	x ABE	124	0,220
ABE	56056	X PLI	124	0,221
PET	57567	X PLI	146	0,254
PET	57567	X ALC	147	0,257
PLI	56306	X PET	146	0,259
ALC	55001	X PET	148	0,269
CIC	56369	X ABE	156	0,277
ABE	56056	X CIC	156	0,278
PLI	56306	X AGO	159	0,282
AGO	55589	X PLI	159	0,286
PET	57567	X ABE	165	0,287
ABE	56056	X PET	165	0,294
PET	57567	X CIC	221	0,384
CIC	56369	X PET	221	0,392
PET	57567	X AGO	244	0,424
AGO	55589	X PET	244	0,439
CIC	56369	X AGO	252	0,447
AGO	55589	X CIC	252	0,453
CIC	56369	X PLI	283	0,502
PLI	56306	X CIC	283	0,503
ABE	56056	X ALC	398	0,71
ALC	55001	X ABE	398	0,724
ABE	56056	X AGO	428	0,764
AGO	55589	X ABE	428	0,77
AGO	55589	X ALC	527	0,948
ALC	55001	X AGO	527	0,958

FIGURE 6.

In all the authors the lowest value is always in relation to Cicero, a phenomenon explicable either by the poor knowledge of his epistles after Augustine or by the relatively atypical phraseology used in his letters. Here as well, a listing by decreasing frequency shows how Augustine/Alcuin and Augustine/Abelard are always the most closely affiliated pairs.[18] The data on locutions over-all shows higher commonality between Augustine, Alcuin, and Abelard. In particular, the ratio of locutions/terms (x 100[19]) be-tween Alcuin and Augustine (2.55) is significantly higher than the pair Alcuin-Pliny (0.45) and Alcuin-Cicero (0.78). The same calculated relations between Abelard and Augustine (2.30) and Abelard and Alcuin (2.14) are higher than the pairs Abelard-Pliny (0.73) and Abelard-Cicero (1.13). This result may suggest a syn-tactic and phraseological distance between classical and medieval authors that is stronger than their lexical divergence.

Turning to a question that intrigued us about vocabulary, among the triple locutions[20] the sole expression genuinely common to Abelard and Petrarch is *ut dictum est*, with a frequency of 0.034% (real); notably lower down we find *et in tantum, quod scriptum est* and *ut scriptum est, ut ita dixerim, dubium non est, et in hoc* and *et in eo, ad id quod*, etc. It is significant that, for example, even in the locutions common to Augustine and Abelard the expressions in-troducing quotations are most common: *sicut scriptum est* (0.02), *quod scriptum est, quod dictum est* – these are traces of an epistolog-raphy marked by structural recourse to intertextuality. If we are able to continue the inquiry for other literary genres as well, we

---

[18] Slight differences between the figures for the same couple, if one starts from either the first or the second author, reveal margins of statistical error, which are around 0.01%.

[19] These data are multiplied by a hundred for greater legibility; the tables preserve the original figures. The low value of the original figures might lead one to suspect that a chi-squared test might indicate a low probability for these statistics. But as we argued before in the paper on the *Epistolae duorum amantium*, we are convinced that Pearson's test does not apply to the realities of artificial and artistic linguistics, where the choices left to chance have been reduced as much as possible.

[20] The list of triple locutions, i.e., sequences of three words, shows matches that as relative frequencies are fairly high but that in reality refer to 2 or 3 occur-rences, a number too low to be significant: which reinforces the point that a mass of statistics in itself does not describe phenomena but simply lists data, which become significant only through subsequent analysis.

may be able to measure the degree to which this pheonomenon is typical either of the epistolary genre or of a group of authors. This result seems to correspond perfectly with the use of proverbs and quotations that Cugusi identified as a regular feature of classical epistolography beyond its formulaic traits.[21] We should add, however, that this characteristic does not extend to other authors in our group, and thus it does not involve Alcuin or Cicero. The triple locutions common to Pliny and Cicero are indeed of a purely phraseological sort, like *etiam atque etiam* (0.027), also shared between Pliny and Petrarch, and *quem ad modum* (0.022) or *nihil est quod* (0.014), while the fourth in rank reveals a political concern absolutely foreign to the postclassical writers: *de re publica* (0.013). Other expressions common to pairs of authors include *gratias ago quod*, which we can take as a marker of genre.

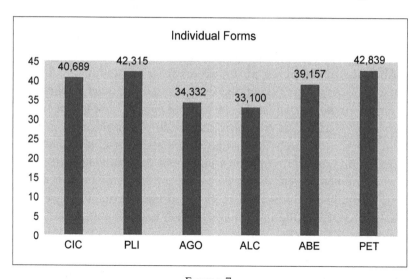

FIGURE 7.

The highest percentage of unique forms in one author with respect to all the others is reported in Petrarch (42.84%) and Pliny (42.31%), as already pointed out above with regard to linguistic variety. But note that Cicero, who has the lowest linguistic variety, still has a high percentage of unique forms (40.69%). This means that he uses a relatively large number of less common words a

---

[21] Cugusi 1989, p. 389-390.

few times and in limited forms. Naturally these data should be purged of spelling peculiarities (like *michi* and *nichil*); but they do reveal for example that *paupertas* and *paupertatem* ("poverty") is unique to Petrarch's language, preoccupied as he is in his private correspondence with economic problems, real or represented, as is *vesperam* ("evening"), showing the poet of Arezzo's fondness for twilight, which is almost as frequent as *querela, fastidii* ("complaint"), and the lexical family of *senectus* ("old age"), while *calamum* ("pen") indicates the self-representing of writing that Cugusi also points to as typical for the genre and for Petrarch in particular; another feature of his is the high frequency of author names like Vergilius, Maro, Varro, Livius, Hieronymus, Socratem (which can also be the nickname of his correspondent Barbato), italis, which accords with an Italo-centric perspective that we have also observed in an analysis of spatial representations in his *Metrical Epistles*.[22]

An important test for the existence of a genre lexicon would require a comparison between the lexicon common to all these epistolographers and the lexicon common, for example, to historical or philosophical writers. With this one could begin to go more deeply into the relationships between choice of diction (i.e., linguistic register) and the form of social and cultural communication (i.e., characteristics of literary genre). We look forward to being able to continue collecting data that will allow these comparisons and will give rise to hypotheses of a general nature regarding literary language; but we also hope that other researchers will use this method for their own comparisons and help to expand the field of data that enables mean values to be calculated and thus makes all the others meaningful.

One can scroll forever through these infinite lists, which shatter the unity of the atom and allow us to enter the orbits of particles that compose it, to learn the secrets of the movements that animate it. If we contemplate its results with a curious and sympathetic eye, statistical linguistics loses all its supposed aridity, and instead unlocks the workroom where an author's thought

---

[22] Stella 2008b.

intersects with the linguistic heritage and the traces of those who have gone before.

Bibliography

D. Baumann & G. Crane (2009), 'Computational Linguistics and Classical Lexicography', in *Digital Humanities Quarterly*, 3.

D. Biber (1991), *Variation across Speech and Writing*, Cambridge: Cambridge University Press.

F. Biville, M.-K. Lhommé & D. Vallat (eds., 2012), *Latin vulgaire-latin tardif IX. Actes du IXᵉ colloque international sur le latin vulgaire et tardif, Lyon, 2-6 septembre 2009*, Lyon: Maison de l'Orient et de la Méditerranée.

J. L. Bybee & P. J. Hopper (eds., 2001), *Frequency and Emergence of Linguistic Structure*, Philadelphia: John Benjamins Publishing Company (Typological Studies in Language, 45).

P. Cugusi (1983), *Evoluzione e forme dell'epistolografia latina nella tarda repubblica e nei primi due secoli dell'impero: con cenni sull'epistolografia ciceroniana*, Rome: Herder.

P. Cugusi (1989), 'L'epistolografia. Modelli e tipologia', in G. Cavallo, O. Fedeli, A. Giardina (eds.), *Lo Spazio letterario di Roma antica*. Vol. 2, *La cirolazione del testo*, Rome: Salerno, p. 379-419.

J. Denooz & S. Rosmordus (eds., 2009), *Natural Language Processing for Ancient Languages*, Traitement Automatique des Langues, 50.

N. Ide (2004), 'Preparation and Analysis of Linguistic Corpora', in S. Schreibman, R. Siemens & J. Unsworth (eds.), *A Companion to Digital Humanities*, Malden: Blackwell Publishing (Blackwell Companions to Literatureand Culture, 26), p. 289-305.

J. Karlgren & G. Eriksson (2007), 'Authors, Genre, and Linguistic Convention', in *Proceedings of the SIGIR 2007 International Workshop on Plagiarism Analysis, Authorship Identification, and Near-Duplicate Detection*, PAN 2007, Amsterdam, Netherlands, July 27, 2007.

M. Lana & C. Basile (2008), 'L'attribuzione di testi con metodi quantitativi: riconoscimento di testi gramsciani', in *AIDA informazioni*, 26, p. 165-183.

C. D. Lanham (1992), 'Freshman Composition in the Early Middle Ages: Epistolography and Rhetoric before the *Ars dictaminis*', in *Viator*, 23, p. 115-134.

X. Luon & S. Mellet (2003), 'Mesures de distance grammaticale entre les textes', in *Corpus*, 2.

T. McEnery (1992), *Computational Linguistics: a Handbook and Toolbox for Natural Processing*, London: Coronet Books.

T. McEnery, R. Xiao & Y. Tono (2006), *Corpus-Based Language Studies: an Advanced Resource Book*, London: Routledge.

R. Morello & A. D. Morrison (2007), *Ancient Letters: Classical and Late Antique Epistolography*, Oxford: Oxford University Press.

M. Passarotti (2011), 'Pratiche di realizzazione e uso di corpora annotati. Il caso del latino', in *Atti del Sodalizio Glottologico Milanese*, Milan: Instituto Glottologia Università di Milano.

J. M. Sinclair (1991), *Corpus, Concordance, Collocation (Describing English Language)*, Oxford: Oxford University Press

J. M. Sinclair (2003), *Reading Concordances: an Introduction*, Harlow: Pearson ESL.

J. M. Sinclair (2004), *Trust the Text: Language, Corpus and Discourse*, London: Routledge.

F. Stella (2008a), 'Analisi informatica del lessico e individuazione degli autori nelle *Epistole duorum amantium (XII secolo)*', in R. Wright (ed.), *Latin vulgaire, latin tardif. VIII*, *Actes du VIIIe colloque international sur le latin vulgaire et tardif, Oxford, 6-9 septembre 2006*, Hildesheim: Roger Wright, p. 560-569.

F. Stella (2008b), 'Spazio geografico e spazio poetico nel Petrarca latino: Europa e Italia dall'*Itinerarium* alle *Epistole* metriche', in *Incontri triestini di filologia classica*, 6, p. 81-94.

J. M. Swales (1990), *Genre Analysis: English in Academic and Research Settings*, Cambridge: Cambridge University Press.

R. Van Deyk, R. Sornicola & J. Kabatec (eds., 2005), *La variabilité en langue: les quatre variations*, Ghent: Communiation and Cognition.

M. Wolters & M. Kirsten (1999), 'Exploring the Use of Linguistic Features in Domain and Genre Classification', in *EACL'99: Proceedings of the Ninth Conference of the European Chapter of the Association for Computational Linguistics*, Bergen: Assocation for Computational Linguistics, p. 142-149.

SECTION 3

INTERTEXTUALITY

LINDA SPINAZZÈ

INTERTEXTUAL RESEARCH WITH DIGITAL VARIANTS IN *MUSISQUE DEOQUE*: A CASE STUDY

Introduction

The *Musisque Deoque, A digital archive of Latin Poetry* was established at the end of 2005. Its purpose is to create a single Latin Poetry Database supplemented and updated by apparatuses and exegetical information. A resource of this kind aims to improve and refine the intertextuality research supporting the literary-historical studies of ancient literature.

Nowadays, the literary scholars of ancient, medieval, and Renaissance literature make large use of computer-assisted *corpora* mainly for intertextual research.[1] But the specialist using digital corpora does not actually search within a corpus of scholarly texts, but within a corpus of 'vulgate' versions of texts, lacking those variants that the history of transmission and editorial criticism have added to the work and that can only be found in the printed editions. Indeed, today's search-engine inquiry to a literary database is limited to providing results of a key inside a fixed, 'authoritarian' text digitized and marked-up from a selected scholarly edition (usually the most popular ones, but not always the most reliable ones). The intention of the *Musisque Deoque Project* is to overcome these limitations, allowing the scholar to locate not only the chosen forms quoted from the reference version, but also the variants proposed in the critical apparatus.

---

[1] An overview regarding different ways to combine 'intertextual research' can be found in the second part of Mastandrea 2011.

10.1484/M.LECTIO-EB.5.102570

For quite some time the question of variants has already been noted as an item of importance for digital humanities. On the one hand, the main projects which deal with digital variants are usually focused on the *collatio* of manuscripts or aim to provide tools that help the philologist make scholarly editions;[2] so these types of instruments are dedicated to the development of pure textual criticism. On the other hand, the point we would like to emphasize is the new trend of philology for classics: it is no longer sufficient to establish a text and a plausible context of origination, although this seems essential to map the path of reception of literary work.[3] Moving this hermeneutic purpose it is necessary to increase rapidly the large *corpus* of scholarly texts with variants. For the time being there are two main types of approaches aimed at broadening lexical and intertextual research with alternative readings of transmission. The former is based on automatic collations of diplomatic editions and is supported by the *Homer Multitext Project*;[4] the latter, endorsed by *Musisque Deoque* team, is focused on the employment of forms filled manually by a team of specialized experts on different authors.[5]

Project MQDQ

The *Musisque Deoque Project* aims to overcome the limit of common authoritative digital archives, creating a Latin Poetry Digital Archive supplemented by apparatuses and with searchable variants.[6]

In order to enrich the database quickly with new variants, some skilled operators prepare the digital *conspectus codicum*, as-

---

[2] Calabretto & Bozzi 1998; Calabretto et al. 2005; Robinson 2010.

[3] This *desideratum* was already highlighted by Contini with this convincing hypothesis: 'supponiamo che occorra determinare in che lezione Dante abbia conosciuto il poema di Lucano'; Contini 1990, p. 46.

[4] ⟨http://www.homermultitext.org/⟩

[5] For a more detailed comparison of the two approaches, see Boschetti 2007; more recently Babeu 2011 describes the different methods and instruments of digital classical philology.

[6] *Musisque Deoque* is the result of the continuous evolution of projects focused on digitization of Latin poetry beginning with two pioneering projects collected in two CD-ROMs, *Aureae Latinitatis Bibliotheca* 1991 and *Poetria nova* 2001, and then in a web project *Italian Poetry in Latin*, whose online archive has been available since 1999.

sisted by dedicated software especially designed for this purpose.[7] The '*Musisque Deoque* editors' – who are usually skilled computer users as well as specialist experts on specific authors – insert the significant variants made up of the alternative readings, which they regard as the most relevant for the study of textual tradition. The concept of 'significant variant' is not as subjective as it might sound. The significant variant is defined by Manca as a '*lectio* we can credit to the author himself, or to an editor, but more often has been introduced by readers or copists still in the ancient phase of the tradition, and which may bring to new perspectives in intertextual research'.[8] A variant tracing the path of the textual tradition must be considered significant, even when this is an error from a metrical, syntactic, pragmatic, or encyclopedic point of view. From the perspective of the *Musisque Deoque* operators, a variant *deterior* or *facilior* – completely useless for the *constitutio textus* – is also significant; in fact, if this different *lectio* somehow spread and propagated itself into literature, this variant has the merit of giving birth to a 'new plausible reading',[9] and so it must be regarded as a significant variant. More often than not corrupted variants as examples of *scriptio continua* or wrong divisions are not significant in our archive.[10]

In order to illustrate the possible method and criterion for editing a text into *Musisque Deoque*, we briefly introduce a specific author.[11]

Case Study: Maximianus

The elegiac couplets on senility used here as an example are the work ascribed to the disputed and contentious author Maximianus. In fact every aspect and feature of this work has been debated among scholars (editors, philologists, historians, and literary

---

[7] For a technical description see Mastandrea & Tessarolo (Mastandrea 2011), 'Introduzione' p. 7-10 and Boschetti 2012.

[8] Manca 2010, p. 703.

[9] Shillingsburg 2006, p. 30.

[10] For further detailed description and some examples of 'significant variants' you can see Manca 2010.

[11] This text was studied for the PhD thesis (L. Spinazzè, 'Per un'edizione critica digitale: il caso di Massimiano elegiaco' (unpublished doctoral thesis, Università Ca' Foscari, 2012) and edited for *Musisque Deoque* in 2012.

critics). There is an abundant bibliography on this elegiac work, therefore we try to propose a summary of the main issues.

1. The identity of the author. The couplets narrate some erotic misadventures in first person, also giving some personal details. The criticism of the nineteenth century examined some crucial points: is Maximianus really an elderly man? Is he really an Italian ambassador? Is the narrator telling us about his real life or is he narrating some fictional episodes? Opinions continue to differ on all of these questions.[12]

2. The time of writing. The elegiac work is usually, though not unanimously, dated between 526 (*terminus post quem:* Boethius, *Consolatio*) and 550 (*terminus ante quem*: Corippus, *Iohannis*); nevertheless some scholars place Maximianus in the ninth century, imagining the writer to be a monk in Carolingian times; though this theory was received with strong opposition, the debate between scholars about a more precise placement in the third or fourth decade of the VI century b. C. is still open.[13]

3. The structure of the elegiac text has also raised a long-standing debate among scholars. Should the text be divided into six separate elegies or is it a continuous single poem, like some manuscripts (especially the most ancient) bear?[14]

4. The meaning of the content itself, and therefore the entire interpretation of the work is still a matter of debate. When summarizing Maximianus' work, Michael Roberts states, 'the Elegies centre on the erotic adventures and misadventures of the speaker of the poems';[15] but he also recognizes that 'formal indeterminacy is matched by uncertainty about the collec-

---

[12] Webster 1900 and Pontiggia 1972 consider Maximianus to be a completely fictional person; Sandquist-Öberg 1999 also believes that Maximianus is the name of a character and not the real author.

[13] The main proponent of a ninth-century dating is Ratkowitsch 1986; about the dating of Maximianus see also Boano 1949, Bertini 1981, Mastandrea 2005, Vitiello 2006.

[14] For a very detailed summary of critical positions see Fo 1986; the most recent editors Sandquist-Öberg 1999 and Schneider 2003 edited the text as a long *carmen continuum*.

[15] Roberts 2010, p. 90.

tion's interpretation'.[16] The couplets have been read by some critics with a serious or moralizing purpose, but by others with a parodic or ironical intent.

Tradition

Obviously, many of these intricate critical issues depend on a very complicated and peculiar transmission of the work. To grasp the tradition of this late Roman elegy under consideration, we have to consider at least these matters:

1. The first witness of some *excerpta* of the elegies appeared in the ninth century, in the codex Paris, Bibliothèque Nationale MS Lat. 2832 (probably more than three centuries after the first circulation of the work).[17] The most ancient manuscript bearing the complete text is the *codex* from Eton, Eton College MS 150, dated to the eleventh century.[18]

2. The work was widely used as a textbook between the tenth and fourteenth centuries. During the Middle Ages, Maximianus' elegies were used as a school handbook and Maximianus was considered one of the *auctores minores* of the canon of classics that Latin learners had to study, as more than one medieval author testified – for example the *Ars Lectoria* by Aimeric, or Eberhard the German in *Laborintus*, etc.[19]

3. A false attribution of the elegies to Cornelius Gallus (Virgil's unhappy friend famous for being the first Roman love elegist) emerged in a group of Italian humanistic codices from the second half of the fifteenth century.

---

[16] Roberts 2010, p. 92.

[17] For a description and detailed references about this manuscript see Alberto 2005, p. 61-65; for discussion of Maximianus' verses in this *codex* see Riou 1972 and Schetter 1970, p. 97-105.

[18] The other *codices antiquiores* dated to the eleventh century – C (Roma, Biblioteca Casanatense, MS 537) and S (Città del Vaticano, Biblioteca Apostolica Vaticana, MS Reg. Lat. 1424) – present an incomplete text.

[19] For Maximianus as a school text see: Glauche 1970, p. 82 and p. 125, Hunt 1991, p. 75 ff., Black 2001, p. 389-390. For Aimeric see Reijnders 1972, p. 168-170; for Eberhard the German see Faral 1924, p. 358 ff.

4. The Venetian printed edition dated 1501 and edited by Pomponio Gaurico proposed the work as fragments of lost work by Cornelius Gallus. This idea rapidly spread not only in Italy but also across Europe and was hard to die.

5. Only in 1794 did Wernsdorf edit the text without mentioning Cornelius Gallus in the title.[20]

The tradition of Maximianus' verses includes sixty-seven manuscripts (from the eleventh to the sixteenth century), several printed editions such as *Cornelii Galli Fragmenta* (between 1501 and the eighteenth century[21]), and five other modern editions. The first modern editor was Baehrens in 1883. In 1890 Michael Petschenig offered a new text of elegies using a unique witness regarded as the most authoritative: the *antiquior* Eton, Eton College, MS 150. In 1900 Richard Webster expanded the list of manuscripts and edited a new text of elegies; another edition was prepared by Giuseppe Prada, who collated the newly discovered *codex antiquus* (Roma, Bibl. Casanatense 537) in 1919. Finally, Christine Sandquist-Öberg prepared a new edition, collecting 57 manuscripts, in 1999. In addition to these there was a pivotal study on the tradition of Maximianus written by Shetter in 1970; this work established once and for all that the transmission of the 686 lines is 'irretrievably horizontal'.[22]

Methodology

The scholarly digital edition adapted by us for the *Musique Deoque Project* is therefore a totally new reconstruction of the text based on:

1. The collation of the five modern editions.

---

[20] *Maximiani etrusci, Elegiarum libri* is the title of edition by Wernsdorf, p. 260.

[21] Fifty-six printed editions have been counted from the first Venetian one (1501) up to the Wernsdorf edition (1794): see Sequi 1995, p. 184-191 including four editions from the seventeenth century where the name of Maximianus near Cornelius Gallus appears in the title (n. 30, 35, 39, 44); during the Nineteenth and Twentieth centuries some publishers insisted in attributing the text to Cornelius Gallus.

[22] Schetter 1970, p. 15.

2. A new analysis of some particularly controversial *loci* carried directly by the *codices antiquiores* – Eton, Eton College, MS 150 [A], Roma, Biblioteca Casanatense, MS 537 [C] and Firenze, Biblioteca Riccardiana, MS 1224 [F] – courtesy of a digital fac-simile or a digital microfilmed copy.

3. Some new humanistic manuscripts, six of thirty-eight, discovered during our study and, therefore, taken into due consideration.[23]

Our choices in editing Maximianus' work for the computer archive of scholarly editions are the result of a sort of methodological compromise. On the one hand, we had to take into account the usual philological reflections on collation of manuscripts and on different critical positions. On the other hand, we had to consider the setting of use.

Regardless of the usual questions that an editor of classical texts must keep in mind, we dealt with some special aspects connected with the final destination of editions: the online database *Musisque Deoque* dedicated to collecting editions of texts in order to assist intertextual research. In particular we focused on two specific topics.

The first consideration is the structure. We are nearly certain that our Late Roman author would have written a long *carmen continuum*, and we focus on the idea of proposing the elegiac couplets as a long continuous single poem (following the choice of the last editor Sandquist-Öberg). Even if the most ancient manuscript – Eton, Eton College, MS 150 (dated to the eleventh century) – presents the elegiac work without division, during early scholastic times the text presented some divisions; indeed, we find six references to Maximianus in the *Ars Lectoria* of Magister Siguinus, and in two occasions the quotation is introduced by the indication *in primo libro* (for verse 242, in the first canonical elegy) and *in secundo libro* (for verse 545, a line usually in the

---

[23] The humanistic manuscripts (which were never considered before in an edition) are the following: Roma, Biblioteca Casanatese, MS 869, 1453-1463 (LT); Padova, Biblioteca Civica, MS CM 422, 1465-1466 (Pm); Padova, Biblioteca Seminario Vescovile, MS 141, 15th c., end (Sp); Milano, Biblioteca Trivulziana, MS Triv. 632, 1451-1475 (Mt); Firenze, Biblioteca Riccardiana, MS 636, 1462 (Fg); San Daniele del Friuli, Biblioteca Guarneriana, MS 105, ante 1455 (Sd).

fifth elegy);[24] this division into two books is also reflected in the *codex* Oxford, Bodleian Library, MS Bodl. 38 (dated to the twelfth century). In the same period, the manuscript Firenze, Biblioteca Riccardiana, MS 1224 (i.e. F, also dated to the twelfth century) presents the reader with a division in several elegies. Thus, we surmised that not only the readings of the text would have had a varying and horizontal pattern of transmission, but also that the arrangement of the elegiac couplets would have varied. Nevertheless, the text is usually presented for non-specialists as a collection of six elegies,[25] and the reference to the 'vulgate'-text is a recommended guideline for quoting using a huge poetic database such as *Musique Deoque*. In the end, having taken into consideration all the pros and cons for an online publication in such a large database of poetic Latin works, we chose a canonical division in six elegies. However, in order to facilitate the occasional users of the latest printed edition as well (Sandquist-Öberg) we put the continuous numbering of verses in brackets on the right. In addition, we inserted an annotation which, when clicked over, reports the further divisions of the titles which can be found in the *Antiquiores* and in the humanistic manuscripts we personally examined (fig. 1).

The second issue regards the variants. As we can infer from some manuscripts, especially humanistic ones,[26] there are often two possible interchangeable readings; this is the sign of a very different and various transmission of text since ancient time. See for instance the *codex La* Firenze, Biblioteca Medica Laurenziana, Plutei 33.26, f. 59r. (fig. 2); the copyist wrote 'corpore' and noted *in margine* the *varia lectio* 'carcere'. In many similar cases we had to decide which variant to put in the text, and often the unique criterion is personal preference. In these instances, from the intertextual point of view, the computer set for edition can represent an improvement in term of quality; in fact, due to the peculiari-

---

[24] Kneepkens–Reijnders 1979.

[25] We can note that when a scholar writes about Maximianus' work while citing a new edition without division of elegies, he puts into bracket the 'canonical' numbering inspired by Baehrens' edition: see on this Consolino 2009, Wasyl 2011, and Welsh 2011.

[26] In the humanistic manuscripts this practice was ever more fashionable, but there are also some examples in the antiquior Eton, Eton College, MS 150.

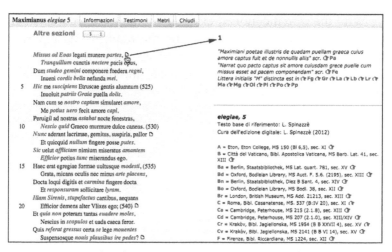

FIGURE 1: Example of annotation: Maximianus, *eleg.* V, *Musisque Deoque* edition (‹http://www.mqdq.it›).

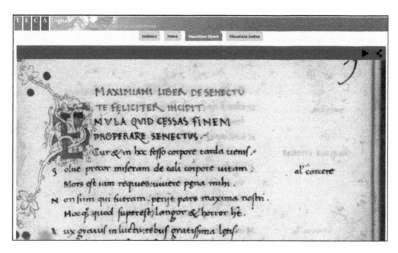

FIGURE 2: Digitized manuscript from *Teca Digitale* (‹http://teca.bmlonline. it›): Firenze, Biblioteca Medicea Laurenziana, ms Plut. 33.26, c. 59r. By permission of the MiBACT; any further reproduction, by whatever means, is forbidden.

ties of the search engine, none of the *varia lectio* is left out even if it is inserted into the apparatus. In fact, in order to discover the transmission of one version within the literary context, the *Musisque Deoque* search engine locates all variants and immediately shows the sources that use one variant rather than another.

With the aforementioned example in mind, one could search for the keywords 'corpore vitam' and the result would report a line with 'carcere vitam':'corpore' is the variant registered only in the apparatus, but even so it is searchable and traced in the right context by the search engine (fig. 3).

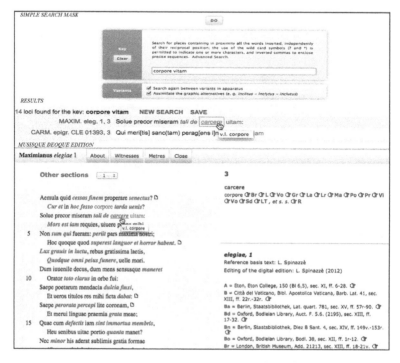

FIGURE 3: Search, results and context of a variant in different pages of *Musisque Deoque* (‹http://www.mqdq.it›).

New feature

The recourse to a manuscript as witness is pivotal and crucial, not only in terms of textual criticism, but also within a context of intertextual research with literary aims.

Indeed, the goal of this project is to build a large collection of editions that can be available for intertextual research, and not to edit a proper 'digital scholarly edition';[27] the constant reference to

---

[27] For a specific and supported definition see Karlsson & Malm 2004 and Shillingsburg 2006 with references.

witnesses has been the *leitmotiv* of the whole philological study as well as for the '*Musisque Deoque* based' edition. During the study of the Maximianus text, we mapped out all of the web resources concerning each manuscript, gathering and organizing the information about the library and the collection as well as the specific *codex* or digitized manuscript. In the case of Maximianus we included certain manuscripts that had already been used by other *Musisque Deoque* editors for other authors (for instance, Statius or Arator in Eton, Eton College MS 150). In such a large database including a large number of authors and works, more often than not the same manuscripts show different works at the same time. Therefore, we introduced a new feature dedicated to organizing the different list of *codices* within the *Musisque Deoque database*.

Even though a strict hypertextual correspondence between digitized text and images of the source manuscripts has not been incorporated in the project, a special feature has been implemented in order to enrich the intertextual database with links providing some further information or other kinds of resources related to the manuscripts. Each of the *Musisque Deoque* editors picks up from the web some information in order to refine his/her personal version of digital text; moreover he/she can also look for a digitalized image of every single witness of his/her *conspectus codicum*; our purpose is to collect and highlight all items referring to manuscripts gathered by our editors so that the links to all resources can be first of all shared with other back-end users, and then published for the benefit of final (front-end) users.

Thus, we have created a further digital catalogue of all manuscripts included in the *Musisque Deoque* archive, assigning them a unique identifier so that each source can be recalled from different works, even if some of the works adopt Latin denominations or idiosyncratic abbreviations. An example is shown in fig. 4 where the Eton, Eton College, MS 150, *codex* titled 'A' for the Maximianus edition, is used by the edition of Arator with abbreviation N; in the edition of *Achilleis* of Statius the same *codex* is known as 'E'.[28]

---

[28] The manuscript Eton College, MS 150 is collated as E by H. W. Garrod, 1906 (Statius, *Achilleis*); A. P. McKinlay for edition of Arator, *Historia Apostolica* (*CSEL* LXXII, 1961) collated the same *codex* as N. See N. Ker 1977, p. 761.

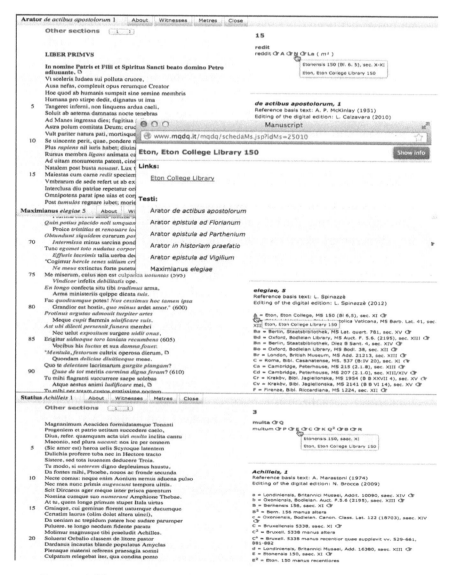

FIGURE 4: The manuscript Eton, College Library, MS 150 in different editions of the *Musisque Deoque* archive (‹http://www.mqdq.it›).

This additional collection and classification of manuscripts provides the opportunity to obtain a unique and unambiguous indication of ancient handwritten sources. We now have the possibility of linking these with external resources on the web correlated to a specific library, collection, or manuscript.

194

Due to this new feature, any user of a *Musisque Deoque* edition can in some lucky cases verify a variant through direct use of a digitized online manuscript. For instance, returning to the text of Maximianus, we can consider, at verse three (v. 3), the *locus* 'carcere vitam'. This collocation is the most attested reading, but the variant 'corpore vitam' is also found in the whole tradition from the twelfth century until the Renaissance, as is shown by the apparatus and *conspectus codicum* of fig. 5.

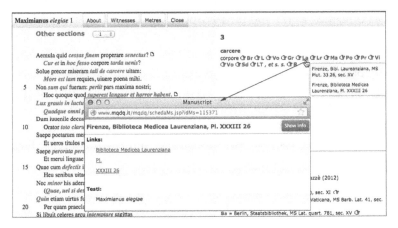

FIGURE 5: *Varia lectio* for *carcere* and a link to a specific manuscript in *Musisque Deoque* archive (‹http://www.mqdq.it›).

If a hypothetical user would like to check the reading in *La* (Firenze, Biblioteca Laurenziana, MS Plut. 33.26), he can click on the abbreviation, opening a new window with three active links referring to:

1. The library that holds the manuscript;[29]

2. A site with detailed information on the collection itself (history, organization, and sometimes lists or digitized volumes

---

[29] You can find the institutional site or, alternatively, some useful information about the library organization or contact. Unfortunately, as in the example of Eton, Eton College, MS 150 shown before (fig. 4), the reference to the library is the unique type of linking for the most of *codices* quoted.

containing descriptions of library collections and single manuscripts);

3. Finally, the link to specific shelf-marks refers the user directly
to information on a specific codex or to the digitized manuscript (as in the current example).

It is possible to search the whole codex; in particular, the user
could check directly in the site *Teca Digitale* (managed by Biblioteca Madicea Laurenziana[30]) the sheet 59r (the beginning of
Maximianus' work) and read 'corpore vitam' into the text (fig. 2).
This last type of link should be recognized as a small qualitative leap for a resource such as *Musisque Deoque*; indeed, the
database offers a reliable edition that can be improved by consult-
ing directly some digitalized sources. Besides, we assume that the
Musisque Deoque search engine could help scholars and researchers to generate knowledge on the keywords they are looking for
and to discover new online information and resources regarding
peculiar texts or authors.

Summary and future development

As of today the *Musisque Deoque* site offers a complete online collection of Latin poetry from its origins to late antiquity. The simplest function of the web interface concerns the retrieval of word
sequences; *Musisque Deoque* inherits, however, the user interface
and query mask (fig. 6) implemented in the previous projects
directed by P. Mastandrea and L. Tessarolo, such as *Italian Poetry
in Latin*, the online archive dedicated to Latin poetry between
the thirteenth and sixteenth centuries.[31] Here, it is possible to
look for words in peculiar positions of the verse (in particular the
beginning and the end), to filter specific metres out (e.g. dactylic
metres), and also to search for words within the extra-text, the
sender of a letter, the speaker of dialogues, etc. The query mask
allows us to look up word sequences (and graphic alternatives)
not only in the reference editions, but also in the collection of
variants as located in the correct context of the verse. This means

[30] ‹http://teca.bmlonline.it/›
[31] ‹http://mqdq.cab.unipd.it/mqdq/poetiditalia/home.jsp?lingua=en›

that a sequence constituted by a word of the reference edition followed by a word registered in the critical apparatus can be recognized as adjacent and finally retrieved.[32]

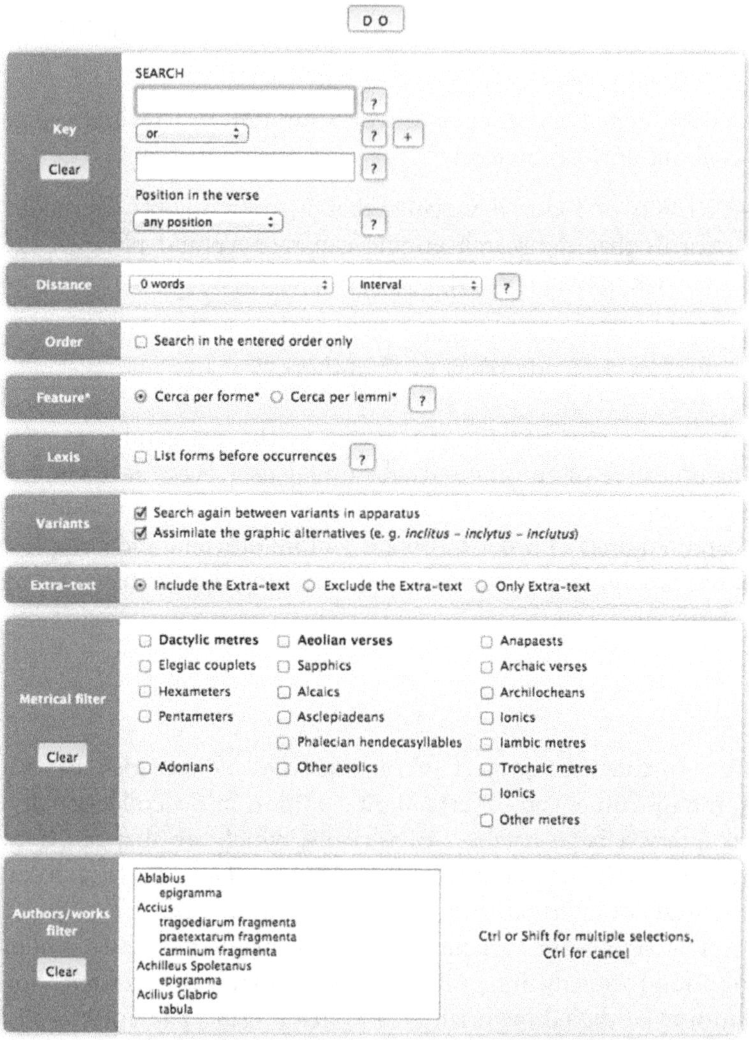

FIGURE 6: Advanced search mask of *Musisque Deoque* (‹http://www.mqdq.it›).

[32] As we have already mentioned, the main aim of the project is the intertextual research, and for this reason we do not pursue the goal of reconstructing a *stemma codicum*. There are currently no user-friendly interfaces dedicated to alignment and classification of the available variants, but in order to extract this type of information the technical experts would be able to manage the XML files.

The database is revised and updated via the addition of new critical apparatuses for each single text. The following outcomes are
presently available:

- 600 poetic Latin texts for 275 authors, with a total of 343,633
  verses;

- 134 revised and annotated works for 124, 837 revised verses,
  about 36% of the total;[33]

- 51,936 of indexed variants; that is, over 50,000 alternative
  forms that the search engine can retrieve and place in the
  correct textual context;

- The conspectus codicum provided with links to external
  sources currently refers to 15 authors.[34]

The same team of *Musisque Deoque* is also responsible for the
maintenance of an online database of *Italian Poetry in Latin*; the
next steps of this project will include combining the separate
search engines in order to obtain a more efficient and complete
intertextual literary overview, and enriching the database of new
editions.

Conclusion

To conclude, the project of *Musisque Deoque* provides us with
some instruments to insert a digital edition into a collection and
to query a large database of variants, which are mapped onto
reference editions. In other words, *Musisque Deoque* is focused on
the study of intertextuality, and for this reason is based on a selection of significant variants recorded in printed critical editions
or found directly into manuscripts. Drawing on an increasing
amount of digital material, such as manuscripts and ancient editions available on the web, the Italian project has begun to create

---

[33] It is possible to know which authors and works are edited by checking the
red-feather icon into the alphabetical or chronological index.

[34] Specifically: Alcimus Avitus, Arator, Avienus, Boethius (*Cons.*), Fulgentius,
Horatius, Iuvencus, Manilius, Maximianus, Prudentius, Reposianus, Seneca (only the tragedies), Sidonius (*carm.* 3-5), Statius (Achilleis), a substantial number
of *Carmina* from *Anthologia Latina*.

a plethora of information on individual *codices* quoted in the database, linking the largest possible amount of information to each abbreviation of each manuscript. In this way, any user who may be interested in reading a text that has been revised through some variants can also check a specific *codex* and discover further details (e.g. its digital reproduction).

Finally, the effort made by the *Musisque Deoque* archive toward the development of bindings between a specific academic resource for philology and the libraries that own the physical sources of its texts represents a prototype for a conceptual collaboration between academic research and other cultural actors in order to build a solid and reliable scholarly cyberspace for classical texts.

Bibliography

A. Babeu (2011), *Rome wasn't digitized in a Day: Building a Cyberinfrastructure for Digital Classicists*, Washington: CLIR Publication.

F. Bertini (1981), 'Boezio e Massimiano', in L. Orbetello (ed.), *Atti del Congresso Internazionale di Studi Boeziani, Pavia 5-8 ottobre 1980*, Roma: Herder Editrice, p. 273-283.

R. Black (2001), *Humanism and Education in Medieval and Renaissance Italy*, Cambridge: Cambridge University Press.

G. Boano (1949), 'Su Massimiano e le sue Elegie', in *Rivista di Filologia Classica*, 27, p. 198-216.

F. Boschetti (2007), 'Methods to extend Greek and Latin Corpora with Variants and Conjectures: Mapping critical Apparatuses onto Reference Text', in *Proceedings of the Corpus Linguistics Conference, University of Birmingham, UK, July 27-30 2007*, Birmingham.

F. Boschetti, et al. (2012), 'Musisque Deoque: Text Retrieval on Critical Editions', in *JLCL: Proceedings of the 'Annotation of Corpora for Research in the Humanities'*, Heidelberg, 5 Jan. 2012, p. 127-138.

S. Calabretto & A. Bozzi (1998), 'The philological workstation BAMBI (Better Access to Manuscripts and Browsing of Images)', in *Journal of Digital Information*, 1.

S. Calabretto et al. (2005), 'The EUMME project: towards a new philological workstation', in *ELPUB*.

F. E. Consolino (2009), 'L'elegia secondo Massimiano', in R. Cardini & D. Coppini (eds.), *Il rinnovamento umanistico della poesia. L'epigramma e l'elegia*, Firenze: Edizioni Polistampa, p. 183-224.

G. Contini (1990), *Breviario di ecdotica*, Torino: G. Einaudi.

Eugenius Toletanus, *Eugenii Toletani Opera Omnia*, ed. P. F. Alberto, Turnhout: Brepols, 2005 (Corpus Christianorum, Series Latina CXIV).

E. Faral (1924), *Les arts poétiques du 12ᵉ et du 13ᵉ siècle: recherches et documents sur la technique littéraire du Moyen Âge*, Paris: Champion.

A. Fo (1986), 'Il problema della struttura della raccolta elegiaca di Massimiano', in *Bollettino di Studi Latini*, 16, p. 9-21.

G. Glauche (1970), *Schullektüre im Mittelalter. Entstehung und Wandlungen des Lektürekanons bis 1200 nach den Quellen dargestellt*, München: Arbeo-Gesellschaft.

T. Hunt (1991), *Teaching and Learning Latin in Thirteenth-Century England. I Text II Glosses III Indexes*, Cambridge: D. S. Brewer.

L. Karlsson & L. Malm (2004), 'Revolution or Remediation? A Study of Electronic Scholarly Editions on the Web', in *Human IT*, 7, p. 1-46.

N. Ker (1969), *Medieval Manuscripts in British Libraries*, vol. II, Oxford: Clarendon Press

Magister Siguinus, *Ars Lectoria. Un art de lecture à haute voix du onzième siècle*, ed. C. H. Kneepkens & H. F. Reijnders, Leiden: Brill, 1979.

M. Manca (2010), 'Database and Corpora of ancient Texts towards the *Second Dimension*: Theory and Practice of *Musisque Deoque Project*', in P. Anreiter & M. Kienpointner (eds.), *Latin Linguistics Today: Akten des 15. Internationalen Kolloquiums zur Lateinischen Linguistik, Innsbruck, 4-9, April 2009*, Innsbruck: Institut für Sprachen und Literaturen der Universität Innsbruck, p. 699-705, (Innsbrucker Beiträge zur Sprachwissenschaft).

P. Mastandrea (2005), 'Per la cronologia di Massimiano elegiaco: elementi interni ed esterni al testo', in M. Diaz & J. Diaz de Bustamante (eds.), *Poesia latina medieval (siglos V-XV): actas del VI Congreso del 'International Mittellateinerkomitee'. Santiago de Compostela 12-14 de septiembre 2002*, Firenze: Sismel, p. 151-179.

P. Mastandrea (2009), 'Gli archivi elettronici di 'Musisque Deoque'. Ricerca intertestuale e cernita fra varianti antiche', in L. Zurli (ed.), *Poesia latina, nuova E-filologia. Opportunità per l'editore e per l'interprete. Atti del convegno internazionale. Perugia 13-15 settembre 2007*, Roma: Herder Editrice, p. 41-72.

P. Mastandrea (ed., 2011), *Nuovi archivi e mezzi d'analisi per i testi poetici. I lavori del progetto Musisque Deoque. Venezia 21-23 giugno 2010*, Amsterdam: Adolf M. Hakkert.

Maximianus, *Maximiani Etrusci Elegiarum Libri*, in *Poetae Latini Minores*, *tomi sexti qui carmina ... amatoria et ludicra complectitur pars prior*, ed. C. Wernsdorf, Helmstedt: C. G. Fleckeisen, 1794.

Maximianus, *Maximiani Elegiae*, ed. E. Baehrens, Leipzig: Teubner, 1883 (Poetae Latini Minores), p. 313-348.

Maximianus, *Maximiani Elegiae*, ed. M. Petschenig, Berlin: Von S. Calvary & Co, 1890 (Berliner Studien für class. Philologie und Archäologie).

Maximianus, *The Elegies of Maximianus*, ed. R. Webster, Princeton: Princeton Press, 1900.

Maximianus, *Maximiani Elegiae*, ed. G. Prada, Abbiategrasso: De Angeli, 1919.

Maximianus, *Versus Maximiani. Der Elegienzyklus textkritisch herausgegeben, übersetzt und neu interpretiert*, ed. C. Sandquist-Öberg, Stockholm: Almquist and Wiksell International, 1999.

G. Pontiggia (1972), 'Massimiano: Elegie', in *Il Verri*, 38, p. 137-138.

C. Ratkowitsch (1986), *Maximianus amat. Zu Datierung und Interpretation des Elegikers Maximian*, Wien: Verlag der Österreichischen Akademie der Wissenschaften.

H. F. Reijnders (1972), 'Aimericus. Ars Lectoria', in *Vivarium*, 10, p. 124-176.

Y.-F. Riou (1972), 'Quelques aspects de la tradition manuscrite des *Carmina* d'Eugene de Tolede: du liber catonianus aux auctores octo morales', in *Revue d'Histoire des Textes*, 2, p. 11-44.

M. Roberts (2010), 'Late Roman Elegy', in K. Weisman (ed.), *The Oxford Handbook of the Elegy*, Oxford: Oxford University Press, p. 85-100.

P. Robinson (2010), 'Editing Without Walls', in *Literature Compass*, 7, p. 57-61.

W. Schetter (1970), *Studien zur Überlieferung und Kritik des Elegikers Maximian*, Wien: Otto Harrassowitz.

W. C. Schneider (2003), *Die elegischen Verse von Maximian. Eine letze Widerrede gegen die neue christliche Zeit*, Stuttgart: Franz Steiner Verlag (Palingenesia, 79).

C. Sequi (1995), 'Bibliographia Maximianea', in P. Mastandrea et al. (ed.), *Concordantia in Maximianum*, Hildesheim-Zurich-New York: Olms Weidmann, p. 178-196.

P. L. Shillingsburg (2006), *From Gutenberg to Google. Electronic Representations of Literary Texts*, Cambridge: Cambridge University Press.

M. Vitiello (2006), *Il principe, il filosofo, il guerriero*, Stuttgart: Steiner (Hermes Einzelschriften).

A. M. Wasyl (2011), 'The Elegy without Love: Maximianus in His

Opus', in *Genres Rediscovered: Studies in Latin Miniature Epic, Love Elegy and Epigram of the Romano-Barbaric Age*, Kraków: Jagellonian University Press, p. 113-163.

J. T. Welsh (2011), 'Notes on the Text of Maximianus', in *Exemplaria Classica. Journal of Classical Philology*, 15, p. 213-224.

SAMUEL RUBENSON

A DATABASE
OF THE *APOPHTHEGMATA PATRUM*

Introduction

The *Apophthegmata Patrum* (AP), the common name used for all collections of sayings of the monastic fathers, is the single most important text corpus emanating from the early monastic tradition. In his magisterial and posthumous work of 1923, *Die Apophthegmata Patrum* – which remains the most important comprehensive scholarly work on their transmission – Wilhelm Bousset has even claimed that they give us access to the authentic voices of the first generation of monks.[1] Subsequent studies of monastic origins, early developments, as well as ideas and practices, have consequently relied heavily upon the AP.[2] In recent revisionist studies of early monasticism, the interpretation has changed – e.g., questioning the idealized image of splendid isolation and attempting to see more of a continuity between classical education and monastic formation – the importance however remains.[3]

The apophthegmata (or sayings) that make up the *Apophthegmata Patrum* are preserved in numerous collections in all the languages of Christian antiquity. These vary from the very large accumulated collections of up to 1,500 sayings, usually organized thematically or alphabetically, to a bewildering variety of smaller

---

[1] Bousset 1923.
[2] Heussi 1936; Burton-Christie 1993; Gould 1993; Regnault 1990.
[3] McVey 1998; Larsen 2006; Rönnegård 2010; Rubenson 2012.

10.1484/M.LECTIO-EB.5.102571

collections, many of which include a variety of hagiographic material known also in their own right.

Two collections, the Latin thematic and the Greek alphabetical, were printed as early as 1615 and 1677 respectively, and both were reprinted in the *Patrologia Graeca* and *Patrologia Latina* of J. P. Migne at the end of the nineteenth century.[4] With their translations into many modern languages these two editions have dominated all scholarly research both on the text itself as well as its use as a source for early monasticism. The large Armenian collection in two recensions, printed in 1721 and again in 1855,[5] as well as the Syriac collection, printed 1897 and again in 1904,[6] have received much less attention. This is also true for the Greek anonymous collection, which was partly edited in a series of articles in the early twentieth century,[7] and more fully in 2013.[8] The Greek thematic collection, closely related to the Latin, has also been edited,[9] as well as three other Latin,[10] two Georgian and five Ethiopic collections.[11]

The complexity of the relations between the collections, even when restricted to the best known, is, as demonstrated by Bousset, daunting. Subsequent studies of single collections, such as the Greek by Jean-Claude Guy,[12] the Latin by André Wilmart and Columba Batlle,[13] and the Syriac by René Draguet, Michel van Esbroeck and Bo Holmberg,[14] have moreover shown that the collections are not stable, and that the printed versions only represent a certain, rather late, stage preserved in single manuscripts, or even created by adding material from different manuscripts. As Guy concludes in his study of a large number of Greek manu-

---

[4] H. Rosweyde 1615; Cotelier 1677.
[5] *Vies et pratiques des saints pères selon la double traduction des anciens* 1855; Leloir 1974, 1975, 1976.
[6] Bedjan 1897; Budge 1904.
[7] Nau 1905, 1907, 1908, 1909, 1912, 1913.
[8] Wortley 2013.
[9] Guy 1993, 2003, 2005.
[10] Freire 1971, 1974; Barlow 1950.
[11] Dvali 1966, 1974; Arras, 1963, 1967, 1984, 1986, 1988.
[12] Guy 1962.
[13] Wilmart 1922; Batlle 1971, 1972.
[14] The presence of apophthegmatic material is mentioned, but never detailed in Draguet 1978 and 1968. For the identification of one important manuscript see Draguet 1953. The importance of Draguet's work on the Syriac manuscripts is emphasised by Gribomont 1987. A survey, with an important analysis of a Sinai ms is Holmberg 2013.

scripts, the transmission of the sayings is characterized by great fluidity caused both by scribes tending to enrich the collections they copied, using different models, deleting or rearranging material and reattributing pieces.[15] Almost every manuscript is a creation in its own right, born of the material available to the scribe and adhering to the preferences of his monastery. It is thus obvious that it is not possible to recreate and edit a single source for all, or probably not even for one of the standard collections. The tradition has grown on the basis of the insertion of new material from a variety of sources, as well as constant rearrangements, exclusions, additions, revisions and reattributions.

Thus the use of only the published versions, generally representing an accumulated late stage of the transmission, neither gives access to a primitive origin of the tradition, nor helps us to understand the history of the transmission, the relations between the various collections, or the factors that have determined the variations. Moreover, the modern editions hide the fact that a larger part of the transmission of the sayings is actually intertwined with other early monastic texts to the extent that it is impossible to draw a sharp line between sayings and other texts, most often hagiographic accounts or excerpts from monastic treatises.[16] The printed versions are further of little help for the growing interest not only in the text, but in discerning the function – or probably changing functions – of the apophthegmata in the monastic tradition.

The Scope of the Database

Against this background the research program Early Monasticism and Classical Paideia – for which the sayings are crucial as sources – decided to create a comprehensive relational database of the textual transmission of the sayings. The aim is to develop and maintain a powerful comprehensive research tool for studies of the textual transmission of the Apophthegmata Patrum in all the languages of Christian Antiquity (Greek, Latin, Syriac, Cop-

---

[15] Guy 1962.
[16] For the close relation to hagiographic text, see Faraggiana 1997 and Dahlman 2013.

tic, Georgian, Armenian, Arabic, Ethiopic and Old Slavonic). The plan is to make this tool available to the scholarly world. As a tool of reference the contents of all printed collections of the sayings in all the languages will be registered, and the full text in the original languages and/or translation inserted in unicode, linking the individual sayings to their parallels across all the versions. This part builds on the work by Bousset, Guy, Batlle, and the editors of the Apophthegmata Patrum and represents a major development of the lists provided by Lucien Regnault and others.[17] In addition, the attempt will be made to register the contents of all relevant manuscripts in all the languages, in most cases with a chronological limit in the Middle Ages.[18] In addition to basic information about the manuscripts themselves, the structure of the apophthegmatic collections in them as well as related material will be registered, and an attempt made to identify all sayings, as far as possible, with their parallels in the printed material or in other manuscripts. For the most important manuscripts of each collection in each language, the actual texts (or at least the incipits) of the sayings are registered in the original language and/or translation, including titles, prologues, and epilogues where appropriate. Other texts important for the textual transmission of the sayings will also be registered and inserted. For easy reference and searches the texts are standardized and annotated.

The database will also include extensive cross-references for individual sayings as well as other texts and structural units. Attempts will also be made to register attestations to the apophthegmata in other ancient Christian texts, and to index personal names, geographical designations, and important concepts. The database will also include scholarly comments and notes on all levels of the texts as well as essential bibliographical information. Each structural element of a manuscript will be registered separately; for each structural element of the manuscript (book, part, section, chapter, group, saying and segment), as well accom-

[17] Regnault 1976, Leloir 1974-1976.
[18] For the Greek and the Latin collections the works by Guy and Batlle, as well as Freire, constitute a basis for the selection of manuscripts. No previous surveys are available for the Syriac collections. For the Arabic collections, the contributions by Sauget are indispensable; see Sauget 1987. I am also grateful to Chiara Faraggiana di Sarzana and Natia Gabrichidze for their suggestions.

panying prologues, epilogues and titles, a unique ID, as well as folio reference is given, including a comment and a bibliography when needed.

The material to be registered into the database is both large and complex, and the project invites all scholars working on the textual transmission to make their work available to the database. In exchange, scholars will be registered as users, and thus able to consult and work with the entire database. All edited as well as unedited material and all data made available in the database will be linked to information about the scholar contributing the material as well as the analysis.

Using the Database

Due to the complexity of the material and the fact that so much of it is unknown, it has been a challenge to create an architecture that will be able to take care of the bewildering variety of the material as well as all different research interests. We have thus found it necessary to create a structure that is open and adaptable to new discoveries and new research questions. In order to achieve this openness and to make it possible for each scholar using the database to experiment by trying out new kinds of analyses and testing various hypothetical explanations, the database has been designed not simply as an archive from which one can retrieve material that has been inserted (although this is of course possible) but rather as an instrument to be used by any scholar working on the apophthegmata.

In order to make this possible a design has been implemented in which scholars store their files, whether text files or tables, in their own personal archive folders. These are the working copies of the individual scholar which the scholar can update at any time using ordinary software. When a scholar wants to share documents, whether texts or tables, copies are saved in a master archive on a common server. From this master archive a master database is created and kept on the server. The actual source of the master database remains the master archive consisting of the documents saved by the scholars. A new master is created when a scholar supplements or replaces her or his files in the master archive with new or updated texts and tables. From this master database, scholars can at any time download a copy on her or his own computer as a basis for the development of a personal database adapted to the needs and interests of the scholar. When a new master database has been created on the server due to new or updated files in the master archive, the scholar is alerted and can upload a new copy to replace the old one.

The personal database is subsequently 'personalized' by the scholar by uploading any files representing work in progress. In the personal database, to which no one else has access, the scholar is then able to do comparisons, searches and calculations, while still working on transcriptions, analyses or hypothetical reconstructions of sources. Whenever the scholar wants to share an updated version of a text file or table, the material is saved in the master archive and a new master database is created from which new copies can be uploaded to update the personal database. Thus the personal database can be kept up-to-date with the results of the other scholars. This design makes it possible to make full use of the database already at the early stage of research and to test material that has not yet reached the stage necessary to be shared with other scholars. The decision about at what point the material is made available to the larger group is entirely up to the individual contributor.

In order to make it possible to process the documents in the database, the texts and tables must be tagged with tags addressing the database columns into which the material goes. To facilitate the tagging, a simple system has been created that can be used in any software that can produce simple text or tables convertible to .csv files. For the creation of an external interface available on internet these tags are replaced by .xml tags according to TEI. Work on creating this interface and possibilities to retrieve texts through CTS protocol are ongoing. An advanced control system in the database checks all input – both on formal and linguistic grounds – to avoid the insertion of mistakes, and alerts the scholar to mistakes made in tagging as well as in typing.

Through the detailed systematic treatment of the material the database will make it possible to study all kinds of relations between manuscripts and collections, developments in language and in organization, as well as modes of translation and cultural transfer. A primary asset of the database is the possibility of identifying parallels between single apophthegma as well as series of apophthegmata in different versions, recensions and collections in manuscripts in all languages by searching for textual similarities as well as similarities in arrangement and attribution. The comparison of how a single saying – attributed to a certain father and arranged with other sayings by that father or according to a certain theme in the Greek standard collections – has been reattributed and combined with other sayings in a variety of collections in e.g. Latin, Arabic or Armenian, may help us to understand both routes of communication and principles of arrangement on a wider scale. Likewise, specific series of sayings appearing together in a diversity of collections will make it possible to identify the smaller units out of which the larger collections have been assembled.

A second use is the identification of kinship between manuscripts on the basis of identifications of similarities in arrangement of material, including non-apophthegmatic texts. Combining data from manuscript catalogues on geographical areas of origin and date with the analysis made when inserting the material such as similar arrangements of material (including non-apophthegmatic texts, similar additions and deletions, similar attributions, etc.) scholars will be able to identify hitherto unnoticed relations and venues of transmission. An important issue is the identification of other principles of organization in addition to the two types of arrangement of the sayings, the systematic and the alphabetic-anonymous, known from the printed Greek and Latin collections. Through comparisons of collections now considered to be without any organizational principle we hope to be able to understand better the process of transmission of these collections. Comparative work on the actual texts inserted may help to analyse developments in language and translation techniques. By being able to study the relations between single manuscripts, groups of manuscripts, and collections on a variety of levels, we further hope to be able to plot contacts and relations in the early monastic tradition.

A set of standard search tools enables the scholar to select with a high degree of flexibility the material to be analyzed or compared. Gradually, we also hope to be able to adapt standard tools of linguistic and statistical analysis to the database. The combination of an interactive database which can be personalized and used by an individual scholar inserting tentative work-in-progress with a systematic treatment of an extremely complex material in many languages makes the database project both unique and indispensable as a tool for future work on the *Apophthegmata Patrum*. For further information on and contact with the research program we refer to our website: ‹http://mopai.lu.se›.

Bibliography

V. Arras (1963), *Collectio Monastica*, Louvain: Peeters (CSCO 238-239).

V. Arras (1967), *Patericon Aethiopice*, Louvain: Peeters (CSCO 238-239).

V. Arras (1984), *Asceticon*, Louvain: Peeters (CSCO 238-239).

V. Arras (1986), *Geronticon*, Louvain: Peeters (CSCO 238-239).

V. Arras (1988), *Quadraginta historiae monachorum*, Louvain: Peeters (CSCO 238-239).

C. W. Barlow (1950), *Martini episcopi Bracarensis, opera Omnia*, New Haven: Yale Univ. Press.

C. M. Batlle (1971), '*Vetera Nova* Vorläufige kritische Ausgabe bei Rosweyde fehlender Vätersprüche', in J. Autenrieth & F. Brunhölzl (eds.), *Festschrift Bernhard Bischoff zu seinem 65. Geburtstag*, Stuttgart: Anton Hiersemann, p. 32-42.

C. M. Batlle (1972), *Die „Adhortationes sanctorum Patrum" im lateinischen Mittelalter*. Überlieferung, Fortleben und Wirkung, Münster Westfallen: Aschendorffsche (Beiträge zur Geschichte des alten Mönchsleben und des Benediktinerordens, 31).

P. Bedjan, ed. (1897), *Acta martyrum et sanctorum Syriace 7*, Paris: Harassowitz.

W. Bousset (1923), *Apophthegmata. Studien zur Geschichte des ältesten Mönchtums*, Tübingen.

E. A. W. Budge, ed. & trans. (1904), *The Book of Paradise*, 2 vols., London.

D. Burton-Christie (1993), *The Word in the Desert. Scripture and the Quest for Holiness in Early Christian Monasticism*, Oxford & New York: Oxford Univ. Press.

J. B. Cotelier, ed. (1677), *Ecclesiae Graecae monumenta 1, 338-712*, Paris, *Patrologia Graeca* 65, p. 72-440.

B. Dahlman (2013), 'The Collectio Scorialensis Parva: an Alphabetical Collection of Old Apophthegmatic and Hagiographic Material', in S. Rubenson & M. Vinzent (eds.), *Early Monasticism and Classical Paideia* (Studia Patristica, LV), Leuven: Peeters 2013, 23-33.

R. Draguet (1953), 'Fragments de l'Ambrosienne de Milan à restituer aux mss syriaques du Sinaï 46 et 16', in J. N. Birdsall and R. W. Thomson (eds.), *Biblical and Patristic Studies in Memory of Robert Pierce Casey*, Freiburg: Herder, p. 167-78.

R. Draguet (1968), *Les cinq recensions de l'ascéticon syriaque d'abba Isaïe*, Louvain: Secrétariat du CorpusSCO (CSCO 289, 290, 293, 294).

R. Draguet (1978), *Les formes syriaques de la matière de l'Histoire Lausiaque*, Louvain: Secrétariat du CorpusSCO (CSCO 389, 390, 398, 399).

M. Dvali (1966, 1974), *Sua saukunet'a novelebis jveli k'art'uli t'argmanebi*, Vols. 1-2, Tbilisi: Mec'niereba.

C. Faraggiana (1997), 'Apophthegmata Patrum: Some Crucial Points of Their Textual Transmission and the Problem of a Critical Edition', in *Studia Patristica*, 30, p. 455-67.

J. G. Freire (1971), *A versão latina por Pascásio de Dume dos Apophthegmata Patrum*, Vols. 1-2, Coimbra.

J. G. Freire (1974), *Comminitiones sanctorum patrum*, Coimbra.

G. Gould (1993), *The Desert Fathers on Monastic Community*, Oxford: Oxford Univ. Press.

J. Gribomont (1987), 'Le vieux corpus monastique du Vatican Syr. 123', in *Le Muséon* 100, p. 131-141.

J.-C Guy (1962), *Recherches sur la tradition grecque des Apophthegmata Patrum*, Brussels: Société des Bollandistes (Subsidia Hagiographica, 36).

J.-C. Guy (1993, 2003, 2005), *Les Apophthegmes des Pères. Collection systématique*, vols. 1-3, Paris: Éditions du Cerf (Sources chrétiennes 387, 474, 498).

K. Heussi (1936), *Der Ursprung des Mönchtums*, Tübingen.

B. Holmberg (2013), 'The Syriac Collection of the Apophtegmata Patrum in MS Sin. syr. 46', in S. Rubenson & M. Vinzent (eds.), *Early Monasticism and Classical Paideia*, Leuven: Peeters (Studia Patristica, LV), 35-57.

L. Larsen (2006), 'The Apophthegmata Patrum and the Classical Rhetorical Tradition', in F. Young, M. Edwards and P. Parvis (eds.), *Papers presented at the Fourteenth International Conference on Patristic Studies held in Oxford 2003. Historica, Biblica, Ascetica et Hagiographica*, Leuven: Peeters, p. 409-416 (Studia Patristica 39).

L. Leloir, ed. (1974-76), *Paterica Armeniaca a PP. Mechitaristis edita*

(1855), *nunc latine reddita a Louis Leloir*, Louvain: Secrétariat du CorpusSCO (CSCO 353, 361, 371, 377).

K. McVey (1998), 'The Chreia in the Desert: Rhetoric and the Bible in the Apophthegmata Patrum', in A. J. Malherbe, F. W. Norris, & J. W. Thompson (eds.), *The Early Church in its Context: Essays in Honour of Everett Ferguson*, Leiden: Brill, p. 246-257.

F. Nau (1905), 'Le chapitre Peri Anachoreton Hagion et les sources de la vie de S. Paul de Thèbes', in *Revue de l'Orient Chrétien*, 10, p. 387-417.

F. Nau (1907), 'Histoires des solitaires égyptiens (MS Coislin 126, fol. 158 ff.)', in *Revue de l'Orient Chrétien*, 12, p. 43-69, 171-189, 393-413.

L. Regnault (1976), *Les sentences des pères du désert, troisième recueil & tables*, Sablé-sur-Sarthe: Solesmes.

L. Regnault (1990), *La vie quotidienne des pères du désert en Égypte du IVe siècle*, Paris: Hachette.

P. Rönnegård (2010), *Threads and Images. The Use of Scripture in* Apophthegmata Patrum, Winona Lake: Eisenbrauns (Coniectanea Biblica 44).

H. Rosweyde (ed.), *Vitae Patrum V-VI* (Antwerpen, 1615), *Patrologia Latina* 73, 855-1022.

S. Rubenson (2012), 'The Formation and Re-formations of the Sayings of the Desert Fathers', in S. Rubenson & M. Vinzent (eds.), *Early Monasticism and Classical Paideia*, (Studia Patristica LV), Leuven: Peeters 2013, 5-22.

P. Sarkissian, ed. (1855), *Vies et pratiques des saints pères selon la double traduction des anciens*, Venice.

J.-M. Sauget (1987), *Une traduction arabe de la collection d'*Apophthegmata Patrum *de 'Enanishô*, Louvain: Peeters (CSCO 495).

A. Wilmart (1922), 'Le recueil latin des *Apophthegmata Patrum*', in *Revue Bénédictine*, 34, p. 175-184.

J. Wortley (2013), *The Anonymous Sayings of the Desert Fathers. A Select Edition and Complte English Translation*, Cambridge: CUP 2013.

CHARLOTTE TUPMAN – ANNA JORDANOUS

SHARING ANCIENT WISDOMS ACROSS THE SEMANTIC WEB USING TEI AND ONTOLOGIES

Introduction

This paper explores the approach of the Sharing Ancient Wisdoms (SAWS)[1] project to the publication and analysis of the tradition of wisdom literatures in ancient Greek, Arabic, Spanish, and other languages. The SAWS project edits and presents the texts digitally, in a manner that enables linking and comparisons within and between anthologies, their source texts, and the texts that draw upon them (referred to here as 'recipient texts'). It is also creating a framework through which other projects can link their own materials to these texts through the Semantic Web, thus providing a focal point for the development of scholarship on these texts and their related manuscripts. The project is funded by HERA (Humanities in the European Research Area) as part of their programme to investigate cultural dynamics in Europe, and constitutes teams at the Department of Digital Humanities and the Centre for e-Research at King's College London, the Newman Institute Uppsala in Sweden, and the University of Vienna.

The wisdom literatures included in the SAWS project are a feature of the broader tendency in antiquity and the Middle Ages to take extracts from larger texts containing wise or useful sayings, and to circulate these anthologies widely. This was done in order to address the problem of the cost and rarity of full, original texts, and was a key method by which ideas and morals were

---

[1] ⟨http://www.ancientwisdoms.ac.uk/⟩

10.1484/M.LECTIO-EB.5.102572

circulated across different countries and languages (Rodríguez Adrados 2009, p. 91-97 on Greek models; Gutas 1981). SAWS focuses on *gnomologia* (or *florilegia*) – manuscripts that collected moral or social advice and philosophical ideas – although its methods and tools are applicable to other manuscript types (such as medieval scientific or medical texts); the ability to extend our methodology beyond *gnomologia* is an important feature of the project (Richard 1962, cols. 475-512).

When new *gnomologia* were created, they tended to be composed of smaller extracts of earlier works, rather than simple copies. The sayings were selected from various manuscripts, reorganised or reordered, words or sentence structures modified, and sometimes an entire saying or part of a saying was attributed to a different author or philosopher from that of the source text. These texts were frequently translated into other languages (such as from Greek into Arabic), and again these tended to be variations rather than simple translations. Such collections were eventually translated into western European languages – in fact, the first book ever published in England (Caxton 1477) was one such collection. This body of texts, therefore, can be regarded as a complex network or graph of manuscripts and individual sayings that are interrelated in a great variety of ways. An analysis of these relationships can reveal much about the dynamics of the cultures that created and used these texts. Here we describe how we digitally encode relationships between texts using TEI XML markup (Text Encoding Initiative Extensible Markup Language) and RDF (Resource Description Framework). We discuss how our representational choices afford new ways of exploring and understanding the texts and their inter-relationships, through Semantic Web tools.

Identifying and representing digitally the relationships between texts

The recording and visualisation of the links within and between the gnomologia, between these collections and their source texts (e.g., Aristotle's writings), and between these collections and their recipient texts (e.g. the eleventh-century Strategikon of Kekaumenos) is a task that must be approached systematically. Crucially, we should do this in a way that can be replicated by others (either using their own tools or ours), so that our collection of texts can act as a starting point for an expandable corpus that takes this approach far beyond our own project.

Before the methodology is explained, we should look at an example of the nature of the texts under consideration. This saying is from *Gnomologium Vaticanum* (no. 87):

Ὁ αὐτὸς ἐρωτηθεὶς τίνα μᾶλλον ἀγαπᾷ, Φίλιππον ἢ Ἀριστοτέλην, εἶπεν· 'ὁμοίως ἀμφοτέρους· ὁ μὲν γάρ μοι τὸ ζῆν ἐχαρίσατο, ὁ δὲ τὸ καλῶς ζῆν ἐπαίδευσεν.'

Alexander, asked whom he loved more, Philip or Aristotle, said: 'Both equally, for one gave me the gift of life, the other taught me to live the virtuous life.'

We can identify that this saying, or section of text, exists in various forms in earlier works, and that there are relationships that can be defined between our saying above and those quoted below (and indeed between the various examples given below):

Plutarch, Life of Alexander 8.4.1:

Ἀριστοτέλην δὲ θαυμάζων ἐν ἀρχῇ καὶ ἀγαπῶν οὐχ ἧττον, ὡς αὐτὸς ἔλεγε, τοῦ πατρός, ὡς δι' ἐκεῖνον μὲν ζῶν, διὰ τοῦτον δὲ καλῶς ζῶν [...]

Alexander admired Aristotle at the start and loved him no less, as he himself said, than his own father, since he had life through his father but the virtuous life through Aristotle [...].

Diogenes Laertius, *Life of Aristotle* 5.19:

Τῶν γονέων τοὺς παιδεύσαντας ἐντιμοτέρους εἶναι τῶν μόνον γεννησάντων· τοὺς μὲν γὰρ τὸ ζῆν, τοὺς δὲ τὸ καλῶς ζῆν παρασχέσθαι.

Aristotle said that educators are more to be honored than mere begetters, for the latter offer life but the former offer the good life.

Pythagoras? Selections from the Sayings of the Four Philosophers: (B) Pythagoras saying 18 (ed. Gutas):

وقال الآباء هم سبب الحياة والحكماء هم سبب صلاح الحياة

(He said: 'Fathers are the cause of life, but philosophers are the cause of the good life.')

In this final example, we can see that the saying has actually been attributed to a different author (Pythagoras), rather than Aristotle or his pupil Alexander. Alternative attributions are a common feature of these kinds of texts, and they add yet another layer of complexity to the types of relationships that can be discovered and described.

We need, therefore, to find suitable methods for:

1. Inserting links between sections of text (both within and between documents, some of which exist in digital form, and some of which do not);

2. Providing a means by which scholarly assertions defining the nature of these relationships can be shared and recorded in a systematic manner; this is particularly important in enabling individual scholars to take credit for (and indeed responsibility for) the assertions that they make in identifying links and defining the nature of those relationships.

The basic unit of interest

We must therefore define, first of all, the basic unit of intellectual interest to us (a 'section' or 'segment' of text), which is the saying (or part of the saying). In order to encode these units, SAWS has chosen to use the Text Encoding Initiative (TEI) Guidelines, which provide guidance as to how to use XML to 'mark up' (i.e., encode) texts of various types.[2] Taking the TEI manuscript schema as a basis, the SAWS team at King's College London has designed its own schema which can be used specifically for the encoding of gnomologia and their related texts. The use of a schema ensures that there is consistency in the markup that we use to encode our texts: as part of the project, the SAWS schema will be made freely available to all scholars who wish to use it for their own purposes.

[2] ⟨http://www.tei-c.org/index.xml⟩

SAWS uses the <seg> (arbitrary segment) element to define the basic unit of intellectual interest (such as a saying [statement] together with its surrounding story [narrative]). For example:

> <seg>*Alexander, asked whom he loved more, Philip or Aristotle, said: "Both equally, for one gave me the gift of life, the other taught me to live the virtuous life".*</seg>

This saying contains both a statement and a narrative, so each of these are therefore marked up in their own <seg> element, using attributes to indicate the nature of the segment ("contentItem" is simply a term that the SAWS project uses to define the whole saying):

> <seg type="contentItem">
> <seg type="narrative">
> *Alexander, asked whom he loved more, Philip or Aristotle, said:*
> </seg>
> <seg type="statement">
> *Both equally, for one gave me the gift of life, the other taught me to live the virtuous life.*
> </seg>
> </seg>

In order to differentiate one <seg> from another, each <seg> element is given an @xml:id attribute whose value is a locally unique identifier (which is automatically generated using simple XSLT: this does not need to be done by hand).[3]

The identifier differentiates one <seg> from all other examples of <seg>, for instance: <seg type="statement" xml:id="KHar_Proclus_ET.ci3.s1">ثالث كل محرّك لذاته فهو راجع على ذاته برهان</seg> ("KHar_Proclus_ET.ci3.s1" is the unique identifier).

This method allows each intellectually interesting unit (as defined by the scholar who is marking up the text) to be distinguished from each other unit, thus providing a means of referring directly to a specific, often very brief, section of the text.

---

[3] The project ultimately decided to adopt the Canonical Text Services (CTS) notation, developed by the Homer Multitext Project for identifying and citing texts and parts of texts: ‹http://www.homermultitext.org/hmt-doc/cite/texts/ctsoverview.html›

Describing textual relationships with an ontology

Next, we must have a systematic way of defining the relationship between one section of text and another. The use of a systematic method is important for two reasons: to ensure consistency in the descriptive terms that we use across the project, and, crucially, to develop a shared vocabulary between SAWS and other projects to which we wish to establish links (and which wish to link their data to ours). We have therefore taken every possible opportunity to explore with other scholars the terms they would use to describe the relationships that they observe within, and between, their texts. Relationships identified include terms such as isCloseRenderingOf, isLooseTranslationOf, isVerbatimOf, and a variety of other terms that represent in an agreed form the different ways in which sections of text are connected to one another. These are stored in the form of an ontology, which lists and gives details of all the types of relationship that have been defined. As ontologies are easily extensible, any relationships of interest identified in the future can also be included: again, the SAWS methodology has been designed to enable its use and modification by others.

We are representing these relationships using an ontology that extends the FRBR-oo model (Doerr and LeBoeuf 2007), which is the harmonisation of the FRBR model of bibliographic records (Tillett 2004) and the CIDOC Conceptual Reference Model (CIDOC-CRM; Doerr 2003). The SAWS ontology,[4] developed through collaboration between domain experts and technical observers, models the classes and links in the SAWS manuscripts. Basing the SAWS ontology around FRBR-oo allows us to reuse much existing vocabulary for both the bibliographic (FRBR) and cultural heritage (CIDOC) aspects being modelled.

Adding relationships to the TEI document

Using this underlying ontology as a basis, relationships between (or within) texts can be added to the TEI documents using the TEI element <relation>. Three entities must be represented: the subject being linked from, the object being linked to, and a de-

---

[4] ‹http://purl.org/saws/ontology›

scription of the link between them. These three entities constitute RDF (Resource Description Framework) 'triples'. The subject entity is represented by the @xml:id of the section of text that is being linked *from*; the object entity is represented by the @xml:id of the section of text that is being linked *to*; and the third entity – the nature of the link itself – is represented by another attribute, @ref, the value of which is drawn directly from the ontology in which we store all the relationships.

In order to insert this information into the TEI document, we use the element <relation>, which has recently been adopted by the TEI community for the purpose of placing RDF markup in TEI documents. When used for this purpose, <relation> takes three main attributes (i.e. the RDF triples), and a fourth that we considered important to include:

- @active – the @xml:id or URI (Uniform Resource Identifier) of the subject being linked from;

- @passive – the @xml:id or URI of the object being linked to;

- @ref – the description of the relationship, which is drawn directly from the list of relationships in the ontology;

- @resp – (responsibility): the name or identifier of a particular individual or resource, such as a bibliographic reference. This enables the recording of the identity of the person(s) responsible for making the assertion about the existence of a relationship between two sections of text. We felt it was important to include this facility, both from the point of view of ensuring proper credit for those who make scholarly assertions about the texts, and also as a means of being able to trace decision-making more easily.

Here is an example of a link that has been identified by one of our teams between two small sections of text in Arabic and Greek manuscripts:

1. Proclus, The Elements of Theology, ed. Dodds
   ```
   <seg type="contentItem" xml:id="Prop-17.ci1">
   Πᾶν τὸ ἑαυτὸ κινοῦν πρώτως πρὸς ἑαυτό ἐστιν ἐπιστρεπτικόν.
   </seg>
   ```

2. Kitab al-Haraka, Hacı Mahmud Efendi 5683
   <seg type="statement" xml:id="KHar_Proclus_ET.ci3.s1">
   برهان ثالث كل محرّك لذاته فهو راجع على ذاته
   <relation active="#KHar_Proclus_ET.ci3.s1"
   ref="http://purl.org/saws/ontology#isVariantTranslationOf"
   resp="EW"
   passive="http://www.ancientwisdoms.ac.uk/cts/urn:cts:
   greekLit:tlg4036.tlg005.saws01:Prop-17.ci1"/

This is equivalent to stating that the Arabic segment identified as "KHar_Proclus_ET.ci3.s1" is a variant translation of the Greek segment identified as "Prop-17.ci1", and that this relationship has been asserted by EW (Elvira Wakelnig) (this could instead be a pointer to a bibliographic reference, if desired).[5]

The definition of 'isVariantTranslationOf' has been agreed upon and documented within the ontology, and the schema has been populated from the ontology so that a drop-down menu appears in the XML editor, from which the required value of @ref can be selected. The <relation> element can be placed anywhere within the TEI document, or indeed in a separate document if required. Several different coding strategies have emerged in our own annotations for SAWS because of personal preferences for different markup approaches, with the most popular strategies being to place each individual <relation> element immediately after the closing tag of the <seg> identified as the active entity, or to include at the end of a TEI file (or in an additional TEI file) a group of all <relation> statements relevant to a particular document. Either method is equally appropriate.

There are clear benefits in linking to external sources where possible, as well as including links within the documents themselves, thereby enhancing the semantic content of our texts by viewing them in the context of other relevant information that is stored externally to our documents. Linking our texts to external sources also provides an alternative point of entry to our texts. For this purpose, the SAWS project also marks up our texts

---

[5] The format of the IDs in the final version of the project varied slightly from this example (this paper was written during the progress of the project) but the principles remained the same.

with semantic links to collections of data on the ancient world where possible, such as the Pleiades historical gazetteer of ancient places,[6] and the Prosopography of the Byzantine World,[7] which aims to document all the individuals mentioned in textual Byzantine sources from the seventh to thirteenth centuries. These links will be supplemented with links to the DBpedia dataset and to the geonames.org modern geographical dataset.[8] Collaborative discussions are also currently underway to identify how we can best mark up links to existing relevant documents such as those stored in the Perseus Digital Library,[9] which holds editions of some of the texts that have been identified as source texts for the *gnomologia*.

Dealing with editorial uncertainty

The relations being expressed about our texts are often subjective; it may be that people will have different opinions about whether or not the assertion of a particular relationship is valid – for example, whether or not one text is sourced from another, or which relationship is most appropriate to use in any particular case. Also, it may be that individual editors see the potential existence of a link between two texts, but are not completely certain about the nature of that link.

The set of link types provided in the SAWS ontology have been developed with the specific vocabulary requirements of our textual scholars in mind, in order to describe relationships using the appropriate terms. Furthermore, explanatory definitions are provided for all terms in the ontology,[10] to assist editors in choosing the appropriate relationship.

In a scenario in which editors disagree on what relationship description is best to use, or where there is disagreement on the validity of asserting a relationship at all, it is vital to be able to record the identity of the individual making the assertion (using the

[6] ‹http://pleiades.stoa.org/›

[7] ‹http://www.pbw.kcl.ac.uk/›

[8] Geonames: ‹http://www.geonames.org/›, DBpedia: ‹http://dbpedia.org/›

[9] ‹http://www.perseus.tufts.edu/›

[10] Definitions can be viewed directly in the OWL ontology at http://purl.org/saws/ontology and also through ontology display and documentation tools such as the LODE tool (‹http://www.essepuntato.it/lode›) at ‹http://www.essepuntato.it/lode/owlapi/reasoner/http://purl.org/saws/ontology›.

@resp attribute in TEI and reification[11] in RDF). As well as crediting scholarly assertions to the appropriate editor, @resp also allows conflicting opinions to be asserted alongside each other without needing to make an artificial choice of one opinion over the other. For example, if we have a damaged manuscript in which some of the text is lost or faded, one editor may think it most likely that this manuscript is a verbatim copy of another manuscript, and so asserts this. Another editor, on the other hand, may disagree, believing this manuscript to be only a close rendering of the other manuscript, and thus can assert this under his own responsibility.

We are currently exploring the best way to handle editorial uncertainty, for instance in cases in which the individual making an assertion about a relationship cannot be completely certain that their assertion is correct due to insufficient corroboratory evidence, or similar reasons. With source material such as ours, and the complexity of the relationships that are being identified, it is inevitable that cases like this will arise. We would like to be able to express these types of uncertainty in a manner that allows the reader to see immediately where a relationship is being identified tentatively, rather than with a high degree of certainty.

There are two main ways in which we might express editorial uncertainty in the markup. One option would be to add a certainty attribute (@cert) to the <relation> element. This would be the simplest method, a particularly relevant concern for editors with less technical proficiency or confidence, and would enable the editor to include the expression of certainty within the same element as the rest of the information about that relationship. For instance:

```
<relation active="#KHar_Proclus_ET.ci3.s1"
ref="http://purl.org/saws/ontology#isVariantTranslationOf"
resp="EW"
passive="http://www.ancientwisdoms.ac.uk/cts/urn:cts:
greekLit:tlg4036.tlg005.saws01:Prop-17.ci1"
cert="low"
/>
```

[11] In RDF, a reified statement is a statement of a subject-predicate-object triple that incorporates higher-order statements about the triple itself, such as who is making the assertion represented by the triple. Reification therefore allows us to represent the @resp attribute of a relationship within the RDF.

However, it could be argued that using this method does not make it sufficiently clear *what* we are ascribing a low certainty to: for instance, does the certainty refer to the existence of a relationship, or to the type of relationship, or to the identity of the passive text?

If we wish to be more explicit about what the expression of uncertainty refers to, we can instead use a <certainty> element, and point this to the specific part of the <relation> that we are describing. So, for instance, if we would like to say that we are uncertain about whether or not a relationship actually exists at all, we can express this in the markup in the following way:

```
<relation active="#KHar_Proclus_ET.ci3.s1"
ref="http://purl.org/saws/ontology#isVariantTranslationOf"
resp="EW"
passive="http://www.ancientwisdoms.ac.uk/cts/urn:cts:
greekLit:tlg4036.tlg005.saws01:Prop-17.ci1"
<certainty match=".." locus="name" cert="low"/>
</relation>
```

Note that here we are placing <certainty> within <relation> (thus it is no longer an empty element), and we are using XPath to match the <certainty> to its parent element (expressed with the two full stops). The @locus allows us to describe what we are not certain about: in this case, the very name of the element (in other words, we are not entirely certain whether or not a relationship exists here).

If we wish to express uncertainty about one of the attributes within <relation>, for instance the type of relationship that exists, we can use a similar method, but point to a specific attribute rather than to the element name:

```
<relation active="#KHar_Proclus_ET.ci3.s1"
ref="http://purl.org/saws/ontology#isVariantTranslationOf"
resp="EW"
passive="http://www.ancientwisdoms.ac.uk/cts/urn:cts:
greekLit:tlg4036.tlg005.saws01:Prop-17.ci1"
<certainty match="../@ref" locus="value" cert="low"/>
</relation>
```

In this example, the @match refers directly to the parent element's @ref, and the @locus expresses that we are uncertain about the value of that attribute – in other words, we are uncertain about the nature of the relationship that has been identified. Similarly we could apply this method to any of the attributes within <relation>.

It is possible to express degrees of certainty using @degree, but at this stage we feel that this would add an unnecessary layer of complexity to the markup. It is, however, something that might be worth exploring in a future stage of the project if it was found to be a useful method of making the editorial process more explicit.

The decision to represent RDF in TEI documents

As described above, we are using RDF triples[12] to mark up information of semantic interest such as relations between the text and links to external entities. Thus our relations can be published as Linked Data on the Semantic Web, where they can be shared, browsed through, searched and queried. Particularly for our purposes (and those of others) concerning TEI XML documents, which are a popular product of digital humanities research, we prefer that RDF annotations should be added to XML documents without extensive changes being required in either the variant of XML being used for the source document, or in the skills and workflow being used in the markup process. This last point is of particular concern for less-technical users who are inexperienced with markup. Keeping structural, syntactical, and semantic information in the same documents where possible also makes the process of markup more simple and less error-prone for non-technical users who wish to mark up documents with their annotations, though it is acknowledged that this is not always possible. To date, no method for accommodating TEI and RDF in the same document has been adopted as standard by the TEI community, though several approaches have recently been offered.

It is desirable (e.g., for SAWS) to be able to mark up triple-like relations directly in TEI, particularly if those relations are specific to the subject domain of the original text and/or if the

---

[12] ⟨http://www.w3.org/RDF/⟩

relations indicate semantic information which cannot currently be encoded using TEI markup. The <relation> element that we have chosen to use in the SAWS project has recently been recommended by the TEI for encoding RDF relations in a TEI document, representing the Subject-Predicate-Object triple format through the values of the attributes of <relation> as described above.

This allows TEI to express more semantic information, through the encoding of RDF triples, without requiring major changes within TEI. Furthermore, RDF can be included directly in TEI markup, allowing researchers to use the workflow and tools they are already accustomed to rather than introducing a requirement for new tools to be learnt and used, external to the existing workflow. This is particularly helpful for those users of TEI who do not have a strong technical background.

The benefits of RDF for information exploration and retrieval

Once information is available in RDF format, it can be queried and reasoned with, leading to the potential generation of new information from reasoning logically with the existing information. We have already seen at least one example within SAWS in which this approach has been helpful. Two of our Arabic texts were linked to one translation but were not linked to each other (in other words, the scholar had made an assertion about the link between each text and the translation, but had not yet asserted a link between the two Arabic texts), but we were able to highlight the links between the Arabic texts by navigating links between the two documents via the translation. New links such as this can be automatically discovered and added to our existing links using Semantic Web tools.

This approach also allows information to be derived from external data sources that are referenced by RDF triples. To illustrate this in the use case of SAWS, information in the Pleiades historical gazetteer can be consulted when constructing queries. Researchers can ask to see, for example, all texts that refer to a particular geographical location, even if they use different place-names to refer to that geographical location (for instance, cases in which places were referred to by different names in different historical periods). For SAWS, this assists us with the frequent issue of manuscripts being in different languages with different character sets (compare for example Ancient Greek and Arabic). By examining the place-names mentioned in the SAWS manuscripts in the context of the information in the Pleiades ontology, we have a precise geographical reference for each place.

For example the place 'Aphrodisias' (URI ‹http://pleiades. stoa.org/places/638753›) was known by the names:

- Νινόη (*c.* 550 BC-330 BC),
- Ἀφροδεισιάς (*c.* 330 BC-AD 300),
- Λελέγων πόλις (no attested dates),
- Σταυρόπολις (*c.* AD 300-AD 640),
- Ἀφροδισιάς (*c.* 30 BC-AD 640).

Developing this example, we can disambiguate between Aphrodisias located in modern-day Turkey and the Aphrodisias located by modern-day Spain (URI ‹http://pleiades.stoa.org/plac es/255978/›), between which the textual information in the TEI alone would not allow us to distinguish.

It is possible that in some cases, the editor might not be able to say whether a place-name refers to one particular location or to another; in this case, the editor could express this by including both possibilities (in other words, including more than one Pleiades reference) and then add an expression of uncertainty to both locations, to indicate that each referenced place could possibly be the place that is mentioned in the text, but that the editor is not sure enough to make either of the assertions with a high degree of certainty. If necessary, an indication of the degree of certainty that the editor has in any particular place-name identification can be added, for instance in cases in which an editor feels that one particular location is more likely to be the place mentioned in the text.

Returning to the issues of the SAWS manuscripts being written in various languages (Ancient Greek and Arabic being the two main languages, and some related documents in Spanish, Latin, and English, to date): although the TEI documents contain transcriptions of manuscripts in the original language, the use of RDF and linking allows the manuscript information to transcend linguistic boundaries to some extent, as parts of the text can be linked to resources which are more language-neutral (e.g., the person 'Aristotle' can be represented by the URI ‹http:// dbpedia.org/resource/Aristotle› independently of whether he is referred to as Aristotle, Ἀριστοτέλης, أرسطو, Aristoteles, Aristóteles or other alternative forms in the original document). This is particularly helpful in studying the transmission of information in the manuscripts across languages, especially if the researcher does not have sufficient skills to navigate between the different languages.

Future work

Having established our methodology and annotated a selection of texts with TEI and RDF for demonstration purposes, the research process of linking our texts and annotating relationships is now continuing in earnest. Currently we have approximately forty-one texts (not including translations) marked up in TEI XML, with more in preparation as the project grows and extends to collaborators. Relationships are being added to these texts on an active and ongoing basis, as the scholars record their knowledge and opinions on how the texts interlink and link to external entities. We are also actively working with existing and potential collaborators – discussing how the ontology suits the needs of other scholars – to establish good practice for linking with other text repositories and to provide training to those who are seeking help in marking up their texts using the SAWS approach.[13]

In terms of publishing our texts as digital editions, we have a functional demonstration version of the online environment in which texts and their relationships will be published. This version is undergoing further development in response to post-demon-

---

[13] One of the key outcomes for the SAWS project of the *Methods and means for digital analysis of ancient and medieval texts and manuscripts* workshop was the connection that we made with the project of Samuel Rubenson and his colleagues at Lund, 'Early Monasticism and Classical Paideia (MOPAI)'. They are approaching the same research questions using a different methodology, and following our meeting in Leuven we have organised a workshop to discuss our respective projects and to discover how best we can work together towards achieving our shared aims.

227

stration feedback from scholars, prior to becoming publicly accessible online at ‹http://www.ancientwisdoms.ac.uk›. We are also exploring alternative ways in which the relationships can be visualised, searched, and analysed, in order to give scholars new visual perspectives on these links.

Bibliography

F. Rodríguez Adrados (2009), *Greek Wisdom Literature and the Middle Ages: the Lost Greek Models and their Arabic and Castilian Translations*, trans. J. Greer, Bern; New York: Peter Lang, p. 91-97.

W. Caxton (1477), *The Dictes and Wise Sayings of the Philosophers*, London: Elliot Stock (repr. 1877).

M. Doerr (2003), 'The CIDOC CRM – an Ontological Approach to Semantic Interoperability of Metadata', in *AI Magazine*, 24, p. 75-92.

M. Doerr & P. LeBoeuf (2007), 'Modelling Intellectual Processes: The FRBR-CRM Harmonization', in C. Thanos, F. Borri & L. Candela (eds.), *Digital Libraries: Research and Development*, Berlin & Heidelberg: Springer (Lecture Notes in Computer Science, 4877), p. 114-123.

D. Gutas (1981), 'Classical Arabic Wisdom Literature: Nature and Scope', in *Journal of the American Oriental Society*, 101, p. 49-86.

M. Richard (1962), 'Florilèges grecs', in *Dictionnaire de Spiritualité*, 5, cols. 475-512.

B. Tillett (2004), 'What is FRBR? A conceptual model for the bibliographic universe', in *Library of Congress Cataloging Distribution Service*, 25, p. 1-8.

MAXIM ROMANOV

TOWARD THE DIGITAL HISTORY OF THE PRE-MODERN MUSLIM WORLD: DEVELOPING TEXT-MINING TECHNIQUES FOR THE STUDY OF ARABIC BIOGRAPHICAL COLLECTIONS

Introduction

Historians of the pre-modern Muslim world are blessed with hundreds of Arabic historical sources, abundant in well-structured biographical records.[1] Largely multi-volume, each chronicle or biographical dictionary includes biographies in numbers that range from several hundred to tens of thousands. The largest source of this kind – *The History of Islam* (*Ta'rīkh al-Islām*) of al-Dhahabī († 748/1347 CE) – comprises 52 volumes, covers 700 years of Islamic history, and includes approximately 30,000 biographies.[2] The overall number of biographies in these sources reaches hundreds of thousands.[3]

A great number of these biographies are rather short notices – they often list only the name of a person with dates of his (more rarely, her) birth and death, whether precise or approximate. However, even onomastic data alone provides historians with a great deal of valuable information, mainly due to the part of the Muslim name known as the *nisba* ('descriptive name'). Let us take a close look at the following name:

---

[1] Paul Auchterlonie's reference – now outdated and incomplete, but still very helpful – lists over two hundred biographical sources. See Auchterlonie 1987.

[2] al-Dhahabī 1990; on this source, see Somogyi 1932.

[3] Over ninety years ago Italian scholars Leone Caetani and Guiseppe Gabrieli collected 250,000 biographical references, see Malti-Douglas & Fourcade 1976. My own biographical databank, which is still in the process of preparation, already includes over 86,000 biographies and biographical records (with only 24 biographical dictionaries processed).

10.1484/M.LECTIO-EB.5.102573

Abū l-Faraj 'Abd al-Raḥmān, the son of (ibn) 'Alī, the son of (ibn) Muḥammad, the son of (ibn) [so-and-so] [...], the son of (ibn) Muḥammad, the son of (ibn) Abī Bakr al-Ṣiddīq, al-Jawzī, al-Qurashī, al-Taymī, al-Bakrī, al-Baghdādī, al-Ḥāfiẓ, al-Mufassir, al-Ḥanbalī, al-Wā'iẓ, al-Ṣaffār.

This name includes nine meaningful descriptive names,[4] which tell us that this particular person belonged to the clan of Taym (al-Taymī) of the tribe of Quraysh (al-Qurashī) and was a descendent of Abū Bakr al-Ṣiddīq (al-Bakrī), the first of the four Rightly-guided caliphs of the Islamic community; a native of Baghdād (al-Baghdādī) and a jurist of the Ḥanbalī school of law (al-Ḥanbalī), he distinguished himself as a knowledgeable transmitter of Islamic tradition (al-Ḥāfiẓ), an exegete of the Qur'ān (al-Mufassir) as well as a public preacher (al-Wā'iẓ); the last nisba (al-Ṣaffār) also tells us that he came from a family that earned its living selling copper utensils.[5] Thus, the onomastic information alone is tantamount to the social profile of a person. Studied as a whole, such social profiles can serve as unique lenses through which the historian can study different aspects of social history, which would otherwise be indiscernible.[6] Additionally, such profiles – in their entirety – form a unique body of data, which is ideally suited to different forms of sociological and spatial analyses.

People who became the subjects of these biographical records, of course, were not simple commoners. By and large, they were representatives of religious, administrative, military and literary

---

[4] In strict grammatical terms, a nisba is an adjective formed from a noun by means of adding suffix 'ī' and thus denoting a relation to the noun from which it was formed (Baghdād + ī => Baghdādī, meaning something or someone related to the city of Baghdād). In historical terms, however, the nisba does not seem to be limited to this particular morphological pattern; the term is rather used for any word that can meaningfully describe a person (including but not limited to such morphological patterns as fā'il, fa'īl, fa''āl[a], dhū shay'[ayn] etc.). This is particularly true in the case of al-Sam'ānī who included all of them in his Kitāb al-ansāb (The Book of Descriptive Names).

[5] In addition, the number of ancestors mentioned in the name (each begins with 'the son of [...]') tends to be proportional to the overall fame of a person.

[6] For a clear conceptualization of the approach, see Bulliet 1970. A somewhat similar approach, although more from a literary studies perspective, was offered in Fähndrich 1973. Unfortunately, the study promised in Fähndrich's work never came to fruition.

elites. Nonetheless, the lives of these notables are often presented with so many details that studying them as a whole will also shed light on the life of rank-and-file believers.

Prior attempts

A number of scholars have realized the potential of Islamic biographical sources, yet very few have ventured to approach them quantitatively. In the 70s and 80s, on the wave of popularity of quantitative methods in history,[7] several scholars from different countries conducted methodologically similar studies, largely independently from each other. Analyzing biographies *en masse*, historians looked for answers to often quite different research questions. In Israel, Hayyim Cohen studied economic backgrounds of the early religious elite (Cohen 1970). In the USA, Richard Bulliet studied the social and religious elite of Nīshāpūr (Bulliet 1972), and later the process of conversion to Islām (Bulliet 1979); Carl Petry studied the civilian elites of Mamlūk Cairo (Petry 1981). In the USSR, a group of Soviet scholars inspired by Piotr A. Griaznevich studied the development of Arabic historical and religious writings in different areas of the Caliphate.[8] The scholars of the Onomasticon Arabicum project produced a series of publications on a number of biographical dictionaries.[9]

Of all these scholars, however, only Bulliet and Petry remained faithful to the quantitative approach and produced more than a single study. The neglect of this kind of approach was mainly due to its extremely laborious and time-consuming nature (even with the help of early computers, which were anything but user-friendly at that time). The abundance of information was – and still remains – unfathomable, so research was extremely time-consuming and even the brave ones soon opted out from this kind of studies. From the middle of the 1980s until the end of the

---

[7] On the fate of quantitative methods in history, see Reynolds 1998.

[8] All from the Leningrad Branch of the Institute of Oriental Studies of the Academy of Sciences of the USSR. Of four planned books, three were published. Unfortunately, written in Russian, they remained unknown to Western scholars. See Boyko 1977; Prozorov 1980; Boyko 1991. All books have summaries in English.

[9] See Graff & Bichard-Bréaud 1971; Pascual 1971; Bichard-Bréaud 1973; Malti-Douglas & Fourcade 1976; Rowson & Bonebakker 1980.

1990s there were almost no studies that relied on this approach. In the late 1990s, advancements in computer technologies and the availability of personal computers stimulated a few more attempts (most notably the Jerusalem Prosopography Project [JPP] founded and directed by Michael Lecker;[10] and the [Netherlands] Ulama Project [NUP] of John Nawas and Monique Bernards),[11] but the potential of the approach is still far from having been realized.

The main problem with the quantitative approach was posed by its very advantage: the limitless data available for analysis. Anyone attempting to implement this approach had to set very strict limits in order to accomplish one's research project: limits on the number of sources, historical periods, geographical areas, and clearly formulated research goals; all this at a time when computers were not widely available and even when they were their use often posed new kinds of problems (no support for Arabic, encoding issues, etc.).[12] Overall, one had to define clearly the research goals, select a limited number of sources, and carefully consider kinds of data required for the research. After careful planning one had to peruse the selected sources, manually extract the required information, and then record it either on paper media or to encode it for transfer to 'the memory bank of a computer'. These technologically imposed limitations also affected the usability of the extracted information: in many cases, the potential of the created databanks was exhausted by the end of the research project, for which they were created. This must have also contributed to the unattractiveness of such endeavors.

---

[10] On Michael Lecker's work and his Jerusalem Prosopography Project, see his webpage: ⟨http://micro5.mscc.huji.ac.il:81/JPP/homepage/⟩. Overall, this seems to be a rather conventional prosopographical project, in many aspects similar to those on Ancient Rome, Byzantium and Medieval Europe. It deals with Early Islamic Administration (c. 622-800) and includes 1,650 persons. For a study based on this project, see Ebstein 2010.

[11] For the technical description of the project, see Nawas & Bernards 1998; for studies based on the NUP database, see Bernards & Nawas 2003; Nawas 2005 and 2006.

[12] Essentially, each project had to develop its own coding system, but in the case of computerized databases it was a particularly important and complex task, especially if a group of scholars was expected to be involved. To appreciate the scale of such an enterprise, see Malti-Douglas & Fourcade 1976, which is a 100 page manual for the Onomasticon Arabicum project.

Needless to say, these technical limitations inhibited the realization of the promises offered by the quantitative approach. Later, when computers became personal and more user-friendly, several more attempts were made to study large bodies of biographical records. (The change in computer standards also played a nasty trick, since previously digitized information now had to be converted to a format readable by new machines, which did not always work out well and some computerized databanks remained on obsolete media.[13])

It was expected that new computerized databases would 'open up a new range of questions that can be asked that would hitherto have been unthinkable "without 500 monks at hand"'.[14] In real life, however, they offered only marginal advantages over the old-fashioned pen-and-paper systems. It is true that they increased the speed and complexity of data retrieval from databases. Yet, they offered no significant improvements for the most tedious process of entering data into databases. Thus, the newcomers continued to suffer from the same limitations as their analog predecessors. Their creation remained equally time-consuming and for this reason a number of projects were never finished.[15] This seems to be true of the above-mentioned JPP and NUP databases: they were created over a rather long period of time, included a relatively small number of biographic profiles (1,650 people in the JPP and 1,000 in the NUP), and their 'coefficient of efficiency' – in terms of numbers of studies based on them and their overall impact on the field – was insignificant, playing well into the hands of the critics of prosopographical and quantitative studies. Another problem with large-scale database projects

---

[13] For example, this happened to Carl Petry's databank, which still remains on magnetic tapes and requires special equipment and expertise in order to be transferred to a modern type of media (from personal conversations with Carl Petry); interestingly enough, old-fashioned analog databases remained immune to these advancements in technology – Richard Bulliet's analog database on Mcbee Keysort cards still serves him almost fifty years after his project began (from personal conversations with Richard Bulliet). For an example of usage of McBee Keysort cards in humanities, see, e.g., Anderson 1953.

[14] The quote is from Mathisen 2007, p. 95. The article is an interesting overview of the use of databases – both analog and digital – in history (prosopography, to be more precise); it is also an excellent representation of the conventional relational database approach with all its advantages and disadvantages.

[15] On this issue, see Mathisen 2007.

is that they often tend to take on a life of their own, gradually transforming from the means into an end in themselves.

I myself had experience in dealing with conventional relational databases when I suggested that the methods used by the above-mentioned Boyko, Griaznevich and Prozorov be computerized. Working with Stanislav Prozorov, my mentor at the St Petersburg Branch of the Institute of Oriental Studies of the Russian Academy of Sciences,[16] I developed a database for the study of Arabic historical sources; however, its earthly manifestation turned out to be quite different from what we both envisioned and hoped for.[17] As always, the bottleneck of the database was the process of entering data, and 'without 500 monks at hand' it was an incredibly inefficient and time-consuming task for a lone graduate student. Eventually, I had to abandon this method and look for alternative ways of analyzing historical data.

New approach

Almost ten years later, however, I am hopeful that there is an efficient way of overcoming these limitations of conventional relational databases. Proposed here is a method that capitalizes on a number of developments in the digital sphere that allow for a very different angle of approach. First, a great number of Arabic historical texts became available in fully searchable format – huge digital libraries are now available on a number of Arabic websites, CDs, DVDs and even dedicated hard drives.[18] Second, the development and wide acceptance of the Unicode standard has made it possible to work efficiently with Arabic texts on personal

---

[16] This is the same academic institution where Piotr Griaznevich's project on the study of the formative period of Arabic historiographical literature took place. Currently, the name of the institution is the Institute of Oriental Manuscripts of the Russian Academy of Sciences («www.orientalstudies.ru»).

[17] The project was described in details in Prozorov & Romanov 2003.

[18] Most of the available texts are very careful reproductions of printed editions, often with pagination and inconsistencies of printed editions faithfully preserved; there are exceptions and one should always collate such electronic texts with their paper editions. It should be noted here that most of the editions published in the Arab world are not critical (at least not in the rigorous sense of European medievalists and classicists), however, they are widely used by the scholars of medieval Islam if only because there are no other editions available and most of the manuscripts are not easily accessible.

computers (although it must be said that quite a few frustrating quirks, especially when dealing simultaneously with Arabic and non-Arabic characters, still remain unsolved). Third, Unicode also made it possible to use powerful tools such as scripting languages and regular expressions in the analysis of Arabic texts. Python is one of the most popular scripting languages for text-mining tasks, while regular expressions are a powerful tool for manipulating patterned text.

The method is meant to overcome two major issues. The first issue is to reduce time costs of laborious data entry by 'delegating' the task as much as possible to the computer. The second issue is to overcome the structural rigidity of conventional relational databases in order to make the database easily adaptable to new tasks, to make it available for research purposes as soon as possible, and to avoid the trap of the database becoming the goal in itself.

The solution for the first issue rests on the premise that we are dealing with highly structured texts where specific kinds of information (e.g., chronological, onomastic, and toponymic data) conform to distinctive textual patterns, which can be described with regular expressions. The solution for the second rests on the following proposition. Keeping in mind that the development of a database structure is a lengthy process that requires advance knowledge of all relevant types of information and their inter-relations (the finished structure does not tolerate well any later alterations), this task should be postponed until the moment when all the required information is extracted and research questions are not only clearly formulated, but also adjusted to the available data. Thus, data are stored in 'source files', which become a databank that can be updated with new kinds of information at any moment; they also serve as the source from which a database could be automatically (re)generated at any time to fit current research agenda.

Given the unique organization and peculiar textual patterns of each individual source, it has to be treated separately and as a whole. First, the source must be tagged in a specific manner, so that a computer (or, more precisely, scripts) may differentiate between its structural elements and split the text of the source into independent data units, such as descriptions of events and texts of biographies/obituaries. These independent units of in-

235

formation become 'source files', where required information is stored in machine-readable format, which can be fed into a database. Mapping the structure is a rather tiresome task, but it allows preservation of the entire text of the source and it need be done only once. Moreover, there are ways to simplify this task, first, by using short tags for the markup of all structural elements (e.g., '|' – for a chapter of the first level; '||' – for a chapter of the second level, etc; '$' – for a biography of a man; '$$' – for a biography of a woman)[19] and, second, by using highlighting schemes, which helps both to avoid typos and to make structural elements easily visible (if tagged correctly, headings are highlighted according to the user-defined conditions, see fig. 1).[20]

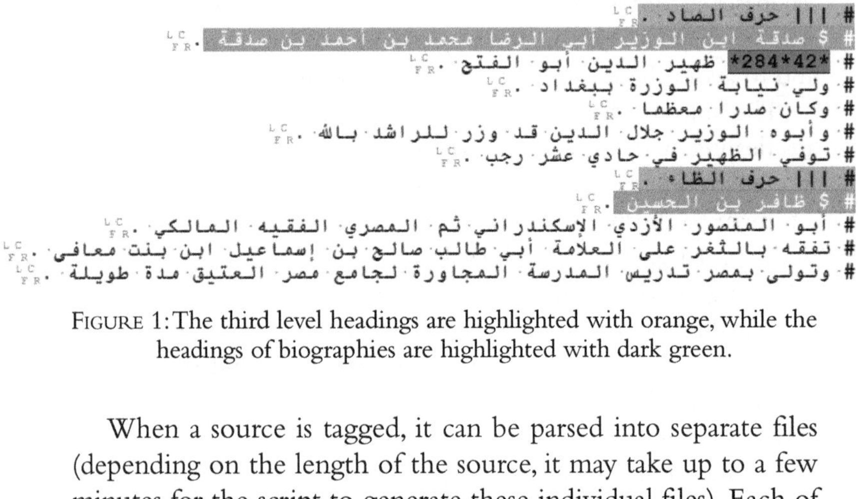

FIGURE 1: The third level headings are highlighted with orange, while the headings of biographies are highlighted with dark green.

When a source is tagged, it can be parsed into separate files (depending on the length of the source, it may take up to a few minutes for the script to generate these individual files). Each of the newly generated files has two parts: the first one is a *cubaron*,[21] the paragraph that contains tagged metadata extracted from the source; and the second one is an *eNass*,[22] the actual text of a bi-

---

[19] These tags can later be easily transformed into TEI tags. In the case of Arabic texts, this is actually the best way to follow, since angle brackets as well as other technical symbols behave erratically when combined with Arabic letters; adding corrections and changes to such text is particularly difficult and annoying.

[20] This functionality is available in EditPad Pro (‹http://www.editpadpro. com/›), the only text editor, which handles long text files, supports Unicode, regular expressions and customizable highlighting schemes.

[21] I borrowed this term from the Onomasticon Arabicum project, where it is used for a paragraph, which 'gathers the totality of biographical and bibliographical information concerning one sole person' (Malti-Douglas & Fourcade 1976).

[22] From an Arabic word *nass* ('text'); the choice of both *cubaron* and *eNass* is

ography or an historical event. Initially, the *cubaron* contains the following information: the name of the source from which it was extracted, the logical path to the *eNaṣṣ* within the source (that is, the names of chapters and subchapters wherein the *eNaṣṣ* was nested), the volume number and page locations of the *eNaṣṣ* text for easy reference, and the type of information that the *eNaṣṣ* contains (e.g., *biography* or *event*). The source files are now ready for text-mining scripts.

Within the Onomasticon Arabicum project, participating scholars extracted and encoded all relevant information from biographies, which included the following rubrics: names with each of their numerous elements coded separately; physical attributes; honorifics; religious affiliations; occupations; scientific and intellectual interests; places of birth, residence, death; affiliated religious institutions; family and tribal relations; age of death; dates of birth and death.[23] Now, significant amounts of this information can be extracted and processed automatically.[24]

In the case of manual data processing each biography is encoded one by one. Computationally, however, it is more efficient to work not with biographies, but with specific kinds of data – i.e. to extract one particular kind of data at a time from all the biographies of a particular source. Each script can be easily adapted to process historical dates, descriptive names (*nisbas*), toponyms, etc.; moreover, dealing with the same type of information makes it easier to discern patterns and thus adjust both text-mining scripts and regular expressions for better performance. Another advantage of such an approach is that it will allow the historian to begin the analysis of data long before the database is complete. Starting the analysis with only a few parameters, the historian will gradually be able to increase the complexity of analysis as new parameters become available.

---

arbitrary, but necessary, since the usage of more common words makes communication very confusing.

[23] For the complete list of rubrics, see Malti-Douglas & Fourcade 1976, p. 133-134.

[24] This is not to say, however, that a computer will do all the work. The main idea behind such automation is to let the computer perform the most laborious tasks and generate information in the form of suggestions, while a human checks the suggested information and manually corrects it if necessary.

Let us return for a moment to our first example of a traditional Islamic name, which included nine meaningful descriptive names (*nisbas*). The issue is how these descriptive names can be extracted and coded automatically. To resolve this issue, we can create a machine-readable list of descriptive names from *Kitāb al-ansāb* of al-Samʿānī († 562/1166 CE), a pre-modern dictionary of descriptive names with over 4,400 entries.[25] First, the structure of the source must be tagged in the same manner as described above and then parsed into individual source files. Each entry from *Kitāb al-ansāb* includes three important units of information: 1) a descriptive name itself, 2) its vocalization, i.e. how this *nisba* should be pronounced,[26] and 3) its definition. Definitions are particularly important, since they can be used for automatic sorting of descriptive names into categories (ancestral, geographical, religious, occupational, tribal, etc.).

```
##### ansab # TITLE # كتاب الانساب للسمعاني
##### Chapter N02 # CHAPTER L1 # باب الألف
##### Chapter N01 # CHAPTER L2 # باب الألفين وما يثلثهما
##### NISBA # TYPE
##### Vol.1 p.60 - Vol.1 p.59 PAGES
##### END OF HEADING
#NIS# الآجري .
# بفتح الألف وضم الجيم وتشديد الراء المهملة هذه النسبة إلى عمل
الآجر وبيعه ونسبة إلى درب الآجر أيضا والمشهور بهذا الانتساب من
القدماء أبو بكر محمد بن خالد بن يزيد الآجري حدث عن أبي نعيم الفضل
بن دكين وسعيد بن داود الزنبري وسريج بن النعمان وعفان روى عنه أبو
بكر الشافعي وأبو عمرو بن السماك وأبو سهل بن زياد وكان ثقة وربما
سماه أبو بكر الشافعي أحمد بن خالد وإبراهيم الآجري يعد في الزهاد
وله كرامات مأثورة وأبو بكر محمد بن الحسين بن عبد الله الآجري ساكن مكة
له مصنفات كثيرة وروايات عن أبي شعيب الحراني وأحمد بن يحيى
الحلواني وغيرهما روى عنه أبو الحسن علي بن أحمد بن الحمامي المقري
والأخوان أبو الحسين علي وأبو القاسم عبد الملك ابنا محمد بن عبد الله
بشران السكري وأبو النعيم أحمد بن عبد الله الحافظ الأصبهاني وكان الآجري
ثقة صدوقا دينا وله تصانيف كثيرة وحدث ببغداد قبل سنة ثلاثين
```

FIGURE 2: A sample entry from the Kitāb al-ansāb of al-Samʿānī.

[25] For a similar task of extracting toponymic data another pre-modern dictionary can be used – *Muʿjam al-buldān* of Yāqūt al-Ḥamawī († 626/1229 CE), which includes over 14,000 entries.

[26] In medieval Arabic handwriting, short vowels and consonantal diacritical dots were often omitted. This could lead to a lot of confusion, especially in cases of words of non-Arabic origin (e.g., without diacritical dots, letters *b*, *t*, *th*, *n*, and *y* in the beginning and in the middle of a word look exactly the same). For this reason authors 'spelled out' difficult words using different descriptors of vowels and consonants.

Fig. 2 illustrates a sample entry from *Kitāb al-ansāb* with the *cubaron* above the line 'END OF HEADING,' and a beginning of the *eNaṣṣ* right below this line. #NIS# is followed by the actual *nisba* – al-Ājurrī, the subject of the entry. Highlighted with light blue, fuchsia and purple are the elements of textual patterns, which are used to extract required information (highlighting is automatic and based on regular expressions).

The line of words highlighted with light blue is the vocalization of the *nisba*, the pattern for which is rather simple – it includes names of Arabic letters, their descriptors, short vowels and a few other technical terms, which can follow each other in any order and make up a phrase of at least three words. Fig. 3 demonstrates how this pattern is rendered into a regular expression. The results of this automatic extraction were quite impressive: I had to correct only about 300 entries (i.e., less than 7%), while over 4,000 vocalizations were extracted correctly. It took about four minutes for the script to parse the entire book.

FIGURE 3: Regular Expression for vocalizations.

The task of extracting definitions is more complicated. It is based on the premise that each thematic section begins with a rather limited number of *technical expressions*, instances of which are frequent enough to make automatic extraction not only possible, but also efficient.

In terms of patterns, the structure of definitions can be described in the following manner. The first common pattern begins with one *technical expression* (TE) and ends with another. In the current example, the *initial* TE is 'this *descriptive name* [refers to]' (*hādhihi l-nisba* [*ilá*], highlighted with fuchsia), while the *terminal* TE is 'and known under this description' (*wa-l-mashhūr bi-hādhā l-intisāb*). This terminal TE is in fact an initial TE for another section of information – the list of people known to bear this name. Thus, the definition itself is the text that starts with the initial TE and ends right before the terminal TE. The second pattern has an initial TE, but does not have a terminal TE; definitions of this pattern are the text of the initial TE plus 10-15 words that follow it. The third common pattern has no initial TE, but does have a terminal TE. Definitions of this pattern are the text from the very beginning of an entry until the beginning of a terminal TE, minus *vocalization*, which was extracted by the previous script and is now available for manipulations.

Instances that do not fall into these patterns are not numerous and can be tagged manually. Fig. 4 shows the results of running the definition script.

```
>>> ============================== RESTART ============
>>>
.........1000.........2000.........3000.........4000....
----------------------------------------------------
Processed definitions:        4450
Unprocessed definitions:         9

----------------------------------------------------

Both topoi:                   3610
Fixed pattern:                  16
Initial only:                  702
Terminal only:                  73
Manually tagged:                39
Without definitions:            10

----------------------------------------------------

Execution time: 0:04:28.878000
```

FIGURE 4: The results of running a script that extracts definitions.

After the application of these two scripts, the updated *cubaron* of each source file looks similar to what is shown in fig. 5, where both the vocalization and the definition of the descriptive name are extracted and tagged.

The last step in text-mining this particular source is to assign each *nisba* to a specific category, or categories, by using sets of keywords. The definition of this particular *nisba*, al-Ājurrī, says the following: 'This descriptive name refers to the production and selling of 'baked bricks', it may also refer to the Darb al-Ājurr ['the Road of Baked Bricks,' a quarter in the western part of Baghdād]'. Thus, this definition contains such keywords as 'production' (*'amal*) and 'selling' (*bay'*), which can be used to automatically assign the *nisba* to the category of *occupation*, and the keyword 'road' (*darb*), which can be used to categorize it also as a toponymic *nisba*. This particular case has to be finalized manually, since the same descriptive name refers to two different entities. However, most descriptive names do not pose such a complication. After these tasks are accomplished, the data from the source files can be converted into formats suitable for other text-mining tasks.

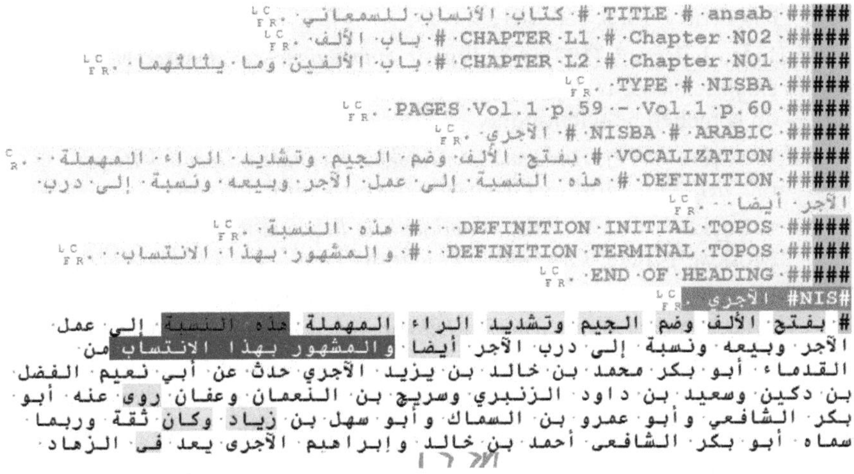

FIGURE 5: The same example from *Kitāb al-ansāb* ('The Book of Descriptive Names') with the updated *cubaron*.

***

The project advanced rather significantly since the paper was delivered in April of 2012. As the work progresses it is becoming clear that text-mining techniques allow not only a realization of the full potential of the quantitative approach, which was proposed over forty years ago, but also opens new, much richer opportunities for the study of classical Arabic sources of various genres. Updates on this ongoing project can be found online at www.alraqmiyyat.org.

Bibliography

al-Dhahabī (1990), *Tārīkh al-Islām wa-wafayāt al-mashāhīr wa-al-a'lām*, Bayrūt, Lubnān: Dār al-Kitāb al-'Arabī.

G. L. Anderson (1953), 'The McBee Keysort System for Mechanically Sorting Folklore Data', in *The Journal of American Folklore*, 66, 262, p. 340-343.

P. Auchterlonie (1987), *Arabic biographical dictionaries: a summary guide and bibliography*, Durham: Middle East Libraries Committee.

M. Bernards & J. Nawas (2003), 'The Geographic Distribution of Muslim Jurists during the First Four Centuries AH', in *Islamic Law and Society*, 10, p. 168-181.

P. Bichard-Bréaud (1973), *Traitement automatique des données biographiques; analyse et programmation*, Paris: Éditions du Centre national de la recherche scientifique.

K. A. Boyko (1977), *Arabskaia istoricheskaia literatura v Ispanii: VIII-pervaia tret' XI v*, Moskva: Glavnaia red. vostochnoi literatury.

K. A. Boyko (1991), *Arabskaia istoricheskaia literatura v Egipte, IX-X vv*, Moskva: 'Nauka,' Glav. red. vostochnoi lit-ry.

R. W. Bulliet (1970), 'A Quantitative Approach to Medieval Muslim Biographical Dictionaries', in *Journal of the Economic and Social History of the Orient*, 13, p. 195-211.

R. W. Bulliet (1972), *The patricians of Nishapur: a study in medieval Islamic social history*, Cambridge, Mass.: Harvard Univ. Press.

R. W. Bulliet (1979), *Conversion to Islam in the medieval period: an essay in quantitative history*, Cambridge: Harvard Univ. Press.

H. J. Cohen (1970), 'The Economic Background and the Secular Occupations of Muslim Jurisprudents and Traditionists in the Classical Period of Islam: (Until the Middle of the Eleventh Century)', in *Journal of the Economic and Social History of the Orient*, 13, p. 16-61.

M. Ebstein (2010), 'Shurṭa chiefs in Baṣra in the Umayyad period: a prosopographical study', in *Al-Qantara (Madrid)*, 31, p. 103-147.

H. E. Fähndrich (1973), 'The Wafayāt al-A'yān of Ibn Khallikān: A New Approach', in *Journal of the American Oriental Society*, 93, p. 432-445.

Graff & P. Bichard-Bréaud (1971), *Documents sur la mise en ordinateur des données biographiques*, Paris: Éditions du Centre national de la recherche scientifique.

F. Malti-Douglas & G. Fourcade (1976), *The treatment by computer of medieval Arabic biographical data: an introduction and guide to the Onomasticum [i.e., Onomasticon] Arabicum*, Paris: Editions du Centre national de la recherche scientifique.

R. W. Mathisen (2007), 'Where are all the PDBs?: The Creation of Prosopographical Databases for the Ancient and Medieval Worlds', in *Prosopography Approaches and Applications: A Handbook*, University of Oxford, Linacre College Unit for Prosopographical Research.

J. Nawas (2005), 'A profile of the mawālī 'ulamā'', in M. Bernards & J. Nawas (eds.), *Patronate and patronage in early and classical Islam*, Leiden & Boston: Brill, p. 484-480.

J. Nawas (2006), 'The birth of an elite: mawālī and Arab 'ulamā'', in *Jerusalem Studies in Arabic and Islam*, 31, p. 74-91.

J. Nawas & M. Bernards (1998), 'A preliminary report of the Netherlands Ulama Project (NUP): the evolution of the class of 'ulamā' in Islam with special emphasis on the non-Arab converts (mawālī) from the first through fourth century A.H', in U. Vermeulen & J. M. F. Van Reeth (eds.), *Law, Christianity and modernism in Islamic society. Proceedings of the Eighteenth Congress of the Union Européenne des Arabisants et Islamisants ... Leuven ... 1996 (Orientalia Lovaniensia Analecta, 86)*, Leuven: Peeters, p. 97-109.

J. P. Pascual (1971), *Index schématique du Ta'rih Baġdād*, Paris: Éditions du Centre national de la recherche scientifique.

C. F. Petry (1981), *The civilian elite of Cairo in the later Middle Ages*, Princeton (NJ): Princeton Univ. Press.

S. M. Prozorov (1980), *Arabskaia istoricheskaia literatura v Irake, Irane i Srednei Azii v VII-seredine X v.: shiitskaia istoriografiia*, Moskva: Izd-vo 'Nauka,' Glav. red. vostochnoi lit-ry.

S. M. Prozorov, & M. G. Romanov (2003), 'Principles and procedures of extracting and processing the data from Arabic sources (based on materials of historic-and-biographical literature) / Original title: Metodika izvlecheniya i obrabotki informatsii iz arabskih istochnikov (na materiale istoriko-biograficheskoi literaturi)', in *Oriens/Vostok*, 4, p. 117-127.

J. F. Reynolds (1998), 'Do historians count anymore? The status of quantitative methods in history, 1975-1995', in *Historical methods*, 31, p. 141-148.

E. K. Rowson & S. A. Bonebakker (1980), *A computerized listing of biographical data from the Yatīmat al-dahr by al-Tha'ālib*, Paris & Los Angeles (CA): Centre national de la recherche scientique & University of California (Onomasticon Arabicum, Série 3).

J. d. Somogyi (1932), 'The Ta'rīkh al-islām of adh-Dhahabī', in *Journal of the Royal Asiatic Society of Great Britain and Ireland*, 4, p. 815-855.

SECTION 4

SCRIPT ANALYSIS

AINOA CASTRO CORREA

PALAEOGRAPHY, COMPUTER-AIDED PALAEOGRAPHY AND DIGITAL PALAEOGRAPHY: DIGITAL TOOLS APPLIED TO THE STUDY OF VISIGOTHIC SCRIPT

Introduction

It is a fact that the development of new technologies and their application to the field of Historiographical Sciences and Techniques – to Manuscript Studies using the Anglo-Saxon term – and especially to palaeography, has irrevocably changed our discipline.[1] But, although palaeography as a science has evolved greatly in recent years, thanks to the establishment of new working methods and the opening of new avenues of research, there is still much to be done in adapting it to current times, to the Digital Age. When I began my training as a pre-doctoral researcher aiming to specialise in Medieval palaeography, I was amazed by the fact that, despite the options now available with digital tools, the working methodology in handling manuscripts remained almost traditional, with all the difficulties that this entails. Even though palaeographers analyse many aspects of a script in order to compile enough evidence to support their study – to date, localise, contextualise the source and establish the script's main graphic characteristics and evolution – very few are usually included in publications, making it difficult, especially for those of us starting our palaeographical careers, to fully understand their speech and to learn from the advances made in these scholarly previous works. The opportunity to participate in this workshop has thus

---

[1] I will focus here on the research process. Regarding teaching palaeography today see Stokes 2010 and Castro 2014b.

10.1484/M.LECTIO-EB.5.102574

led me to think thoroughly about how palaeographic work can be improved and aided by digital tools, and to make some reflections using a specific Visigothic case study which might be useful for future works.

Traditional palaeography

Since the late eighteenth century, when the science of palaeography was born,[2] the elementary objectives of the discipline have changed considerably. Following a logical progression, palaeography is today not only a science devoted to the study of writing, with the basic purpose of reading 'old' texts accurately, to date and locate them geographically, but a science dedicated, alongside with Diplomatics and Codicology, to understanding texts in all their complexity. From the first distinctions and classifications between different types of writing used in Antiquity and the Middle Ages, through the specific study of the abbreviation systems and the emerging interest in establishing the origin of each type of script and its graphic evolution, palaeography has been understood, especially since the mid-twentieth century,[3] as an independent science, as a discipline that, using its own methodological procedures, focuses on the study of writing not as static entity but as a living reflection of the society to which it belongs.[4] Palaeography is a science that tries to discover when, where, by whom, how and for whom, from a historical perspective, a manuscript was made, and the vicissitudes through which it has passed since its production.[5] It is a discipline studying writing and also the object that contains it, and, as a science, is based on the application of a specific methodology for the correct graphic analysis of each document. But, how has this methodology changed, and how can it be changed, in the so-called Digital Age?

---

[2] Mabillon 1681, improved by Maffei 1727 and Tassin and Toustain 1750–1765.
[3] Further advances on the scripts of the Late Roman Empire were made, leading to a better understanding of the evolution of early medieval (national) scripts. See Schiaparelli 1930; Millares 1941; Mallon 1952; Cencetti 1954.
[4] See Petrucci 1991 and 1999.
[5] Bately 1993, p. 47.

Methodology

The required starting point for any research aiming not only to read the text of a handwritten document, but also to answer the aforementioned questions – when, where, by whom, how and for whom, from a historical perspective, a manuscript was made –, is the graphical analysis of the writing, namely the literal meaning of palaeography or micro-palaeography. Without a correct analysis of the morphological and brachygraphic characteristics of each scribe or copyist's writing, with particular attention to its specific features in relation to the canon of each graphic type, any conclusions reached during the development of the research may be unreliable.

The constituent elements of the script on which the palaeographic analysis is focused were defined by Mallon in 1952[6] and since then have been revised, enhanced and adjusted by each researcher[7] in order to analyse the particular characteristics of the specific manuscript source under study in as much detail as possible. Given the case study in question here, manuscript sources in Visigothic script, and in particular the typological variants employed in charters – cursive, semi-cursive and minuscule – the following elements can be considered fundamental:[8]

i.   Graphic quality (calligraphic to rudimentary)[9]

ii. Stroke speed (cursive versus minuscule)

---

[6] 'Pour étudier les écritures de monuments paléographiques déterminés, il faut tenir compte des notions suivantes : formes, angle d'écriture, ductus, module, « poids » de l'écriture, enfin matière subjective, sans négliger les caractères internes et notamment la nature du texte', Mallon 1952, p. 22-23. Mallon was the first scholar to determine the constituent elements of writing in order to analyse and study their characteristics and morphological evolution. His work was completed by Gilissen 1973.

[7] See Aussems 2006, p. 53-69, for a detailed historiographical revision.

[8] Aspects such as ruling, size of the writing material, material aspects (characteristics of the parchment), margins or decoration are not listed here as they are especially useful for the study of codices – and therefore codicological study – not for charters.

[9] It depends on the purpose of the document. Some palaeographers prefer to distinguish between usual writing and calligraphic style, and indeed this differentiation should be taken into account for other types of corpora (*epistolae*, inventories, catalogues, notes, etc.).

iii. Angle of inclination, distinguishing between straight and leaning to the right or left

iv. Contrast of the strokes, expressed according to the subdivisions 'pronounced', 'moderately pronounced' and 'slightly pronounced'

v. Modulus – the proportions of the letters – expressed according to the subdivisions 'flattened', 'rounded' and 'slender'

vi. Letter forms[10] – all forms and allographs, not just those traditionally considered to be representatives, should be examined, particularly for the cursive variant[11]

vii. Ductus – the sequence and direction of the different strokes that make up each graphic sign

vii. Ligatures and connections, between letters and between words

ix. Abbreviations (signs and forms)

x. Punctuation (signs and forms)

xi. Text structure – aesthetic separation between each part of the diplomatic structure, proportion of the space left within the parchment for signatures, etc. – and variations in the course of the base line[12]

xii. Linguistic features (orthography and influences)

xiii. Flourishes and other signs (symbolic *invocatio* and signatures).

The resulting graphic profile based on a detailed analysis of all these elements defines the writing of each scribe and is the starting point for the study of a particular manuscript source. Following a comparative statistical method,[13] that is, comparing the graphical features of the script used in a particular manuscript

---

[10] Regarding aspects vi, ix and x, Aussems (2006, p. 74-75) makes an important point: if a scribe is copying a text, to what extent does he copy these aspects from the archetype or does he simply use their own? When working with a copy of a charter whose original still exists, this observation must be taken into account.
[11] Only by comparing an alphabet with another it can be established which letter forms are indeed the key to identifying a scribe.
[12] See Aussems 2006, p. 73.
[13] Method proposed by Mundó (1982, p. 53-58) to replace the traditional 'direct ocular' comparison. See also Millares 1983, p. 7.

whose date and origin are unknown with those shown in a manuscript with similar characteristics[14] that can be dated and securely located – codices with colophon, charters with date and geographical references – one can answer as to when and where it was made. Extrapolating this information to the historical context, with the assistance of Codicography and Diplomatics, one can understand how the writing process of a particular manuscript was developed and for whom or for what purpose it was prepared. At the same time, studying the writing itself without comparing examples provides information about its author. The greater or lesser perfection of his script, its refinement, differentiation among calligraphic, semi-calligraphic, rudimentary or semi-rudimentary – or, if one prefers, among 'professional', 'usual' and 'elemental' – reflects the scribe's competence and dedication to his work. The angle of inclination and the modulus shown by the script has proven useful not only for differentiating hands but also regional variants of Visigothic script.[15] The way in which a scribe makes and marks the abbreviations is essential to assessing exogenous influences; for example, the use of superscripted letters indicates an increasing influence of Carolingian script and the existence of routes of cultural exchange throughout Europe. The analysis of the text, form and content, from a textual and philological view, and the punctuation system likewise provides information about the cultural level of the schools and the circulation of books and ideas in the scribe's environment during his career.[16] Also, regarding the signs, for example the study of the Christogram symbol, usually included at the beginning of the texts in charters as well as preceding the signatures, not only helps to differentiate a hand but has also shown interesting results for dating and localizing manuscript sources.[17]

As can be seen, the palaeographic research process certainly involves approaching the text from a global perspective of the cultural history within which it is located (the history of writing,

---

[14] Manuscripts presumed to pertain to the same period, country and region, from the same cultural context and, obviously, written in the same typological variant of a particular script. See Mundó 1982, p. 54.

[15] See del Camino 2012.

[16] See Díaz y Díaz 1997.

[17] See Castro 2014b.

books and reading, the history of written culture), considering the artefact not just as a graphic example, but also as a social, economic, political, linguistic and artistic representation of a specific place in a specific historical period. That is, palaeography is an obviously interdisciplinary science which is of fundamental importance to the study of each source in all its complexity.

Problems

A specific methodology to be followed in order to perform the palaeographic study of a manuscript source represents an improvement, but also involves difficulties in obtaining and sharing the results.

The first problem of applying the method of analysis discussed above is the subjective nature and judgmental descriptive terms of some of the criteria to be analysed. Using words alone, it is not a simple task to scientifically define the aesthetic quality of the writing, the contrast of the strokes or the modulus, for all researchers in order that they can compare graphic examples from different sources.[18] Consequently, palaeographic science has been considered 'an authoritarian discipline, the pertinence of which depends on the authority of the author and the faith of the reader';[19] an inexact science based in the reliability and demonstrated expertise of the researcher. The solution to this problem has been seen in the so-called 'quantitative palaeography', statistical method that entails employing numerical values for measuring the significant features of handwriting, largely discussed.[20] But regardless of whether the researcher adapts numerical data on the criteria of analysis, there are still drawbacks to consider.

Published palaeographical studies based on sources in Visigothic script do not tend to include enough detailed images or

---

[18] See Treharne 2011, especially note 13, which offers a compendium of several ways to define these criteria.

[19] Derolez 2003a, p. 7-9 (9).

[20] See Gilissen 1974. Regarding the debate on 'quantitative palaeography' following Bischoff's foresight ('With the aid of technological advances palaeography, which is an art of seeing and comprehending, is in the process of becoming an art of measurement', 1990, p. 3), see: 'Commentare Bischoff'; Derolez 2003a, p. 2, 7-9, and 2003b; and Stokes 2009.

specific quantitative data to support their conclusions.[21] That is, these studies lack the full graphic profile in addition to measures relating to the writing slant or modulus in each graphic form, which would be essential for any expert to assess the conclusions proposed by their author and to provide the objective data that would allow hand differentiation given another source. The specialist undoubtedly takes all these aspects into consideration, but manually preparing them for inclusion in a piece for publication is an arduous task. As a result, one must rely on the palaeographer's experience when he says, for example, that a scribe is characterised by the use of a grapheme or sign with a specific form that does not exactly match the standard of each graphical mode. But what about the other elements? Must we assume that they are of no interest just because the researcher did not, or could not, present them in his publication? As Derolez has openly stated, 'when an extremely experienced palaeographer [...] fails to indicate the criteria on which his statement is based, he may be a perfect connoisseur, but he is not being an effective teacher.'[22] Regarding the study of Visigothic script, there are brilliant published studies that go further than the basic characteristics of this script to the specific features that may indicate regional variants and chronology, but to clearly understand the specialist work, one must be a specialist oneself in this script to appreciate the complexity of the details provided and read between the lines without seeing them. Thus, the investigation continues from these works, moving slowly and including the subjective assumptions of each reader.[23]

Another obstacle is the question of how to organise large bodies of sources. Working with a corpus of a couple of hundred documents, it is a slow but feasible task to develop the full record of each of the manuscript samples considered and to compare the results looking for examples that may correspond, within reasonable doubt, to the same hand; if the sample is a corpus much larg-

---

[21] This is not always the case when working with sources written in other scripts. See the *Digipal* project.

[22] Derolez 2003a, p. 2.

[23] Exceptions that should be a model for future works on Visigothic script are compiled in Alturo 2012; as an example, del Camino 2012 highlights that the subjectivity of previous works, in which specific and quantitative data were not included, prevents her from presenting more reliable conclusions.

er than that, the task becomes unrealistic.[24] All the features that a palaeographer sees when examining a manuscript source must be retained in order to use them later when drawing conclusions, and the specialist needs to see everything available. Visual memory is indispensable in traditional palaeography to identifying concordances between scribes. Going back to the study of Visigothic script, how can one retain thousands of sources in memory, or in the 'palaeographic eye', when trying to distinguish a regional variant?[25]

So, could the use of any type of software help us to include a complete graphic profile based on the elements analysed, which would allow others to understand, evaluate and criticise our findings, and to use the data in future studies on other sources? Would it be possible to incorporate some application of digital analysis that would make the critical process faster, easier and more objective without losing quality? To what extent can palaeography benefit from recent advances in software development?

Palaeography and new technologies

The introduction in the last few years of digital applied techniques to the great range of disciplines that can be considered in any palaeographic investigation marks the logical evolution of this science. Indeed, the potential use of computer programs in palaeography was advocated and evaluated by several researchers long before the software became a reality.[26] But how does the study of manuscript sources benefit from applying these advances?

'Computer-aided' palaeography

With the arrival of the Digital Age, the possibilities for the study of manuscript sources have grown significantly. As a result of advances in the fields of digitisation and cataloguing of

---

[24] See, for example, the study of 350,000 fragments to establish groups coming from the same source, explained in Wolf 2010.

[25] See Castro 2012b.

[26] Mundó 1982, p. 58.

manuscript sources, and because there is now at our disposal a wealth of online resources to work with, it is easier to access digital reproductions of those sources of interest and to study them outside the confines of archives or libraries.[27] Having these digital 'surrogates'[28] marks the beginning of a change in palaeographic research, but it is up to the researcher to make the most of them.

Term 'computer-aided palaeography' is understood as the integration of text manipulation programs or digital image processing tools into the traditional methods of analysing and transcribing manuscript sources. Applications designed to interact directly with the text (to transcribe, edit or comment on it) provide flexibility to the editing work and also serve as collaborative tools allowing to participate in ongoing online projects such as 'T-Pen: Transcription for palaeographical and editorial notation' or 'eLaborate'. Image manipulation applications, such as Adobe Photoshop or its free counterpart GIMP, facilitate the incorporation into published work of samples of the study process, like graphics or pictures from a given source, as will be discussed below. Both programs allow one to enlarge or reduce the image to see in greater or lesser detail, but also to digitally calculate distances and all the measures needed instead of using a protractor and a ruler in the traditional way; likewise, to alter the image in order to facilitate the segmentation of graphical forms, or even to carry out restoration or recovery of corrupted text that is illegible or difficult to read with the naked eye.[29]

In addition to facilitating the preparation and presentation of an improved edition of the text, these tools permit the scholar to include in his or her work, with patience and investment of time, a complete record of every hand, covering all the constituent elements of its script. Computer-aided palaeography provides a degree of objectivity – though it is still the researcher who selects the graphic forms to be considered and takes measurements ap-

[27] See Sexy Codicology's map of digitised medieval manuscripts. For Spanish manuscripts online see PARES (Portal de Archivos Españoles). For virtual libraries see Uhlíř 2009 (*Manuscriptorium*). And, for a guide to resources, see also Castro 2014.
[28] See Terras 2010.
[29] See Craig-McFeely 2010.

propriate to his study – and results in a clearer and more open ex-
position to the scientific community. The aspects analysed when
working with primary sources do not change, nor does the way
we approach them. But could the software take the role of the
researcher? That is, could it automatically extract the graphic segments of each of the representative elements?

'Digital palaeography'

The term 'digital palaeography' (coined by Ciula in 2005) refers
to a range of research projects aimed at developing software or
applying existing software from other disciplines to handwriting
analysis,[30] which helps the palaeographer to incorporate quantitative – and not just qualitative – data in his work when presenting the research process undertaken. As a result, these tools can
also extend the corpus under study and help manage the large
number of sources that are now available in digital format.

Based on the digital image of a manuscript source, the main
objectives already tested with these applications have focused on:
recovering text that is hidden to the naked eye by applying specific techniques, such as Hyperspectral Image Analysis (HSI),[31]
and the automatic identification of scribes, differentiating their
work in a manuscript source and automatically obtaining transcriptions.[32]

---

[30] *Ex.* forensic Graphology (Stokes 2007-2008).

[31] This technique measures the reflectance of a document at a high spatial and
spectral resolution allowing the non-invasive recovery of text which, in its current state, is totally or partially damaged and unreadable by direct manipulation,
such as palimpsests (Salerno 2007). See also Shiel 2009; Giacometi 2012. HSI can
be used to check if there is text on the back of those charters to which a sheet
of paper or parchment has been added as reinforcement without having to remove it, something that is very common in the manuscript sources in Visigothic
script and for which the traditional method used to highlight ink, ultraviolet
lamps, is not possible. HSI also has application in relation to identification of
scribes since it can allow the separation of text layers; it can identify where different hands have intervened in a document, which part of the text corresponds
to one hand or another, and the chronological order in which they were involved
in its production, differentiating inks by their specific spectral signature.

[32] Applications developed for this purpose are based on image binarization
and segmentation followed by character (graphic symbol) analysis, and ink analysis. Examples: Fusi 2009 (application of an Artificial Neuronal Network); Ciula

Applying programs to provide graphic profiles of a scribe's writing can make palaeographical studies easier, but to select features and extract specific numerical values for each example are still semi-automatic processes that require the palaeographer's interpretation at each step.[33] Identification of scribes through ink analysis seems to have more potential.[34] HSI speeds up the analytical process and provides information that could not otherwise be accessed, as well as objectivity in relation to the study of the handwritten sources analysed, and the data obtained, for example, in the differentiation of ink/hands, since it can provide specific numerical values and measurements that do not depend on the scholar's perception. Its application to the study of Visigothic script sources, or any kind of manuscript source, will definitely mark a turning point working with palimpsests or, for example, charters written by several scribes. It can even help to analyse the writing process itself since it can highlight emendations. However, not all the archives provide the use of this technique.

Digital tools applied to the study of Visigothic script

The development of new digital tools designed to analyse the formal features of writing seems very promising, but there is still a long way to go in terms of testing before they can be fully applied to palaeographical research. With the exception of *Graphoskop*,[35] the tools referred to are not open access. Also, and despite its great potential, based on the examples mentioned, it is difficult to obtain good results applying these prototypes to the study of Visigothic script and particularly to the cursive variant due to its specific characteristics.[36] In the meantime, the tools mentioned in the first group ('computer-aided palaeography'),

2005 and 2009 (SPI/JSPI software); Tomasi 2009 (BIT-Alpha plus OCR/ICR); Aussems 2009 (ink analysis: *Quill*).

[33] See note 32. For example, in an ANN (also applying SPI/JSPI) the specialist must manually extract samples to feed the neural recognition system 'library'. BIT-Alpha segments the samples itself, but it still needs validation.

[34] See Ira Rabin's chapter within this volume.

[35] Gurrado 2009.

[36] In the minuscule variant, allographs, ligatures and/or connections are used less frequently, making feasible the graphic segmentation of features and the eventual automatic recognition of them as well as the differentiation of hands.

such as the image-processing ones, can improve palaeographic analysis even using only the most basic of the available functions. The process is slow and laborious, but, as will be discussed below, it can provide good results.

Working on identifying regional variants

'Visigothic script' refers to the Latin script used between about the eighth and thirteenth centuries in the territories that once formed the ancient Visigothic kingdom [fig. 1 and 2].

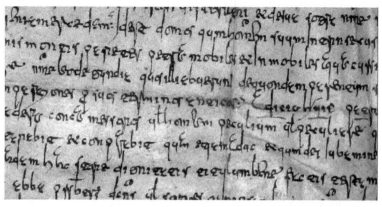

FIGURE 1: Example of cursive Visigothic script. ACLu., Libro X de pergaminos, legajo 2, n° 3.

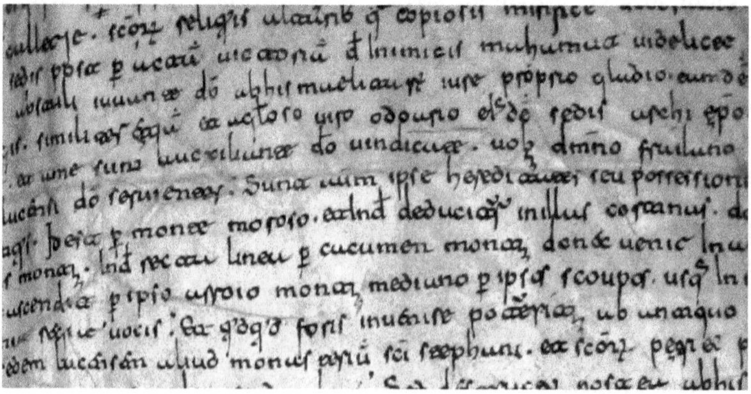

FIGURE 2: Example of minuscule Visigothic script. ACLu., Libro X de pergaminos, legajo 2, n° 1.

In the last century, palaeographers established the basic graphical characteristics of the script (variants, morphology, abbreviations, evolution, etc.) and discussed its possible origin (genetic, chronological and geographical). Since then research on this script has focused on further analysis of regional characteristics. The study of this aspect is very important for setting the geographical location of all those sources which, if analysed in isolation, could not be ascribed with certainty to a specific production centre, such as codices without colophon, or fragments. Their graphic features can be compared with those of the scripts for which a provenance and date has been determined, such as those used in charters, in order to provide a complete context in which to continue with the study of this script, its evolution, and all the cultural aspects related to these sources.[37]

The first two areas to be differentiated were the Mozarabic and the Leonese, in the late nineteenth century, and afterwards also the Portuguese, Catalan and southern French.[38] But there is still work to be done. Despite the large volume of documentation from the ancient kingdom of Galicia preserved in Visigothic script, a detailed examination of these sources has not yet been undertaken. Consequently, the scientific community has accepted the idea that this type of script does not have enough specific features relating to this area to merit a separate study and to be considered independent of the Leonese form, in which it has traditionally been included. Thus, the main goal of my doctoral thesis was to begin the study of the Galician manuscript sources written in Visigothic script, through the representative sample of the diocese of Lugo.[39]

---

[37] See Millares 1935, p. 18; *id.* 1941, p. 40.

[38] See Alturo 2004.

[39] Of the four Galician provinces, Lugo preserves the most documentation in Visigothic script (see Castro 2012a). In addition, it has traditionally been considered the province freest from outside influences from a graphical point of view (see Lucas 1991). The project, aiming both to analyse the script and place the sources preserved within their historical/cultural context, was divided into the following tasks: (i) making a corpus, (ii) identifying the major production centres (cathedral and monastic training schools), (iii) distinguishing the material authors of these sources and relating them to each centre or school, (iv) specifying a timeline for the use of the Visigothic script in its main variants by centre, (v) determining the percentage of use of each variant within this period, (vi) identifying those characteristics which look like specifics to this area, (vii)

The first useful tool: The database

The first step in the study was to gather the necessary corpus encompassing all the Galician charters and codices preserved in Visigothic script.[40] Before directly considering all archives that might hold relevant sources, I searched for references to documentation already published in archive catalogues and in other publications related to the early medieval history of Galicia.[41] Once this guide was complete, the task was to explore the relevant archives looking for the references already found as well as for unpublished[42] material from coeval holdings. Also, to avoid as far as possible the omission of sources, I searched for documentation preserved by those institutions founded before the year 1200 – the *terminus ante quem* of use of Visigothic script in Galicia. Following these steps the manuscript sources for Lugo diocese were selected: over 150 charters, four cartularies, two fragments and a codex [fig. 3 and 4]. The good state of preservation of these testimonies meant that almost all of the sources compiled (approximately 80%) could be worked with.

ARCHIVES	ORIGINALS	TIMELINE	COPIES	TOTAL
Archivo de la Catedral de Lugo	52	918-1156	5	57
Archivo Histórico Nacional de Madrid	83	917-1196	22	105
Archivo del Monasterio de Ferreira de Pantón	4	1075-1099	–	4
Schoyen Collection	1	1115	–	1
	140	917-1196	27	167

FIGURE 3: Charters in Visigothic script from Lugo diocese by archive.

studying the evolution of each variant and (viii) comparing the results, dating and graphic features with the peculiarities of this script in other centres or of other regional variants.

[40] The inscriptions were to be collected too, but the lack of previous studies on them and the investment of time required to travel to Galician museums and archaeological sites made me postpone their study. Manuscript sources in Carolingian script dated up to 1200 were also collected in order to analyse the influences between both scripts.

[41] The main results were published in Castro 2009 and 2011.

[42] The published sources are in some cases only 20% of the total.

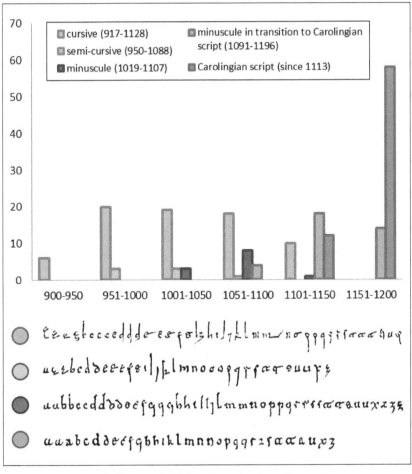

FIGURE 4: Charters in Visigothic script from Lugo diocese.
Timeline by types.

In order to manage all this information, manuscript sources and
bibliography, I decided to create a database using Microsoft Access with the following fields: (i) (ID and job status: edited, revised, etc.); (ii) archive; (iii) signature; (iv) notes on palaeographic
analysis: type of writing, particularities, etc.; (v) notes on diplomatic analysis: document type, action, etc.; (vi) historical context;
(vii) content analysis: grantor, addressee, toponyms and anthropo-
nyms; (viii) date; (ix) place; (x) summary; (xi) date (by scribe); (xii)
scribe; (xiii) documentary tradition (updated); (xiv) bibliographic
references with the attached PDF/link; and (xv) transcription.

As in an archive catalogue, each document in the corpus has its own ID which includes all the available information about it: that which comes from my study and from existing works, and that which comes directly from the document. This tool has proven very useful because it allows quick and easy searches, avoids repetition of entries or the confusion of published an unpublished documents, highlighths previous works to be kept in mind (and reviewed before starting the analysis), is easy to update with information on each document, allows completion of the fields as one works, automatically creates indexes and, most importantly, provides the option of sharing the work (online) to make it available to others.[43]

Palaeographic analysis aided by Adobe Photoshop

Some of the aforementioned constituent elements of the script in which the palaeographic analysis is based can be explained in words, but others (letter forms, ligatures and connections, abbreviations, punctuation and signatures) also require the use of images and quantitative data in order to be as objective as possible and present a complete study that other researchers can use.

The benefits of the Microsoft Access database led me to consider the option of making a database of images, a graphic catalogue of all the elements to be analysed in each written testimony. This 'library', to use the term applied in automatic recognition software, would allow further analysis of the particularities of each variant and each hand, obtain more specific information about scribes (training schools, educational level and environment), identify anonymous hands, chronologically and geographically locate a source (for example, a copy), study in detail the evolution of writing and, most importantly, add detailed visual support to the work. But, given that the software tools are not yet adapted to the palaeographer's purposes, the only option is to use programs like Photoshop, segmenting the features manually and with a lot of patience, and the same applies to obtaining quantitative data (measurements, etc.).

---

[43] Part of this information has been uploaded to CODOLGA. An edited volume of these sources is also planned.

Thus, for each analysed source I started to build a complete catalogue of graphic forms, including the percentage of use of each one in each different hand, not only for the general forms shared by all the Visigothic documents, but also for the aspects that seemed to be peculiarities of this area or of a particular scribe: forms of each letter, examples of each ligature and connection, all the abbreviations, signs indicating abbreviation and punctuation sign. To enable comparison of these images (the characteristics of each hand) I organised the segments by folders and then made tables both for each centre (cathedral, monastic and parish), variant (cursive, semi-cursive, minuscule and transition to Carolingian script) and scribe and aspect (letter forms, abbreviations, signs and so on).

The process of developing both the catalogue and the charts was very slow and laborious. However, their detail has been critical for the identification of scribes, the specific characteristics of their writing and their relation to each production centre or school.

By looking at the graphic features in the tables of analysis it is also easy to observe a number of issues that change according to the chronological period and school. For example [fig. 5], in

DISTINCTIVE FEATURES[44]		PERIOD	
		917–1017 11 scribes	1023–1128 18 scribes
slant		levorotatory 40%; dextrorotatory 20%; without slant 40%	levorotatory 17%; dextrorotatory 17%; without slant 66%
use of uncial *a*	⅄	36%	33%
use of *c* starting or ending with wavy line	e	commonly used by 80% of scribes	used only in 11% of the scribes and, likewise, with little use
use of *c* with stroke to the left	ℓ	commonly used by 60% of scribes	77% (with little use in each hand)
use of *e* with stroke to the left	ʃ	commonly used by 90% of scribes	88% (with little use in each hand)
use of *e* 'caudate'	ꝫ	18%	22%

[44] The images given show the most common version of each case.

use of *t* cursive after a or *n* (ligatures)		90%	66%
difference between the two forms of *ti/tj*		100%	88%
use of *u* cursive (ligatures)		100%	61%
abbreviation for indicating nasal		20%	33%
vertical stroke for -*um*		0%	39%
s indicating -*us*		3%	50%
'G-clef' -*us*		100%	89%
'G-clef' -*um*		80%	22%
stroke for -*is*		45%	72%
abbreviation for *que*		0%	28%
use of the Visigothic form for *per*		100%	83%
use of the Visigothic form for *qui*		90%	83%

FIGURE 5: Evolution of writing. Example: cursive Visigothic script at Lugo's Cathedral.

analysing the cursive variant used by the scribes of Lugo Cathedral (main centre) between 917-1017 and 1023-1128[45] useful in-

---

[45] These two chronological stages are distinguished given the date of the first example preserved in minuscule variant, considering the influence reflected in the cursive one.

formation is obtained relative to the slant, use of graphemes like *e* or *c* with stroke, or forms for the ending *-um/us* that will help to place the graphic example in context against other manuscript sources from the same area.

Also, doing the segmentation manually, conclusions that would be difficult to achieve with specific automatic recognition software became clear. In fig. 6 are gathered the minuscule alphabets which two contemporary scribes used in three different charters: at the top, those belonging to Nuño – in cursive Visigothic script – and, at the bottom, those of Menendo – in minuscule (in transition to Carolingian script) variant. Nuño described himself as a *diaconus* and *lucensis notarii* working from Lugo Cathedral at least between January 1084 and March 1104. Only these three charters by his hand have been preserved.[46] Comparing the characteristic features shown by Nuño's writing without looking at the whole document, that is, as a computer would do, it is unlikely that one would realise that the change in the development of the descenders in

Nuño (1084-1124).

Menendo (1091-1124).

FIGURE 6: Comparing alphabets from the same hand.

[46] These are: AHN., Sección Clero, Lugo, Catedral, carp. 1325B, n° 17 (private donation to the Cathedral); AHN., Sección Clero, Lugo, Catedral, carp. 1325B, n° 24 (exchange of lands between the cathedral and a family); and ACLu., Libro X de pergaminos, leg. 2, n° 19 (royal donation to the cathedral).

the last alphabet corresponds to a change in the social level of the grantor and not to a different hand. Menendo also worked for the cathedral, between February 1091 and May 1124. From his hand three originals and a copy have survived.[47] In this case the scribe changed the slant, used different forms for *a*, added the *e* caudate for *ae*, and the final stroke of some letters and the descenders also changed. He did not adjust his writing depending on the grantor; his style varied naturally from one document to another. Reading the texts in each document, analysing their structure and peculiarities, adding all the information included in the charts and the graphical support, it becomes easier to find similarities even when dealing with anonymous scribes and copies.

Conclusions

At the beginning of this paper the elements of writing that are analysed to build a scribe's graphic profile as a starting point for the complete study of a particular manuscript source were discussed. Some of the aspects considered, such as the slant, contrast and writing module, are themselves numeric values, while others, like the shape of graphic signs or the ductus, are issues that traditionally have been shown through graphic examples. It is a laborious task to analyse and include the first set of issues in published work, but it is possible and it is rendered far easier with the aid of certain software. Presenting detailed empirical data for the less easily measurable second group is more complicated. In order to build a complete graphic profile, it is necessary to include all the variations of the graphical forms used by the scribe and not just those considered most representative by the researcher. The incorporation of digital tools into the methodology applied to palaeographic analysis facilitates this task, but does it bring objectivity to the study of each hand's script? Manuscript analysis by computer software provides metadata for each graphic sample beyond the capability of the human eye: it is objective, high-precision and can be extrapolated so much faster than using the traditional manual

---

[47] Originals: AHN., Sección Clero, Lugo, Catedral, carp. 1325B, n° 18 (will to the cathedral); AHN., Sección Clero, Lugo, Catedral, carp. 1325C, n° 11 (royal donation); AHN., Sección Clero, Lugo, Catedral, carp. 1325C, n° 13 (private sale of a village). Copy: ACLu., Libro X de pergaminos, leg. 2, n° 2 (royal donation).

method. However, most of these tools are still in development, their creators seeking the algorithm that, with the appropriate modifications, will provide higher quality results. Leaving aside the inherent difficulties posed by the programming of software for the specific purpose of analysing writing or correctly tran-scribing text, the interaction between palaeography and digital tools applied to – or developed specifically for – the analysis of digital images of manuscript sources, must also overcome another set of constraints arising mainly from the prerequisite of bringing together specialists with advanced knowledge on both subjects. The main problem is the lack of communication, or little fluid communication, between developers and users. Palaeographers often do not fully understand the tools, so while they are able to obtain results they are unable to interact with the software using their own terminology to influence the way the system works and communicate with it. In the future, the software should allow in-teraction in order to improve both the preparation and the proper interpretation and communication of results. While technology is crucial to making of palaeography a 'true evidence-based disci-pline'[48], it is also crucial for such tools, understood both as 'objec-tive' support to the analysis conducted by the palaeographer and as a method to expedite his work, to become really useful.

Although it is true that the use of software in obtaining the metrological data of different graphic signs used by a given hand is a breakthrough, it remains uncertain whether the same soft-ware could perform the whole analytical process and study of a chosen source based on this information. The writing of any given scribe is not invariable; it depends on several factors, both conscious – for example, the intention to conform to a certain style of document – and unconscious – variation of writing tool, fatigue, etc. – that cannot be properly considered by quantitative analysis alone. If two manuscripts of the same hand produced at the same time are digitally analysed, the quantitative varia-tions of the script in both examples may be sufficiently limited for the software to relate the two and attribute both to a single scribe. But, if looking at two examples produced by the same hand, say, five years apart, the software may infer that the writing

[48] Hassner 2012, p. 185.

characteristics indicate two different hands, because it is unable to infer the graphic evolution of the scribes. Using ANN or SPI, one can establish a prototype of every shape and consider the extent of deviation to determine whether two examples correspond to the same hand. But how to quantitatively determine the likely degree of variation? The software is useful when linking identical samples, but not (at least yet) when performing the complete study of a corpus. Before Mallon established the elements of a graphic example to be analysed, palaeography was an art based solely on experience. With the addition of digital tools, the traditional methodology does not change,[49] but speeds up and gains objectivity. The starting point for the study of manuscript sources, which involves the analysis of the graphical features of writing, can now be measured in quantitative data, but the expert must consider them and draw conclusions to answer the questions of who, when and where. The 'art' of palaeographic science is 'the palaeographic eye', which judges based on experience and knowledge accumulated through working with manuscript sources,[50] analysing everything it sees. In this sense, new technologies can transform data collection quantitatively and objectively and allow sharing of a 'vision' of the manuscript, but cannot replace traditional methods, contextualise the numerical results or draw conclusions. If, however, we strive to take full advantage of the many tools now at our disposal and to continue looking for ways to improve and accelerate our research, we will benefit not only ourselves as researchers, but also enable others to better understand our work and to contribute to it with their knowledge.

Bibliography

J. Alturo (2004), 'La escritura visigótica. Estado de la cuestión', in *Archiv für Diplomatik*, 50, p. 347-386.

J. Alturo, A. Castro & M. Torras (eds.) (2012), *La escritura visigótica en la Península Ibérica: nuevas aportaciones*, Bellaterra: UAB Servei de Publicacions.

---

[49] A possible exception is the application of techniques such as DNA analysis to date and locate manuscript sources (Stinson 2010), which may also contribute to improving our understanding of parchment production and trade routes.

[50] See also Canart 2006.

M. Aussems (2006), 'Christine de Pizan and the scribal fingerprint: a quantitative approach to manuscript studies', MA thesis, University of Utrecht.

M. Aussems & A. Brink (2009), 'Digital Palaeography', in M. Rehbein, P. Sahle & T. Schaβan (eds.), Codicology and Palaeography in the Digital Age, Norderstedt: Books on Demand, p. 293-338.

J. Bately, M. P. Brown & J. Roberts (eds.) (1993), A Palaeographer's View. The selected writings of Julian Brown, London: Harvey Miller.

B. Bischoff (1990 [1979]), Latin Palaeography. Antiquity and the Middle Ages, Cambridge: Cambridge Univ. Press.

C. del Camino (2012), 'La escritura visigótica de los centros mozárabes en su período primitivo', in J. Alturo, A. Castro & M. Torras (eds.), La escritura visigótica en la Península Ibérica: nuevas aportaciones, Bellaterra: UAB Servei de Publicacions, p. 115-144.

P. Canart (2006), 'La Paléographie est-elle un art ou une science?', in Scriptorium, 60/2, p. 185.

A. Castro (2009), 'Fuentes bibliográficas para el estudio de la documentación Altomedieval gallega', in CODOLGA: Corpus Documentale Latinum Gallaeciae, 6.

A. Castro (2011), Colección diplomática altomedieval de Galicia I: documentación editada en escritura visigótica (662-1234), A Coruña: Toxosoutos.

A. Castro (2012a), 'La escritura visigótica en Galicia. Diócesis lucense y mindoniense: Cuestiones metodológicas y estado de la investigación', in A. Castro et al. (eds.), Estudiar el pasado: aspectos metodológicos de la investigación en Ciencias de la Antigüedad y de la Edad Media. Proceedings of the First Postgraduate Conference on Studies of Antiquity and Middle Ages, Oxford: British Archaeological Reports, p. 370-375.

A. Castro (2012b), 'La escritura visigótica en Galicia. I. Diócesis lucense' (unpublished doctoral thesis, Universitat Autònoma de Barcelona, 2012).

A. Castro (2014a), 'Observations on the Chrismon symbol in Visigothic script charters of Lugo diocese (917-1196)', in Scriptorium, 68/2.

A. Castro (2014b), 'Latin Palaeography: resources for teachers and students or about how not to get lost on the Internet', in Espacio, Tiempo y Forma. III. Historia Medieval, 27.

G. Cencetti (1954), Lineamenti di storia della scrittura latina, Bologna: Pàtron.

A. Ciula (2005), 'Digital palaeography: Using the digital representation of medieval script to support palaeographic analysis', in *Digital Medievalist*, 1.

A. Ciula (2009), 'The Palaeographical Method Under the Light of a Digital Approach', in M. Rehbein, P. Sahle & T. Schaβan (eds.), *Codicology and Palaeography in the Digital Age*, Norderstedt: Books on Demand, p. 219-325.

G. Costamagna et al. (1995) 'Commentare Bischoff', in *Scrittura e Civiltà*, 19, p. 325-348.

G. Costamagna et al. (1996) 'Commentare Bischoff', in *Scrittura e Civiltà*, 20, p. 401-407.

G. Costamagna et al. (1998) 'Commentare Bischoff', in *Scrittura e Civiltà*, 22, p. 397-417.

J. Craig-McFeely (2010), 'Finding What You Need, and Knowing What You Can Find: Digital Tools for Palaeographers in Musicology and Beyond', in F. Fisher, C. Fritze & G. Vogeler (eds.), *Codicology and Palaeography in the Digital Age 2*, Norderstedt: Books on Demand, p. 307-339.

A. Derolez (2003a), *The Palaeography of Gothic Manuscript Books: From the Twelfth to the Early Sixteenth Century*, Cambridge: Cambridge Univ. Press.

A. Derolez (2003b), 'Possibilités et limites d'une paléographie quantitative', in P. Defosse (ed.) *Hommages à Carl Deroux*, Brussels: Latomus, p. 98-102.

M. C. Díaz y Díaz (1997), 'La cultura medieval y los mecanismos de producción literaria', in J. I. de la Iglesia Duarte (coord.), *VII Semana de Estudios Medievales*, Nájera, p. 281-296.

D. Fusi (2009), 'Aspects of Application of Neural Recognition to Digital Editions', in M. Rehbein, P. Sahle & T. Schaβan (eds.), *Codicology and Palaeography in the Digital Age*, Norderstedt: Books on Demand, p. 175-195.

A. Giacometti et al. (2012), 'Cultural Heritage Destruction: Documenting Parchment Degradation via Multispectral Imaging', in *Electronic Visualisation and the Arts (EVA 2012)*, London, p. 301-308.

L. Gilissen (1973), *L'expertise des écritures médiévales. Recherche d'une méthode avec application à un manuscrit du XIᵉ siècle: le Lectionnaire de Lobbes*, Gand: Éditions scientifiques.

L. Gilissen (1974), 'Analyse des écritures: manuscrits datés et expertise des manuscrits non datés', in J. Glénisson & L. Hay, *Les techniques de laboratoire dans l'étude des manuscrits*, Paris: Centre national de la recherche scientifique, p. 25-35.

M. Gurrado (2009), '*Graphoskop*, uno strumento informatico per l'analisi paleographica quantitativa', in M. Rehbein, P. Sahle & T.

Schaβan (eds.), *Codicology and Palaeography in the Digital Age*, Norderstedt: Books on Demand, p. 251-259.

T. Hassner et al. (2012), 'Computation and Palaeography: Potentials and Limits (Dagstuhl Perspectives Workshop 12382)', in *Dagstuhl Reports*, 2/9, p. 184-199.

M. Lucas (1991), 'Paleografía gallega. Estado de la cuestión', in *Anuario de Estudios Medievales*, 21, p. 419-469.

J. Mabillon (1681), *De re Diplomatica libri VI*, Paris.

S. Maffei (1727), *Istoria diplomatica che serve d'introduzione all'arte critica in tal materia*, Mantova.

J. Mallon (1952), *Paléographie romaine*, Madrid.

A. Millares (1983³ [1932]), *Tratado de Paleografía Española*, Madrid.

A. Millares (1935), *Los códices visigóticos de la catedral toledana. Cuestiones cronológicas y de procedencia* (Discurso en la Real Academia de la Historia), Madrid.

A. Millares (1941), *Nuevos estudios de Paleografía Española*, México.

A. M. Mundó (1982), 'Méthode comparative-statistique pour la datation des manuscrits non datés', in *Paläographie 1981. Colloquium des Comité International de Paléographie*, München, p. 53-58.

A. Petrucci (1991), 'Storia della scrittura e storia della società', in *Anuario de estudios medievales*, 21, p. 309-322.

A. Petrucci (1999), *Alfabetismo, cultura y sociedad*, Barcelona: Gedisa.

E. Salerno, A. Tonazzini & L. Bedini (2007), 'Digital image analysis to enhance underwritten text in the Archimedes palimpsest', in *International Journal on Document Analysis and Recognition*, 9/2, p. 79-87.

L. Schiaparelli (1930), 'Note paleografiche. Intorno all'origine della scrittura visigotica', in *Archivio Storico Italiano* ser. VII, XII, p. 165-207.

P. Shiel, M. Rehbein & J. Keating (2009), 'The Ghost in the Manuscript: Hyperspectral Text Recovery and Segmentation', in M. Rehbein, P. Sahle & T. Schaβan (eds.), *Codicology and Palaeography in the Digital Age*, Norderstedt: Books on Demand, p. 159-174.

T. Stinson (2010), 'Counting Sheep: Potential Applications of DNA Analysis to the Study of Medieval Parchment Production', in F. Fisher, C. Fritze & G. Vogeler (eds.), *Codicology and Palaeography in the Digital Age 2*, Norderstedt: Books on Demand, p. 191-208.

P. A. Stokes (2007-2008), 'Palaeography and Image-Processing: Some Solutions and Problems', in *Digital Medievalist*, 3.

P. A. Stokes (2009), 'Computer-Aided Palaeography, Present and Future', in M. Rehbein, P. Sahle & T. Schaβan (eds.), *Codicology and*

Palaeography in the Digital Age, Norderstedt: Books on Demand, p. 309-338.

P. A. Stokes (2010), 'Teaching manuscript in the Digital Age', in F. Fisher et al. (eds.), *Codicology and Palaeography in the Digital Age 2*, Norderstedt: Books on Demand, p. 229-245.

R.-P. Tassin & C.-F. Toustain (1750-1765), *Nouveau Traité de Diplomatique*, 6 vols., Paris.

M. Terras (2010), 'Artefacts and Errors: Acknowledging Issues of Representation in the Digital Imaging of Ancient Texts', in F. Fisher et al. (eds.), *Codicology and Palaeography in the Digital Age 2*, Norderstedt: Books on Demand, p. 43-64.

G. Tomasi & R. Tomasi (2009), 'Approche informatique du document manuscript', in M. Rehbein, P. Sahle & T. Schaβan (eds.), *Codicology and Palaeography in the Digital Age*, Norderstedt: Books on Demand, p. 197-218.

E. Treharne (2011), 'Writing the Book: Cambridge, University Library, MS Ii. 1. 33', in *New Medieval Literatures*, 13, p. 299-308.

Z. Uhlíř & A. Knoll (2009), '*Manuscriptorium* Digital Library and EN-RICH Project: means for dealing with digital Codicology and Palaeography', in M. Rehbein et al. (eds.), *Codicology and Palaeography in the Digital Age*, Norderstedt: Books on Demand, p. 67-78.

L. Wolf et al. (2010), 'Automatic Palaeographic Exploration of Genizah Manuscripts', in F. Fisher et al. (eds.), *Codicology and Palaeography in the Digital Age 2*, Norderstedt: Books on Demand, p. 157-179.

Internet

Codicology and Palaeography in the Digital Age, ⟨http://kups.ub.uni-koeln.de/2939/ - ⟨http://www.i-d-e.de/kpdz2-online⟩

CODOLGA, ⟨http://corpus.cirp.es/codolga/⟩

DIGIPAL, ⟨http://digipal.eu/⟩

eLaborate, ⟨http://www.elaborate.huygens.knaw.nl/⟩

GRAPHEM, ⟨http://liris.cnrs.fr/graphem/⟩

GRAPHOSKOP, ⟨http://www.palaeographia.org/graphoskop/index.htm⟩

Manuscriptorium, ⟨www.manuscriptorium.com⟩

PARES, ⟨http://pares.mcu.es/⟩

Sexy Codicology - map ⟨http://sexycodicology.net/blog/digitized-medieval-manuscripts-online/⟩

T-Pen: Transcription for paleographical and editorial notation, ⟨http://t-pen.org/TPEN/⟩

EUGENIO R. LUJÁN – EDUARDO ORDUÑA

IMPLEMENTING A DATABASE FOR THE ANALYSIS OF ANCIENT INSCRIPTIONS: NEW DEVELOPMENTS IN THE HESPERIA ELECTRONIC CORPUS OF PALAEOHISPANIC INSCRIPTIONS

Introduction*

The purpose of the Hesperia databank of Palaeohispanic languages is to collect, organize and process all the ancient linguistic materials pertaining to the Iberian peninsula (and any related materials in southern France), with the exception of Latin, Greek and Phoenician inscriptions.[1] More than 2,000 Palaeohispanic inscriptions are known to date and, fortunately, the number increases every year. These inscriptions, which can be dated from at least the sixth century BC[2] to the beginning of the second century AD, were written in at least five different languages: Iberian, Celtiberian, Lusitanian and two unidentified languages.[3] For

---

* This paper is part of the research projects FFI2009-13292-C03-02 and FFI2012-36069-C03-02, which have the financial support of the Spanish Ministry of Economy and Competitiveness. We are very grateful to two anonymous reviewers for their comments and suggestions.

[1] The term 'Palaeohispanic' is employed here in the sense of 'old languages and inscriptions from *Hispania*'. The languages attested on those inscriptions are frequently referred to as 'Pre-Roman' languages of Spain. However, this name is misleading, given that, in fact, most inscriptions are later than the Roman settlement in Spain; 'Palaeohispanic' is thus preferable.

[2] The date can only be approximate, since most of the oldest inscriptions (the Southwestern inscriptions) have not been found in their original archaeological context. See De Hoz 2010, p. 358-361.

[3] Recenlty, Koch 2009 and 2011 has argued that the language of the Southwestern inscriptions – the oldest ones – is Celtic. However, most scholars working on Palaeohispanic languages and inscriptions have not accepted his proposal, since Koch's analyses and arguments are far from cogent. See De Hoz 2010, p. 386-402, for a reliable discussion of our current knowledge about the language of these inscriptions.

10.1484/M.LECTIO-EB.5.102575

these inscriptions several varieties of Palaeohispanic scripts were employed over time and space,[4] but we also have texts written in the Greek and Latin scripts.[5] Besides the inscriptions, for the study of Palaeohispanic languages we must also take into account the indigenous names (personal names, place names, ethnonyms, and god names) and additional information about the Palaeohispanic languages, such as glosses, that has been transmitted by a number of Greek and Latin sources, both literary and epigraphic. This kind of information is fundamental, e.g., for our knowledge of the languages related to Basque in Antiquity.[6]

The study of Palaeohispanic inscriptions poses problems of different kinds that we had to bear in mind when designing and developing a database that would allow us to digitize and process them in an appropriate way.[7] Two of the identified languages belong to the Indo-European family of languages (Lusitanian and Celtiberian), one of them being specifically Celtic. The third, Iberian, remains an isolate one, in spite of different proposals. All of them are only partially understood, especially as far as longer documents are concerned, and many aspects of their grammar and vocabulary are still unclear. This difficulty is amplified in the case of Iberian, for which the recourse to comparison to other genetically related languages is not possible. As for the scripts, the Iberian Levantine script is totally deciphered, as well as its adaptations for Celtiberian. However, the values of a certain number of signs of the Southern and Southwestern varieties remain highly controversial.[8]

---

[4] Palaeohispanic scripts originated from Phoenician script; see De Hoz 2010, p. 485-517. Several varieties were employed over time: Southwestern script, Southern script and 'Classical' Iberian Levantine script, from which two slightlty different adaptations were made for the writing of Celtiberian. Updated tables of these scripts can be found in De Hoz 2010, p. 618-625.

[5] There are Iberian inscriptions written in a variety of Ionian alphabet, and Celtiberian inscriptions written in the Latin script. All known Lusitanian inscriptions are written in Latin script as well.

[6] The fundamental work to date is Gorrochategui 1984. For a recent review of what we know about Basque in Antiquity see Gorrochategui 2009.

[7] The standard edition for these inscriptions to date is Untermann's *MLH*.

[8] This is one of the basic problems with Koch's proposals (see fn. 3). His interpretations are based on values of the signs of the Southwestern script that are not assured.

Therefore, one of the primary goals of the database must be to contribute to the advancement of our knowledge of these languages and scripts, allowing for complex searches that may shed light on the grammar of the Palaeohispanic languages and the interpretation of the texts, providing a quick and reliable means of testing hypotheses about debated aspects of these languages, and making it easier to confirm or reject possible phonetic values for the still undeciphered signs of some of the Palaeohispanic scripts, among other various possibilites. The database must also be useful for a better understanding of certain phenomena in the history and distribution of these languages, such as identifying lexical isoglosses, patterns of spread of some of the epigraphic features, and regional or diachronic biases of certain phenomena, in order to gain a deeper insight into the dynamics of these languages and inscriptions.

The Hesperia databank is now a joint project of several research teams of the Complutense University at Madrid, the University of the Basque Country, and the Universities of Zaragoza and Barcelone.[9] It is hosted on a dedicated server of the Faculty of Philology of the Universidad Complutense at Madrid and it is accesible through the web site of the project (⟨http://hesperia. ucm.es/⟩).

The Hesperia databank was originally a FileMaker database developed by Fernando Quesada, from whose design it still retains its graphical aspect – viz., most of the original fields and the distribution in tabs with a heading. Now Hesperia is implemented internally as a MySQL database containing several tables, corresponding to the different sections: Epigraphy, Numismatics, Onomastics, Lexicon, and Bibliography. The graphical user interface is an HTML form,[10] built using the PHP programming language, each form corresponding to a MySQL table. Only the Numismatics section has two tables, and we will refer to them later. Each section, except Lexicon and Bibliography, has tabs in

---

[9] For a presentation of the project in previous stages see Luján 2005.

[10] Here we use 'form' in the technical sense of the HTML tag. In the rest of this paper we will prefer 'section' or 'tab', as our graphical user interface is divided in tabs, each one containing one HTML form. Each 'section' corresponds to a MySQL table.

order to keep all the fields in the screen without the need to scroll down to see all of them.[11]

Some of the databases are now in an advanced state of development. However, given the diversity of the materials that had to be integrated into the databank and the technical complexity of dealing with all the different types of materials (e.g., fonts for the transliteration of the scripts, photographs and drawings of the inscriptions, cartography, and so on), the various parts of the databank will be fully operational in different phases. The goals of the databank have also evolved since its initial conception and we now have more ambitious prospectives. This has led us to make certain improvements in the databank by integrating additional tools and implementing new ways of dealing with the information that we have compiled. We thus believe that the Hesperia database can provide interesting methodological cues for other digitized corpora of ancient inscriptions.

We have provided general descriptions of the databank and all of its sections in previous works (Orduña, Luján and Estarán 2009, Orduña and Luján in press),[12] so we will focus here in more detail on some parts of the Epigraphy section that can be seen as more innovative in certain aspects, or that have a deeper complexity. We will focus especially on those features related to the storing and representation of transcriptions of Palaeohispanic texts and their critical apparatus, the search engine, and the dynamic generation of maps. We will also provide some more detail about certain new improvements in the Hesperia databank that were not described in our previous works – in particular the new way of presenting bibliographic references, as well as the bibliographic impact searcher. We will also describe the new way to display the lexical references that correspond to a certain text, as this was still work in progress at the time of our prior publications.

---

[11] The entry of new data into the database is only allowed for users with privileges, so in this paper we will mainly focus on what a normal user will see.

[12] The original posters presented at the Lisbon conference can be accessed on the Internet (‹http://eprints.ucm.es/8672/›) and provide a general overview of the main features of the databank.

Browsing the database

We will first discuss a simple but, in our view, important feature of the Hesperia databank: it is easy to navigate. Unlike many databases on the Internet, in which the user must start from a search engine,[13] in Hesperia it is possible to browse all the records in the same way as in other desktop applications such as Filemaker. Once the users enter the database, they find the first record, and they can browse through the records with the 'next/previous' buttons with which all tabs are provided, thus navigating through all of the records in the order that they were entered. Every user can thus have a glimpse of the database without any previous knowledge, as would be required if they were confronted first with a search engine. It is also possible to filter the records according to simple criteria, for example 'language = Iberian' or 'archaeological site = Empúries'. Once the filter has been selected, the navigation buttons act only over the matching records.

Another way of navigating the database is by using the search engine, which allows the user to enter search criteria for every field, in a multi-filter way that could be labelled as 'faceted browsing':[14] all the matching results are displayed as a table with the contents of some important fields (e.g. 'text'), and each result has a link to the complete record. The results are sorted in ascending or descending alphabetical order according to the field selected by the user.

Last, but not least, it is possible to navigate 'geographically': the MapServer program, which we will discuss later, allows the user to see the points corresponding to all the archaeological sites that have provided Palaeohispanic inscriptions. The user can then click on them to see the list of the inscriptions found at that site, with links to the relevant records.

We will now turn specifically to the Epigraphy section, focusing on its more innovative aspects. As a general background, it will suffice to say that it is organized in tabs, with a heading

---

[13] This is the case, e.g., with the 'Epigraphische Datenbank Heidelberg' (‹http://www.uni-heidelberg.de/institute/sonst/adw/edh/index.html.en›), which contains Latin inscriptions.

[14] 'Faceted browsing' is a technique for accessing information that allows users to browse that information applying multiple filters at the same time.

always visible over them that contains some general information about the inscription, such as the name of the archaeological site, its location, or its references in epigraphic corpora. There are six tabs, which contain other general information about the epigraphic object itself, the text and its critical apparatus, illustrations, epigraphy and palaeography, archaeological context, and bibliography. The Illustrations tab allows the uploading of an un-limited number of image files of the inscriptions, and they appear as a table containing the images as thumbnails, which are links to the full size images (fig. 1) and are automatically generated whenever an image is uploaded. These image files are not stored in the MySQL database, but in folders or directories whose names correspond to the record id numbers, so that the database files remain small in size and are easy to back up.

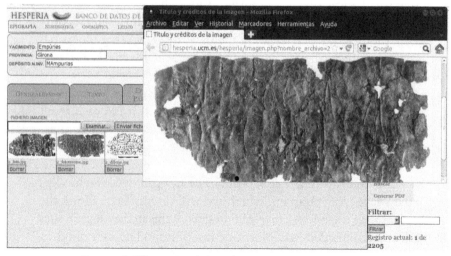

FIGURE 1: 'Illustrations' view for inscriptions in Hesperia.

Text and critical apparatus

In the Epigraphy section there is a tab devoted exclusively to the transcription of the Palaeohispanic text and its variant readings. Palaeohispanic inscriptions are, for the most part, unique and we thus lack different versions of the same text, so in this context 'variant' is intended to refer to an alternative reading proposed by a scholar that is not the one selected for the main text. In Palaeo-hispanic epigraphy it is especially important to provide the variants since, as we have remarked in above, we still have a limited knowledge of these languages and in many cases we lack cogent reasons to definitively reject certain proposals. It is thus crucial to have a way of presenting the alternative readings in such a fashion that, on the one hand, they do not intrude upon the user when reading the text, and on the other hand, they are not neglected because the user would need to look away from the main text every time that there is a variant for a word.

We have found a solution that, in our view, fulfills both requirements: each section of text with alternative readings is marked in blue, and a floating bubble appears over this section, containing the variant spellings, all in a single window (fig. 2).

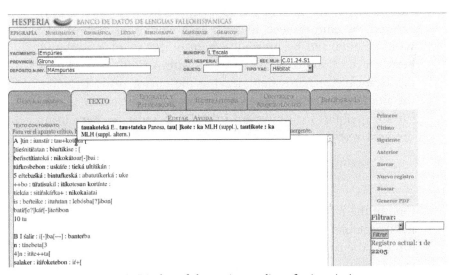

FIGURE 2: Display of alternative readings for inscriptions.

We refer to sections of text which have alternative spellings as 'words', in the sense of a section of text separated by punctuation marks. We use them as a natural way of segmenting the text, since this is how the Iberian and Celtiberian scribes proceeded themselves, whether or not it corresponds to our concept of a word; this is convenient because in this way variant spellings are easily found by the search engine. Let us suppose that we have selected as the preferred transcription for a text *tautintibas*, while other scholars have read *boutintibas*. If we marked only *$ta&utintibas* (the

$ and & signs enclose the text with an alternative reading in our notation),[15] corresponding to *$bo&* in the critical apparatus, this would be useless: a user looking for *boutintibas*, or *boutin*, would not be able to find it, as the field containing the variants would have only *bo*. As we can see, the longer the texts that we mark as variants, the easier it will be for a user to find these variants. Punctuation marks are usually a good splitting point when they exist, but sometimes it is better to cut shorter sections.

We have said that the text and its variants both appear in a single window. In fact, this is not a true HTML form field, but a white table cell that allows formatting. The real HTML form, only accessible to the team members,[16] contains two fields, one for the transcription selected as the preferred reading, and the other for the critical apparatus. Once the main text is entered, the editor selects in order each word or section of text with variants, and by pressing a button, this word is enclosed between the $ and & marks and then automatically copied into the Critical Apparatus field, leaving the cursor ready to enter the alternative readings. A semicolon is used at the end of all the variant spellings for one word in order to separate them from the next word.

Lexical references

One of the tables upon which Hesperia is internally built is the Lexicon table, which stores the lexical entries and is accessible through the corresponding section. The lexical entries are 'words' in the sense described in the previous paragraphs. Due to the current state of knowledge of the Palaeohispanic languages – which is very limited in terms of semantic meaning, and in the case of the Iberian language, practically nil – the contents of these lexical entries have little to do with what one would expect in the case of better known languages. These entries typically contain little

---

[15] These signs were chosen arbitrarily at the first stages of the project because they do not correspond to any other sign used in the transcription of Palaeohispanic languages, and they can thus be safely ignored by the search engine.

[16] The same approach is used in other tabs.

more than bibliographic references[17] or a list of other possibly related words or segments.[18]

One advanced feature of Hesperia is the simplicity with which one may consult this lexicon through the text itself: one link in the Epigraphy and Palaeography tab opens a window with the transcription of the text, in which each word, in the sense already explained, is a link to its lexical entry (fig. 3). This is made possible by means of a function that stores the text in an array, using the punctuation marks as separators, so that each word is an array element. Before comparing each array element with the entries in the lexicon, some functions are internally used in order to allow the match even if the transcription system has not been the same in the lexicon and in the text, or if there are some other anticipated differences. For example, the text transcription or the lexical entry can be outdated regarding the transcription of a sign previously thought to be **bo**, the correct value of which is, however, **ta**.

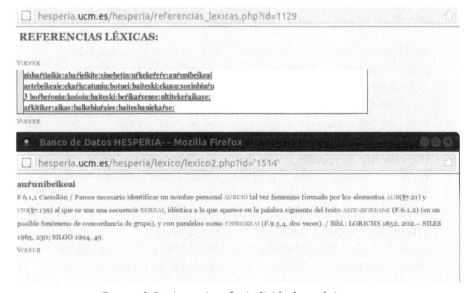

FIGURE 3: Lexicon view for individual words in a text.

[17] These bibliographic references are manually entered, in the author-year format, pointing to the full reference included in the general bibliography, which is also manually entered.

[18] See De Hoz 2011, p. 290, n. 127 for a survey of the existing Iberian lexicons and its problems. As he points out, they do not usually propose a segmentation of the lexical entry.

The links in the text open a side window with the lexical entry, in which every word in bold (which we usually employ only to transliterate Iberian words) is transformed also into a link to this entry. In this case we have provided a simple option of creating a link to this word without previously checking if this entry exists or not, so that it is possible that the link sometimes points only to a 'There is no entry for...' message. This occurs when the lexical entry mentions suffixes or other text strings smaller than those used as lexical entries. On the other hand, this system is very useful when the lexical entry simply points to another entry and also in order to keep different readings or transcriptions of a word in the lexicon. Such entries are also employed in the few cases in which we are certain enough to separate a lexeme from one or several affixes: e.g., for the frequent Iberian word *śalir* (most probably 'silver') we have an entry *śalir*, and the entries *śalirg*, *śalirban*, *śalirnai* simply point to the first one.

Bibliography

In Hesperia we have developed a new way to present bibliographic references. There is a Bibliography table that contains all the bibliographic records cited in the different sections of the database. One of the fields of this table contains the short citation form, in the author-year style that will be used to cite each bibliographic record. There is also a link for each record that displays the number of records in the Epigraphy, Onomastics or Numismatic sections that cite this bibliographic entry, followed by the list of links to each of these records.

In the Bibliography tab of the Epigraphy, Numismatics or Onomastics section, we enter only the short form of the references, usually followed by page number(s), and the user can see these short references in form of a link that shows a floating window with the complete reference (fig. 4).

The search engine

All the sections in the Hesperia databank are provided with a search engine that supports searches on matching criteria entered in any field of the database – or in several fields at a time – with

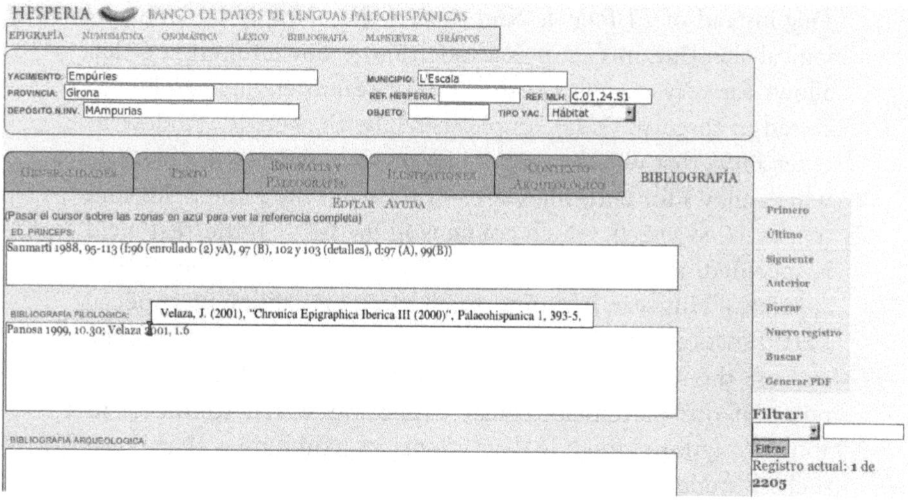

FIGURE 4: Display of full reference in a bibliographical entry.

the option of looking for records that match the criteria provided in any one of the fields, or alternatively in all of them (fig. 5). For each field it is also possible to look for an exact match or for a 'regular expression' match. As we have already said, the results appear in the form of a table, with links to each record.

In its more common use, the regular expression search simply involves the ability to look for parts of the contents, for example

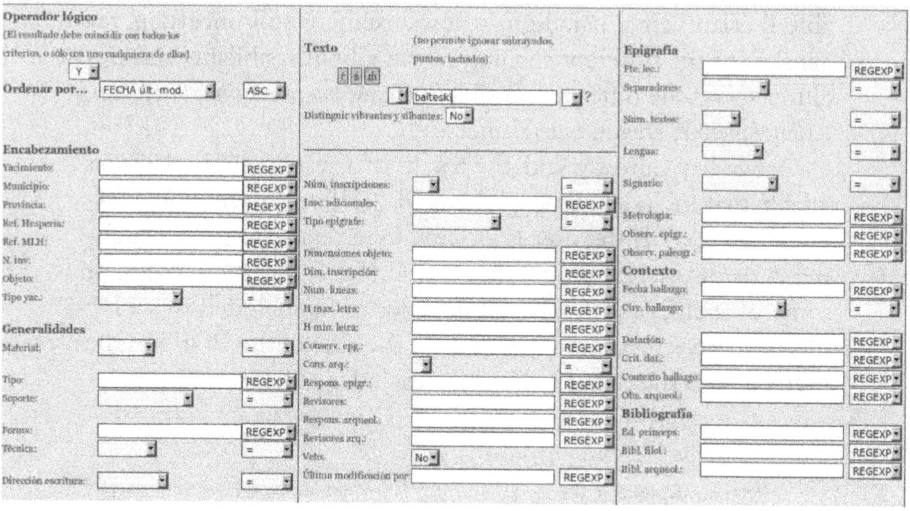

FIGURE 5: The Hesperia search engine.

Puig instead of *El Puig de Sant Andreu*, the name of an archaeological site. But, in fact, it is a much more powerful engine that
allows for very complex searches. Our search engine can be accessed in three ways: (a) simple search, with a single window to
enter a text that will be searched for in every field; (b) easy search,
which allows for entering search criteria in only some fields; and
(c) advanced search, which contains all the fields. If the 'text' field
is specified, the engine also automatically searches the critical
apparatus. This search engine, in all three modalities, uses special
PHP functions that emulate the Perl regular expression engine
and use the same regular expression language.[19] One important
point of this particular regular expression search feature is its
ability to ignore Unicode diacritic marks (combining characters)
such as 'underline' or 'dot under', used in our transcriptions for
marking uncertain signs or signs only partially preserved but with
assured reading. The match is thus possible without using these
marks in the search string.

The regular expression search engine provides the user with
a set of wildcard symbols such as \b (boundary), \w (word character, i.e., an alphabetical character), \s (white space), etc., which
can form very complex expressions when combined with text
strings.[20] One example will suffice to show the power of the
regular expression language: the expression *(baś)?b?i[td]?[ei][ŕ]
ok(an|ar|e)(te)?(tine)?* can match all the different forms of a prob-
able Iberian verbal paradigm whose lexeme is still uncertain, regardless of the different spelling of the vibrants, sibilants and oc-
clusives, and the different possible suffixes: *biteŕoketetine, biteŕokan,
basbiteŕoketine, eŕokar, bideŕokan*, etc.

As we have already said, the results of a search are displayed as
a table that includes some of the fields (archaeological site, reference, and text). If the user is looking for a text string, the matching parts of the text are marked in red (fig. 6). All the records, or
some of them, can be selected in order to be included in a PDF
file, or to be represented in a map. In the case of the PDF file, the
user can also select the fields to be included.

---

[19] Perl is considered the programming language with the most powerful
regular expression engine.
[20] The standard book about regular expressions is Friedl 2002.

Resultado de la búsqueda:
(El botón de la parte inferior genera un archivo pdf con los registros marcados)
MARCAR TODOS | NO MARCAR NINGUNO
VOLVER

Yacimiento	Ref. MLH	Ref. Hesperia	Texto	Enlace a ficha
El Puig de Sant Andreu	C.02.03		(a) 1 ar : basiarebe 2 ebarik'ame : r'uik'esiŕa : b'orste : abaŕkeb'orste : r'eŕ 3 tifs : b'aitesbi : neŕ'ekeŕu : bośb'eliorku : r'imor 4 k'iŕ : bartasko : amb'eiku : baitesar' : saltuko : kulebobeŕku+ 5 bikiŕŕuŕ'e : eŕeśu : kotib'anem : eberka : bośk'alir' 6 loŕsa : batibi : biurboneś : saltukilerku : ki (b) tarun : abobaker : abaśaker : bosbeŕiun : erna : b'orak'au	VER FICHA Incluir en PDF ☐
La Serreta	G.01.03		ki+++(+):++[- - -]+[boadesirbilosg+ r'ebiosikiun	VER FICHA Incluir en PDF ☐
La Punta de Orleyl (Orleyl III)	F.09.03		biurŕiki:tuskitar: abaolIII:beledbifeto rosair'baitesir 3 kaeśakin[	VER FICHA Incluir en PDF ☐

MARCAR TODOS | NO MARCAR NINGUNO
[Generar PDF o Mapa (seleccionados)]
3 resultados encontrados
[Generar mapa (todos)]

FIGURE 6: View of search results.

Dynamic map generation with MapServer

One of the most interesting features of our database is its ability to show dynamically generated maps with MapServer. This is an open source CGI program, developed by the University of Minnesota, that takes geographical information from a 'shapefile'[21] or a database and represents it on a map, allowing access to all the information contained in the 'shapefile' or the database related to a geographical point. The program requires certain files for every MapServer application: one or several HTML templates that act as a graphical user interface, and a 'mapfile' or configuration file that tells the program where to find the geographical information, the templates, or other files such as icons, and contains the layers that will appear in the map. These layers can be set by default or selected by the user. In our case, a physical map of the Iberian Peninsula always appears by default, and the user can select the other layers: point layers showing the distribution of archaeological sites, for example, or raster WMS (Web Map Server) layers obtained from external servers showing aerial orthophotos.

We use this program in two different ways: statically, to show layers with all the inscriptions, or dynamically, to generate maps that contain all or some of the results of a search.

---

[21] A 'shapefile' is a multifile format consisting of three files, a .shp file containing the geographical coordinates of the objects, a .shx one whith the indexes, and a .dbf one with the attributes of the objects.

285

The first method is accessible through the link 'MapServer', which provides a map in which the user can select different layers, some of them corresponding to external WMS servers that provide satellite photos or cartographic maps, and the rest corresponding to the different sections (i.e., tables) of the database: Epigraphy, Onomastics, and Numismatics. Selecting one of these layers, the user can see all the points that have provided Palaeohispanic inscriptions, Latin inscriptions with Palaeohispanic personal names, or the distribution of Palaeohispanic mints. In the case of epigraphic points, there are different icons according to the writing system employed at that site (fig. 7).

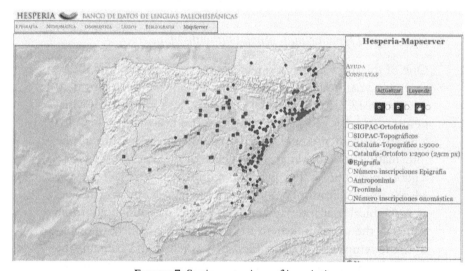

FIGURE 7: Static map view of inscriptions.

In the second method, the search engine generates a table with all the matching records, and each one has a check-box used to select the records to be included in a PDF file or in a map. There is also a button that provides direct generation of the map with all the results. A map is generated only with the points corresponding to the matching results, and the list of records with their corresponding links is shown below the map.

Regardless of the method used, the generated map has different controls, and two main working modes: navigation or information. In the navigation mode the user can zoom or move the map. Starting from the first level of zoom, labels appear next to the points showing the name of the place: that is, the archaeological site in the epigraphical layer, the town or city in the onomastic layer, and the mint name in the numismatic layer (fig. 8). In the information mode the user may click on the icon of a point to obtain the list of all the records located in that point and the links to each record. It is very easy to use MapServer in this way to browse the database in a geographical approach.

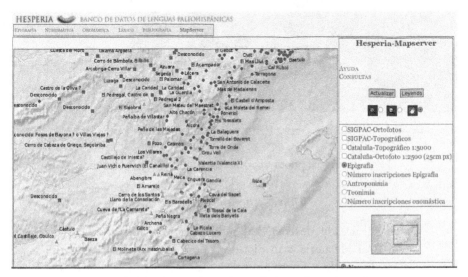

FIGURE 8: MapServer dynamic rendering of search results.

Both the static point layers and the dynamic search result point layers are preserved by default while using the zoom feature or after clicking for information on a point. In this way we can see the points over the aerial orthophotos of the archaeological sites, which can have a resolution of up to 25cm/pixel (fig. 9), so that when, in the near future, we have more precise geographic coordinates for each inscription inside an archaeological site, we will be able to see the distribution of the inscribed objects over the site.

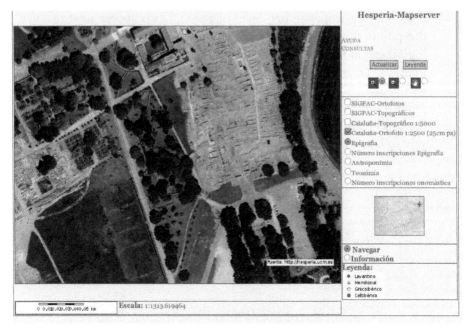

FIGURE 9: Aerial photo of an archaeological site in MapServer.

Other sections of Hesperia

We have already described the Bibliography and the Lexicon sections of Hesperia, and discussed how they interact with the Epigraphy section. There are two other important sections, Numismatics and Onomastics, which we have already described in detail in previous works, so we will only provide a short overview here.

Their graphical user interfaces work in a very similar manner to the one already described for the Epigraphy section, and both Numismatics and Onomastics have a complex search engine that allows for dynamic map generation and PDF file generation as well. The Numismatics section is internally organized in two tables, the main one containing mints and general information about them, and the other, the coin legends corresponding to each mint. The Onomastics section is organized in four tabs: Anthroponymy-Corpus, Anthroponymy-Analysis, Theonymy-Analysis and Toponymy, each one corresponding to a MySQL table. The first of these tabs contains all the names and the geographical coordinates studied in more detail in the next two ta-

288

bles, and the last one contains all the place names mentioned by ancient sources. This last section is less directly connected to the other three. Searches in each of the first three tabs allow for dynamic map generation, taking the geographical information from the first one. The 'mapfile' or configuration file used by the MapServer program allows for setting different layers from only one MySQL table, using filters that in this case take a form similar to 'type = anthroponym' or 'type = theonym', 'type' being one field in the Anthroponymy-Corpus table.

Finally, there is a Charts section that consists of a search engine similar to the one described above. Here the user may view the distribution of the results according to a given feature (such as the type of material of the inscriptions), which is presented as a pie chart showing percentages. It is thus very easy to detect certain interesting facts: for example, a chart representing the distribution of the frequent Iberian word *śalir* according to the material of the inscription clearly shows that this word, apart from coins, appears only on lead tablets.

Bibliography

J. De Hoz (2010), *Historia Lingüística de la Península Ibérica en la Antigüe-dad, I. Preliminares y mundo meridional prerromano*, Madrid: Consejo Superior de Investigaciones Científicas (Manuales y Anejos de Emerita, 50).

J. De Hoz (2011), *Historia Lingüística de la Península Ibérica en la Antigüe-dad, II. El mundo ibérico prerromano y la indoeuropeización*, Madrid: Consejo Superior de Investigaciones Científicas (Manuales y Ane-jos de Emerita, 51).

J. Friedl (2002), *Mastering Regular Expressions*, Sebastopol: O'Reilly (2nd edition).

J. Gorrochategui (1984), *Onomástica indígena de Aquitania*, Bilbao: Uni-versidad del País Vasco.

J. Gorrochategui (2009), 'Vasco antiguo: algunas cuestiones de geo-grafía e historia lingüísticas', in F. Beltrán et al. (eds.), *Acta Palaeo-hispanica X. Actas del X Coloquio sobre Lenguas y Culturas Paleohis-pánicas* (= Palaeohispanica, 9), Zaragoza: Institución Fernando el Católico, p. 539-555.

J. T. Koch (2009), *Tartessian: Celtic in the South-west at the Dawn of His-tory*, Aberystwyth: Celtic Studies Publications - David Brown.

J. T. Koch (2011), *Tartessian 2. The Inscription of Mesas do Castelinho. ro and the Verbal Complex. Preliminaries to Historical Phonology*, Oxford: Oxbow.

E. R. Luján (2005), 'Hesperia. The electronic *corpus* of Palaeohispanic inscriptions and linguistic records', in *Review of the National Center for Digitization* (Belgrade) 6, p. 78-89.

MLH = J. Untermann (1975-2000), *Monumenta Linguarum Hispanicarum*, 4 vols., Wiesbaden: Reichelt.

E. Orduña, E. R. Luján & M. J. Estarán (2009), 'El banco de datos Hesperia', in F. Beltrán et al. (eds.), *Acta Palaeohispanica X. Actas del X Coloquio sobre Lenguas y Culturas Paleohispánicas* (= Palaeohispanica, 9), Zaragoza: Institución Fernando el Católico, p. 83-92.

E. Orduña & E. R. Luján (in press), 'Philology and technology in the Hesperia databank', in *Journal of History, Literature, Science and Technology* (*JHLiST*).

SECTION 5

CODICOLOGY

IRA RABIN

INK IDENTIFICATION TO ACCOMPANY DIGITIZATION OF MANUSCRIPTS*

Introduction

To date, the field of codicology (i.e., the study of manuscripts as physical objects) has not addressed the question of chemical composition of writing materials. Recent advances in non-destructive testing provide us with tools for investigating physical and chemical properties of manuscripts. Combining the expertise of codicologists and palaeographers with that of experimentalists in the fields of chemistry and physics may add a further valuable dimension to the study of manuscripts and their historical context.

The color of inks (often characterized as brown, black, or gray) is not a suitable criterion for distinction and identification, since its appearance is prone to changes due to variants resulting from production and to the phenomena of corrosion and aging. One of the goals of our research at the Bundesanstalt für Materialforschung und -prüfung in Berlin, Germany (BAM) is to work out a simple, mobile method for the typological identification of various writing materials that cannot be differentiated by visual appearance alone. In the future, this method should be integrated into the procedure used to digitize manuscripts and make palimpsests visible.

Digitization of manuscripts usually employs the entire visible spectrum of light; to read palimpsests, reflectographic procedures

* My thanks go to my colleagues at the BAM, Emanuel Kindzorra and Oliver Hahn, and at the SFB 950, Christian Brockmann, Claire MacDonald and Boryana Pouvkova. Permission to publish preliminary results of our investigation of the Ms. BYU 091G811 was granted by Roger T. Macfarlane of the BYU. His active participation in the measurements is gratefully acknowledged.

10.1484/M.LECTIO-EB.5.102576

use light of various wavelengths, generally from UV to the close IR range (multi-spectral imaging, henceforth: MSI). MSI is based on the specific physical and chemical characteristics of the writing materials: although it does not allow for material classification, it can be used to recognize tannin-, iron-gall- and soot-based inks. Usually, not even such a coarse classification is carried out during manuscripts digitization. Therefore, we believe that a simple routine for ink identification accompanying digitization would be highly desirable.

The information gained from such routine identification should be included as a matter of course in the documentation or object description, because it is an important component of the item's materiality. Further analyses to address specific cultural-historical questions can be carried out subsequently with appropriately calibrated and more complex analytics.

Different ink types: overview

Soot, plant, and iron gall inks form different typological classes of historical black writing materials. Soot ink is a fine dispersion of carbon pigments in a water-soluble binding agent; plant-based ink consists of tannin solution; and iron gall-ink presents a boundary case between soot and plant ink – a water-soluble preliminary stage (belonging to the second group), followed by insoluble black material that develops through oxidation when the writing is exposed to air (belonging to the first group). Each ink class has distinct properties that would readily permit their easy differentiation, if only these historical inks always belonged to just one of the classes above. In reality, inks may contain additives that obscure a clear picture. Nevertheless, we believe that a coarse identification can be made using optical properties of the main component that would be representative of the class. Experience and knowledge of the ink type will improve accuracy of the identification.

Soot inks

According to its generic recipe, one of the oldest writing and drawing pigments is produced by mixing soot with a binder dissolved in a small amount of water. Thus, along with soot, binders such as gum Arabic (ancient Egypt) or animal glue (China) belong to the main components of soot inks. From Pliny's detailed account on the manufacture of various soot-based inks (Pliny, *Naturalis historia*, Book XXXV, 25) we learn that, despite its seeming simplicity, the production of high quality pure soot was not an easy task in antiquity. Therefore, we expect to find various detectable additives that might be indicative of the time and place of production. Carbon inks do not penetrate the substrate (papyrus, parchment or paper) and stay well localized on the surface. Their deep black color does not change under infrared light.

Plant inks

Plant or tannin inks are solutions of tannins extracted from various plants and are of brown color. The best-known one is the thorn or Theophilus' ink[1] whose elaborate recipe is recorded in Theophilus' twelfth century work *De diversis artibus* (Dodwell 1961, p. 34-35). Another recipe is offered in the book of Dionysios from Mount Athos (Malerbuch 1983, p. 33). Unfortunately, no systematic study of the historical use of these inks has been compiled: their use has been only occasionally reported in different scriptoria. Inks of brown-reddish color in oriental manuscripts were also identified as pure vegetable extracts (Zerdoun 1983, p. 117).

Plant inks are absorbed by the substrate; the degree of absorption depends to a great extent on the nature of that substrate. They have a characteristic homogeneity and show no crystallization. They gradually fade under light of growing wavelength and become transparent for light of *c.* 750 nm. They are best identified by their physical and optical properties.

Iron-Gall inks

Iron-gall inks are surely among the most commonly used writing materials and dominate the black to brown palette of many manuscripts.

---

[1] Zerdoun 1983, p. 156-165 offers a detailed discussion of this ink that could be a plant or an imperfect iron-gall one if one translates 'atramentum' as carbon black or vitriol, respectively.

Though the origin of the use of a mixture of iron salts and tannins to produce a blackening fluid can be traced back to Antiquity (Pliny, *Naturalis historia*, Book XXXIV, 43, 48), the earliest evidence of recipes that unambiguously mention a reaction between iron sulfate and tannins to produce writing inks does not appear before the twelfth century (Zerdoun 1983, p. 218-224). By that time, however, iron-gall ink was used almost universally throughout Europe and the Orient and numerous recipes have come down to us from that time on.

Iron gall inks are produced by mixing natural iron vitriol with gall nuts extracts. Iron(II) sulfate (also known as 'green vitriol' because of its color and its glassy appearance) is the most frequently named ingredient in ink formulas. In medieval writings, however, other names like 'atramentum' and 'chalcanthon', derived from ancient sources, are often used.[2] Gall nuts are diseased formations on the leaf buds, leaves, and fruits of various species of oak, caused when parasitoid wasps deposit their eggs in them. They contain gallic acid and a number of other tannins, in various amounts.

When iron(II) sulfate and gallic acid are mixed, initially a colorless, soluble complex results. Its oxidation through contact with air results in black, water insoluble pigment. The inks usually contain other organic materials such as tannins, as well as a water-soluble binding agent, e.g., gum Arabic. Solvents like water, wine, or vinegar are used to take extracts from the gall nuts.

Since the ingredient substances are mostly naturally occurring raw materials, the inks display a very heterogeneous composition. On the one hand, gall nuts contain varying amounts of gallic acid; on the other, other tannin-containing components are used along with gall nuts – tropical woods, sumac, oak bark, pomegranate skin, or crushed peach pits (Fuchs 1999). Natural vitriol usually contains a mixture of metal sulfates (e.g. iron sulfate, copper sulfate, manganese sulfate, zinc sulfate) with relative weight contributions characteristic of the source or purification procedure (Krekel 1999). We use this very property of the iron-gall inks to compare and to distinguish between them (Hahn et al. 2008).

---

[2] For a detailed discussion of medieval terminology see the monograph by M. Zerdoun Bat-Yehouda 1983.

It should be mentioned that the color of iron-gall inks perceived today might be significantly different from what was originally intended. This color is attributable to the ageing-related processes, as already reported in the eighteenth century. Inks with too much iron vitriol change color in the direction of yellow to red; those with too much gall nut are more lasting, but soon turn brown (Ribeaucourt 1797). So it can be assumed that only some of the originally black iron gall inks have kept their original hue. Microscopically, these inks appear highly inhomogeneous in color and texture, with traces of dark crystals. They gradually lose opacity in the near infrared region and become invisible under infrared light. Their elemental composition is rich in metals that are easily detected by the XRF-technique. Finally, they display a characteristic spectrum when investigated by Raman spectroscopy (Lee et al. 2008).

Inks of a mixed composition

In addition to inks of pure classes, mixed inks containing components of different classes are well-known. In such cases, one usually has a type-defining component and 'picture smearing' additives. In this respect, a recipe from Dioscurides is remarkable among ancient Roman recipes for the production of soot inks. Along with soot ('condensed smoke') and gum, the recipe mentions a copper compound (chalcanthon).[3] Indeed Particle Induced X-ray Emission (PIXE)[4] studies of ancient Greek papyri from the Louvre collection identified copper in the inks. Without supporting evidence from other analyses, these inks were erroneously classified as metal-gall[5] ones (Delange et al. 1990).

PIXE and micro-X-Ray Fluorescence (μ-XRF) studies of the Dead Sea Scrolls also revealed a number of documents written with inks containing large amounts of copper. In this case, however, the use of infrared reflectography unequivocally proved the

---

[3] Cf. Zerdoun 1983, p. 80.

[4] PIXE, similar to XRF, measures X-rays emitted by the chemical elements present in a material irradiated with heavy particles such as protons.

[5] In contrast with iron, no insoluble black results from the reaction of copper sulfate with gallic acid. Therefore, the confusing expression 'metal-gall ink' should be avoided.

soot nature of the inks and helped avoid erroneous classification (Nir-El and Broshi 1996).

The difficulty and high costs of soot ink production resulted in various attempts to replace them. We believe that the early appearance of the plant inks can be correlated with such attempts. In some cases, small quantities of soot were added to improve the color of those inks. Some medieval Arabic and Jewish recipes for soot inks contain such additives as vitriol and tannins.

Even more continuous is the transition from the purely plant (i.e., tannin) inks to the iron-gall inks since a small addition of vitriol to a tannin ink would produce an imperfect iron-gall one. Moreover, metals like iron and copper can be occasionally present in the tannin inks due to the water or tools used in the production process. A full elucidation of the composition of such inks requires the use of complex instrumental diagnostics (Rabin et al. 2012). Nevertheless, the determination of the main components can be accomplished using their optical properties alone.

Analytic procedures

Based on their principle, the most popular non-contact mobile techniques for ink identification can be categorized into molecular, elemental and optical analysis methods.

Vibrational (Infrared [IR] and Raman) spectroscopy allows identification of the molecules and their structure by supplying specific information on vibrations of atoms in molecules. In the first technique, a molecule absorbs a portion of the irradiated infrared light, hence its name. In the second technique – named after the Indian physicist Sir Chandrasekhara Venkata Raman – monochromatic light in the ultraviolet, visible, and near infrared ranges of the electromagnetic spectrum is used. Since the mechanisms of the interaction with light differ from one technique to the other, the techniques complement each other. This type of spectroscopy seems to be the most straightforward way to identify and distinguish between different types of inks. It has also been proved useful in studies of illuminated manuscripts and paintings, since tabulated Raman data allow for a quick and unequivocal identification of pigments. Unlike the case of pigment identi-

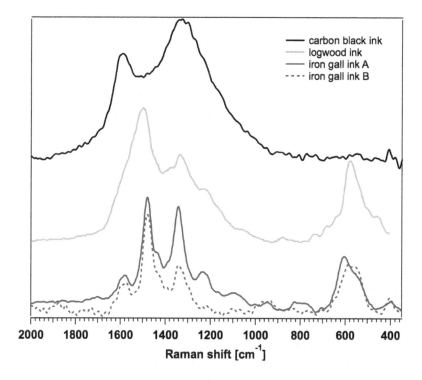

FIGURE 1: Raman spectra of soot inks of the Temple scroll first century ad (top), logwood ink with iron sulfate (middle, reprinted from Bicchieri et al. 2008), and iron gall inks (bottom, A – modern self-made, B – Coptic manuscript from tenth century ad).

fication, however, reliable experimental methods for the identification of medieval black inks started to emerge only during the last decade. From the comparison of the Raman spectra of soot, plant and iron-gall inks in fig. 1 we can conclude that each type has its characteristic fingerprint that provides a recognition pattern. Unfortunately, mobile tools designed for on-site use by non-specialists are not yet available. Nevertheless it is to be hoped that the ongoing analysis of historical ink samples by means of conventional techniques will ultimately lead to improvements in the mobile equipment and the establishment of a database of different inks.

Elemental analysis by *X-ray fluorescence technique (XRF)* relies on the study of patterns of X-rays emission from chemical elements

299

present in a material irradiated with high-energy X-rays. Here, the situation differs dramatically from the case of vibrational spectroscopy. This technique benefits from the availability of a variety of transportable instruments ranging from single spot to high-resolution scanning equipment, as well as from a wealth of knowledge and experience that has been accumulated in the characterization of historical inks via this technique. Specifically, the development and use of the fingerprint model based on the qualitative and quantitative detection of inorganic components of iron gall inks allows their reliable classification (Hahn et al. 2004). In table 1 we compare three mobile XRF (Bruker) spectrometers used for manuscript studies. The low-resolution portable TRACER (column 1) is relatively cheap, light and easy to operate. In many cases it provides one-shot recognition of the iron gall inks and can even be used for the comparison of different inks in the same document. Its major shortcomings are low sensitivity and low spatial resolution. When used in tandem with an optical imaging system it should be a first choice for ink recognition in collections. ARTAX (middle column) was specially designed for the studies of art objects and has proved its efficiency for no less than a decade. It is a robust device that can be transported to the site of the studies. A 70 μm X-ray beam and scanning facility enables the study of fine differences between the inks and their properly classification; it also allows for the determination of their provenance (Rabin et al. 2009). Jet stream M6 presents a further development in the XRF field. Fast scanning in combination with higher resolution allow one to obtain large images accompanied by spatial elemental distributions. Therefore, one scan provides information on all the materials simultaneously, including degradation patterns of each material. Since the device is rather new on the market its full capabilities have not yet been explored. In the future, small optical multi-colored imagers will be integrated into XRF equipment leading to a simultaneous test of the optical properties.

Optical properties reflect the interaction of the material with light covering ultraviolet (UV), visible (VIS), and infrared (IR) regions of the electromagnetic spectrum. Therefore, IR reflectography has been traditionally used to study soot-based pigments or car-

INSTRUMENT	TRACER SD-III	ARTAX	JET STREAM M6
	Portable (2.5 kg + tripod)	Transportable (~70 kg)	Transportable (150 kg)
MEASURE-MENT TYPE	Single spot	Line scan	x,y scan
AREA	unlimited	unlimited	unlimited
BEAM SIZE	~ 8 mm	70 μm	50-850 μm (adjustable)
ACQUISITION TIMES	Adjustable; Minutes	Adjustable; high resolution scan can last for few hours	Adjustable; high resolution scan can last up to 12 hours
OUTPUT	Qualitative composition	Elemental distribution & average quantitative composition based on line scans	Image & spatial elemental distribution throughout the area measured
	Iron gall inks identification and comparison	Inks fingerprint	Composition and distribution of inks on both sides of the parchment/paper
			Degradation pattern

TABLE 1: Comparison of three mobile XRF spectrometers.

bon inks. As shown in fig. 2, the color of soot inks is independent of the wavelengths (lower row); plant inks lose opacity between 750 and 1000 nm whereas iron-gall inks become transparent only at the wavelength › 1000 nm. Similarly, multi-spectral imaging for the visualization of palimpsests or hyper-spectral imaging for document monitoring would allow one to differentiate between soot-based and tannin-based inks, since only the latter become transparent in the infrared region of the spectrum. Conventional multi-spectral imaging setup employs LED illumination with up to 13 different wavelengths ranging from UV to near IR region (Christens-Barry et al. 2011). Using broad-spectrum lamps and filters, the lesser known hyper-spectral technique produces continuous reflectance curves of the surface in addition to the images (Klein et al. 2006). In order to incorporate ink differentiation into manuscript digitization workflows, one could adopt a simplified version, where only 2-3 wavelengths are monitored, since the main goal is to investigate the opacity in the spectral range 700-1000 nm.

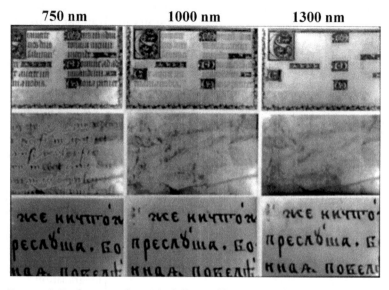

FIGURE 2: Reflectography with different filters (750, 1000 and 1300 nm). From top to bottom: iron-all inks, plant (tannin inks) and soot inks. Reprinted from Mrusek et al. 1995).

Coarse identification by a handheld multi-color microscope

An easy way to add such functionality to the routine inspection of manuscripts by scholars is to use a handheld USB microscope equipped with a NIR (940 nm) light source. It should be stressed that pure soot inks can be unambiguously identified by IR-reflectography alone. It is distinguishing between plant and iron gall inks that is challenging and requires NIR reflectography in addition to IR reflectography.

FIGURE 3: Images made with the USB microscope Dinolite AD413T-I2V in the vis-ible region (left) and near infrared (right, ~940 nm), respectively. From top to bottom: self-made soot inks, inks from a page of a medieval manuscript, inks from a Hebrew manuscript.

Fig. 3 presents micrographs in visible (left column) and near infrared (right column) illumination, respectively. At 940 nm, soot ink characters (top) preserve their color, plant inks (middle) disappear completely, whereas iron gall-inks (bottom) are still discernible, though they change their color considerably. Visual examination of the inks can also help to identify their nature. Light colored plant inks cover the parchment uniformly, in contrast to iron-gall ink whose partial degradation causes inks to appear in varying

303

colors in one single word. The corresponding elemental distributions unequivocally confirm the identification of plant and iron gall inks. A scanning μ-XRF spectrometer (Artax, Bruker) was used for the present study of the elemental composition. In fig. 4a we see element distributions along a line scan across a character from the middle portion of fig. 3. Iron (Fe) and potassium (K) are abundant in the inked area. Common vitriol components like copper (Cu) and manganese (Mn) are also present in the sample, but they are equally distributed in parchment and ink. Therefore they do not belong to the ink ingredients. In contrast, in fig. 4b elements copper, zinc (Zn) and nickel (Ni) are clearly associated with iron and the inked area that corresponds to the inks from fig. 3 (bottom). Since these very elements usually accompany iron in a natural vitriol mixture it can be safely concluded that vitriol constitutes an ink ingredient. Therefore, the first ink is of a plant nature and only the second ink belongs to the iron-gall type.

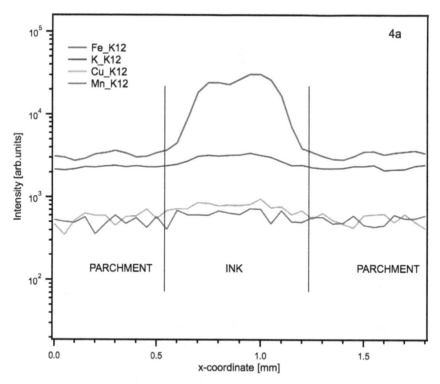

FIGURE 4a: μ-XRF line scans of the inks shown in fig. 3, middle portion.

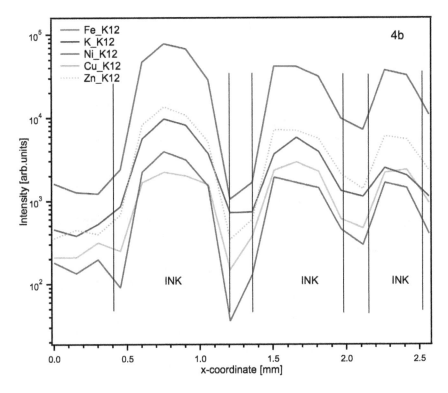

FIGURE 4b: μ-XRF line scans of the inks shown in fig. 3, bottom portion.

Conclusion

Detailed knowledge of writing materials is indispensable for advanced manuscript studies. Such knowledge, if available and stored in an accessible database, would provide correlations between the manuscripts stored in different collections and allow dating of the manuscripts and geographic attributions. One of the first steps toward the creation of such a database would be a routine recognition of the ink type that can accompany digitization programs and primary manuscript assessment. This paper suggests that such recognition protocols do not require expensive and complicated equipment but can be accomplished with a help of a simple USB microscope equipped with NIR light source.

Bibliography

M. Bicchieri, M. Monti, G. Piantanida & A. Sodo (2008), 'All that is iron-ink is not always iron-gall!', in *Journal of Raman Spectroscopy*, 39, p. 1074-1078.

W. A. Christens-Barry, K. Boydston & R. L. Easton (2011), 'Some Properties of Textual Heritage Materials of Importance in Spectral Imaging Projects', in M. Hakkarainen, A. Nurminen, V. Vahtikari (eds.), *EIKONOPIIA: Digital Imaging of Ancient Textual Heritage – Proceedings of the International Conference, Helsinki 28-29 November, 2010*, Finnish Society of Sciences and Letters (Commentationes Humanarum Litterarum, 129), p. 35-50.

E. Delange et al. (1990), 'Apparition de l'encre métallogallique en Égypte à partir de la collection de papyrus du Louvre', in *Revue d'Égyptologie*, 41, p. 213-217.

C. R. Dodwell (1961), *Theophilus, De diversis artibus. Theophilus, the various arts. Translated from the latin with Introduction and Notes*, London: Thomas Nelson, p. 34-35.

R. Fuchs (1999), 'Der Tintenfraß historischer Tinten und Tuschen - ein komplexes, nie enden wollendes Problem', in G. Banik & H. Weber (eds.), *Tintenfraßschäden und ihre Behandlung, Werkhefte der staatlichen Archivverwaltung Baden-Württemberg*, Stuttgart: Kohlhammer (Serie A Landesarchivdirecktion, 10), p. 36-75.

O. Hahn, W. Malzer, B. Kanngießer & B. Beckhoff (2004), 'Characterization of Iron Gall Inks in Historical Manuscripts using X-Ray Fluorescence Spectrometry', in *X-Ray Spectrometry*, 33, p. 234-239.

O. Hahn et al. (2008), 'The Erfurt Hebrew Giant Bible and the Experimental XRF Analysis of Ink and Plummet Composition', in *Gazette du Livre Médiéval*, 51, p. 16-29.

M. E. Klein et al. (2006), 'The quantitative hyperspectral imager a novel non-destructive optical instrument for monitoring historic documents', in *International Preservation News, IFLA*, 40, p. 4-15.

C. Krekel (1999), 'Chemische Struktur historischer Eisengallustinten', in G. Banik & H. Weber (eds.), *Tintenfraßschäden und ihre Behandlung, Werkhefte der staatlichen Archivverwaltung Baden-Württemberg*, Stuttgart: Kohlhammer (Serie A Landesarchivdirektion, 10), p. 25-36.

A. Lee, V. Otieno-Alego & D. Creagh (2008), 'Identification of iron-gall inks with near-infrared Raman microspectroscopy', in *Journal of Raman Spectroscopy*, 39, p. 1079-1084.

Malerhandbuch vom Berge Athos vom Mönch Dionysios (1983), Slavisches Institut München, p. 33

R. Mrusek, R. Fuchs & D. Oltrogge (1995), 'Spektrale Fenster zur Vergangenheit', in *Naturwissenschaften*, 82, p. 68-79.

Y. Nir-El & M. Broshi (1996), 'The black ink of the Qumran Scrolls,' in *Dead Sea Discoveries*, 3, p. 158-167.

Pliny the Elder, *The Natural History*, ed. H. Rackham, 10 vols., Loeb Classical Library, London: William Heinemann; Cambridge, Mass.: Harvard Univ. Press, 1949.

I. Rabin et al. (2009), 'On the origin of the ink of the Thanksgiving Scroll (1QHodayot[a])', in *Dead Sea Discoveries*, 16, p. 97-106.

I. Rabin et al. (2012), 'Identification and classification of historical writing inks in spectroscopy', in *Comparative Oriental Manuscript Studies Newsletter*, 3, p. 26-30.

H. Ribeaucourt (1797), 'Über die gewöhnliche schwarze Tinte', in *Crells chemische Annalen*, 28, p. 41-54.

M. Zerdoun Bat-Yehouda (1983), *Les encres noires au Moyen Âge*, Paris: CNRS.

PATRICK ANDRIST

GOING ONLINE IS NOT ENOUGH! ELECTRONIC DESCRIPTIONS OF ANCIENT MANUSCRIPTS, AND THE NEEDS OF MANUSCRIPT STUDIES*

How important is the date of a manuscript for scholarship?

While preparing this paper, I asked a few colleagues – philologists, historians, codicologists, but also managers of manuscript collections – what information they most want to find when looking at an online catalogue of ancient manuscripts. The question was: 'When you look at such a catalogue, which are the five pieces of information you would most like to find?' Depending on their need or their specialty, some mentioned the bindings or the materials, others the decorations, the miniatures, or the availability of reproductions. The content was always important, even if one respondent did not mention it. But the one piece of information that was consistently mentioned, one way or another, was the date of the manuscript or, more precisely, the date of the manuscript part one was working on.

In a spirit of humour, I sometimes asked: 'Do you just need a date? Or do you need a correct date?' In other words, how important is it that the date of a manuscript is more or less correct? For manuscript scholars, the answer is crystal clear. As everyone knows, in most cases it is crucial to know or at least to have a good idea of when a manuscript was copied or painted because most of the manuscript-related disciplines – if not all of them – are historical ones.

* I am very thankful to the organisers of the conference for their initiative, particularly to Tara Andrews, who very nicely reviewed the language in depth; to the ESF and the Interedition for their financial support; to Marilena Maniaci and André Binggeli for usefully discussing several points with me. Of course, I alone assume responsibility for the many shortcomings of this article.

10.1484/M.LECTIO-EB.5.102577

For example, for a book historian studying the development of book techniques, it is obviously useful to know when the books are dated. For an art historian studying paintings at the court of Otto I the Great, it certainly makes a difference if a miniature was painted in the tenth or the eleventh century. If one is editing ancient texts and there are several witnesses to this text, the dates of the manuscripts play a major role in sorting out the variants one way or another. It is even more critical if one for example studies the reception of a work in the fourteenth century. In a word, as soon as there is some kind of historical approach, the date of the object is significant for the overall scholarly appreciation of the codex.

(1) Thus, our first, obvious claim is:
Manuscript studies need information that is as correct as possible, particularly about the dates of the manuscripts.
... but this is not enough!

A situation scholars are frequently faced with is the fact that many manuscripts do not have one, but several dates. This is not a question of undated manuscripts because one can often figure out more or less when they were copied or painted by analysing the materials or the script. Nor is it a question of bindings, which are almost always much younger than the written or painted part of the volume. Rather, it is a question of volumes made up of several parts, with not all of them produced at the same time or in the same place.

The difficulty of cataloguing manuscripts in a way that complex manuscripts are also satisfactorily described is not new; scholars have often pointed this out and made suggestions to solve the problem.[1] This paper extends the debate to online descriptions and discusses several ways to prepare them, in order to present clearly and unambiguously relevant chronological information. This is not a comparison of database formats (EAD, Marc, etc.), specific software or databases, even though some software solutions make it easier to unambiguously describe a codex. This is about ways to organise the information visually – and, when

[1] Thorndike 1946, p. 94-95; Robinson 1980, p. 61-69; Derolez 1995, p. 381-383; Gumbert 1997; Munk Olsen 1998, p. 128-129; Andrist 2006; Gumbert 2009 etc.

possible, structurally – so that the users of the online description can (1) immediately and easily understand which data (concerning content, writing support, layout, ink, etc.) belong to the same production unit, and do not confuse them with data belonging to other production units,[2] and can (2) automatically retrieve correct information when including a date in their search queries.

The case of the multi-date codex Barocci 33

To illustrate the problem of multi-date manuscripts, let us consider a very clear example, albeit one already used elsewhere:[3]

> Barocci 33 is a Greek manuscript in the Bodleian Library in Oxford. It is made up of three main parts, which can be called 'Production Units' (or PUs).
> The oldest PU is B, the second part of the current volume. It was copied by Michael Lygizos in the second half of the fifteenth century (see figure 1 below).
> A, the PU that makes up the first part of the volume, was copied in the first half of the sixteenth century by two scribes, one of whom was called Kônstantios, and was prepended to the older PU. It may even have been copied with this intention, but this is difficult to demonstrate.
> Finally, in 1595, Nicolaos Labros copied C, the third PU, and added a colophon at the end, including his name and the date. Eventually, or perhaps even immediately, it was appended to the other PUs of the current volume.

A. s. XVI$^{1/2}$	A. (f. 1-116) hands a-b.: incl. Kônstantios Text 1: M. Blastaris
B. s. XV$^{2/2}$	B. (f. 117-244) hand c.: Michael Lygizos Texts 2-6: incl. Georgius Gemistius Plethon, *opera misc.*
C. a. 1595	C. (f. 245-⟨421⟩) hand d.: Nikolaos Labros Texts 12-13 f. 418v: colophon including the date and the scribe name

FIGURE 1: Overview of Barocci 33.

---

[2] On the concept of Production Units, see Andrist, Canart & Maniaci 2010, and 2013, especially p. 59-61. See also Gumbert 2004. Summarised explanations in English can also found in Andrist 2011.

[3] Andrist 2010, p. 19-21.

The result is a volume that ends with the name of a scribe and a date. By browsing the bibliography of the codex, it becomes apparent that more than one scholar believed the date applied to the entire manuscript, and mistakenly attributed information from PU A and PU B to 1595. What difference does it really make? Does it make a difference if these texts are linked to the date of PU B or PU C for a philologist preparing the edition of Plethon? Again, the answer is obvious. In the first case, this manuscript would have been copied a few years after the author's death in 1452; in the second case, it would have been copied some 150 years later.

In reality, these scholars are victims of the description of Henry Coxe in 1853 (see figure 2 below)[4], who plainly states at the beginning of his description that the codex was written in 1595. One cannot, however, say that his date is wrong because it can be found in the manuscript. In reality, this is a problem of correctly linking the information about the date with other pieces of information from the codex, such as the content, the scribes, and so forth.

(2) Our second claim is:
Manuscript studies need the various types of information in a description to be correctly linked to each other.
... it is already good, but it could even be better!

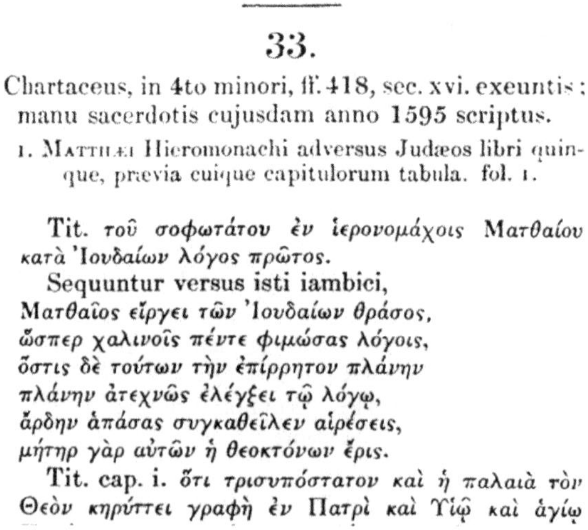

33.

Chartaceus, in 4to minori, ff. 418, sec. xvi. exeuntis :
manu sacerdotis cujusdam anno 1595 scriptus.

1. Matthæi Hieromonachi adversus Judæos libri quinque, prævia cuique capitulorum tabula. fol. 1.

Tit. τοῦ σοφωτάτου ἐν ἱερονομάχοις Ματθαίου κατὰ Ἰουδαίων λόγος πρῶτος.
Sequuntur versus isti iambici,
Ματθαῖος εἴργει τῶν Ἰουδαίων θράσος,
ὥσπερ χαλινοῖς πέντε φιμώσας λόγοις,
ὅστις δὲ τούτων τὴν ἐπίρρητον πλάνην
πλάνην ἀτεχνῶς ἐλέγξει τῷ λόγῳ,
ἄρδην ἁπάσας συγκαθεῖλεν αἱρέσεις,
μήτηρ γὰρ αὐτῶν ἡ θεοκτόνων ἔρις.
Tit. cap. i. ὅτι τρισυπόστατον καὶ ἡ παλαιὰ τὸν
Θεὸν κηρύττει γραφὴ ἐν Πατρὶ καὶ Ὑιῷ καὶ ἁγίῳ

FIGURE 2: Beginning of Henry Coxe's description, in 1853.

---

[4] Coxe 1853.

How frequently do these kinds of situations occur? Where Greek manuscripts are concerned, experience shows that manuscripts quite frequently contain multiple PUs comprising their main written or painted parts.[5] When I was curator of the Bongarsiana in Bern, I took some time to look into Arabic, Hebrew, German and old Latin manuscripts, and found that many of them were affected by the same phenomenon. As far as medieval manuscripts are concerned, as soon as one starts looking for these kinds of situations, one seems to find them almost everywhere.

Online description type 1a:
A bad interpretation of the mono-layer model

Before considering a third claim, let us see how the information about Barocci 33 might be correctly presented in an online description. We will consider the two most widely used models for preparing description patterns – although several other models are possible.

The first one is the standard mono-layer model,[6] which has been in use in printed catalogues since the middle of the twentieth century and is the most frequently used model on the Internet today. In this model, the various descriptive categories follow each other, each one in one and only one field per description (cf. below).

Let us consider four different ways to work with such a model, taking Barocci 33 as an example. In the following (incomplete) simulations, the same exact pattern, based on the mono-layer model, is completed in four different ways.

The first way represents the worst solution and should never be used:

In this first example, the fields were completed following the same principle as the catalogue of Coxe (but including some extra information). Failure to mention the applicable limits of the given date and to give a correct dating for PU A and PU B makes this description very flawed. The structure of the manuscript can

---

[5] This means excluding the notes and the bindings; otherwise about 100% of the manuscripts would be concerned.

[6] I no longer use the expression 'analytic model' because of the expression 'catalogo analitico' in Italian, which is used to refer to a "full-scale" catalogue; see Petrucci 2001, p. 93-104.

1a. - A bad example

Signature
Barocci 33

Extent
(3) 421 (1) folios

Date
March 14, 1595

Content
1. (f. 1r-116r sup.) Matthaeus Blastaris, Adversus iudaeos 2. (f. 117r-209v sup.) Gennadius Scholarius, Adversus iudaeos 3-5. (f. 210r-230v) Georgius Gemistius Plethon, opera misc., cf. cat. 6. (f. 231r-241v) Isocrates, Ad Demonicum oratio paraenetica 7-11. (f. 244v) notes, by Andreas Dônos, cf. cat. 12. (f. 247r-414v) Gennadius Scholarius, Apologia pro quinque cpp. concilii Florentini 13. (f. 415r-418v sup.) Definitio synodi Florentini

Material
Several kinds of paper: including watermarks "Cardinal Hat", "Pair of scissors" ...

Scripture and hands
a. (f. 1-24) unknown hand b. (f. 25-116) hand of \<Kônstantios> c. (f. 117-244) hand of \<Michael Lygizos> d. (f. 247-421) hand of \<Nicolaos Labros> (see colophon, f. 418v)

Etc.

FIGURE 3: An unsatisfactory method to describe Barocci 33 using the mono-layer model.

only be deduced if the reader notices that both the hands and the texts change at the same point in the manuscript. Only readers who know the activity dates of the scribes can form an idea about the chronological distance between these parts.

Unfortunately, a fair amount of examples of this description type can still be found online, as well as in printed catalogues.

Online description type 1b:
An acceptable interpretation of the mono-layer model.

A different method to complete the same simulated scheme in an acceptable way, which is not software-dependent and can be set up in any XML or SQL type of database, is offered below. It is simply a matter of awareness, standards and systematics.

1b. - An acceptable example

Signature
Barocci 33

Extent
(3) 421 (1) folios

Date
(f. 1-116) S. XVI 1/2 ; (f. 117-244) S. XV 2/2 ; (f. 245-421) a. 1595, 14th of March

Content
1. (f. 1r-116r sup.) Matthaeus Blastaris, Adversus iudeaos 2. (f. 117r-209v sup.) Gennadius Scholarius, Adversus iudaeos 3-5. (f. 210r-230v) Georgius Gemistius Plethon, opera mis, cf. cat. 6. (f. 231r-241v) Isocrates, Ad Demonicum oratio paraenetica 7-11. (f. 244v) notes, by Andreas Dônos, cf. cat. 12. (f. 247r-414v) Gennadius Scholarius, Apologia pro quinque cpp. concilii Florentini 13. (f. 415r-418v sup.) Definitio synodi Florentini

Material
Several kinds of paper: including watermarks "Cardinal Hat", "Pair of scissors" ...

Scripture and hands
a. (f. 1-24) unknown hand b. (f. 25-116) hand of <Kônstantios> c. (f. 117-244) hand of <Michael Lygizos> d. (f. 247-421) hand of <Nicolaos Labros> (see colophon, f. 418v)

Etc.

FIGURE 4: An acceptable way of describing Barocci 33 following the standard mono-layer model.

In this second example, the three PUs and their extent are mentioned in the 'date' field. The reader can immediately understand the basic structure of the codex. He must then remember this structure when reading the other fields of the description; he should not, for example, take for granted that the text of Matthaeus Blastaris was originally copied into this same manuscript

315

with the texts of Plethon, even though they are bound together today.[7]

Thankfully, a fair number of such acceptable descriptions can already be found on the Internet.

Online description type 1c:
An improved example

Provided that the programmers did not limit the available space of the database field, the same pattern can be used slightly differently to better underline the natural structure of the manuscript. Because it implies that one reads, understands and reflects on the physical features of the codex, this constitutes a so-called 'syntactical descriptions'.[8] Again, this improved method is not software-dependent and can be set up in any XML or SQL type of database.

In this third example, not only are the extent and the dates of the PUs mentioned at the beginning, but the separate parts are also numbered from A through C. To prevent mistakes and confusion, this numbering is repeated in every field and used as a way to structure the information. As a result, readers can always very clearly know which PU in the manuscript should be associated with the given information.

In spite of this important improvement, this type of description still has some disadvantages.

First, repeating the structure in every field takes up time, energy and space. And there is always the risk of mistakes because of imperfectly repeated information. One can easily imagine what happens if there are 20 PUs in a manuscript.[9]

Second, it does not allow the reader to take in all the characteristics of a PU at once. One has to browse all the description

---

[7] Another 'danger' this type of description poses – though not illustrated by the example above – is the tendency of the cataloguers to mention two subsequent PUs from the same date in one shot, even if they were produced in a very different context.

[8] 'Syntactical description type C' in Andrist 2015; on the concept of 'syntax of the codex', see Andrist, Canart & Maniaci 2013, p. 9.

[9] In the below scheme, the displays of the 'content' and 'material' fields were limited by the programmer, but this kind of problem does not normally occur in standard Internet software. In the above example, it was compensated through use of a scrollable field.

1c. - An improved example

Signature
Barocci 33

Extent
421 f. = (3) 116 + 128 + 177 (1) folios

Date
A. (f. 1-116) S. XVI 1/2 B. (f. 117-244) S. XV 2/2 C. (f. 245-421) a. 1595

Content

A. (f. 1-116)
  1. (f. 1r-116r sup.) Matthaeus Blastaris, Adversus iudeaos
B. (f. 117-244)
  2. (f. 117r-209v sup.) Gennadius Scholarius, Adversus iudaeos
  3-5. (f. 210r-230v) Georgius Gemistius Plethon, opera mis
  6. (f. 231r-241v) Isocrates, Ad Demonicum oratio paraenetica

Material
Paper A. (f. 1-116)   Watermarks: 2 series of "Cardinal's hat" with countermark "B" ... B. (f. 117-244)

Scripture and hands

A. (f. 1-116)
  a. (f. 1-24) unknown hand
  b. (f. 25-116) hand of <Kônstantios>
B. (f. 117-244)
  c. (f. 117-244) hand of <Michael Lygizos>
C. (f. 245-421)

Etc.

FIGURE 5: An improved way to describe Barocci 33 following the standard mono-layer model.

fields if he wants to link the date, the hand, the layout, the decoration, etc., of the PU he is interested in.

I have not been able to find examples of systematic use of this model online, although it has been successfully used in printed catalogues.[10] There are, however, hybrid solutions between type 1b and 1c, both online and in print, where the PUs are systematically and clearly distinguished only in the content field.[11]

---

[10] See, e.g., Kerstin 2003; also Kouroupou & Géhin 2008.
[11] See, e.g., the description of Zürich Rh. 97 in Mohlberg 1952, p. 206, or Charfet, Rahmani 151 (Catalogue SONY 775) in the database e-ktobe of Syriac manuscripts (⟨http://www.mss-syriaques.org/⟩).

Online description type 1d:
Another improved way of interpreting the mono-layer model

Another way to clearly distinguish the PUs of a manuscript, which does not require illustration here, is to prepare one description per PU, instead of one description for the entire manuscript. This solution entirely avoids the risk of 'mislinking' pieces of information that do not belong together, without overcharging the fields. In the case of Barocci 33, this would mean writing three descriptions. This is another type of 'syntactical description'.[12]

Where should one then describe the common elements like bindings, running notes, common history, bibliography, etc.? Several options are possible:

- An ill-advised solution would be to repeat the general information in every description.
- A better solution would be to for example add this to the first or the last description in the series. One must then design or complete the scheme in such a way that users clearly know they are not accessing the entire description, but just one PU, even though all the fields are completed.
- A third solution would be to create an extra description specifically for the common elements. The reader would then only see partly completed descriptions – either with information about the volume or about the individual PUs.

In any case, a one-to-one relationship between the number of descriptions and the number of volumes being described would be lost. In many situations, however, this need not pose a problem.

More problematically, it is then much more difficult to get an overview of the manuscript, particularly when the online description was obtained through a search query. If there is no internal link to the other description records within the series that make up the manuscript, there is no way of accessing them without completing a new search. Again, this is very much tied to how the database was designed in the first place.

---

[12] 'Syntactical description type B' in Andrist 2015.

This type of solution has sometimes been used for online catalogues, in particular for descriptions of volumes containing fragments, but also occasionally for other types of multi-PU volumes.[13] For example, interesting cases can be found in the Marburger Repertorium, a specialised catalogue dedicated to German manuscripts from the thirteenth and the fourteenth century, where fragments currently found in the same binding are described separately from each other but, when relevant, together with the other fragments of the same original manuscript now dispersed among different libraries.[14]

Introduction to the bi-layer model

As we just saw, satisfactory descriptions can be achieved through proper use of the mono-layer model, no matter what kind of database is being used. However, each way of representing the structure of the manuscript results in some visibility loss of information, and/or a loss of time. To move beyond these shortcomings, one needs another model based on a different approach to the description, such as the bi-layer model.

Conceptually, it is an archaeological or stratigraphic approach: the manuscript is considered a physical object made up of several other embedded physical objects, which must be separately described. In the upper level, there is only one object: the current volume, which is also a Circulation Unit. In the second level, there are either Production Units or older Circulation Units which, again, can comprise simple Production Units or even older Circulation Units, etc. Of course, the reality can be more complex, but this simplified explanation satisfactorily underlines the two main objects of a complex manuscript: the current vol-

---

[13] For a very interesting, systematic and compact use of this approach in a printed catalogue, see Gumbert 2009a and 2009b. For a hybrid solution between type 1d and 2a in the database e-ktobe, see below footnote 18.

[14] ‹http://www.mr1314.de/›; see for example the descriptions of Berlin, Staatsbibl., mgf 734 in nine entries. When users click the first one (mgf 734 Nr. 1), they get the independent description of the first fragment. However, when they click the second entry (mgf 734 Nr. 2), they very interestingly receive a description of three fragments of the same codex, today in Berlin, Nürnberg and Stuttgart. For another description of the same current volume in Berlin, see below, footnote 18; concerning the Marburger Repertorium, see Andrist 2010, p. 22-26.

ume and the several embedded Production Units. Each of them is then separately described.

In practice, the result is to set up two description patterns: one pattern for the volume and its general information, the other pattern for the PUs. Consequently, a codex description comprises a single volume description using the volume pattern and one PU description for each PU in the manuscript, making repeated and subsequent use of the PU pattern. Information about the production date and contents are given in the PU layer only. In a sense, the PUs – not the manuscript – are the main entities to be described.

Of course, one can think of an improved multi-layer approach, in which each level is separately described, no matter how many there are. So far, I have seen no Internet or print solution do this, even though recursion is very common in computer programming. Multi-layered descriptions are somewhat easier to prepare for a printed description, but not necessarily always easier to understand.

I have also done some tests with a five-pattern solution, including one specific pattern for the binding, directly linked to the volume layer; another for the texts, underneath the PU layers; and a fifth one for supplementary elements such as notes or added slips, also linked to the volume layer.[15] However, this has often resulted in online descriptions that are difficult to set up and understand.

It is worth again emphasising that this bi-layer model is not tied to any specific software or database. Although, of course, not every software package or database allows for it. It is entirely independent of implementation technology and can be achieved through storing descriptions in a relational database, or through extensive XML tagging. It is very suitable for any type of electronic approach and, indeed, it has already been used online with many different software packages in many different ways – some examples are given below.

It is indeed noteworthy that the rules for the software Manuscriptum XML, dedicated to the description of manuscripts, en-

---

[15] Even though the binding and the notes can be considered separate levels, this is not the case for texts. It was convenient, however, to describe them with their own pattern. For ways to treat notes in a bi-layer approach, see below p. 326-327.

tirely integrate the concept of multi-part manuscripts, and that the software provides means to describe complex manuscripts at various levels through the notion of 'Blocks'.[16] Let us hope that cataloguers will use it with the same understanding of a multi-part manuscript and, as a result, produce coherent multi-layer descriptions!

Online description type 2a: An all-inclusive interpretation of the 'bi-layer' model

In this first type, all the information relating to one PU is simply grouped in one occurrence of the PU pattern, including all its texts, its paintings, its scripts, its material aspect, etc. This is the most simple and basic type of syntactical description.[17]

There are then two basic ways of linking the information about a PU and its containing volume:

- They can all be displayed in the same window, one after the other. If the software allows for this, the PU information can even be embedded into the general information, so that the applicable parts of the general description (e.g. the signature, the material information and the binding) come at the beginning; followed by the PUs and with the remaining general information such as history and bibliography at the end.

- Alternatively, the catalogue can apply a 'click-and-jump' technique: one obtains the description of a particular PU by clicking the appropriate link in the volume description or in another PU description. This technique is often easier to realise, but it is then more difficult to keep an overall view of the current codex. In any case, it is clearly useful to repeat the codex signature at the top of each PU description.

For example, conceptually, an all-inclusive bi-layer description of Barocci 33 would look like this:

---

[16] Riecke 2009 (available online at ‹http://www.manuscripta-mediaevalia. de/hs/handbuch.pdf›). On this project, funded by the Deutsche Forschungsgemeinschaft (DFG), see Giel 2010.
[17] 'Syntactical description type A' in Andrist 2015.

Layer 1

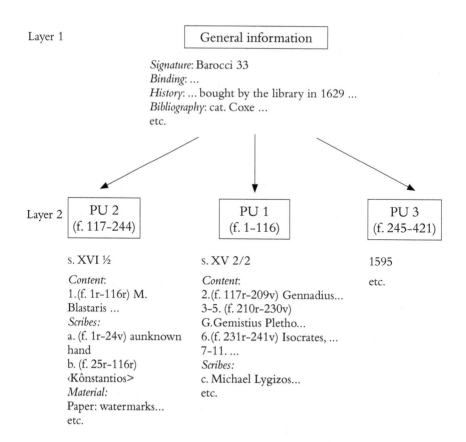

General information

Signature: Barocci 33
Binding: ...
History: ... bought by the library in 1629 ...
Bibliography: cat. Coxe ...
etc.

Layer 2

| PU 2 | PU 1 | PU 3 |
| (f. 117-244) | (f. 1-116) | (f. 245-421) |

s. XVI ½   s. XV 2/2   1595

Content: Content: etc.
1.(f. 1r-116r) M.   2.(f. 117r-209v) Gennadius...
Blastaris ...   3-5. (f. 210r-230v)
Scribes: G.Gemistius Pletho...
a. (f. 1r-24v) aunknown   6.(f. 231r-241v) Isocrates, ...
hand   7-11. ....
b. (f. 25r-116r)   Scribes:
<Kônstantios>   c. Michael Lygizos...
Material: etc.
Paper: watermarks...
etc.

FIGURE 6: The basic structure of a bi-layer stratigraphic description of
Barocci 33.

An online description could then look like this:
First, the overall volume description:

2a – Overall volume description

Signature

Barocci 33

Extent

421 f. = (3) 116 + 128 + 177 (1) folios
A. (f. 1-116) Matthaeus Blastaris
B. (f. 117-244) Gennadius Scholarius; Isocrates
C. (f. 245-421) Gennadius Scholarius; Definitio synodi Florentinae

Etc.

(including the description of the Binding, Notes, History, Bibliography...)

Then the three descriptions of the three Production Units follow:

2a – Description of Production Unit A

Heading
A. (f. 1-116) Matthaeus Blastaris

Date
(f. 1-116) S. XVI 1/2

Content
1. (f. 1r-116r sup.) Matthaeus Blastaris, Adversus iudeaos

Material
Paper with watermarks: 2 series of "Cardinal's hat" with countermark "B" ...

Scripture and hands
a. (f. 1-24) unknown hand b. (f. 25-116) hand of <Kônstantios>
Etc.

2a – Description of Production Unit B

Heading
B. (f. 117-244) Gennadius Scholarius; Isocrates

Date
S. XV 2/2

Content
2. (f. 117r-209v sup.) Gennadius Scholarius, Adversus iudaeos 3-5. (f. 210r-230v) Georgius Gemistius Plethon, opera mis 6. (f. 231r-241v) Isocrates, Ad Demonicum oratio paraenetica 7-11. (f. 244v) originally empty; today with notes, cf. infra Supplementary elements

Material
Paper with watermarks: 2 series of "pair of scissors" ...

Scripture and hands
c. Hand of <Michael Lygizos>
Etc.

2a – Description of Production Unit C

Heading
C. (f. 245-421) Gennadius Scholarius; Definitio synodi Florentinae

Date
a. 1595 (see colophon, f. 418v)

Content
12. (f. 247r-414v) Gennadius Scholarius, Apologia pro quinque cpp. concilii Florentini 13. (f. 415r-418v sup.) Definitio synodi Florentinae

Material
Paper with watermarks: not recognised

Scripture and hands
d. Hand of <Nicolaos Labros> (see colophon, f. 418v)

Etc.

FIGURE 7: A stratigraphical way to describe Barocci 33 following
the bi-layer model.

The result is very clear, and it is difficult to mix information
that is not contextually relevant – as is also illustrated by the following description. It was created in the database 'Archives et
manuscrits' of the Bibliothèque nationale de France for codex
Paris gr. 1823.[18]

[18] (⟨http://archivesetmanuscrits.bnf.fr/⟩); unfortunately, there is no permalink to these descriptions. See also, on the website for the project 'Bibliotheca
Laureshamensis-digital' (⟨http://www.bibliotheca-laureshamensis-digital.de/de/
index.html⟩), the description of codex Vaticanus Pal. lat. 554, in two 'Faszikel'.
Remarkably enough, this project entirely takes into account the multi-part
manuscripts, as explained in the online presentation: 'Handelt es sich um einen
Codex, der aus mehreren ursprünglich selbständigen Teilen zusammengesetzt ist,
wozu auch Fragmente gezählt werden, weichen die Beschreibungen im Aufbau
etwas ab [...]' (⟨http://www.bibliotheca-laureshamensis-digital.de/de/projekt/
erschliessung.html⟩). Let us again hope that these principles will be applied in a
very systematic way! A convincing hybrid solution between type 2a and 1d is
sometimes found in the database e-ktobe (see above footnote 11), where the two
layers are in fact realised with the same pattern; see for example the description
of manuscript Paris BnF syr. 434. An interesting use of the bi-layer model can
also be found in the presentation of Berlin, Staatsbibl., mgf 734 in Manuscripta Mediaevalia (⟨www.manuscripta-mediaevalia.de⟩; permalink: ⟨http://www.
manuscripta-mediaevalia.de/dokumente/html/obj31250686,T⟩). The layers for
each fragment are made by repeatedly using two embedded standard fields and
increasing their numbering. Concerning Manuscripta Mediaevalia, see Andrist
2010, p. 27-31.

{ BnF	Archives et manuscrits

Olympiodore/Damascius + Psellos + Timée de Locres + Théophraste

---

Paris BnF Grec 1823

[II] + 176 + (6) + [III]
345 × 235 × 50 (feuillet : 328 × 230)
Manuscrit formé par la réunion de quatre parties dues à des copistes différents.
Toutes les parties du recueil sont constituées de papiers filigranés à fines vergeures et pliées in-folio.
Reliure François Ier à couvrure de maroquin vert sombre virant au brun sur le dos. Technique alla greca : dos plat, coiffes saillantes sur les tranchefiles, pas de chasse, chants rainurés, vestiges de quatre fermoirs montant du plat inférieur vers le plat supérieur (deux en gouttière, un en tête et en queue). Décoration des plats : combinaison d'un décor imprimé à froid de filets dessinant trois rectangles emboîtés et d'un décor doré s'insérant dans ces rectangles : entrelacs, fleurs de lys, monogramme F surmonté d'une couronne et, au centre des plats, grand fer aux armes de France entourée du collier de l'ordre de Saint-Michel et avec la salamandre dans un brasier, emblème de François Ier ; la dorure se présente en deux couleurs, l'une plus jaune l'autre plus grise, les éléments

. . . .

Informations sur le traitement

Notice rédigée par Jocelyn Groisard (août-septembre 2007).

. . . .

Olympiodore/Damascius

I = ff. 1-130

1536

13 cahiers, tous des quinions. Signatures de α' à ιγ' de première main dans l'angle inférieur externe du premier recto du cahier. Réclame verticale dans l'angle inférieur interne du dernier verso du cahier.
Filigranes : I.1) Deux flèches croisées surmontées d'une étoile : cahiers 1-5 ; paire distincte aux ff. 10 et 25 ; = Harlfinger Flèche 21 (et non Flèche 19 comme indiqué par erreur dans ce répertoire), papier utilisé par le même copiste en 1538 et 1539 ; I.2) Deux flèches croisées surmontées d'une étoile, différent du précédent : cahier 6 ; paire distincte aux ff. 56 et 60 ; I.3) Ancre inscrite dans un cercle surmonté d'une étoile : cahier 5 ; paire distincte aux ff. 41 et 42 ; probablement identique à Harlfinger Ancre 12, papier attesté en 1534 à Venise ; I.4) Ancre : cahiers 7, 9 et 11 ; paire distincte aux ff. 61 et 63 ; I.5) Échelle inscrite dans un cercle surmonté d'une

. . . .

Toutes les notes marginales sont des scholies copiées de première main à l'encre rouge, ou de plus rares corrections également de première main mais à l'encre noire (par ex. ff. 29r, 44v, 50r, 59v, 76r).

Présentation du contenu

(ff. 1r-29r) Olympiodore, Commentaire sur le Phédon de Platon, éd. L. G. Westerink, The Greek Commentaries on Plato's Phaedo. Volume I : Olympiodorus, Amsterdam-Oxford-New York, 1976 : [titre dans marge externe] ὀλυμπιοδώρου φιλοσόφου σχόλια εἰς τὸν πλάτωνος φαίδωνα, suivi de l'indication d'une lacune initiale de 6 feuillets : λείπει δὲ τούτοις τὰ ἐξ ἀρχῆς φύλλα ἕξ ; [explicit f. 29r, l. 17] οὐ ζωοῦσιν αὐτά.

(ff. 29r-82r) <Damascius>, Commentaire sur le Phédon de Platon, éd. L. G. Westerink, The Greek Commentaries on Plato's Phaedo. Volume II : Damascius, Amsterdam-Oxford-New York, 1977, pp. 25-285 :

. . . .

Psellos

II = ff. 131-142

Début des années 1540

2 cahiers : 1 × 8 (138). 1 × 4 (142). Signatures de α' àβ' au milieu de la marge inférieure du premier recto du cahier.
Filigrane : II) Deux flèches croisées orientées vers le bas et surmontées d'une grande étoile, avec la contremarque 3M surmonté d'un trèfle ; paire distincte aux ff. 142 (contremarque f. 139) et 131 (contremarque f. 138) ; = Harlfinger Flèche 24a-b, papier attesté à Venise en 1542.
Un seul copiste dont l'écriture présente quelques similitudes avec celle de Georges Basilikos (à qui cette partie

etc.

FIGURE 8: An online description of Paris gr. 1823 following the all-inclusive interpretation of the bi-layer model.

In the above example, the general information comes first. There is no date at the beginning, but a note explains that the codex comprises four parts copied by three scribes. Each of the four parts is then described separately, with the date included toward the beginning of the description. In printed catalogues, this type of solution has been advocated as early as 2003[19] and is becoming more and more widespread.[20]

In the last few years, with the help of some colleagues, I have had the opportunity to test different systems. I was able to write syntactical descriptions using very different databases such as HAN, based on a Marc format system; scopeArchiv, which is close to the EAD philosophy; Nuova Biblioteca Manoscritta (NBM), a MySQL database with a Java front end; or e-codices, which strictly follow the TEI XML standards.[21]

It is important to stress that, contrary to a widespread idea, a bi-layer syntactical description is not necessarily a long one.[22] It is simply a matter of organising what little information there might be in a meaningfully structured way.

There is always some question about where to describe any reader and owner notes. Since they are always physically written on folios that belong to a PU (or to elements of the binding), should they be put in the PU layer (or with the binding)? This would usually make sense for notes relating to a particular text or to a particular owner of the PU before it was bound with the other PUs. Or should they be described in the volume layer, since they usually were not produced at the same time as the texts and because they often relate to the current volume and not to a

---

[19] Andrist 2003.

[20] See, for example, Andrist 2007, Stutzmann & Tylus 2007, Bobichon 2008, Dukan 2008, Di Donato 2011, Del Barco 2011.

[21] Unfortunately, most of these tests are no longer available online. Concerning these systems: HAN: ⟨http://aleph.unibas.ch/F?con_lng=GER&func=file&local_base=DSV05&file_name=verbund-han⟩; scopeArchiv: for exemple in the Burgerbibliothek Bern, ⟨http://katalog.burgerbib.ch/suchinfo.aspx⟩; on this experiment, see Andrist 2010, p. 40-43; NBM: ⟨www.nuovabibliotecamanoscritta.it⟩. For more about NBM, see Andrist 2010, p. 35-40. A few syntactical descriptions are available in e-codices, for example in Basel, Universitätsbibliothek, Cod. A VII 3: ⟨http://www.e-codices.unifr.ch/en/description/ubb/A-VII-0003⟩.

[22] See for example, the description of Bodm. 115 on e-codices, ⟨http://www.e-codices.unifr.ch/fr/description/cb/0115⟩ (soon to be replaced by a longer description).

specific PU? One could even think of describing them as independent Production Units (but this mostly gives them a undue importance), or to present some notes at one level, and some other notes at the other level, depending on their nature and content (it is then frequently difficult for readers to find them). For practical reasons, I usually describe them in one specific field in the volume layer only.

Before presenting another very important advantage of type 2a below, as far as searching is concerned (see p. 329), another type following the bi-layer model must be presented. It was conceived by people interested in texts or paintings, who are sometimes unsatisfied not to find all their description in the same place and are thus unable to at once see the volume contents in their last configuration.

Online description type 2b:
A content-focused interpretation of the 'bi-layer' model

How can one give a unified overall presentation of the contents in an online description of the codex that outlines the individual PUs? The easy solution is to move the contents field from the PU layer to the volume layer.[23] In the case of Barocci 33, the overall volume description would then look like in figure 9 below.

The PU descriptions would look like in figure 7, without the Content field. This description result more than sufficiently meets the basic conditions for a clear representation of the codex, provided the PUs are also distinguished in the content field. Otherwise, the repeated call of specialists to clearly show which texts are on which part of the manuscript[24] will not be heeded, and there will be a big risk that the readers do not correctly link the contents and the other types of information, like in the 1b type described above (see above, p. 315-316). Besides, setting apart

---

[23] This could be done for any feature the cataloguers want to stress. For example, in a catalogue of illustrated manuscripts, one could be tempted to group all the paintings in one field only.

[24] See above p. 310 footnote 1. For an example of model 2b in printed catalogue, see the description of cod. Quart. Eccl. Slav. 17 in Cleminson, Moussakova & Voutova 2006, p. 97.

2b – Second part: Material aspects of Unit A

Heading
A. (f. 1-116) Material Description

Date
(f. 1-116) S. XVI 1/2

Material
Paper with watermarks: 2 series of "Cardinal's hat" with countermark "B" ...

Scripture and hands
a. (f. 1-24) unknown hand   b. (f. 25-116) hand of <Kônstantios>   Etc.

2b – First part: Description of all the content

Signature
Barocci 33

Extent
421 f. = (3) 116 + 128 + 177 (1) folios

Content

A. (f. 1-116)
   1. (f. 1r-116r sup.) Matthaeus Blastaris, Adversus iudaeos
 B. (f. 117-244)
   2. (f. 117r-209v sup.) Gennadius Scholarius, Advrsus iudaeos
   3-5. (f. 210r-230v) Georgius Gemistius Plethon, opera misc.
   6. (f. 231r-241v) Isocrates, Ad Demonicum oratio paraeneti
   7-11. (f. 244v) originally empty; today with notes, cf. infra Supplementary elements
 C. (f. 245-421)
   12. (f. 247r-414v) Gennadius Scholarius, Apologia pro quinque cpp. concilii Florentini
   13. (f. 415r-418v sup.) Definitio synodi Florentinae

FIGURE 9: Beginning of the description of Barocci 33 following the content-focused interpretation of the bi-layer model.

the texts makes the relation between text and script, or text and layout, much less spontaneously visible.

However, the main problem of this approach to online descriptions becomes apparent with the need to search for and retrieve information. We will now turn to this problem.

A goal for future databases: the possibility to always automatically retrieve correctly linked information

Several types of description were presented above, including various forms that allow for easy (and correct) linking of information pieces that belong together. However, most of the time, while the correct links are visible to the reader, there is no such internal linking at the computer database level. Consequently, if a database user searches a specific text (or a painting, scribe, etc.) from a specific time, the results usually include incorrectly linked information in the case of multi-date manuscripts[25].

(3) Our third claim is:
Manuscript studies require that online searches offer complete and correct results, particularly when chronological limits are entered, so that only information within the given time range is retrieved.

In a standard mono-layer model, it is not difficult to understand why the computer cannot easily discern, for example, which texts belong to which dates: all the dates are in one field and all the texts in a different one. The same problem applies to a bi-layer model of type 2b, because the content information is split from the date information and grouped in a single field. A powerful parsing method could conceivably compensate for this situation, especially if the PUs are clearly indicated in each of the relevant fields (type 1c above), but this has not been the case so far, and it would not be a reliable solution because the ability to parse individual PU information would then depend on the internal layout of the field freely set up by the cataloguers.

Theoretically, of the description types presented above, only type 2a can easily solve the problem. This is why use of type 2a is strongly recommended.

As we saw, catalogues based on a type 2a model should be able to display correct information when a user enters multiple search criteria. But is this the case with the existing online databases following this model? A series of tests yielded somewhat disappointing results. The tests were based on searches for texts recurring in several manuscripts, including multi-part ones. With the text and a date range, the search function should find those copies of the text that were copied within the given date range – and only those! Unfortunately, all but one of the tested databases failed to give correct results, with NBM the exception (see above). In the other cases, the search results usually offered all the manuscripts with the given text and a date specification falling into the given

---

[25] See also Gippert 2015.

date range, even if this date had nothing to do with the PU containing the searched text. For example, in the case of the Barocci 33, the text of Plethon would be retrieved even when the search query was limited to the sixteenth century. This, of course, is not satisfactory and shows that correct retrieval of information, which is structurally easy to implement, should in any case be included in the instructions for the database programmers. This is theoretically the case, for example, with the German software Manuscriptum XML.[26] It raises quite a few hopes among scholars, but this potential for scholarly research will only be realised if the software is always used in a coherent way, and when the resulting structured descriptions are not mixed in a single database with unstructured ones (or can be isolated from them).

Readers should understand that these remarks do not aim to criticise or discourage the efforts of those who put this information on the web. On the contrary, as a user, I am very thankful to those who continue this work. I wish only to underline one common limitation of the current databases and thereby point to one major improvement that should be included in the next generation of databases.

Conclusion

As explained above, manuscript studies need:

(1) *Online information that is correct: this is a question of the basic ethics of scholarship.*

This does not rule out that less reliable pieces of information are also given as pieces belonging to the 'historiography' of the manuscript, such as data from old or outdated publications/descriptions. But they should be clearly separated from the systematic and more reliable information, and not interfere with this. For the same reason, there is no space in scholarly databases for

---

[26] See above p. 320-321. See Riecke 2009, p. 113: 'Dabei sollte in MXML die Struktur der Handschrift durch die Hierarchisierung der Blöcke möglichst genau abgebildet werden, um bei Recherchen genau zu dem relevanten Faszikel oder Text bzw. zu dem bestimmten Faszikel- oder Textblock leiten zu können.'

obviously wrong or 'quick and dirty' types of information or descriptions.

(2) *Online information that is correctly linked: a user of a manuscript description must always be able to correctly relate information pieces that belong to the same PUs, particularly the dates of the PUs.*

As explained above, there are multiple, very simple ways in which these goals can be satisfactorily achieved, no matter which software is being used. They do not necessarily require much time and are also perfectly suitable for 'small-scale' descriptions. No matter whether the software allows for stratigraphic descriptions and no matter what software is being used, the most important consideration is the capacity and willingness of the cataloguer to see the significant discontinuities in a manuscript and to report them to users. Again, this is not primarily a question of software, but of awareness, organisation and systematics.

(3) *Online information that can be completely and correctly retrieved: this criterion primarily depends on the software and the database design. Unfortunately, this condition is currently only very rarely met.*

Historiographical pieces of information should not be included in standard 'factual' searches; or there should at least be an easy way to exclude them.

Imagine what power manuscript sciences could have if every online database were to allow a correct retrieval of information that could be accessed through a portal, so that it became possible to retrieve correct information from all the databases at once? This is a dream, but as we saw, it is a dream that can be realised.

There is an old adage in computer science: 'Garbage in... garbage out'! Manuscript databases are not exempted from this rule – the more correct and correctly linked information is entered, the better the database will meet the needs of manuscript studies.

Merely going online is definitely not enough.

Bibliography

P. Andrist (2003), '*Catalogus codicum graecorum Helveticorum. Règles de catalogage, élaborées sous le patronage du Kuratorium „Katalogisierung der mittelalterlichen und frühneuzeitlichen Handschriften der Schweiz"*, version 2.0', Bern: Burgerbibliothek Bern, reviewed by P. Augustin, *Scriptorium,* 58 (2004), p. 122-127.

P. Andrist (2006), 'La descrizione scientifica dei manoscritti complessi: fra teoria e pratica', in *Segno e testo*, 4, p. 299-356, + 8 plates.

P. Andrist (2007), *Les manuscrits grecs conservés à la Bibliothèque de la Bourgeoisie de Berne – Burgerbibliothek Bern. Catalogue et histoire de la collection*, Dietikon-Zurich: Urs Graf.

P. Andrist (2010), 'La description des manuscrits médiévaux sur Internet: un regard critique', in E. Crisci, M. Maniaci & P. Orsini (eds.), *La descrizione dei manoscritti: esperienze a confronto*, Cassino: Università degli Studi di Cassino (Studi e ricerche del Dipartimento di Filologia e Storia, 1), p. 19-45.

P. Andrist (2011), 'The Physiognomy of Greek contra Iudaeos Manuscript Books in the Byzantine Era. A Preliminary Survey', in R. Bonfil, O. Irshai, G. G. Stroumsa et al. (eds.), *Jews in Byzantium. Dialectics of Minority and Majority Cultures*, Leiden, Boston: Brill (Jerusalem Studies in Religion and Culture, 14), p. 549-585.

P. Andrist, (2013), *La syntaxe du codex. Essai de codicologie structurale*, Turnhout: Brepols (Bibliologia 32).

P. Andrist (2015), 'Syntactical description of manuscripts: a powerful tool for understanding, communicating and searching ancient books' in A. Bausi et al. (eds.), *Comparative Oriental Manuscript Studies. An Introduction*, Hamburg.

P. Andrist, P. Canart & M. Maniaci (2010), 'L'analyse structurelle du codex, clef de sa genèse et de son histoire', in A. Bravo García & I. Pérez Martín (eds.), *The legacy of Bernard de Montfaucon: Three Hundred Years of Studies on Greek Handwriting. Proceedings of the Seventh International Colloquium of Greek Palaeography (Madrid - Salamanca, 15-20 September 2008)*, Turnhout: Brepols (Bibliologia 31A), p. 289-299.

P. Bobichon (2008), *Hébreu 669 à 703. Manuscrits de théologie*, Turnhout: Brepols (Manuscrits en caractères hébreux conservés dans les bibliothèques de France. Catalogues, 1).

R. Cleminson, E. Moussakova & N. Voutova (2006), *Catalogue of the Slavonic Cyrillic Manuscripts of the National Széchényi Library*, Budapest, New York: Central European University Press (CEU Medievalia, 9).

H. Coxe (1853), *Catalogus Codicum Manuscriptorum Bibliothecae Bodlei-*

anae Pars Prima Recensionem Codicum Graecorum Continens, Oxford; reprinted with handwritten corrections from N. Wilson (1969), Oxford, col. 50-52.

J. Del Barco (2011), *Hébreu 1 à 32*, Turnhout: Brepols (Manuscrits en caractères hébreux conservés dans les bibliothèques de France. Catalogues, 4).

A. Derolez (1995), 'La codicologie et les études médiévales', in J. Hamesse (ed.), *Bilan et perspectives des études médiévales en Europe. Actes du premier Congrès européen d'études médiévales, Spoleto, 27-29 mai 1993*, Louvain-la-Neuve, p. 371-386.

S. Di Donato (2011), *Hébreu 214 à 259: Commentaires Bibliques*, Turnhout: Brepols (Manuscrits en caractères hébreux conservés dans les bibliothèques de France. Catalogues, 3).

M. Dukan (2008), *Fragments bibliques en hébreu provenant de Guenizot*, Turnhout: Brepols (Manuscrits en caractères hébreux conservés dans les bibliothèques de France. Catalogues, 2).

R. Giel (2010), 'Cataloging for the Web. Manuscriptum XML and Manuscripta Mediaevalia', in E. Crisci, M. Maniaci, P. Orsini (coord.), *La descrizione dei manoscritti: esperienze a confronto*, Cassino: Università degli Studi di Cassino (Studi e ricerche del Dipartimento di Filologia e Storia, 1), p. 47-60.

J. Gippert (2015), 'Catalogues and cataloguing of Oriental manuscripts in the digital age', in A. Bausi et al. (eds.), *Comparative Oriental Manuscript Studies. An Introduction*, Hamburg.

J. P. Gumbert (1997), 'Codicological Descriptions – Why Short, and Why Long?', in J. Vodopivec & N. Golob (eds.), *Book and Paper Conservation. Proceedings*, Ljubljana, p. 51-62.

J. P. Gumbert (2004), 'Codicological Units: Towards a Terminology for the Stratigraphy of the Non-Homogeneous Codex', in E. Crisci & O. Pecere (eds.), *Il codice miscellaneo, tipologia e funzioni. Atti del convegno internazionale (Cassino, 14-17 maggio 2003)*, Cassino: Università degli studi di Cassino (Segno e testo, 2), p. 17-42.

J. P. Gumbert (2009a), *Illustrated Inventory of Medieval Manuscripts. Leiden, Universiteitsbibliotheek, BPL:* Hilversum.

J. P. Gumbert (2009b), 'IIMM – A completely new Type of Manuscript Inventory', in *Gazette du livre médiéval*, 55, p. 43-46.

K. Hajdú (2003), *Katalog der griechischen Handschriften der Bayerischen Staatsbibliothek München*, Bd. 3. Codices graeci Monacenses 110-180, Wiesbaden: Harrassowitz.

M. Kouroupou & P. Géhin (2008), *Catalogue des manuscrits conservés dans la Bibliothèque du Patriarcat Œcuménique: les manuscrits du monastère de la Panaghia de Chalki*, 2 vols., Turnhout: Brepols.

L. C. Mohlberg (1952), *Katalog der Handschriften der Zentralbibliothek Zürich 1, Mittelalterliche Handschriften*, Zürich: Berichthaus.

B. Munk Olsen (1998), 'L'élément codicologique', in P. Hoffmann (ed.), *Recherches de codicologie comparée. La composition du codex au Moyen Âge, en Orient et en Occident*, Paris (Collection Bibliologie), p. 105-129.

A. Petrucci (2001), *La descrizione del manoscritto: storia, problemi, modelli*, Roma: Carocci, p. 93-104.

A.-B. Riecke (2009) *Die Erstellung von Handschriftenbeschreibungen nach den Richtlinien der DFG mit Hilfe von Manuscriptum XML*, Version 1.1, ‹http://www.manuscripta-mediaevalia.de/hs/handbuch.pdf›.

P. R. Robinson (1980), 'The "Booklet": A Self-Contained Unit in Composite Manuscripts of the Anglo-Saxon period', in A. Gruys & J. P. Gumbert (eds.), *Codicologica 3, Essais typologiques*, Leiden (Litterae textuales), p. 46-69.

D. Stutzmann, P. Tylus (2007), *Les manuscrits médiévaux francais et occitans de la Preussische Staatsbibliothek et de la Staatsbibliothek zu Berlin – Preussischer Kulturbesitz*, Wiesbaden: Harrassowitz (Staatsbibliothek Preussischer Kulturbesitz. Kataloge der Handschriftenabteilung: Reihe 1. Handschriften; Bd. 5).

L. Thorndike (1946), 'The Problem of the Composite Manuscript', in *Miscellanea Giovanni Mercati*, VI, Città del Vaticano (Studi e testi, 126), p. 93-10.

JORIS J. VAN ZUNDERT

BY WAY OF CONCLUSION: TRULY SCHOLARLY, DIGITAL, AND INNOVATIVE EDITIONS?

Most contributions in this volume in some way refer to scholarly edited texts. Given the theme of the workshop from which these proceedings arise, they tend to show or consider how digital technologies may improve our capabilities for scholarly editing and analysis. Many of the texts we deal with in a scholarly fashion are now being remediated in a digital environment that allows the representation of textual resources in a multitude of varying forms and formats other than the makeup of the physical book with which we are so very familiar. This raises questions about the configuration and the properties of digital scholarly editions: on what sets them apart from analogue editions, and what sets them apart from non-scholarly editions. The reconfiguration of the scholarly edition in a digital form may have methodological ramifications too. I am not referring to the mere conveniences of scale that are associated with online editions – the obvious expedients of online discovery and transfer of digital materials. There is methodological gain in that, but I would hesitate to say that there is methodological *innovation* in it. The issue is: what could the true methodological innovation of digital scholarly editions be? In concluding these proceedings I would like to offer a short reflection on that question.

At the workshop a discussion under the tongue-in-cheek title 'Ten (10) reasons why we should only produce digital editions from now on...' explored the advantages of digitally published scholarly editions. This quickly yielded far more than ten advan-

10.1484/M.LECTIO-EB.5.102578

tages. I list but a few that are named with some regularity.[1] Digital editions offer the possibility to include almost any extant data, which can be of almost any type. This provides the potential for all witnesses, both in machine readable and in facsimile format, and all paratext pertaining to a particular tradition to be contained by a digital scholarly edition, with virtually none of the limitations of the print medium. Digital editions also offer the possibility to include various kinds of enriching media such as images, sound, and video. This promises to change quite dramatically our experience of the digital scholarly edition. The technologies underpinning the digital edition facilitate the indexing of its contents by internet search engines, which increases the visibility of editions considerably. The discovery of editions becomes less dependent on the abilities of readers and users to navigate different library catalogues and predict the right metadata and keywords. Even given a quote or paraphrase, the search engines will yield pointers to related editions. Digital editions also make it far easier for readers to navigate the text of the edition itself: full-text search provides an easy means to find words and phrases, faster than and superior to an analogue index or concordance. The digital environment enables us to share our editions instantly and to publish them globally in an instant. Moreover, digital editions are so called 'multi-platform editions': they can be published in print on demand, to eReaders, and on websites. Future capabilities of digital editions could include publishing an edition in a distributed way – that is, to have one's online edition be partly or wholly included in other digital editions while still being tied to its originating digital source, so that updates and corrections would be automatically propagated. One potential innovation that is already being realized is the ability to create, update, correct, and revise editions in a collaborative fashion – perhaps even through crowdsourcing – using web-based environments developed for the creation of digital editions.[2]

Yet on closer inspection, fundamentally these capabilities do not constitute methodological innovation in the sense that they add new functions to the text itself, functions that could not

[1] Cf. e.g. Fischer 2012.
[2] Cf. Brumfield 2013.

possibly have been realized through the print edition. Rather, these capabilities are re-inventions or re-mediations in a digital environment of the functions of text that we already know from the print paradigm. Collaborative editing, revisions, indices, even transclusion (the incorporation of text in another text)[3] are not unheard of in print. Again the digital medium 'only' adds speed and scale – speed, for instance, through the ability of real time updates; scale, for example, when we crowdsource the transcription phase of an edition. These benefits of speed and scale of the digital medium facilitate great convenience, but in essence do not entail methodological change. For all its richness and for all the heralding of methodological revolution, the digital medium in fact has not fundamentally altered the scholarly edition. All digital scholarly editions still by and large follow the conventions of the print medium: they are digital metaphors of the book. The production workflow is also 'merely' conventional – more scalable and flexible due to the digital work environment perhaps, but in essence unchanged.

Should this worry the scholarly community? Is it at all problematic that the digital scholarly edition is nothing more or less than the re-invention of the codex in a digital environment? On the one hand it is not. There is true and undeniable merit in establishing the digital construct that most faithfully and critically represents a codex in the digital environment so that scholarly work benefits maximally from the digitally scaled convenience of discovery and exchange. On the other hand the question is: should the digital medium serve us only as a tool of scale, or do we find in it an opportunity – even an obligation – to explore the ways in which its idiosyncrasies can influence and alter our methodology? To approach the same question from another angle: what do we express when we publish a digital edition that, for all practical purposes, is mimicking the process and product of the print scholarly edition as closely as possible? The implication is that there is no essential difference between the physical edition and the digital edition, that the methodological process is identical, that the product is functionally identical, and that the scholarly merit should be identical.

[3] Cf. Nelson 1993.

If this is what we want to imply for digital scholarly editions then why not create PDF files and call them digital scholarly editions, since they give us an exact digital copy of print editions? We clearly have not stopped at this, and so we evidently appreciate there must be essential differences between the digital and the print paradigm. There is an analogy for this in the history of scholarly editing itself. The majority of philological practitioners have accepted that a reconstruction of a text according to authorial intent is fundamentally impossible. Reverse engineering any authorial text, if it is even vaguely possible, can only be an interpretative approximation.[4] The analogy then is that because there is intentionality in the configuration and materiality of a print scholarly edition too, any attempt to remediate the scholarly edition as an exact copy of this scholarly intentionality in the digital medium will necessarily result in only an approximation of the original material and functional intentionality of the scholarly print edition. And so I would argue that it cannot be the primary intent of a digital scholarly edition to represent a scholarly edition that is better represented by a print publication. Rather, the intent ought to be to render a text in such a fashion and with such functionality of use that it becomes a representation of the scholarly edited text that exploits the idiosyncrasies of the digital environment to enhance its scholarly character and purpose.[5] This necessarily implies methodological changes to the scholarly editorial process. Our current methodologies are aimed specifically at print scholarly editions. It is an obvious fallacy to think that the exact same methodology would lead to digital scholarly editions that exploit the idiosyncratic scholarly potential of the digital environment.

Supposing that we follow this line of argument, what are the idiosyncrasies? What would make a scholarly edition sufficiently different form a print edition to judge it inherently and essentially digital? Examples that come to mind are the Hyperstack model[6] and the Maximal edition defined by Vanhoutte.[7] The Hyperstack ideal centres around the end-user and his or her engage-

---

[4] Wimsatt 1954; cf. Greetham 1994, Chapter 8.
[5] Cf. Robinson 2014; Sahle 2013.
[6] Fischer 2011.
[7] Vanhoutte 2011.

ment with the 'actual text'. The text in question is presented in an initial form; from there a user can drill down to every conceivable level of criticism provided by the collected and linked witnesses to the text, including existing editions with their apparatuses. Further possibilities for engagement and understanding are provided by the contextualization of materials and audio translation. The Maximal edition model also engages first of all from the end-user perspective, advocating a minimal edition as a reader's text for initial engagement and a maximized view with all variance and apparatus presented for highly specific scholarly scrutiny. Could we conclude then that a true digital scholarly edition is one such as these, that collects and presents in a critical scholarly fashion multiple user-oriented visualizations of a text or a work?

Recently Peter Robinson has tried to develop a rationale for such editions, working from the statement that 'text is the site of meaning which links the document and the work'.[8] The work is always there, shadowy but omnipresent, as Robinson puts it. However, that work as a cognitive construct cannot be directly represented through any edition, whether physical or digital. Rather, I would say, we are left with unsatisfactory options for representation. Either we represent the text-as-document and concentrate on the painstaking reproduction of each witness in the highest possible material detail, or we aspire to the approximation of a representation of the text-as-work. We must call the latter approximate at best, because it remains unclear what a representation of text-as-work entails. This is also arguably why, as Robinson concludes, we have actually seen a move over the past decades from trying to represent the text-as-work – with proponents like McGann[9] and Shillingsburg[10] – towards representing the text-as-document as put forth for instance by Hans Walter Gabler[11] and Elena Pierazzo.[12] Remediation of the scholarly edition as a digital metaphor of the book – a digital facsimile of the scholarly print edition – is satisfactory insofar as it seems to yield

---

[8] Robinson 2012.
[9] McGann 2001.
[10] Cf. Jones 2010.
[11] Gabler 2010.
[12] Pierazzo 2011.

clearer and more obvious limits that are tied to the scholarly print edition as a physical object. To take those boundaries as constraints and represent the physical object as a digital simulation facilitates the digital editorial task by providing a practical and concise set of clear objectives, even if (as can be inferred from the extensive literature on the subject) these objectives can be problematic in themselves. But to represent 'the work' on the other hand... what does that actually entail?

Yet, the forms that the Maximal and Hyperstack editions take are not entirely congruent with a text-as-document approach. Their forms suggest a tendency – or is it an ambition? – to present as many documents as possible that are witness to the text (preferably all of them), and subsequently to add as much contextualizing material as is relevant in the eyes of the editors. Rather than text-as-document this signals a text-as-work approach. Rather than telling the user 'here is a virtual book with the text' they seem to express: 'here is all that we can offer you to get to know the work'. Regardless of how disappointingly unfinished such projects may tend to be in the end,[13] these ambitious endeavours show what we intuitively appreciate as representing the text-as-work. All-in representations such as these are sites of knowledge visualisation that focus on a particular work.[14]

But do these sites of knowledge visualization take our methodology beyond that of print? Probably not, insofar as that knowledge could still theoretically be presented in print as well. Indexing, referencing, annotation, typesetting, and so on would perhaps be almost insurmountably complex and error-prone jobs in such cases – but not, in principle, impossible. Obviously these tasks are greatly facilitated by the digital medium. But in themselves they still do not add an intrinsic digital aspect to the scholarly edition.

If we want to venture beyond that point we must ask ourselves: what capabilities does the digital medium add to our scholarly repertoire that print could not, even in theory? Two of these key capabilities are interactivity and processing. Interactivity is the ability of a scholarly edited text to be susceptible to dialogue, to be susceptible to change, addition, and subsequent

---

[13] Fischer 2012.
[14] Shillingsburg 2006.

digital re-publication. This is distinct from being susceptible or open to annotation. Print text can be annotated in the margins, between the lines, or with post-it notes. But printed text cannot be changed: there is no way to seamlessly delete or add characters. Although it might not always be desirable, digital models do make this possible; in practice it can even be done in a 're-sponsible scholarly' fashion as long as a sensible form of version management is implemented. Digital scholarly editions of the same text could then branch off from a common initial scholarly edition to represent different intellectual arguments about that text, but with a guaranteed traceable provenance. The second key capability is processing, that is: analysis and the ability to infer information and interpretation from a text representation through computational means. As Buzzetti has pointed out, stylometric analysis and authorship attribution are based on this kind of pro-cessing, but digital editions ought to allow us to go far beyond these analytical applications.[15] Here it suffices to note that for algorithmic computational processing, one obviously needs the text in a machine-addressable and machine-readable form.

When we look at the digital scholarly editions in existence we see that exactly these two key features are hardly if at all supported, not even in acclaimed editions such as the Saint Pat-rick's *Confessio* Hypertext Stack Project[16] or the edition of the Van Gogh Letters,[17] both of which stand as exemplars of good practice. Interactivity in the sense of openness to changes and additions is virtually never a feature. Even the lesser openness of annotation is seldom supported. Likewise, it is hardly ever pos-sible to negotiate the text in an automated way – that is, to cir-cumvent the graphical interface and approach the text through a computer-to-computer exchange protocol. Yet it is exactly these intrinsic capabilities, available only in the digital space, that could drive a real change in our methodologies. Interactivity, for instance, could lead to editorial workflows, as in the case of crowdsourcing[18] where the editor's role becomes that of a fa-cilitator and guide through the process rather than executive, so

---

[15] Buzzetti 2009.
[16] Fischer 2011.
[17] Jansen et al. 2009.
[18] Brumfield 2013.

that both 'use' and 'user' are redefined in relation to the scholarly edition, turning it from a site of knowledge visualization to a site of knowledge production.[19] Likewise machine access to editions or editorial sources greatly facilitates new forms of analysis such as topic modelling and stylometry,[20] analytic approaches that may even be aggregated over large corpora of textual data through 'algorithmic reading' to push our methodological abilities powerfully forward.[21]

Thus there is ample room for methodological innovation above and beyond the simple gains of easy access and sharing. Yet perhaps the current state of affairs is not all that surprising. First of all, the openness that is required for interactivity does not sit well with our feeling of responsibility and ownership. Be they digital or not, scholarly editions are considered scholarly primarily because they are produced by a community that takes responsibility for the scholarly quality of process and product. This does not need to preclude a more open variant of scholarly methodology and its resulting editions. Nevertheless, digital editions have a relatively short history and we have almost no inkling of how their scholarly adequacy is to be warranted. Thus we are not very eager to amend our methodologies. As McGann said 'philology is the fundamental science of human memory'.[22] We are rightfully careful about how we operate that memory in order to ensure that it continues to function. Even so, that does not in any way relieve us from the task to engage with the digital environment and to explore how its specific variant of 'philological memory' addresses our scholarly needs and practices. Obviously we cannot ignore the increasing digitalization of society, academy, and thus also scholarship.

Secondly, we do not yet have the digital text models that would be needed to propel these kinds of serious methodological innovations. The models we would need resemble the vision of Theodor Nelson[23] for Hypertext and his ideas for a virtual space for linked documents (the Docuverse). It was not Nel-

[19] Cf. Beaulieu et al. 2013.
[20] Cf. Van Zundert 2012.
[21] Ramsay 2011.
[22] McGann 2013.
[23] Nelson 1993.

son, however, but Tim Berners Lee who implemented an actual functioning protocol for hyper-linking documents – a protocol whose model is only a shallow implementation of the Hypertext vision.[24] It does not allow for robust reciprocal linking, annotation, or versioning. Nevertheless as a result of the adoption of the latter vision for the World Wide Web we must make do with the broken symmetry of this particular hypertext model. Also for this reason there is not a great deal of sense in abandoning too quickly our current digital sandbox, where we remediate the scholarly edition as a digital metaphor of the book. We need to give the pioneers of digital scholarship[25] time to figure out more suitable digital text models.

What this all serves to say – to come finally to a conclusion – is that the digital medium does not automatically boost, inspire, or even support methodological innovation. In fact, at closer inspection, when it comes to our scholarly editions in the digital environment, apart from the scale upon which we can operate much of our methodology seems to be the same as it ever was. Real methodological innovation is hard to define, and hard to identify. I should carefully stress that this reflection is not meant to say that the current convergent applications of digital technology is not an advance, or that it should be deemed pointless failure. Far from it! There is no question that the majority of digital technologies currently applied in our field scale the availability, the discoverability, and the convenience of exchange of scholarly editions up to a level whose merit cannot be overestimated.

But what this reflection also suggests is that we have only just begun to incorporate the potential of the truly digital into our methodologies. The current state of affairs, which is predominantly remediation but not innovation of methodology, strikes me as merely the first step of a longer journey. There are ways to view this as the metaphor of the half-empty glass. Robinson found that in the case of the digital scholarly edition we actually shifted away from an explorative focus on text-as-work to a conventional focus on text-as-document. In this sense con-

---

[24] Berners Lee 1999.
[25] E.g. Haentjens Dekker & Middell 2011; Andrews & Macé 2013; Schmidt & Colomb 2009.

ventional methodologies brought into the digital environment have a certain cloaking or regressive effect. That which is in truth re-representation poses as methodological innovation. This re-representation taken as innovation partly eclipses a further major challenge: the exploration of the idiosyncratic methodological merit of the digital environment. Exploring that potential is obviously in itself not a trivial task, nor one that can be undertaken without methodological peril. However, it is a task we are obliged to undertake. As experts on text it is up to us to identify its true digital characteristics, limits and functions. Thus we have a glass half full. Good, now let us fill it further.

Bibliography

T. L. Andrews & C. Macé (2013), 'Beyond the Tree of Texts: Building an Empirical Model of Scribal Variation through Graph Analysis of Texts and Stemmata', in *Literary and Linguistic Computing*, 28 (4), p. 504-521.

A. Beaulieu, S. de Rijcke & B. van Heur (2013), 'Authority and Expertise in New Sites of Knowledge Production', in P. Wouters, A. Beaulieu, A. Scharnhorst & S. Wyatt (eds.), *Virtual Knowledge: Experimenting in the Humanities and the Social Sciences*, Cambridge MA, USA: MIT Press, p. 25-56.

T. Berners-Lee & M. Fischetti (1999), *Weaving the Web: The Original Design and Ultimate Destiny of the World Wide Web by Its Inventor*, New York: Harper.

B. Brumfield (2013), 'The Collaborative Future of Amateur Editions', in *Collaborative Manuscript Transcription*, ⟨http://manuscripttranscription.blogspot.nl/2010/12/nabpp-transcription-user-survey-results.html⟩.

D. Buzzetti, (2009), 'Digital Editions and Text Processing', in M. Deegan & K. Sutherland (eds.), *Text Editing, Print and the Digital World*, Farnham (UK) & Burlington (USA): Ashgate, p. 45-61.

F. Fischer, (2011) 'About the HyperStack', in *St. Patrick's Confessio*, ⟨http://www.confessio.ie/about/hyperstack#⟩.

F. Fischer (2012), 'All Texts Are Equal, But... Textual Plurality and the Critical Text in Digital Scholarly Editions', in *Variants*, 10, p. 77-92.

H. W. Gabler (2010), 'Theorizing the Digital Scholarly Edition', in *Literature Compass*, 7 (2), p. 43-56.

D. Greetham (1994), *Textual Scholarship: An Introduction*, Oxford & New York: Taylor & Francis.

R. Haentjens Dekker & G. Middell (2011), 'Computer-Supported Collation with CollateX: Managing Textual Variance in an Environment with Varying Requirements', in *Supporting Digital Humanities 2011*, University of Copenhagen, 17-18. Nov. 2011.

L. Jansen, H. Luijten & N. Bakker (eds.) (2009), *Vincent van Gogh: The Letters*, Amsterdam: Amsterdam University Press.

S. Jones, P. Shillingsburg & G. Thiruvathukal (2010), 'E-Carrel: An Environment for Collaborative Textual Scholarship', in *Journal of the Chicago Colloquium on Digital Humanities and Computer Science*, 1 (2), ⟨https://letterpress.uchicago.edu/index.php/jdhcs/article/view/54/65⟩.

J. McGann (2001), *Radiant Textuality: Literature after the World Wide Web*, New York: Palgrave Macmillan.

J. McGann (2013), 'Philology in a New Key', in *Critical Inquiry*, 39 (2), p. 327-346.

T. H. Nelson (1993), *Literary Machines. The Report On, and Of, Project Xanadu Concerning Word Processing, Electronic Publishing, Hypertext, Thinkertoys, Tomorrow's Intellectual Revolution, and Certain Other Topics Including Knowledge, Education and Freedom* (First published 1981), Sausalito CA, USA: Mindful Press.

E. Pierazzo (2011), 'A Rationale of Digital Documentary Editions', in *LLC*, 26 (4), p. 463-477.

S. Ramsay (2011), *Reading Machines: Toward an Algorithmic Criticism (Topics in the Digital Humanities)*, Chicago: University of Illinois Press

P. Robinson (2004), 'Where We Are with Electronic Scholarly Editions, and Where We Want to Be', in *Jahrbuch für Computerphilologie Online 3*, p. 123-143, ⟨http://computerphilologie.uni-muenchen.de/jg03/robinson.html⟩.

P. Robinson (2012), 'Towards a Theory of Digital Editions', in *Variants*, 10, p. 105-131.

P. Sahle (2013), *Digitale Editionsformen, Zum Umgang mit der Überlieferung unter den Bedingungen des Medienwandels – Befunde, Theorie und Methodik*, Vol. 8, Norderstedt: Norderstedt Books on Demand (Schriften des Instituts für Dokumentologie und Editorik).

D. Schmidt & R. Colomb (2009), 'A Data Structure for Representing Multi-Version Texts Online', in *International Journal of Human-Computer Studies*, 67 (6), p. 497-514.

P. L. Shillingsburg (2006), *From Gutenberg to Google: Electronic Representations of Literary Texts*, Cambridge: Cambridge Univ. Press.

E. Vanhoutte (2011), 'So You Think You Can Edit? The Masterchef Edition', in *The Mind Tool: Edward Vanhoutte's Blog*, ⟨http://edward-vanhoutte.blogspot.nl/2011/10/so-you-think-you-can-edit-mas-terchef.html>.

W.K. Wimsatt (1954), 'The Intentional Fallacy', in W.K. Wimsatt (ed.), *The Verbal Icon: Studies in the Meaning of Poetry*, Lexington: The University Press of Kentucky, p. 3-20.

J. van Zundert (2012), 'If You Build It, Will We Come? Large Scale Digital Infrastructures as a Dead End for Digital Humanities', in *Historical Social Research-Historische Sozialforschung*, 37 (3), p. 165-186.